The Tarot Café

By
Sang-Sun Park
Volume 4

TOKYOPOP®

HAMBURG // LONDON // LOS ANGELES // TOKYO

The Tarot Cafe Vol. 4
created by Sang-Sun Park

Translation - Sukhee Ryu
English Adaptation - Kristin Bailey Murphy
Retouch and Lettering - Gloria Wu
Production Artist - Rafael Najarian
Cover Design - Kyle Plummer

Editor - Julie Taylor
Digital Imaging Manager - Chris Buford
Production Managers - Jennifer Miller and Mutsumi Miyazaki
Managing Editor - Lindsey Johnston
VP of Production - Ron Klamert
Publisher and E.I.C. - Mike Kiley
President and C.O.O. - John Parker
C.E.O. - Stuart Levy

A  Manga

TOKYOPOP Inc.
5900 Wilshire Blvd. Suite 2000
Los Angeles, CA 90036

E-mail: info@TOKYOPOP.com
Come visit us online at www.TOKYOPOP.com

ISBN: 1-59532-814-9
First TOKYOPOP printing: December 2005
10 9 8 7 6 5 4 3 2 1
Printed in the USA

Story so far...

A sultan who has fallen in love with a young slave... A poor student who drives away a lake fairy over doubt and jealousy... A dragon that seeks to avenge the death of a dear friend... These are just a few of the supernatural beings that Pamela, owner of The Tarot Café, has welcomed through the doors of her mysterious establishment. But can she help them while dealing with a deep, dark secret of her own?

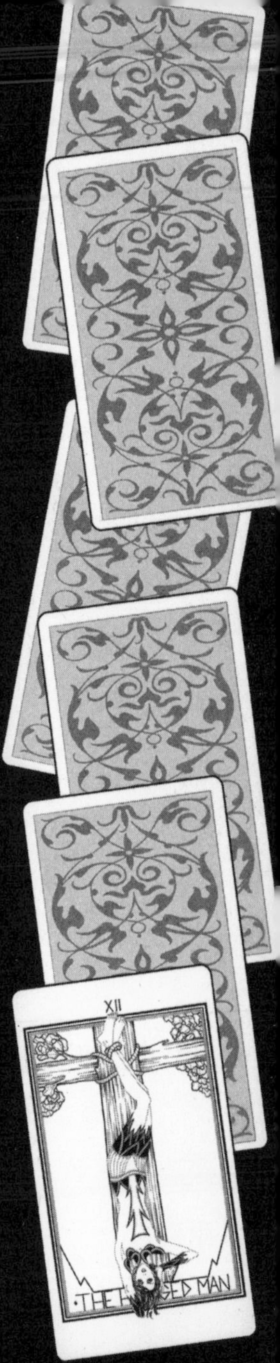
XII

Table of Contents

XVII The Stars

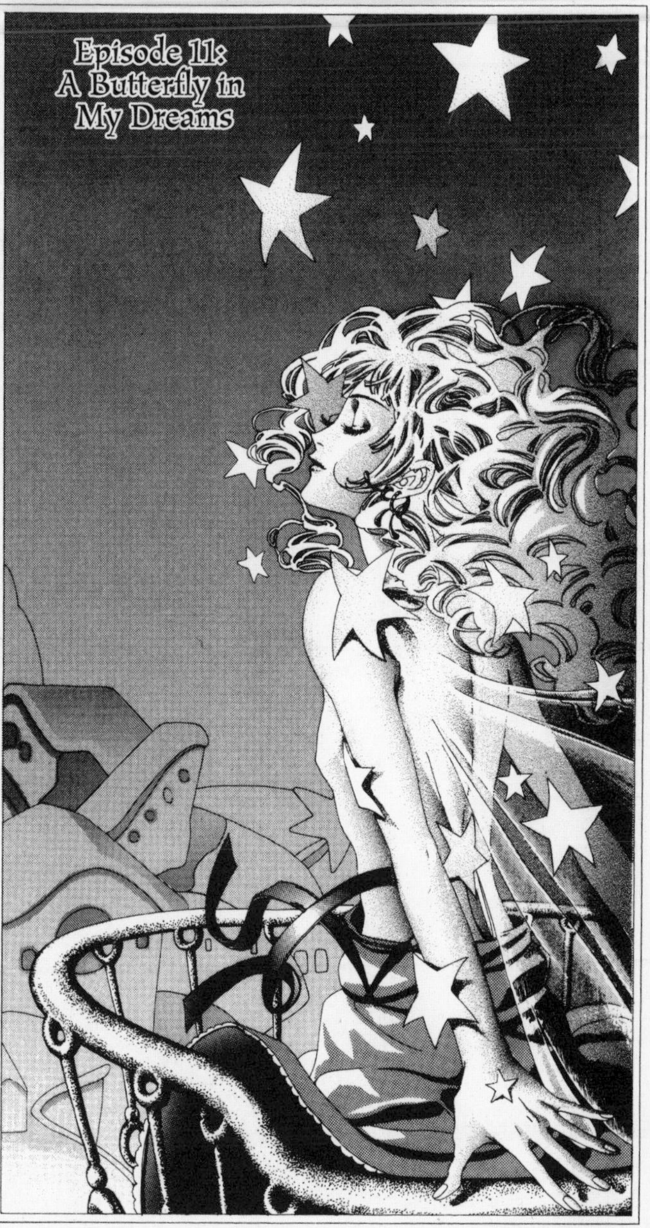
Episode 11:
A Butterfly in
My Dreams

Le Stelle Der Stern

Les Étoiles La Estrella

The Stars: This card represents inspiration, a feeling of wanting to give back, hope at the end of the tunnel, and serenity during times of upheaval.

ILLUSTRATION FROM FEY TAROT

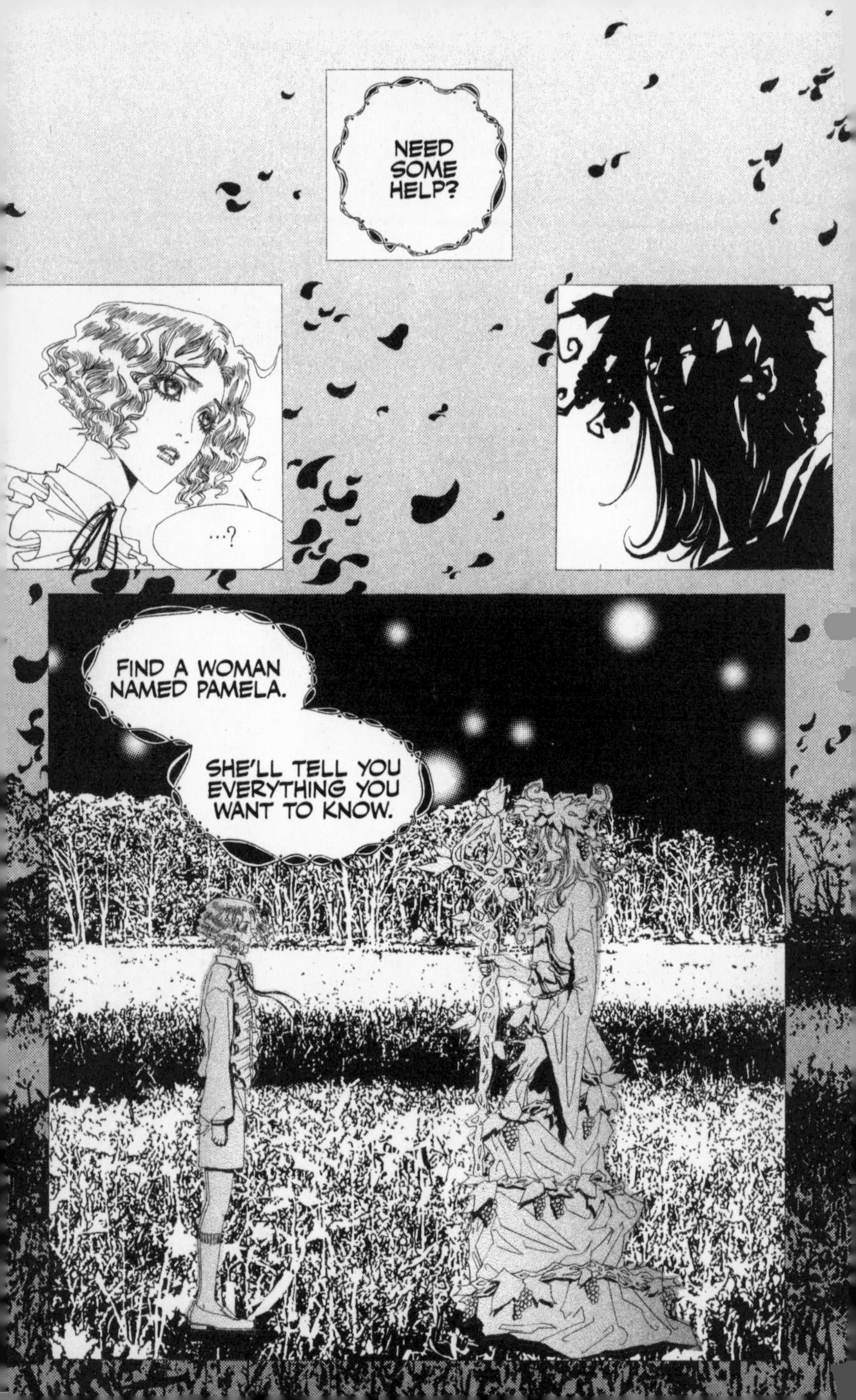
NEED SOME HELP?
...?
FIND A WOMAN NAMED PAMELA.
SHE'LL TELL YOU EVERYTHING YOU WANT TO KNOW.

A VACATION IN A QUIET PLACE UNTIL THE REPAIRS ON THE CAFÉ ARE FINISHED... I GUESS IT'S A NICE ENOUGH PLACE.

I WISH BELUS HADN'T DECIDED TO TAG ALONG.

YOU'RE ALWAYS SO TOUCHY AROUND BELUS, PAMELA.

YOU SAY YOU HAVE A "CONTRACTUAL RELATIONSHIP" WITH HIM, BUT I WONDER IF YOU REALLY LIKE HIM.

DIDN'T I TELL YOU I'D SELL YOU TO THE BUTCHER IF YOU SAID THAT AGAIN?

AAAH! I'M SORRY, I'M SORRY!

SHE'S JUST BEING A CRAZY OLD SPINSTER. I'M OUTTA HERE BEFORE SHE EXPLODES.

WELL, THEN, I'M GOING OUT TO MEET BELUS.

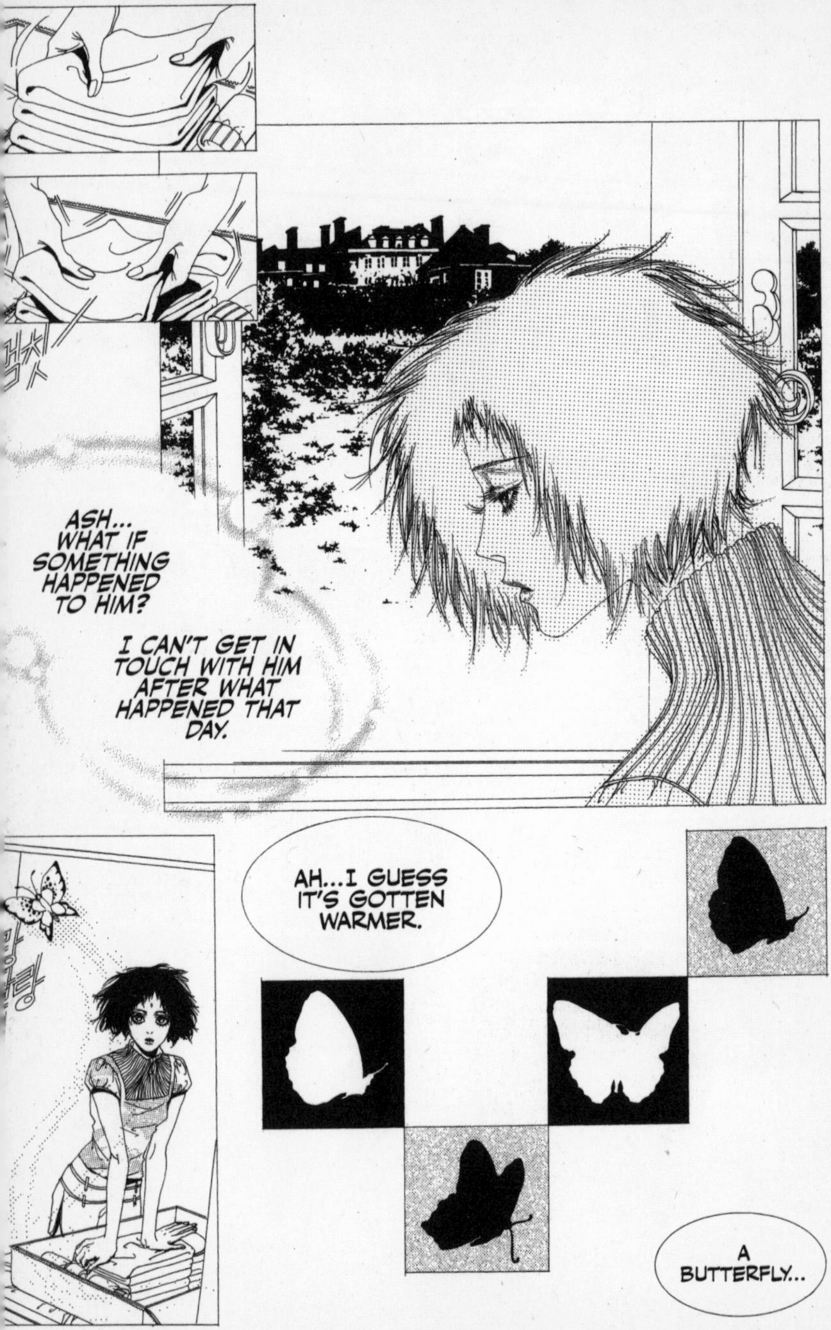
ASH... WHAT IF SOMETHING HAPPENED TO HIM?
I CAN'T GET IN TOUCH WITH HIM AFTER WHAT HAPPENED THAT DAY.
AH...I GUESS IT'S GOTTEN WARMER.
A BUTTERFLY...

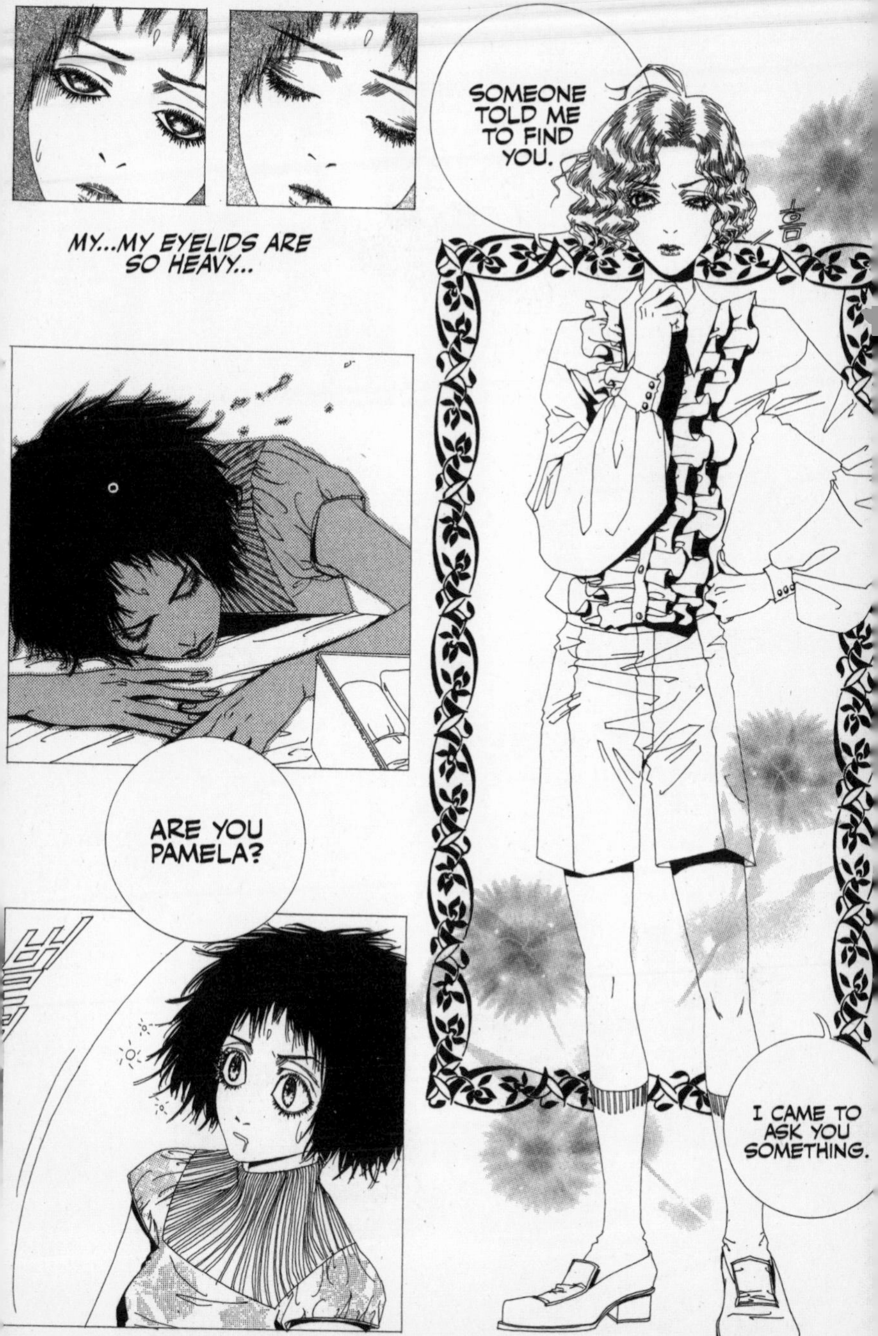
MY...MY EYELIDS ARE SO HEAVY...
ARE YOU PAMELA?
SOMEONE TOLD ME TO FIND YOU.
흠
I CAME TO ASK YOU SOMETHING.

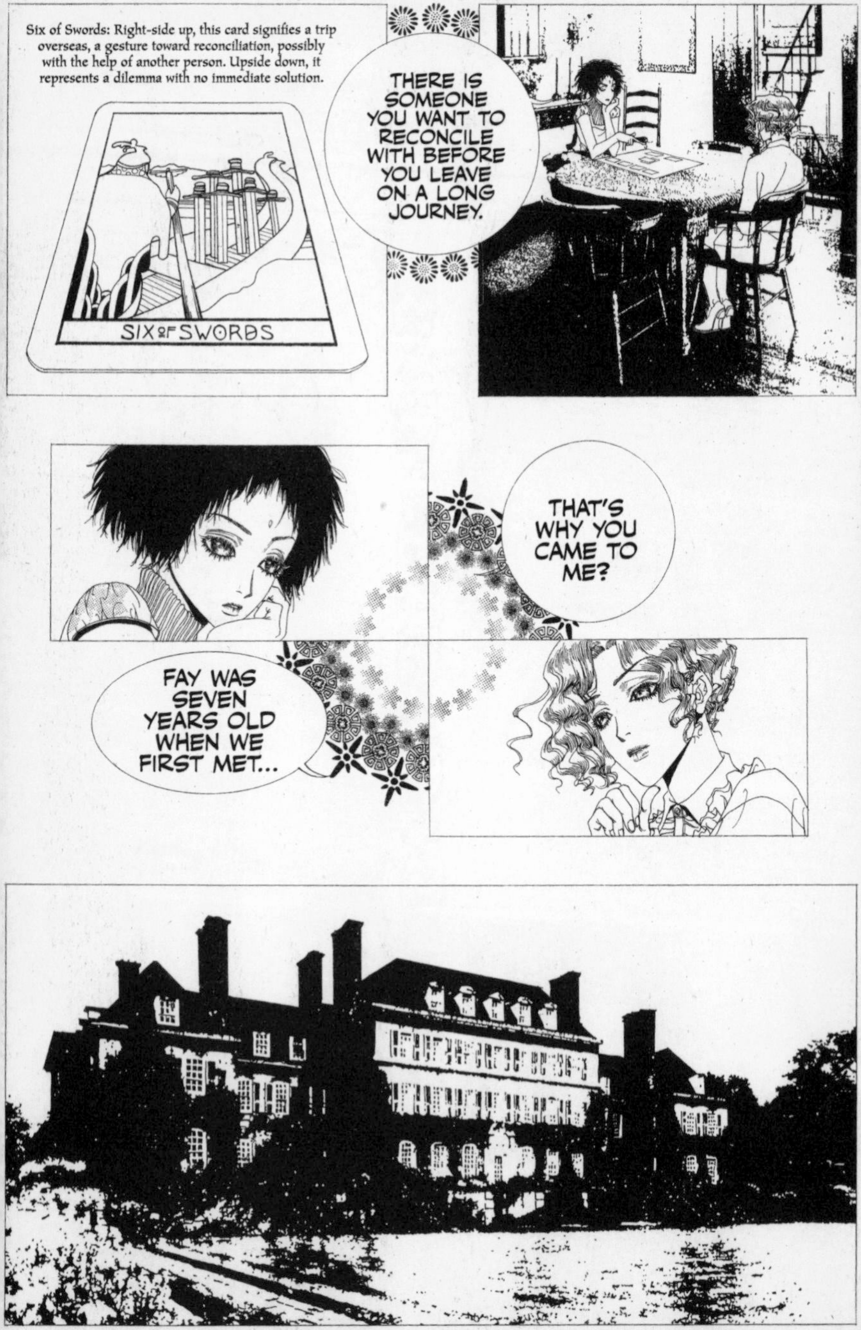
Six of Swords: Right-side up, this card signifies a trip overseas, a gesture toward reconciliation, possibly with the help of another person. Upside down, it represents a dilemma with no immediate solution.
SIX OF SWORDS
THERE IS SOMEONE YOU WANT TO RECONCILE WITH BEFORE YOU LEAVE ON A LONG JOURNEY.
THAT'S WHY YOU CAME TO ME?
FAY WAS SEVEN YEARS OLD WHEN WE FIRST MET...

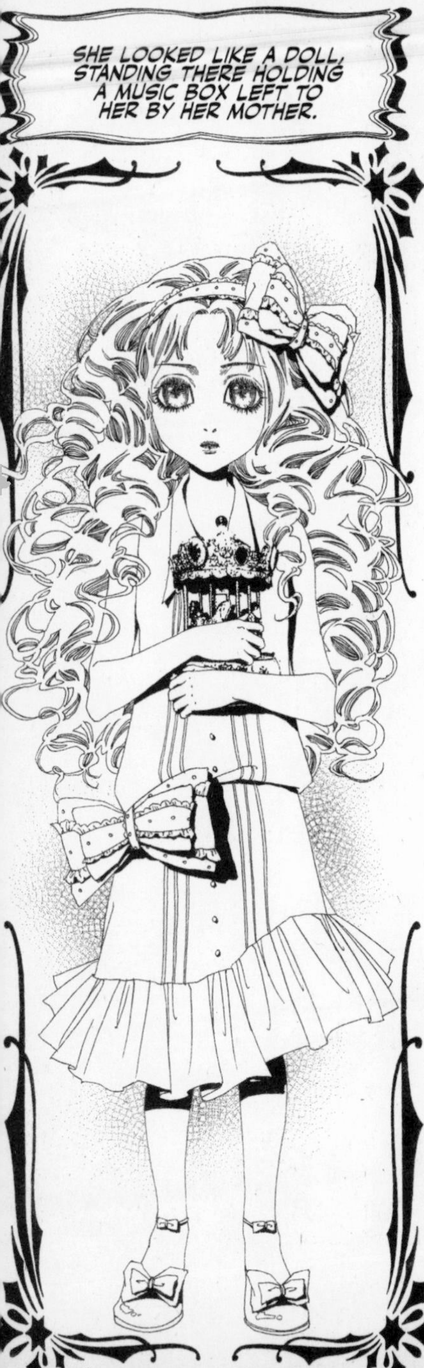
SHE LOOKED LIKE A DOLL, STANDING THERE HOLDING A MUSIC BOX LEFT TO HER BY HER MOTHER.

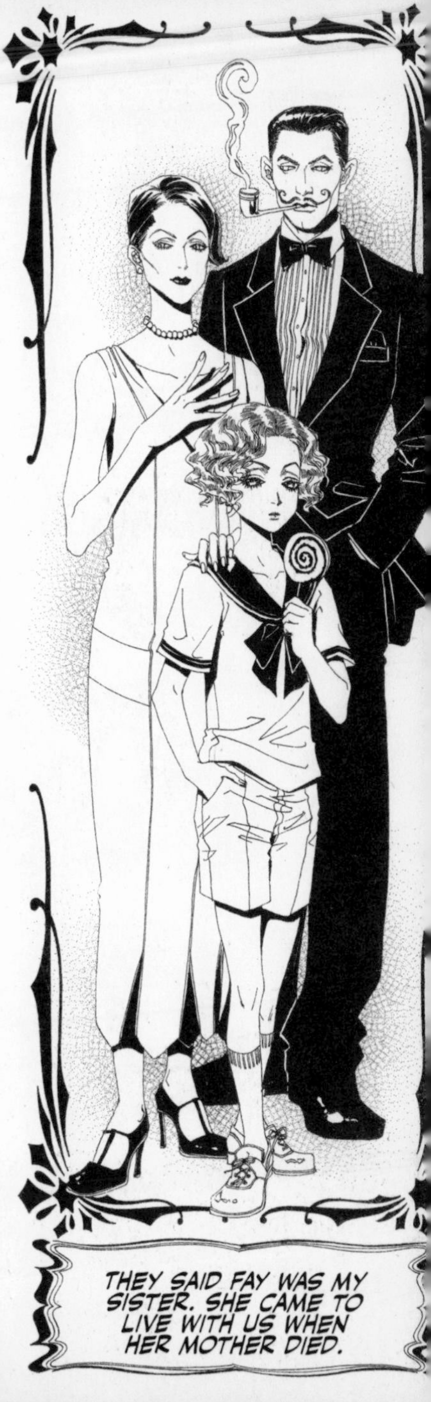
THEY SAID FAY WAS MY SISTER. SHE CAME TO LIVE WITH US WHEN HER MOTHER DIED.

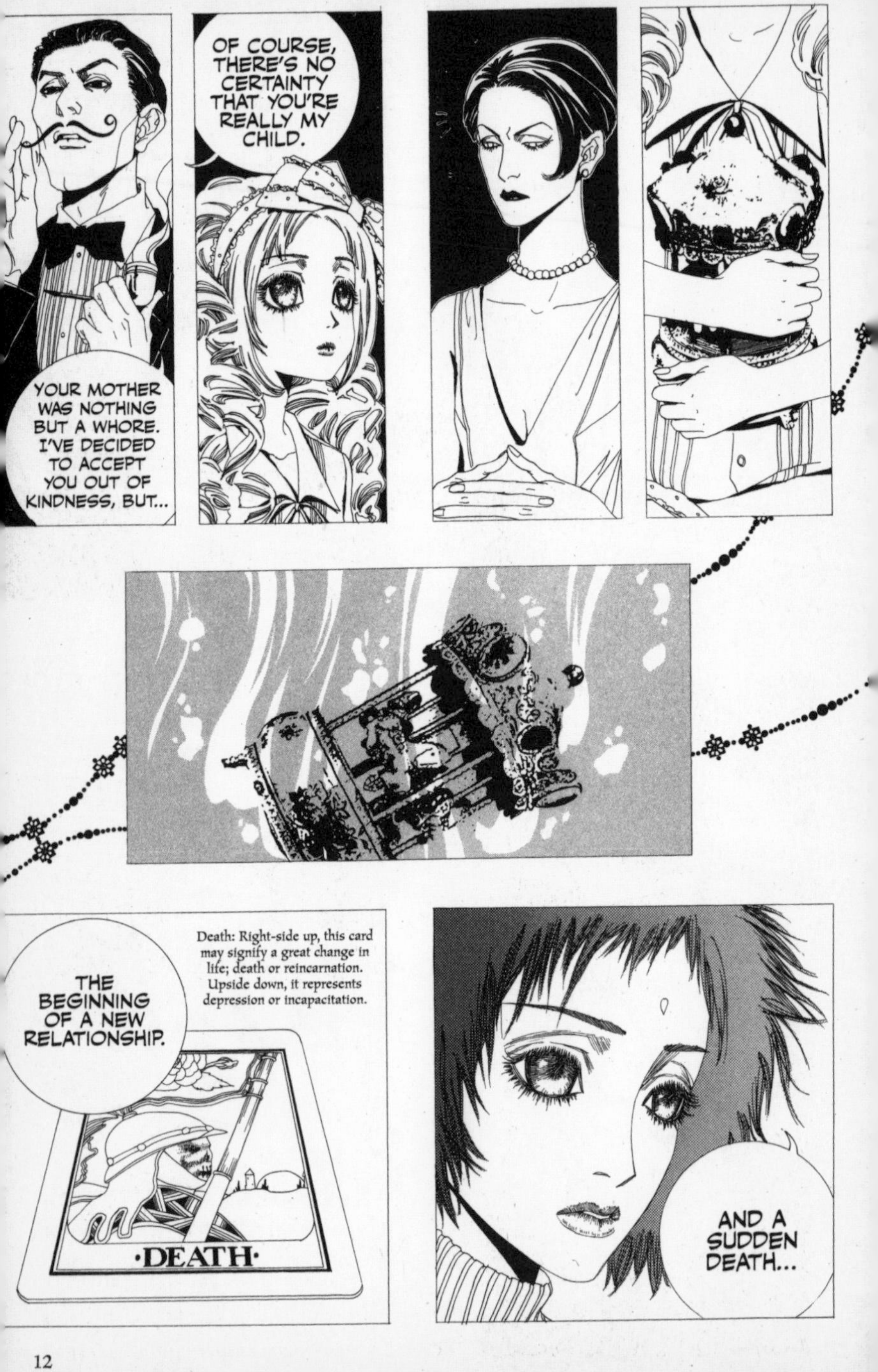
YOUR MOTHER WAS NOTHING BUT A WHORE. I'VE DECIDED TO ACCEPT YOU OUT OF KINDNESS, BUT...
OF COURSE, THERE'S NO CERTAINTY THAT YOU'RE REALLY MY CHILD.
THE BEGINNING OF A NEW RELATIONSHIP.
Death: Right-side up, this card may signify a great change in life; death or reincarnation. Upside down, it represents depression or incapacitation.
·DEATH·
AND A SUDDEN DEATH...

YES, MY FATHER DIED.

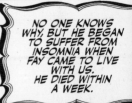

NO ONE KNOWS WHY, BUT HE BEGAN TO SUFFER FROM INSOMNIA WHEN FAY CAME TO LIVE WITH US. HE DIED WITHIN A WEEK.

SOME SAID THAT FAY'S MOTHER DIED THE SAME WAY.

MY MOTHER HATED FAY. SHE HAD HER LOCKED UP IN THE ATTIC TO LIVE IN ISOLATION, LIKE A LEPER.

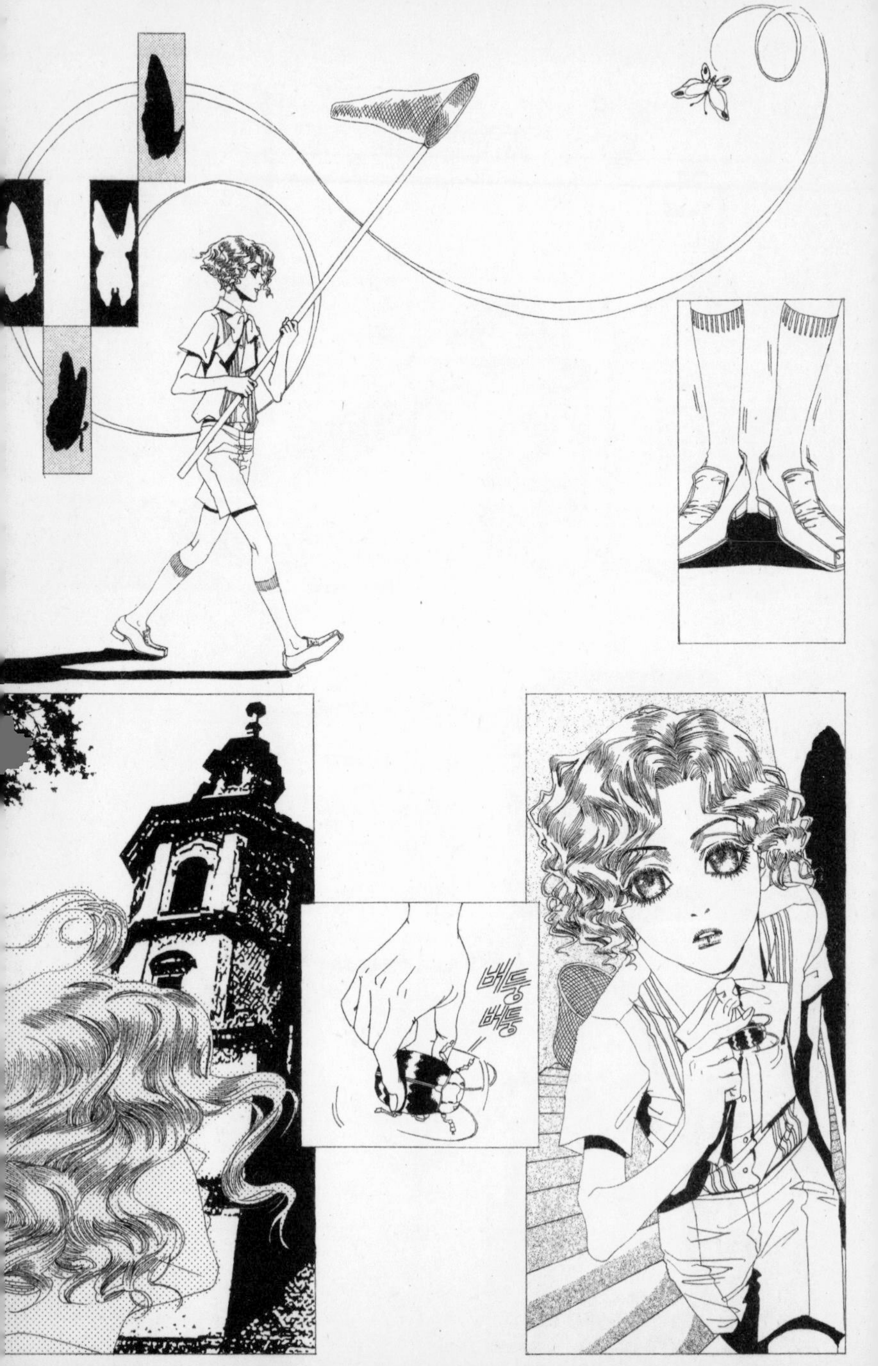
버둥
버둥

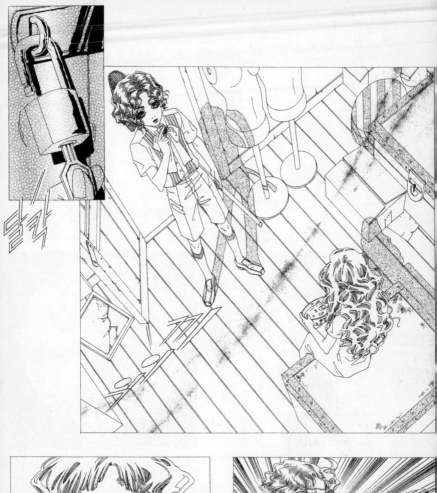

YOU FILTHY LITTLE THING!

HERE, EAT THIS!

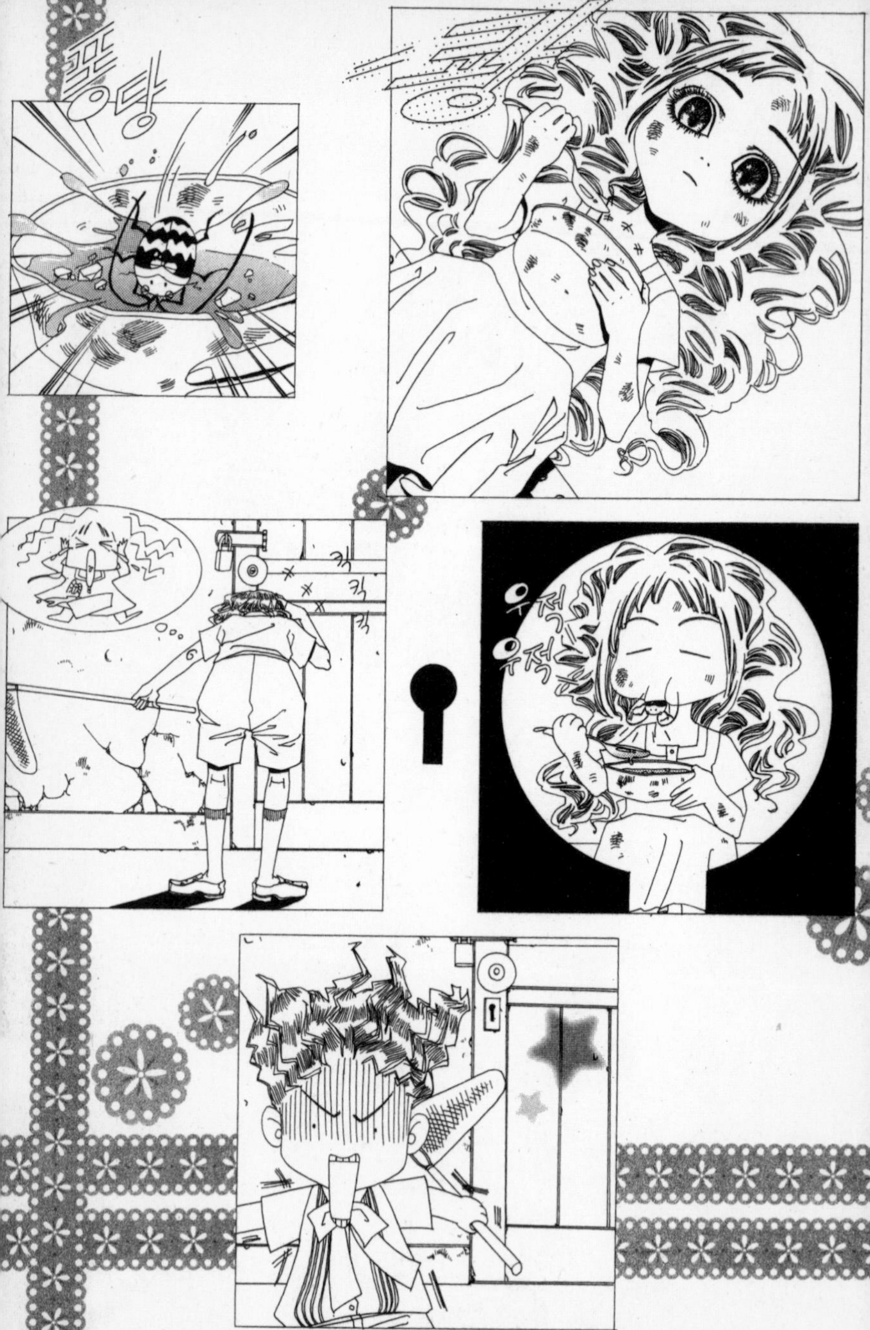
퐁당
우적
우적

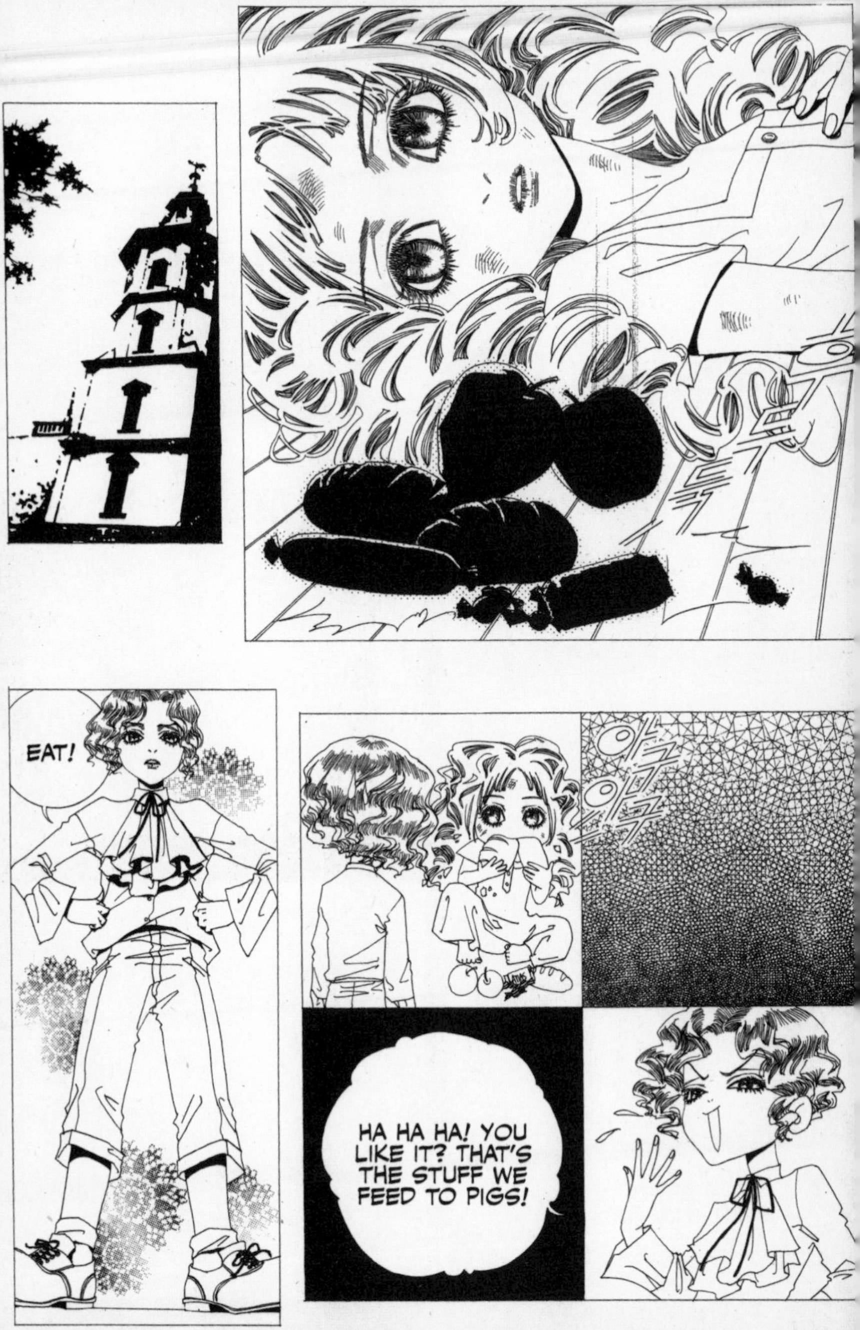
EAT!
HA HA HA! YOU LIKE IT? THAT'S THE STUFF WE FEED TO PIGS!

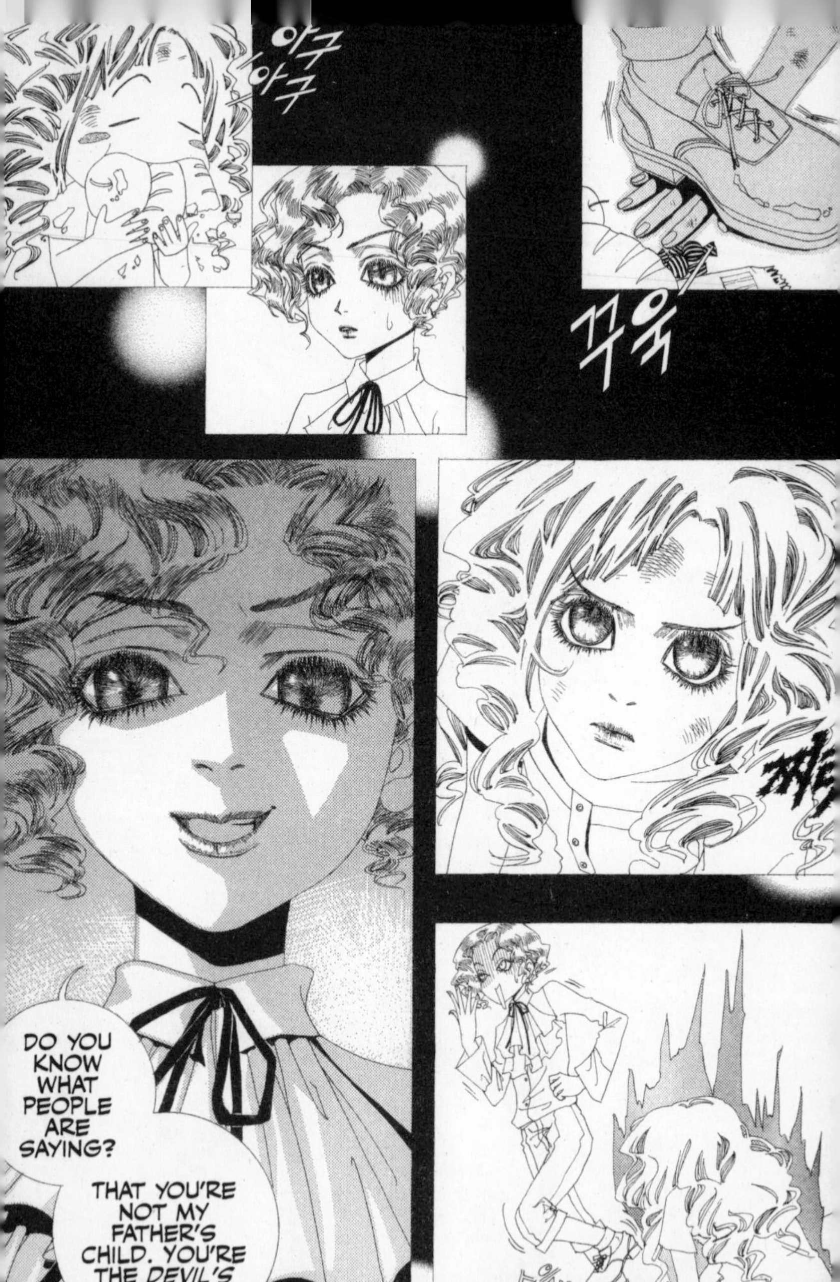
아구 아구
꾸욱
DO YOU KNOW WHAT PEOPLE ARE SAYING?
THAT YOU'RE NOT MY FATHER'S CHILD. YOU'RE THE *DEVIL'S* CHILD.
스윽..

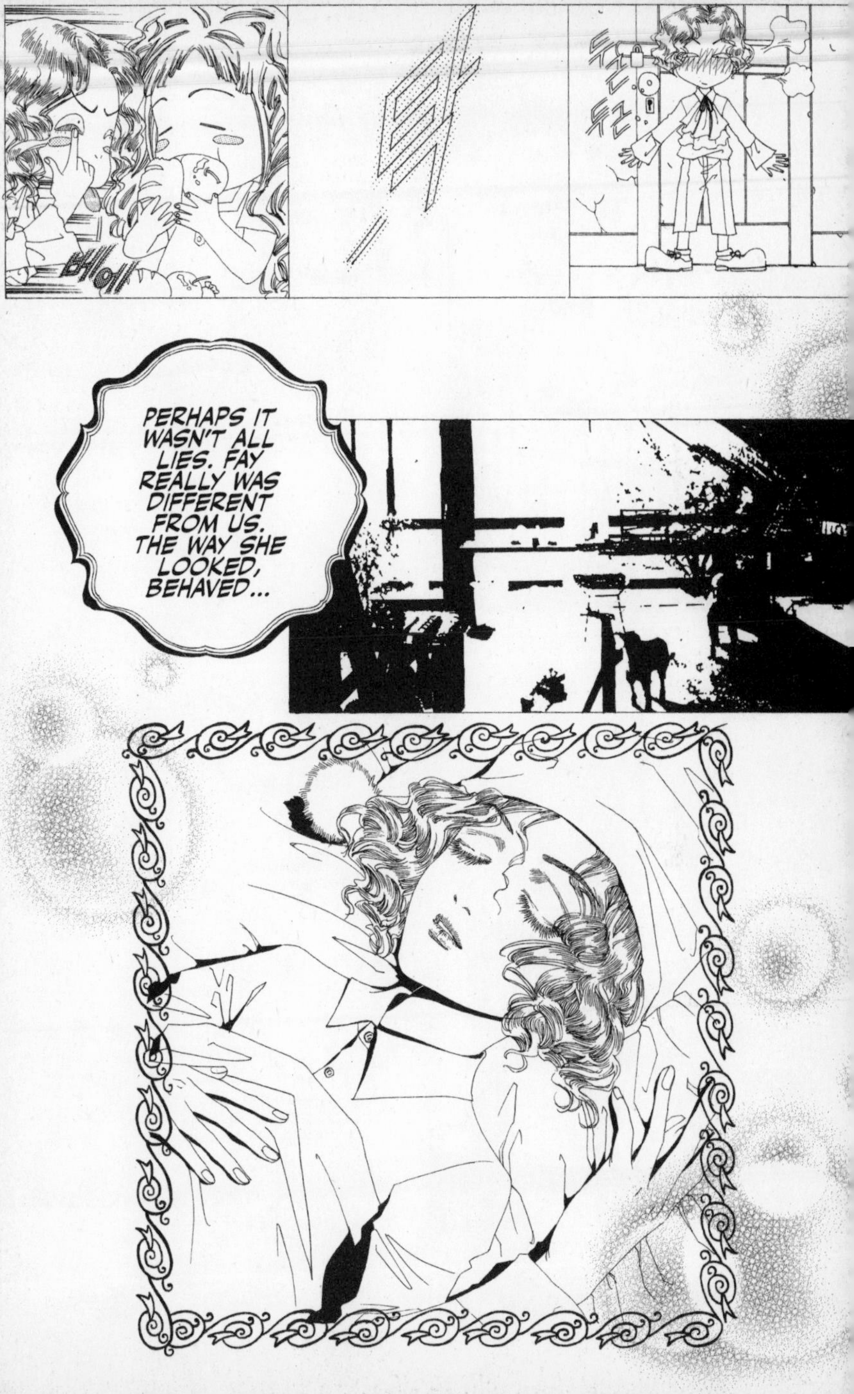
PERHAPS IT WASN'T ALL LIES. FAY REALLY WAS DIFFERENT FROM US. THE WAY SHE LOOKED, BEHAVED...

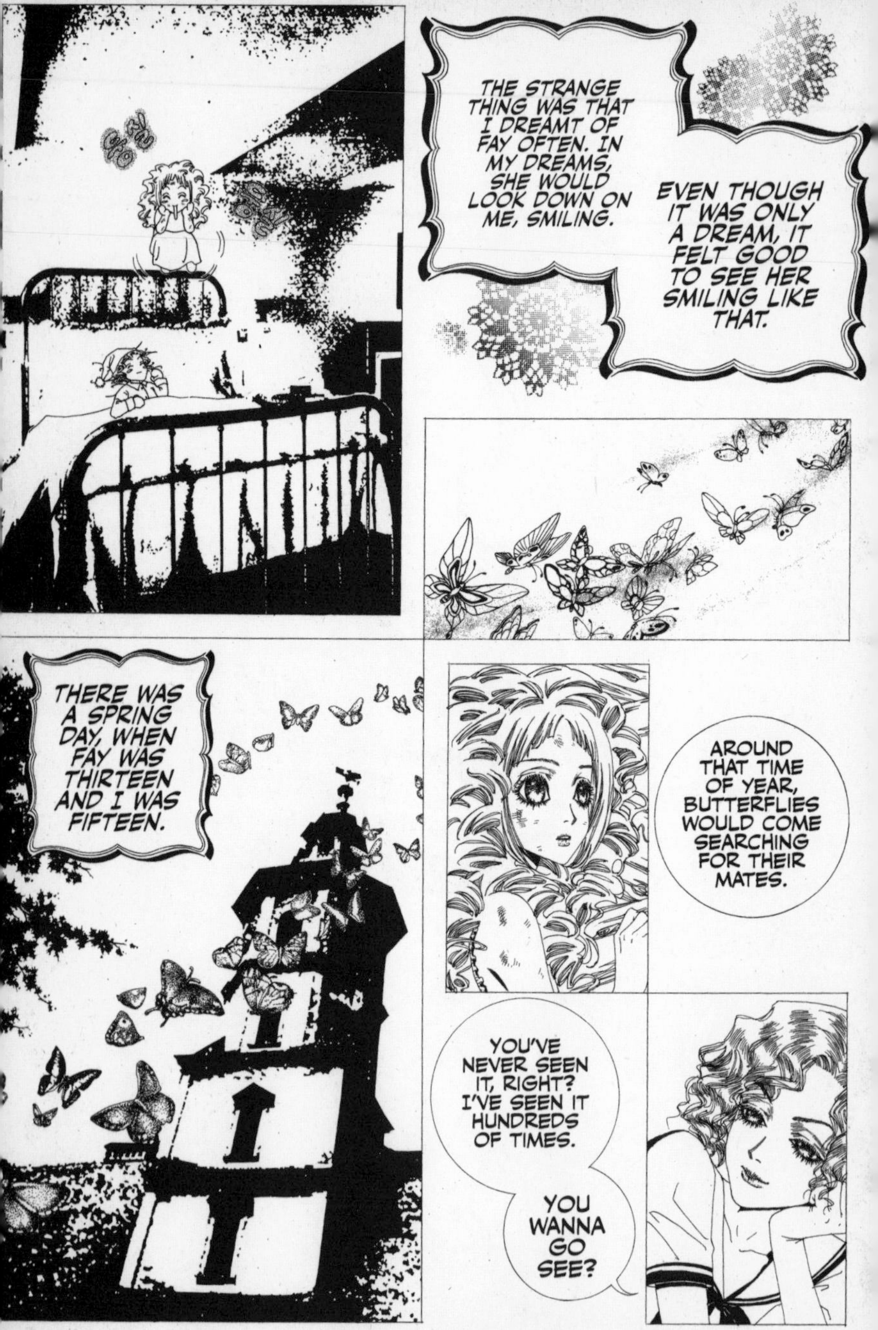
THE STRANGE THING WAS THAT I DREAMT OF FAY OFTEN. IN MY DREAMS, SHE WOULD LOOK DOWN ON ME, SMILING.
EVEN THOUGH IT WAS ONLY A DREAM, IT FELT GOOD TO SEE HER SMILING LIKE THAT.
THERE WAS A SPRING DAY, WHEN FAY WAS THIRTEEN AND I WAS FIFTEEN.
AROUND THAT TIME OF YEAR, BUTTERFLIES WOULD COME SEARCHING FOR THEIR MATES.
YOU'VE NEVER SEEN IT, RIGHT? I'VE SEEN IT HUNDREDS OF TIMES.
YOU WANNA GO SEE?

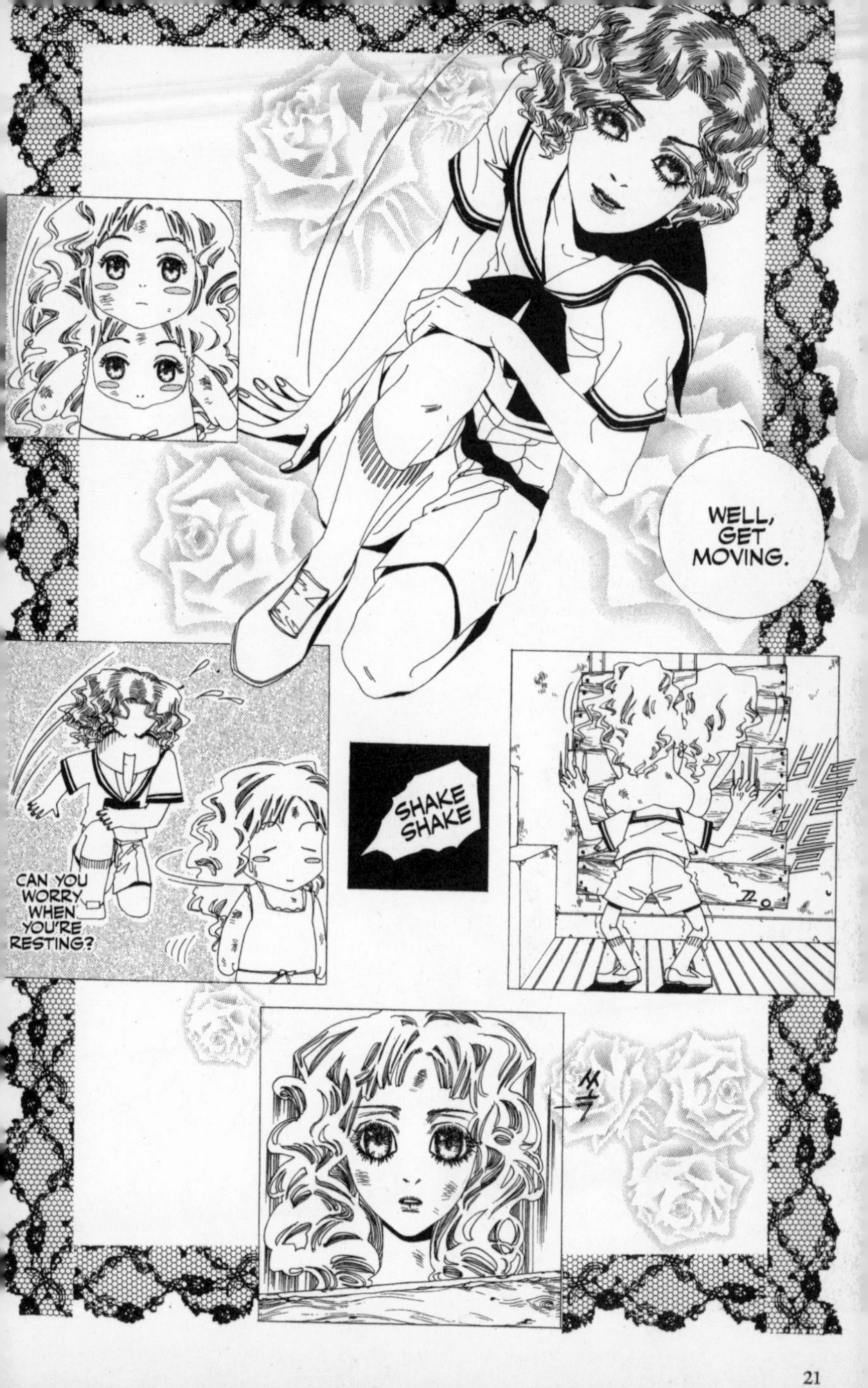
WELL, GET MOVING.
CAN YOU WORRY WHEN YOU'RE RESTING?
SHAKE SHAKE

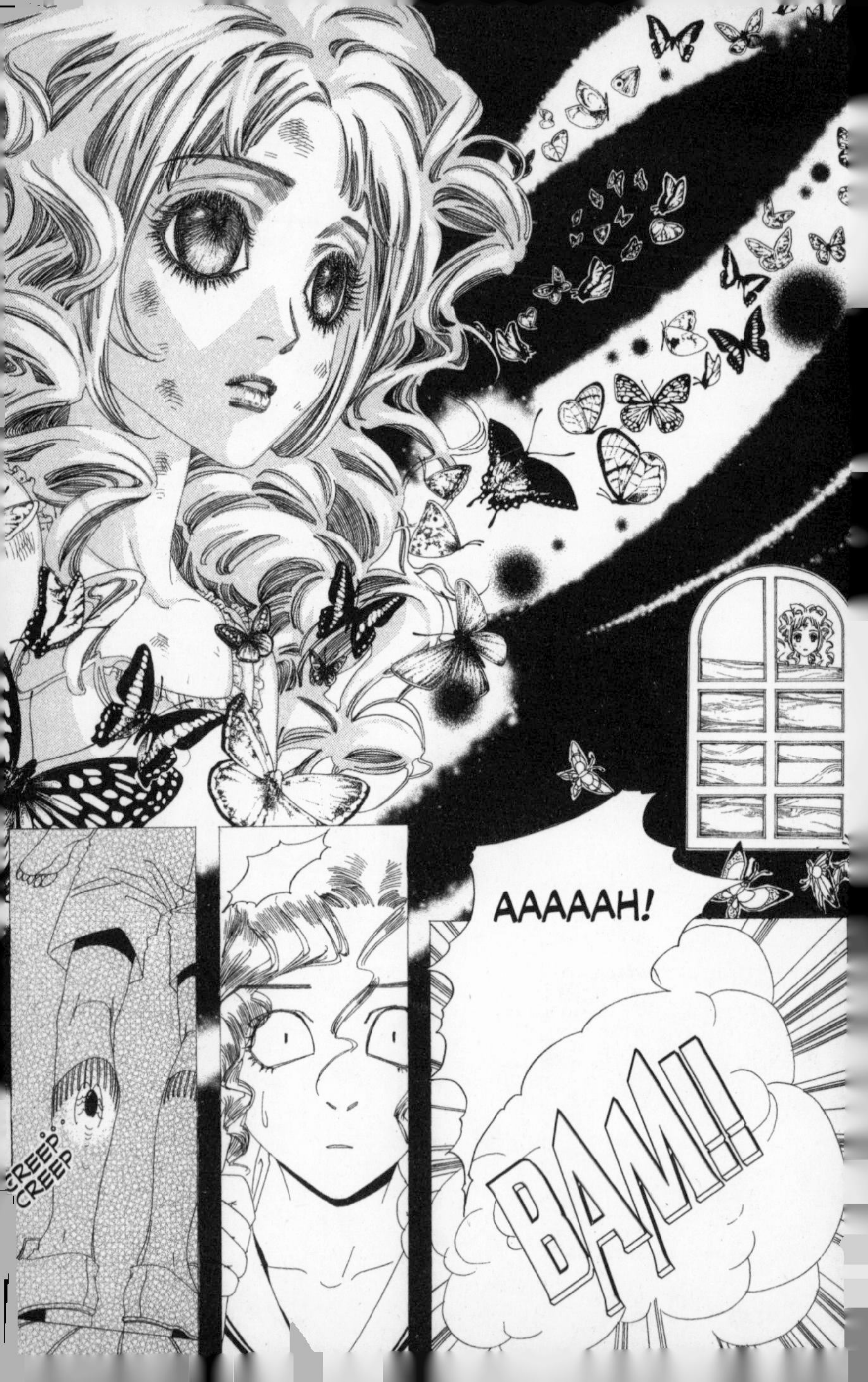
CREEP CREEP
AAAAAH!
BAM!!

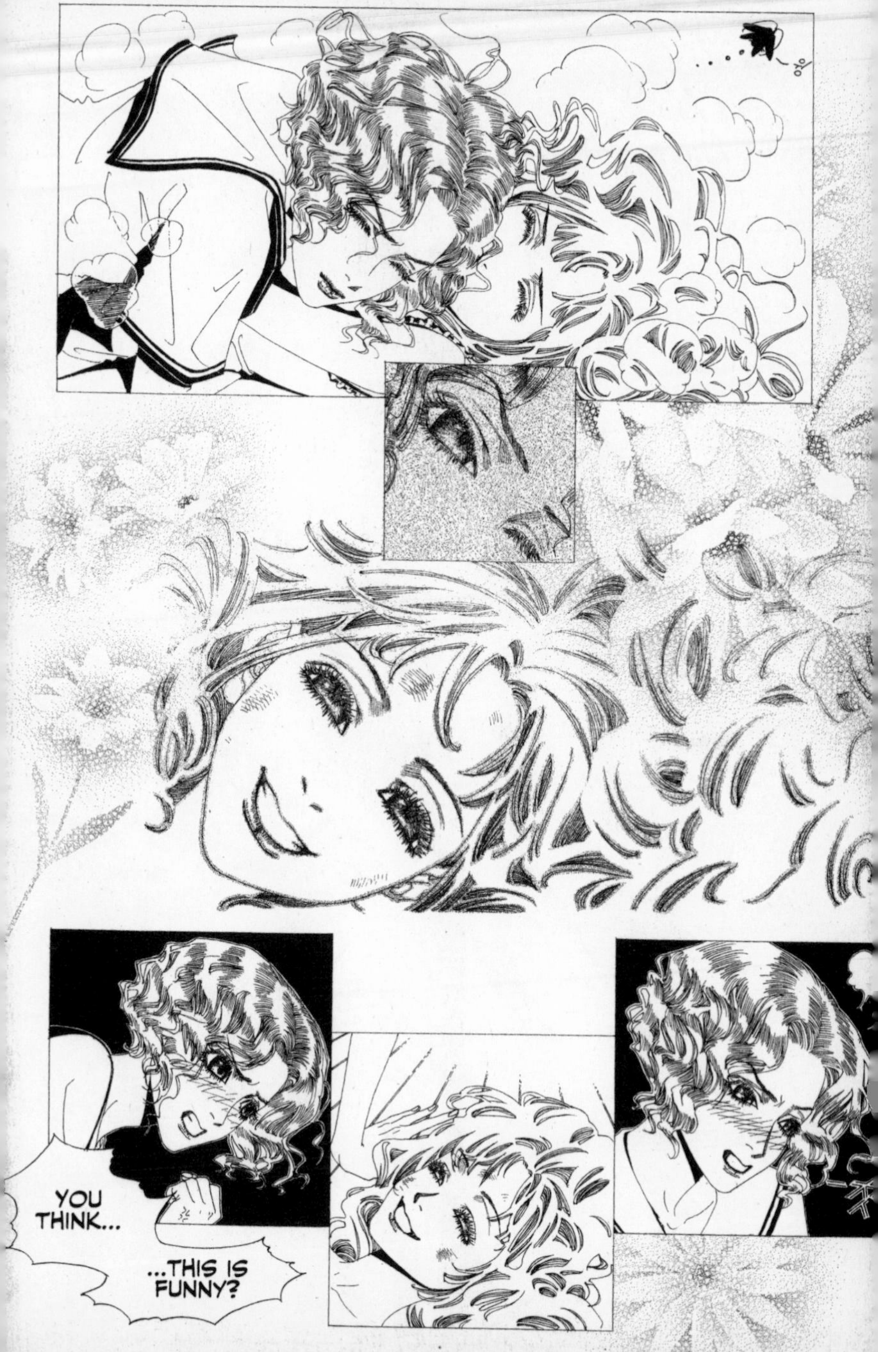
YOU THINK...
...THIS IS FUNNY?

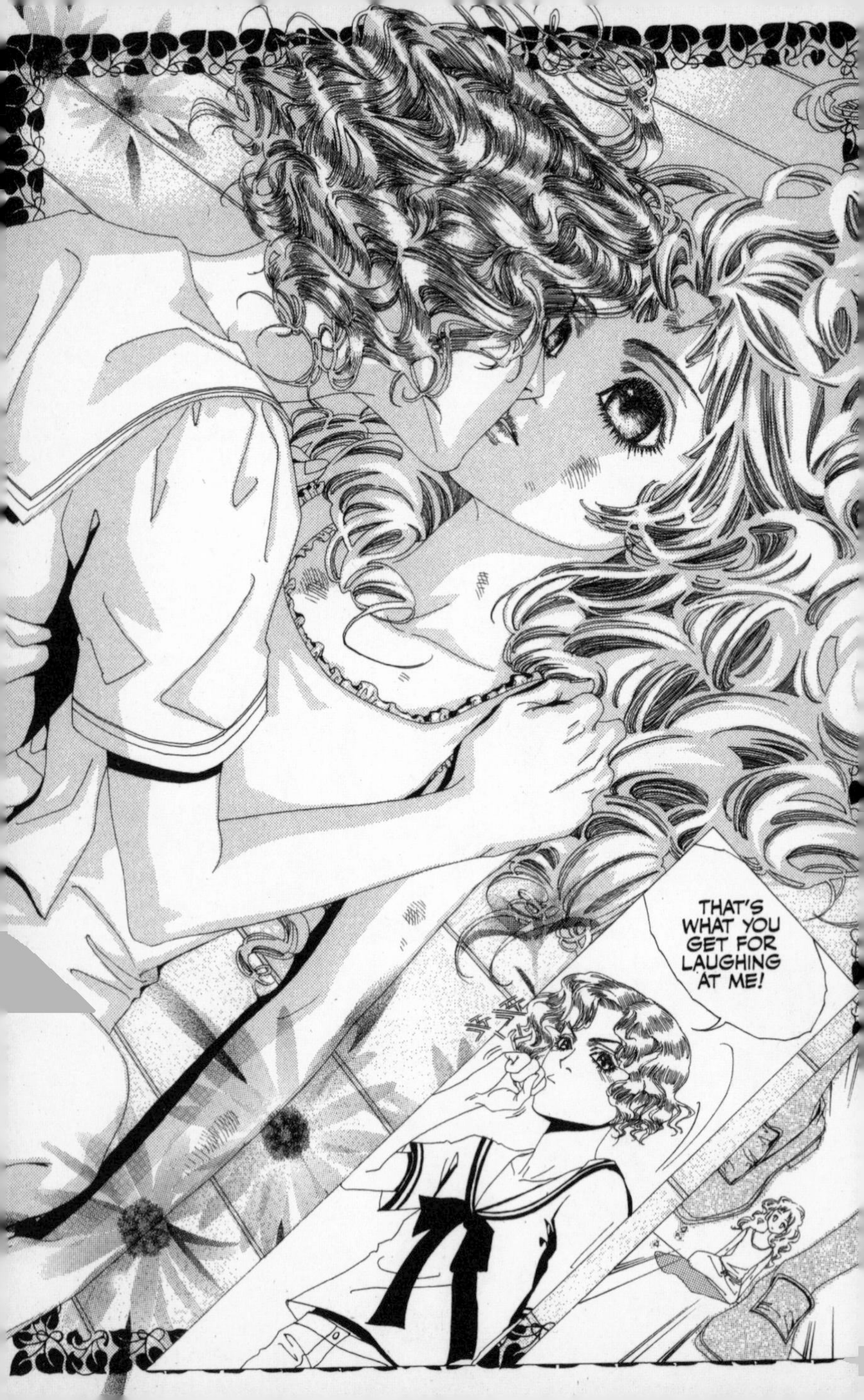
THAT'S WHAT YOU GET FOR LAUGHING AT ME!

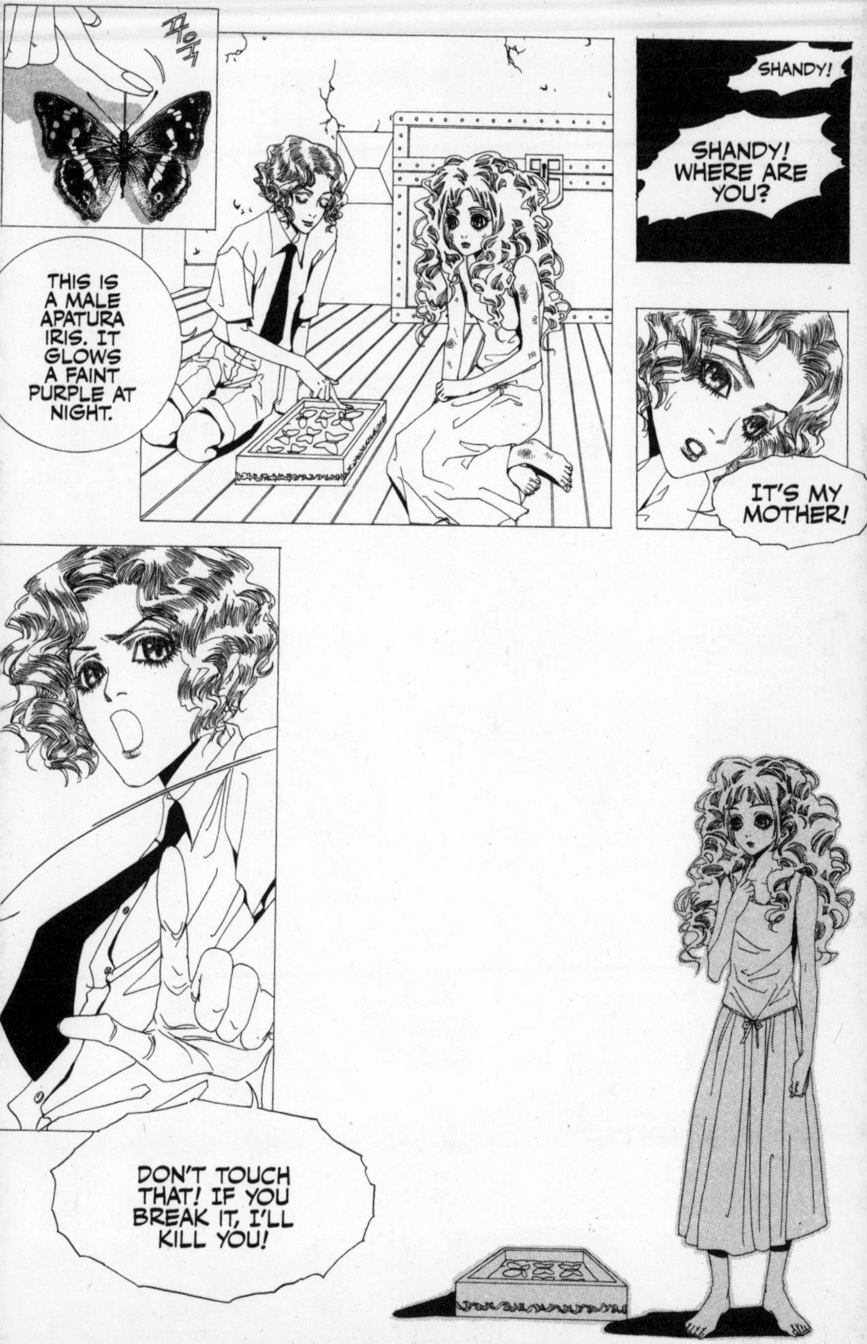
THIS IS A MALE APATURA IRIS. IT GLOWS A FAINT PURPLE AT NIGHT.
SHANDY!
SHANDY! WHERE ARE YOU?
IT'S MY MOTHER!
DON'T TOUCH THAT! IF YOU BREAK IT, I'LL KILL YOU!

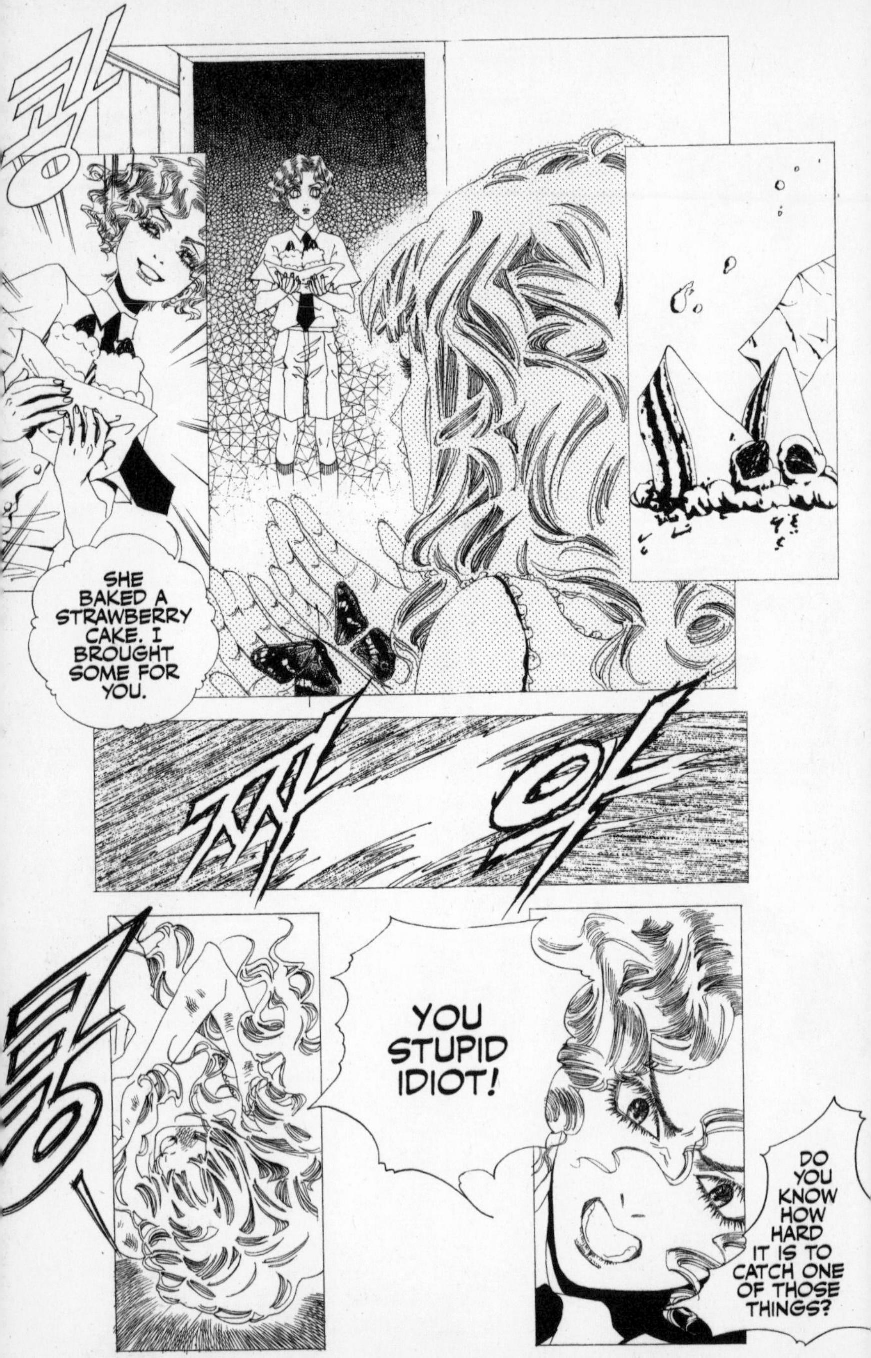
SHE BAKED A STRAWBERRY CAKE. I BROUGHT SOME FOR YOU.
YOU STUPID IDIOT!
DO YOU KNOW HOW HARD IT IS TO CATCH ONE OF THOSE THINGS?

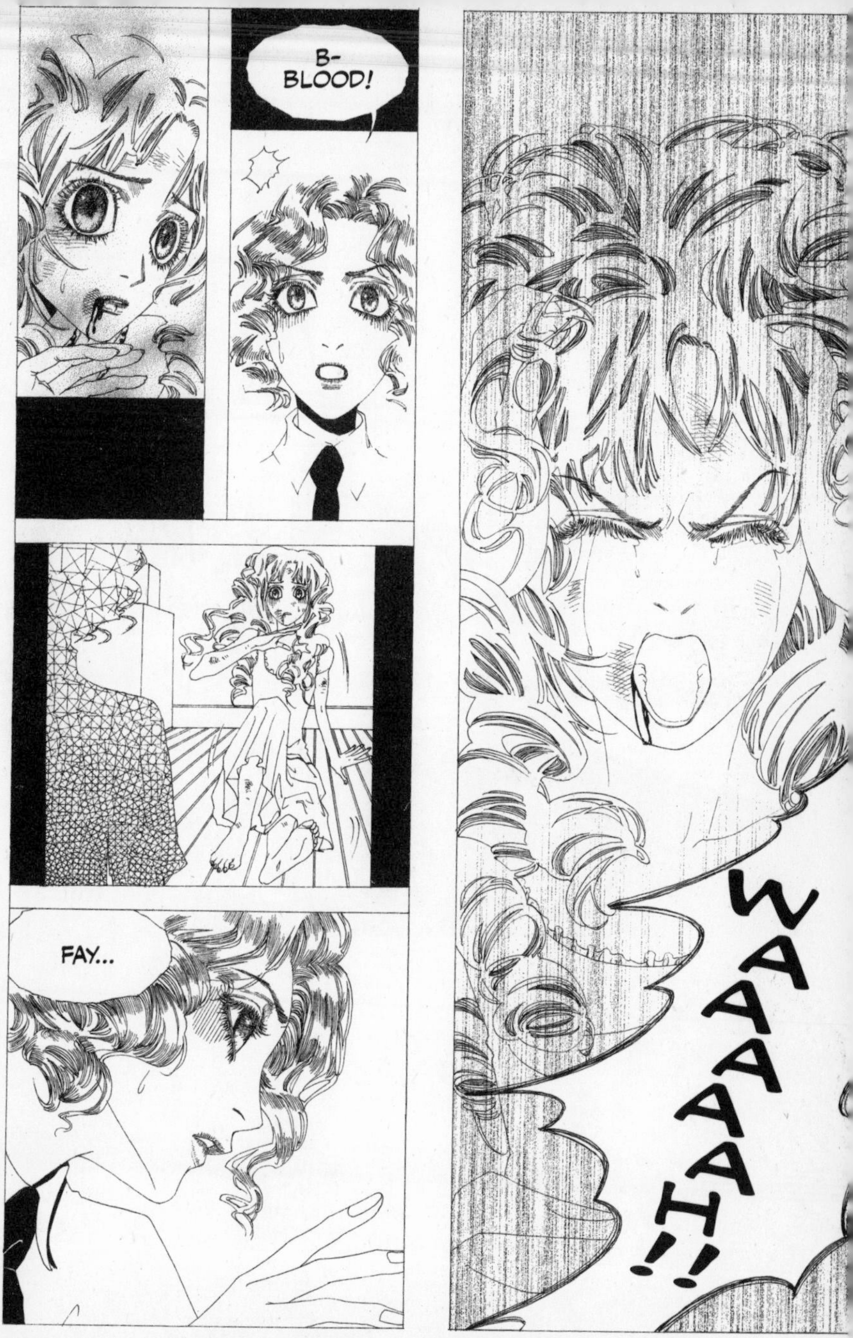
B-
BLOOD!
FAY...
WAAAAAH!!

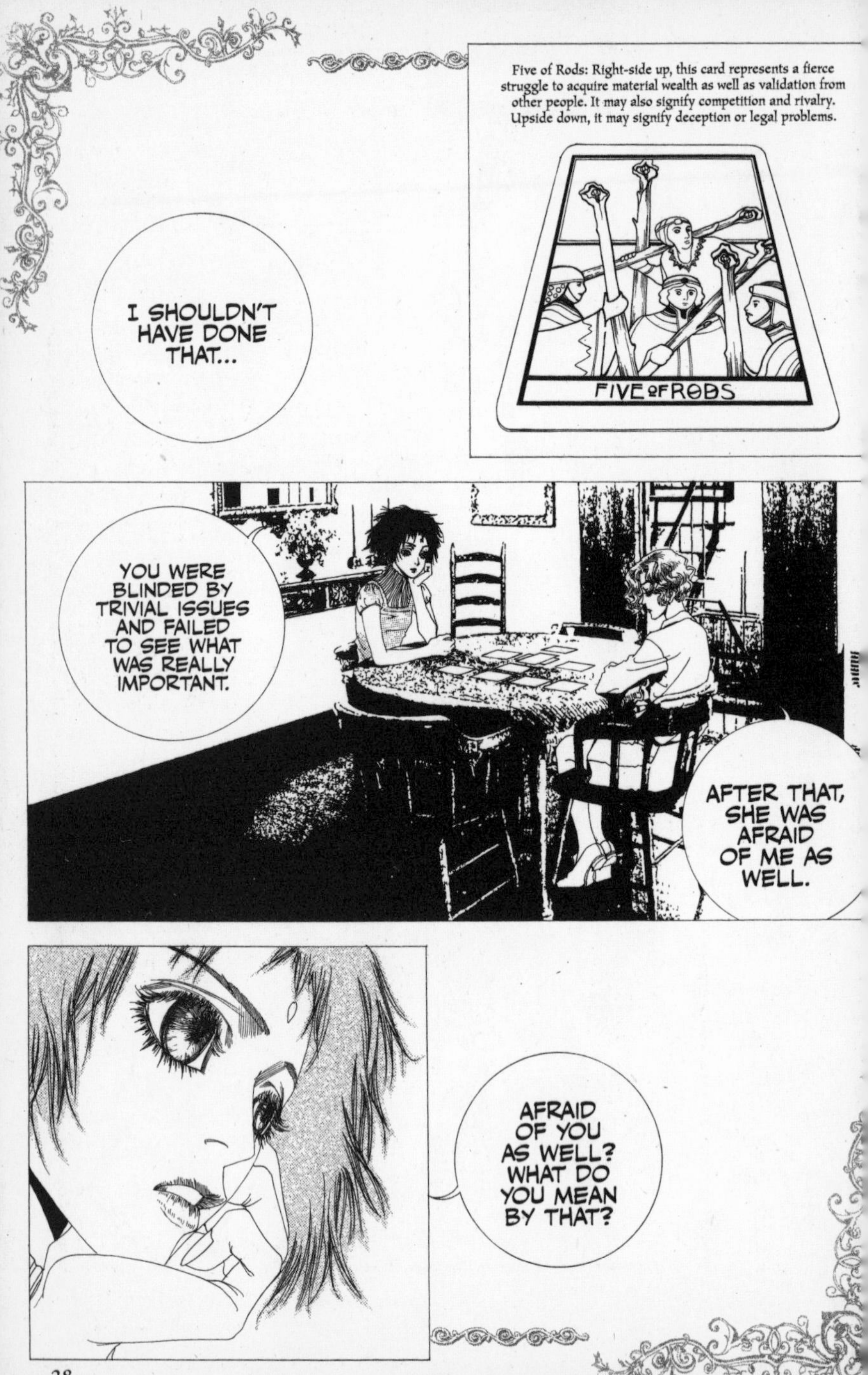
I SHOULDN'T HAVE DONE THAT...
Five of Rods: Right-side up, this card represents a fierce struggle to acquire material wealth as well as validation from other people. It may also signify competition and rivalry. Upside down, it may signify deception or legal problems.
FIVE OF RODS
YOU WERE BLINDED BY TRIVIAL ISSUES AND FAILED TO SEE WHAT WAS REALLY IMPORTANT.
AFTER THAT, SHE WAS AFRAID OF ME AS WELL.
AFRAID OF YOU AS WELL? WHAT DO YOU MEAN BY THAT?

8 Swords

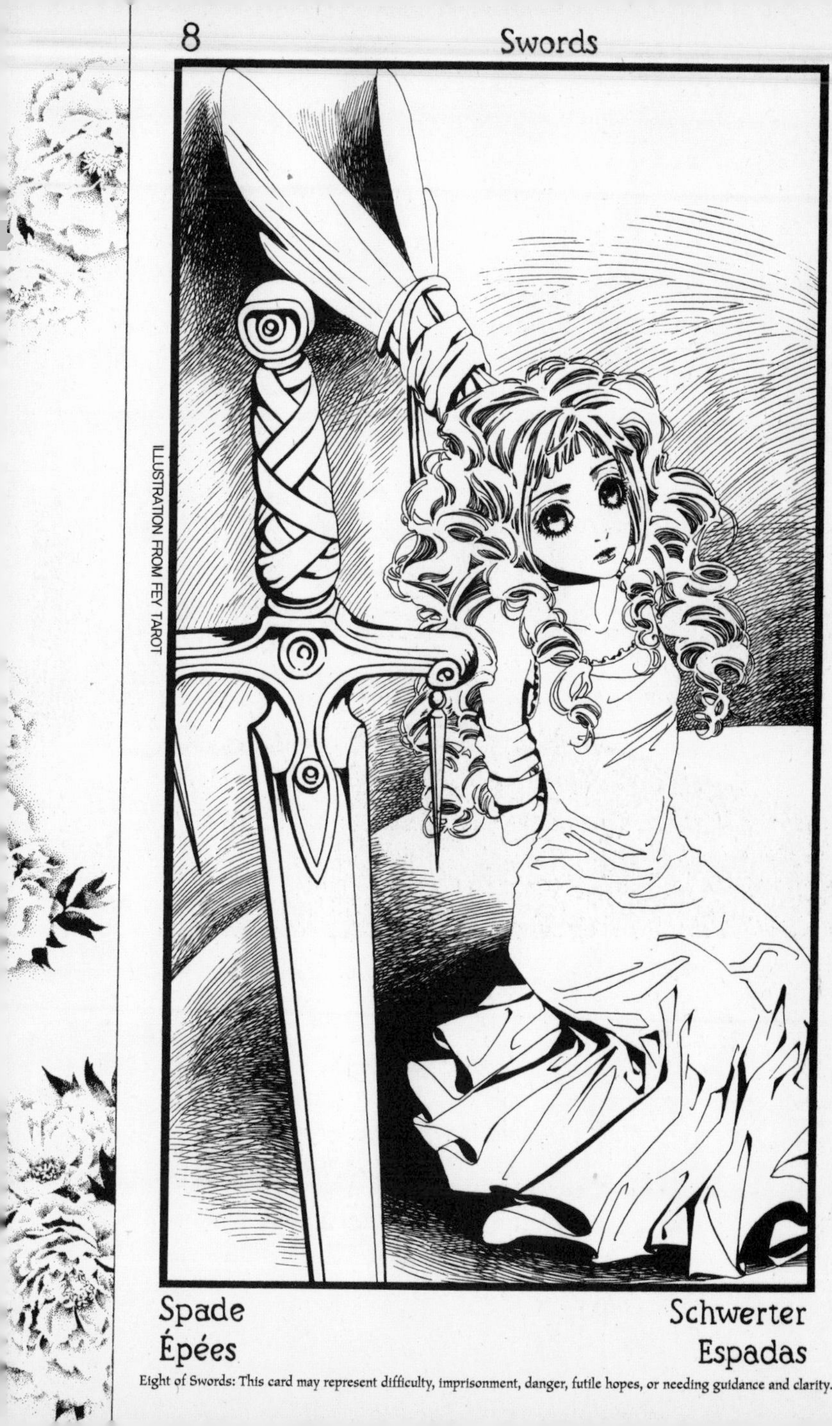

ILLUSTRATION FROM FEY TAROT

Spade
Épées

Schwerter
Espadas

Eight of Swords: This card may represent difficulty, imprisonment, danger, futile hopes, or needing guidance and clarity.

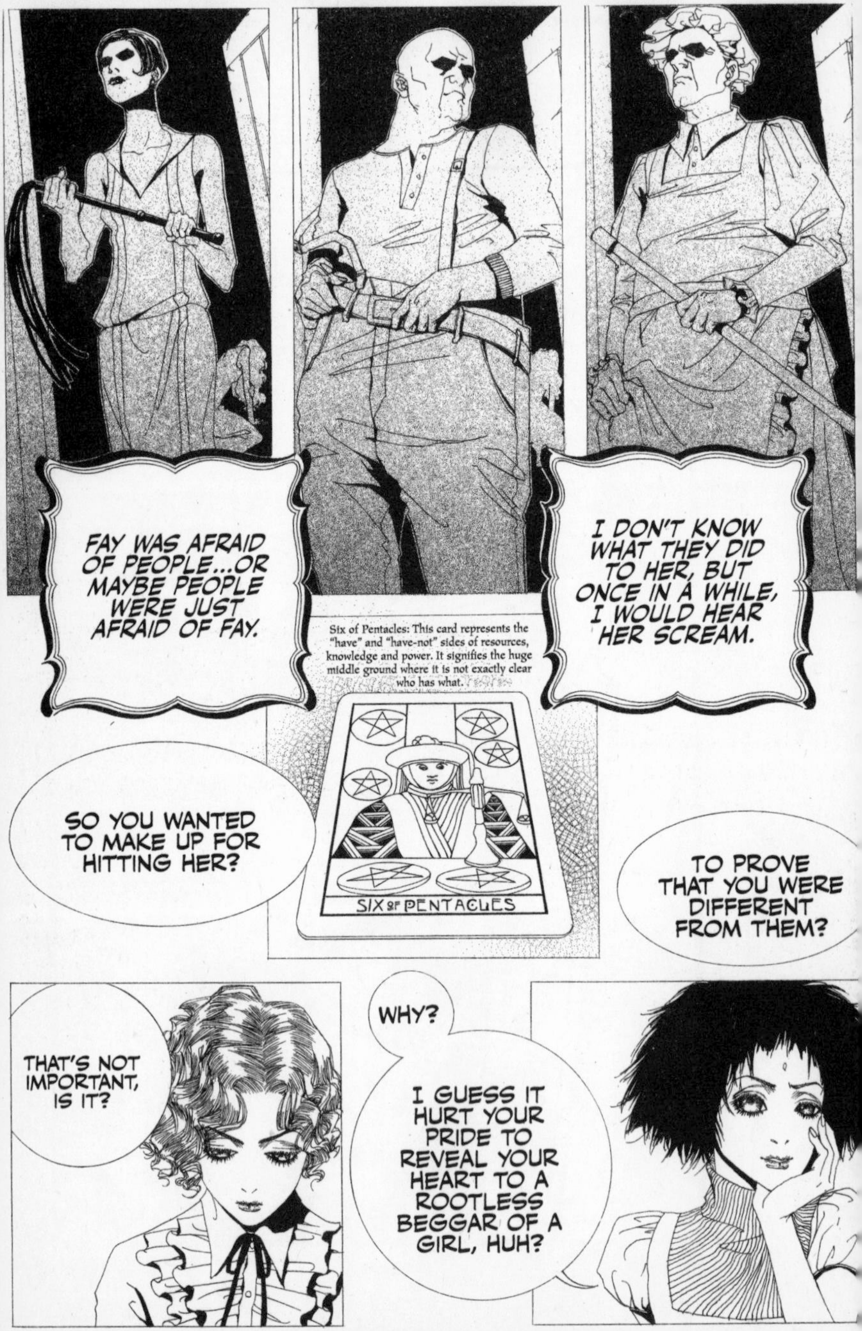
FAY WAS AFRAID OF PEOPLE...OR MAYBE PEOPLE WERE JUST AFRAID OF FAY.
I DON'T KNOW WHAT THEY DID TO HER, BUT ONCE IN A WHILE, I WOULD HEAR HER SCREAM.
SO YOU WANTED TO MAKE UP FOR HITTING HER?
Six of Pentacles: This card represents the "have" and "have-not" sides of resources, knowledge and power. It signifies the huge middle ground where it is not exactly clear who has what.
SIX OF PENTACLES
TO PROVE THAT YOU WERE DIFFERENT FROM THEM?
THAT'S NOT IMPORTANT, IS IT?
WHY?
I GUESS IT HURT YOUR PRIDE TO REVEAL YOUR HEART TO A ROOTLESS BEGGAR OF A GIRL, HUH?

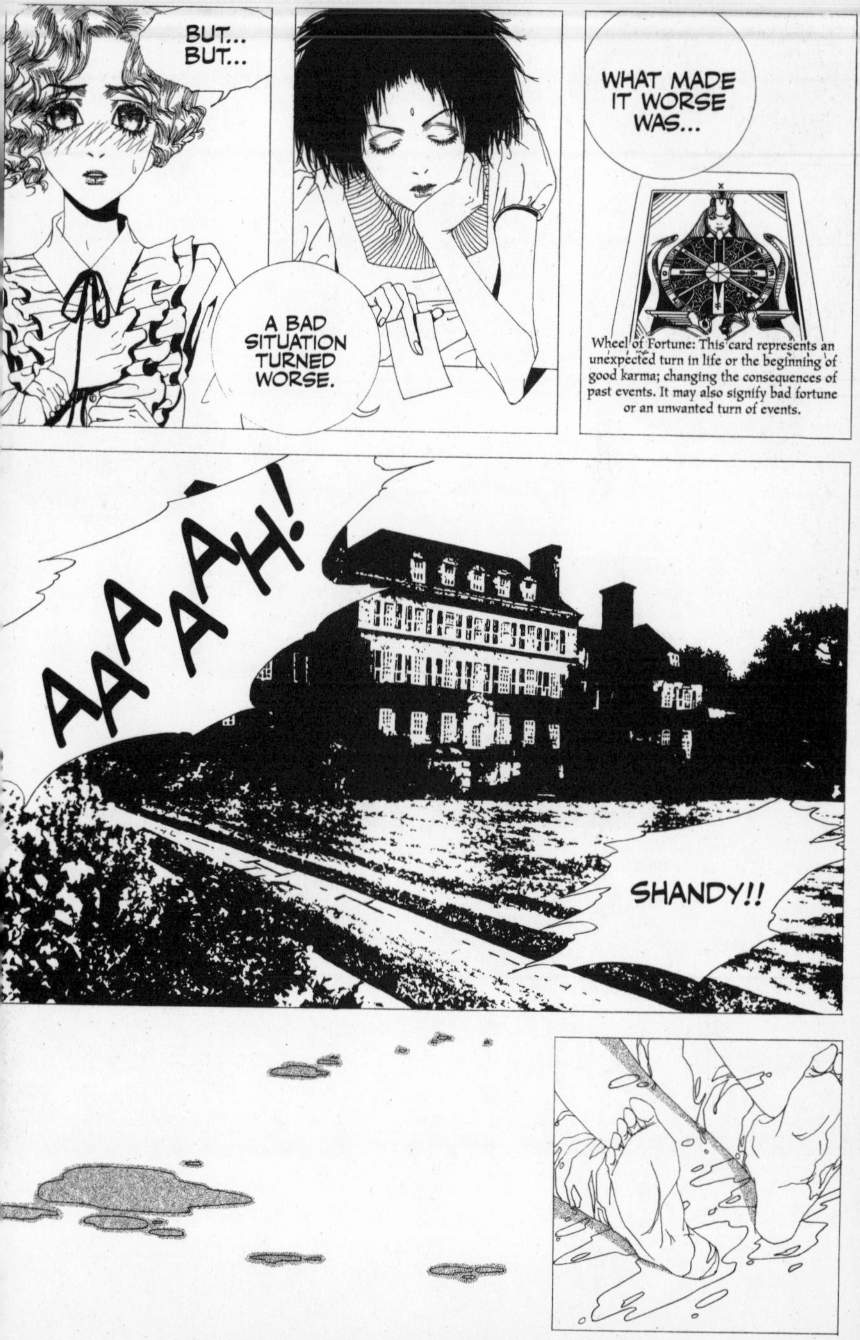
BUT...
BUT...
A BAD SITUATION TURNED WORSE.
WHAT MADE IT WORSE WAS...
Wheel of Fortune: This card represents an unexpected turn in life or the beginning of good karma; changing the consequences of past events. It may also signify bad fortune or an unwanted turn of events.
AAAAAH!
SHANDY!!

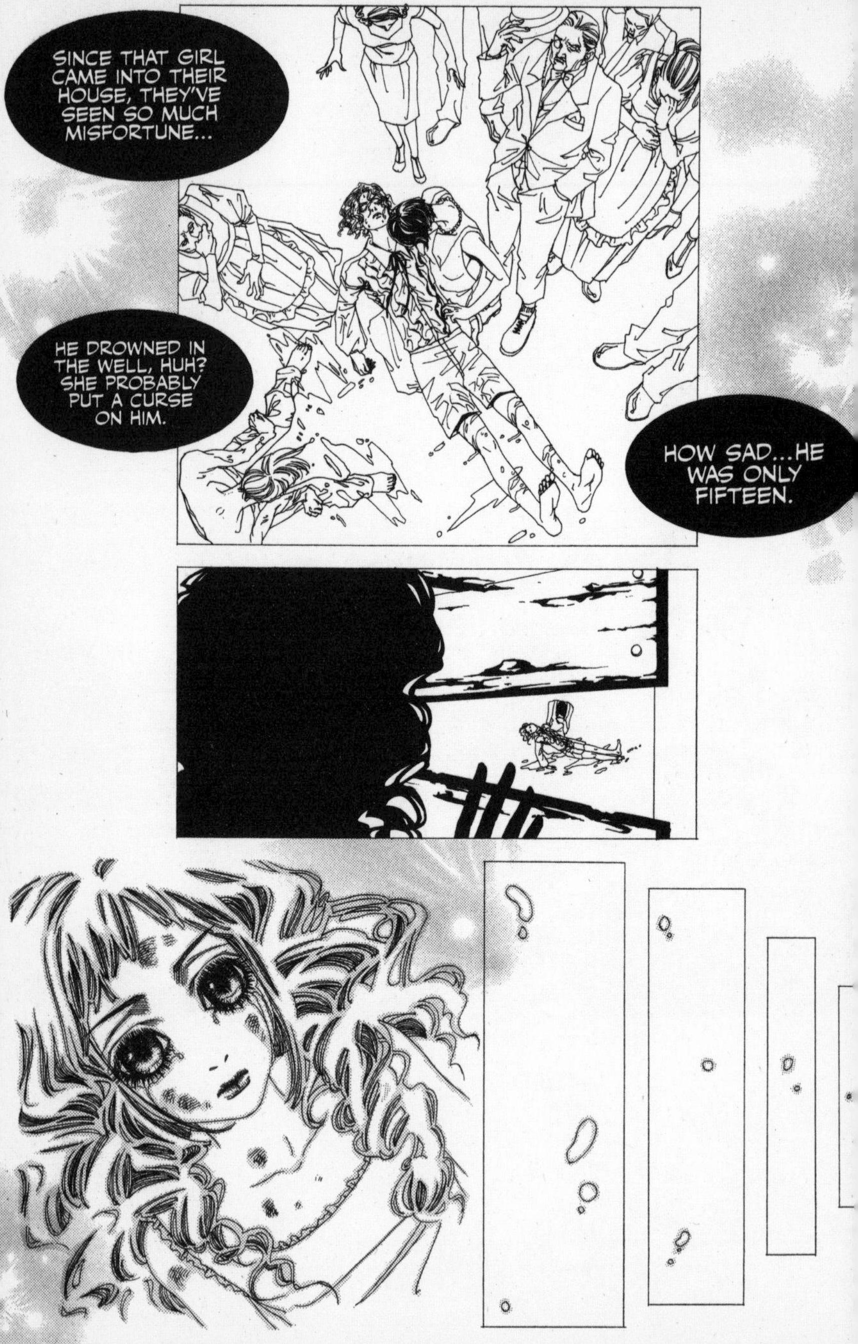
SINCE THAT GIRL CAME INTO THEIR HOUSE, THEY'VE SEEN SO MUCH MISFORTUNE...
HE DROWNED IN THE WELL, HUH? SHE PROBABLY PUT A CURSE ON HIM.
HOW SAD...HE WAS ONLY FIFTEEN.

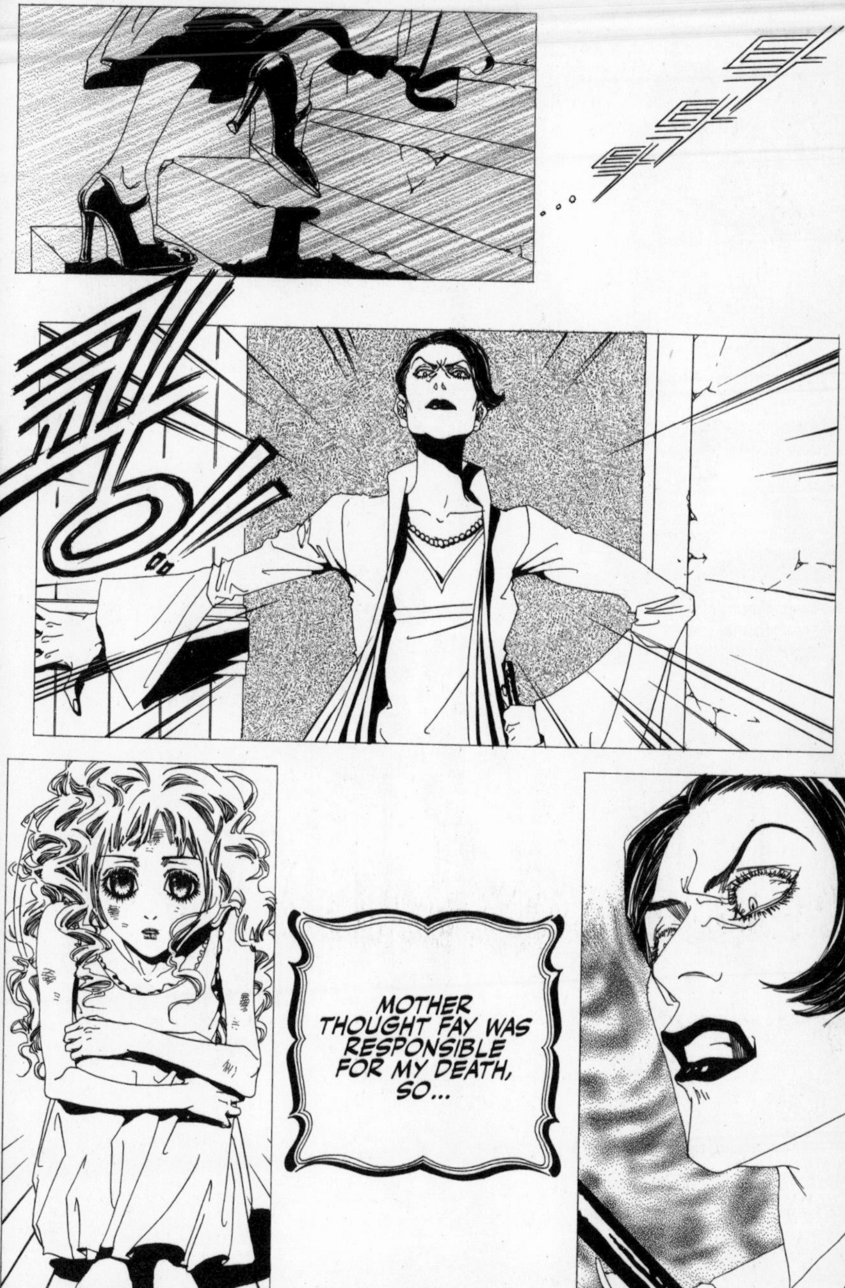
MOTHER THOUGHT FAY WAS RESPONSIBLE FOR MY DEATH, SO...

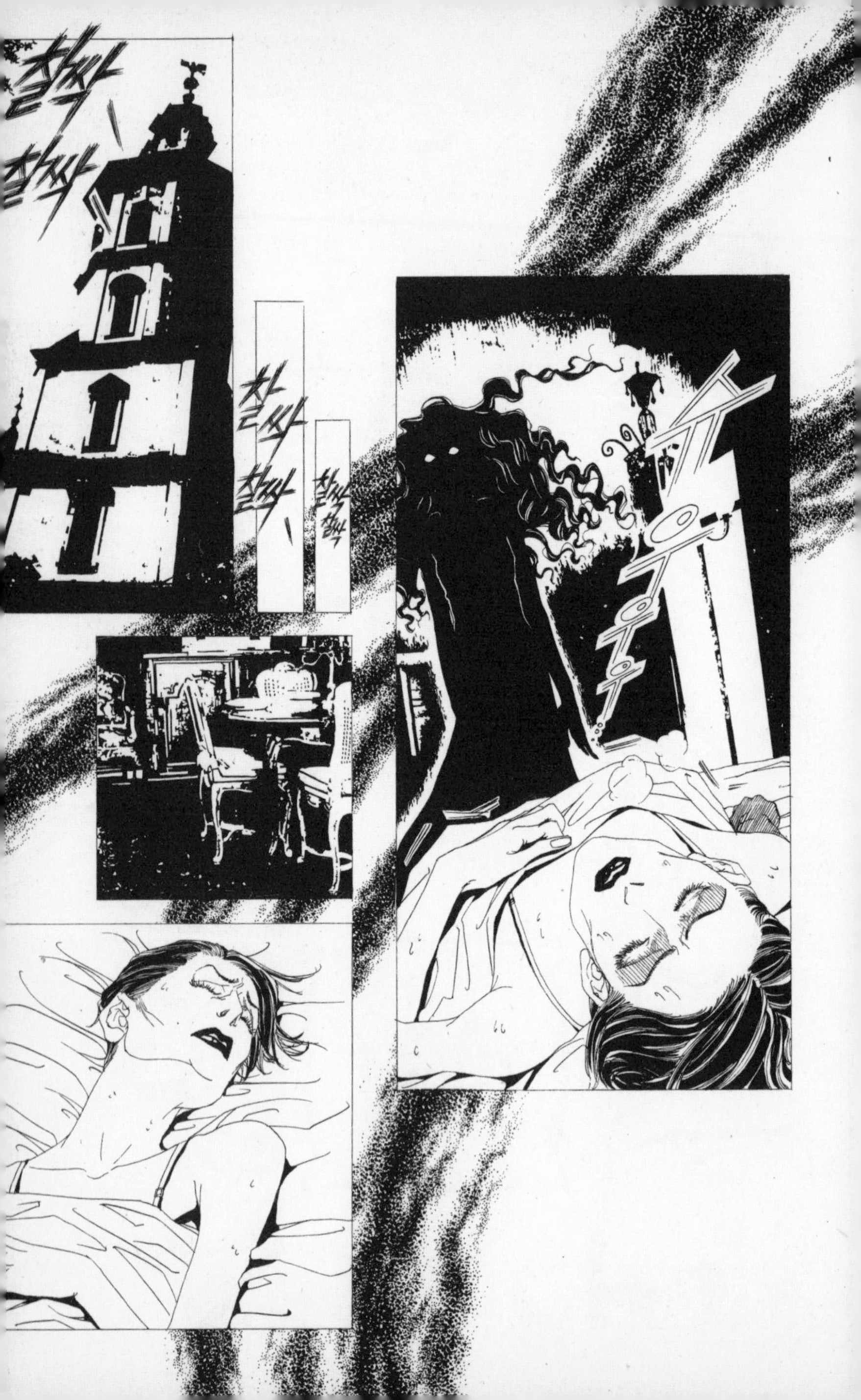
철썩 철썩
철썩 철썩
철썩 철썩
스으으으

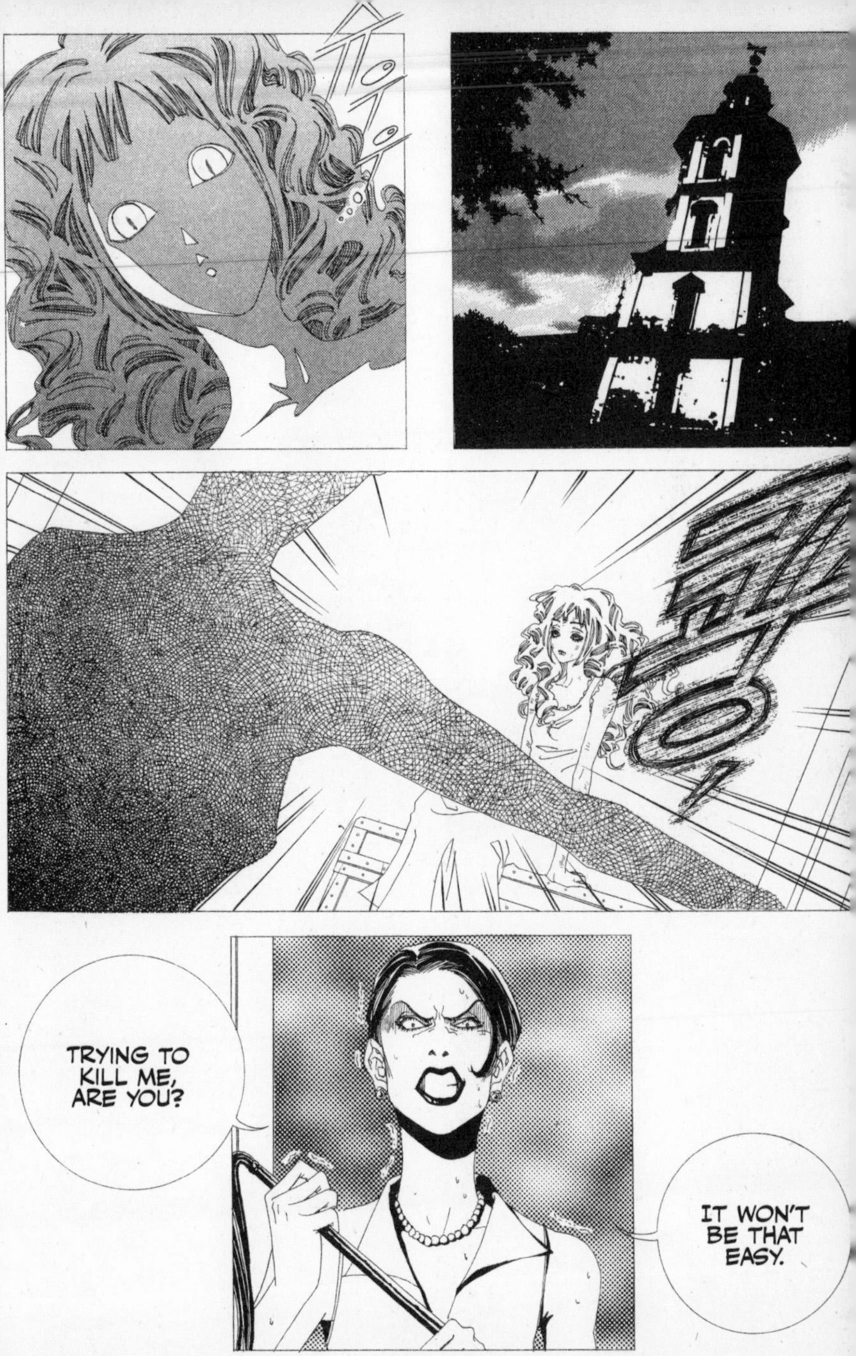
TRYING TO KILL ME, ARE YOU?
IT WON'T BE THAT EASY.

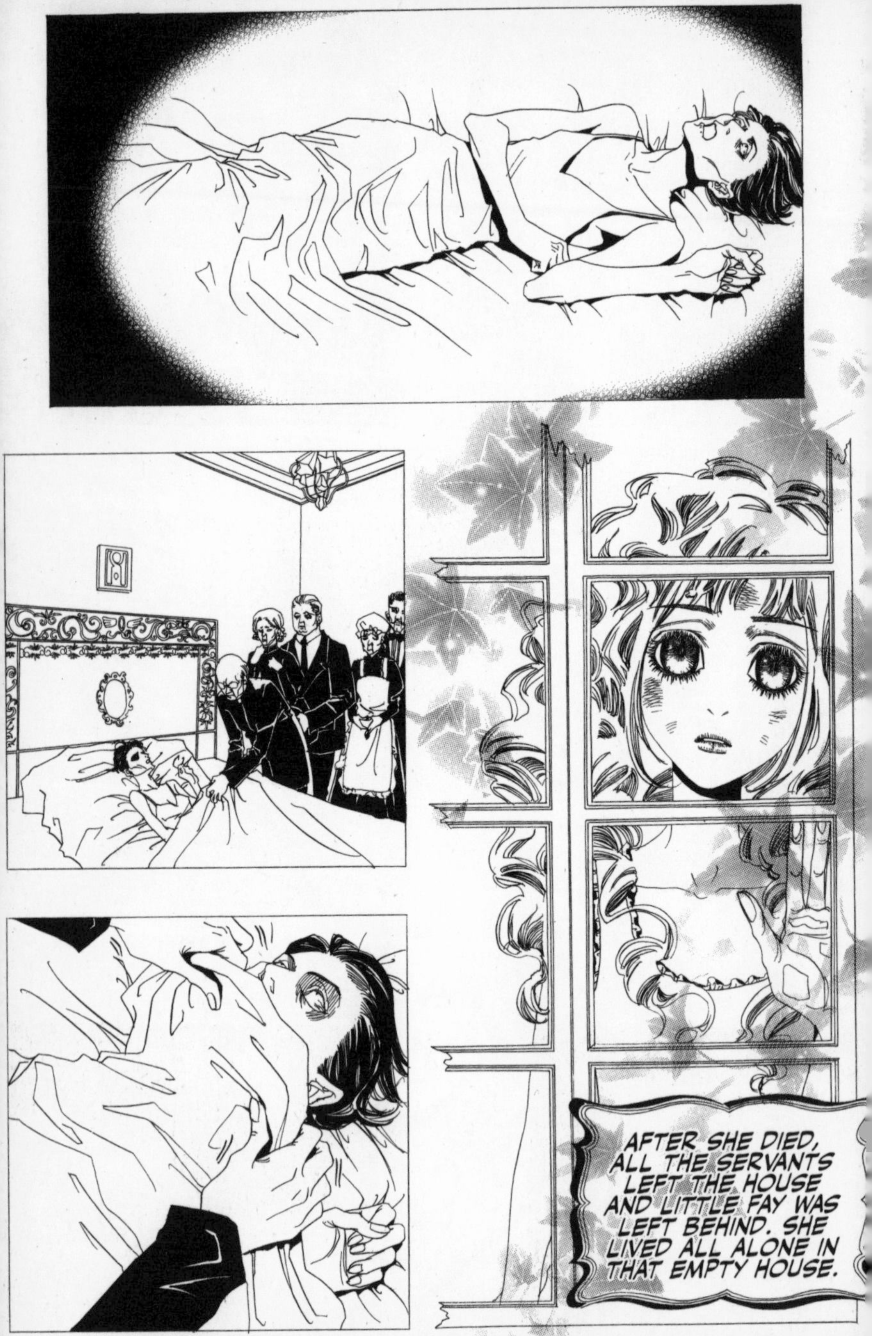
AFTER SHE DIED, ALL THE SERVANTS LEFT THE HOUSE AND LITTLE FAY WAS LEFT BEHIND. SHE LIVED ALL ALONE IN THAT EMPTY HOUSE.

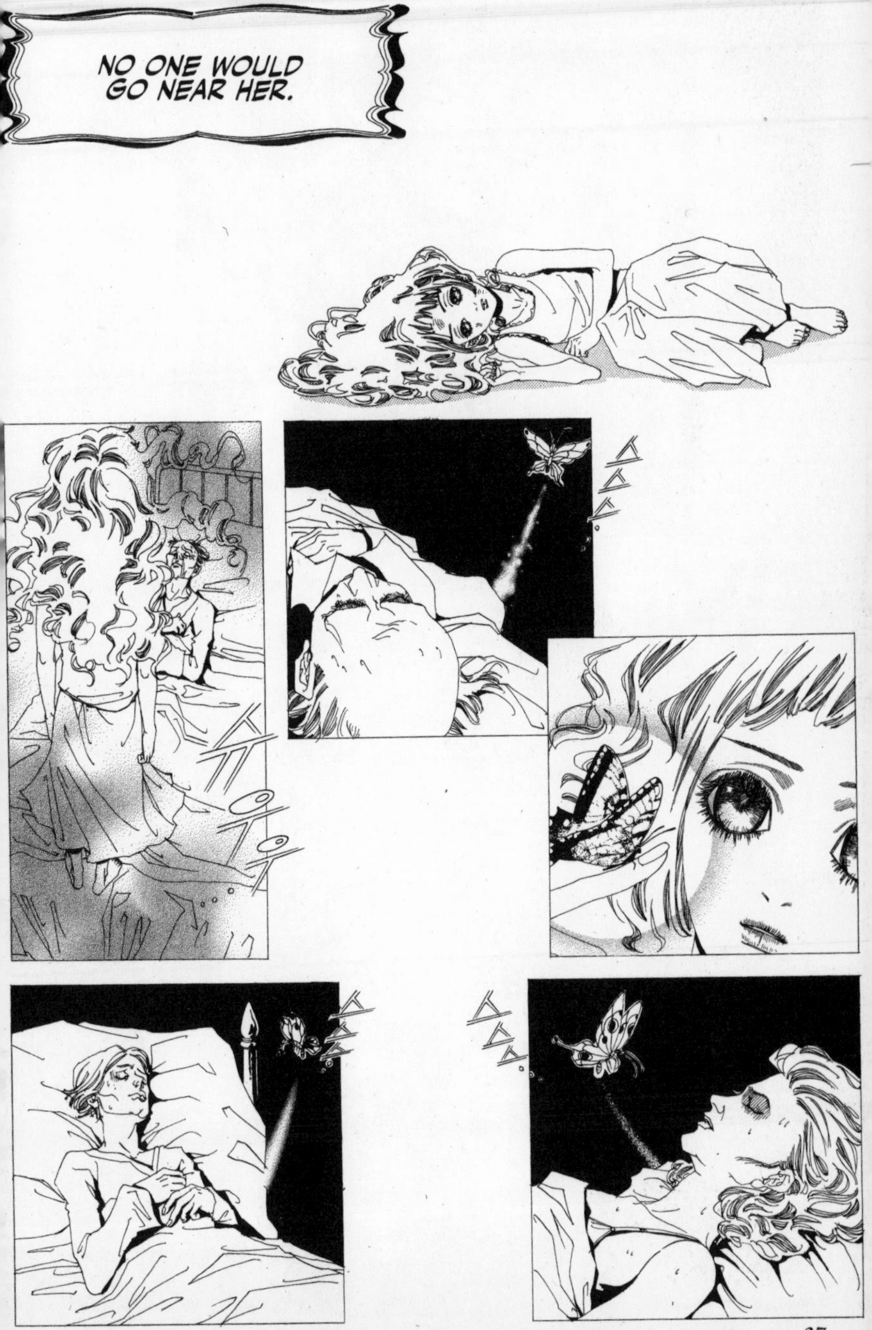
NO ONE WOULD GO NEAR HER.

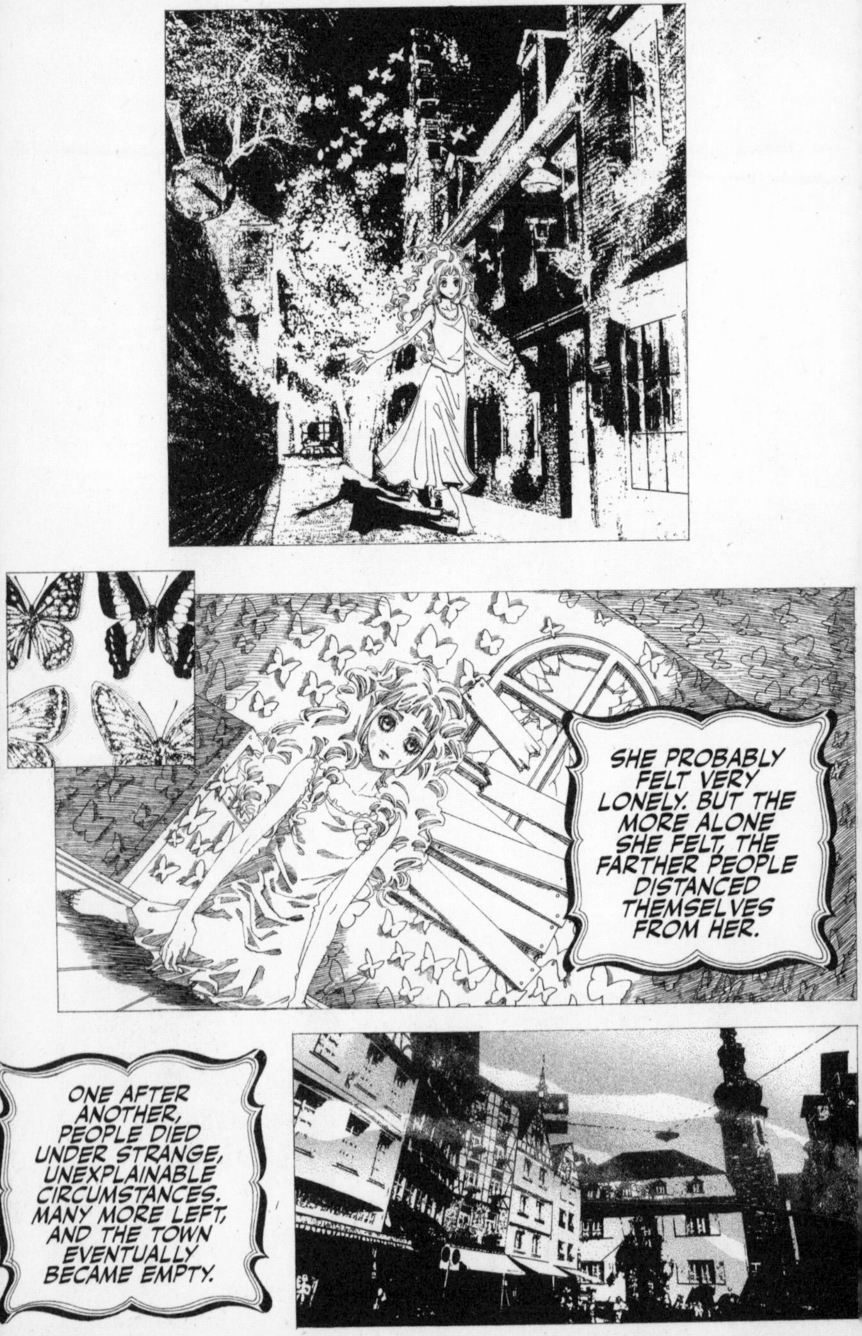
SHE PROBABLY FELT VERY LONELY. BUT THE MORE ALONE SHE FELT, THE FARTHER PEOPLE DISTANCED THEMSELVES FROM HER.
ONE AFTER ANOTHER, PEOPLE DIED UNDER STRANGE, UNEXPLAINABLE CIRCUMSTANCES. MANY MORE LEFT, AND THE TOWN EVENTUALLY BECAME EMPTY.

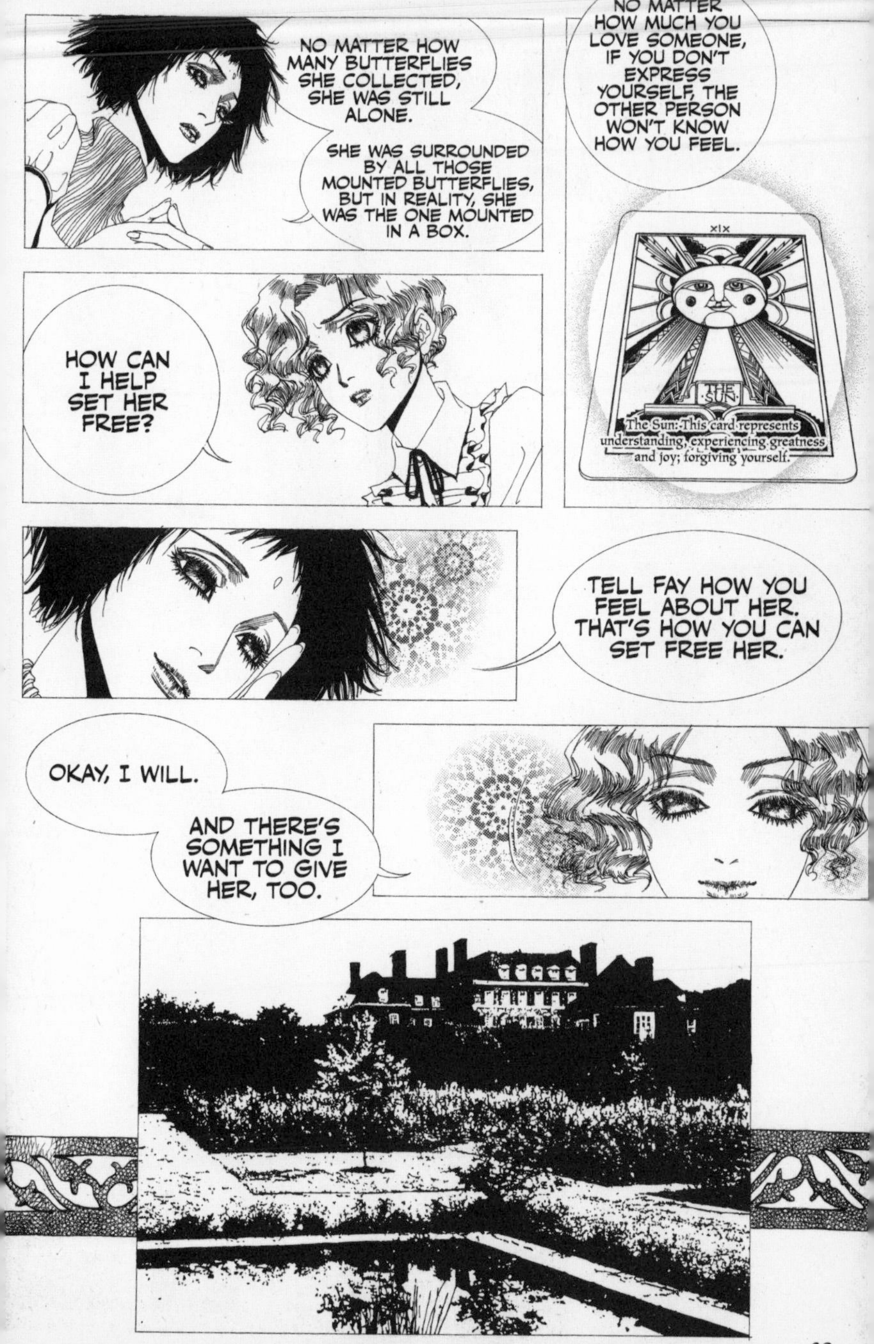
NO MATTER HOW MANY BUTTERFLIES SHE COLLECTED, SHE WAS STILL ALONE.
SHE WAS SURROUNDED BY ALL THOSE MOUNTED BUTTERFLIES, BUT IN REALITY, SHE WAS THE ONE MOUNTED IN A BOX.
HOW CAN I HELP SET HER FREE?
NO MATTER HOW MUCH YOU LOVE SOMEONE, IF YOU DON'T EXPRESS YOURSELF, THE OTHER PERSON WON'T KNOW HOW YOU FEEL.
XIX
THE SUN
The Sun: This card represents understanding, experiencing greatness and joy; forgiving yourself.
TELL FAY HOW YOU FEEL ABOUT HER. THAT'S HOW YOU CAN SET FREE HER.
OKAY, I WILL.
AND THERE'S SOMETHING I WANT TO GIVE HER, TOO.

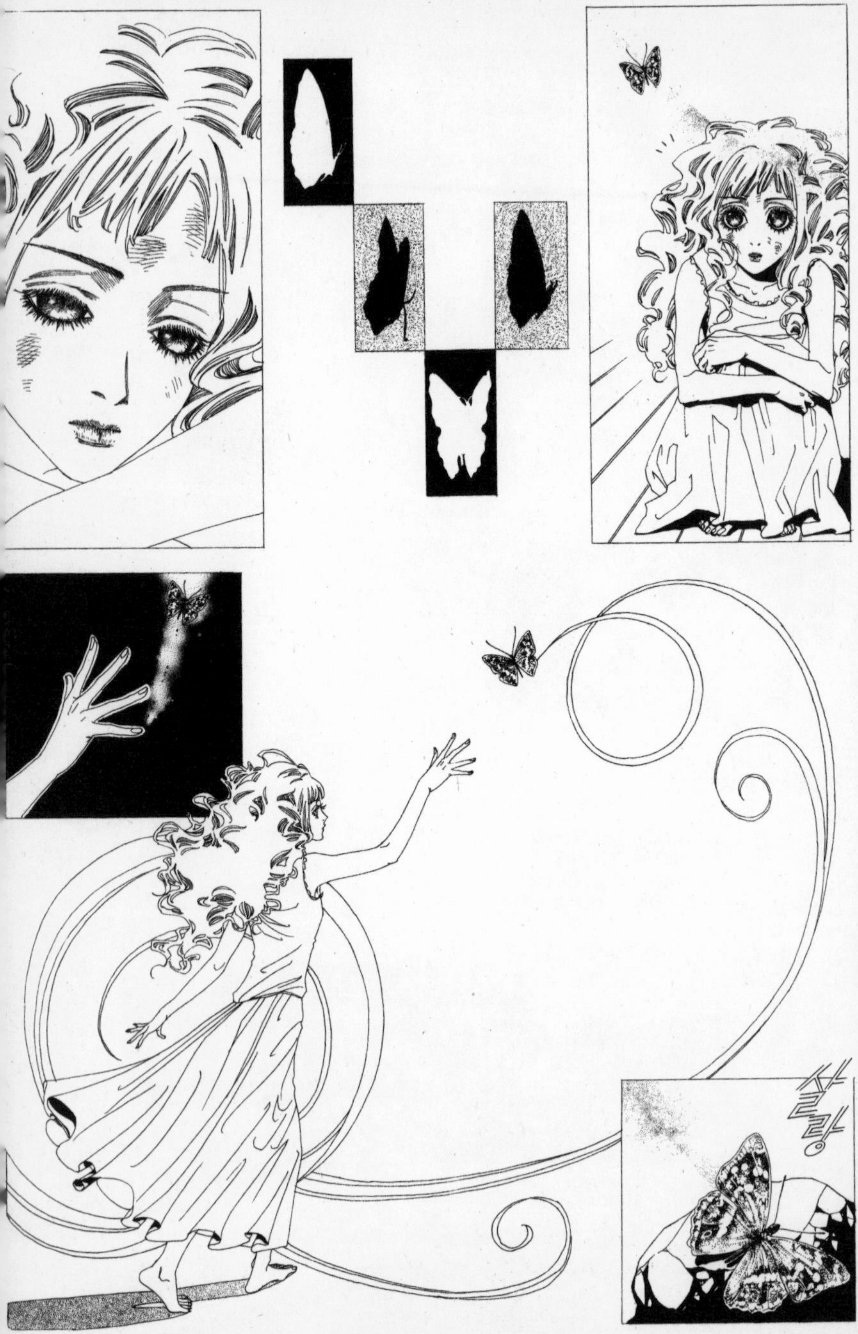
살랑

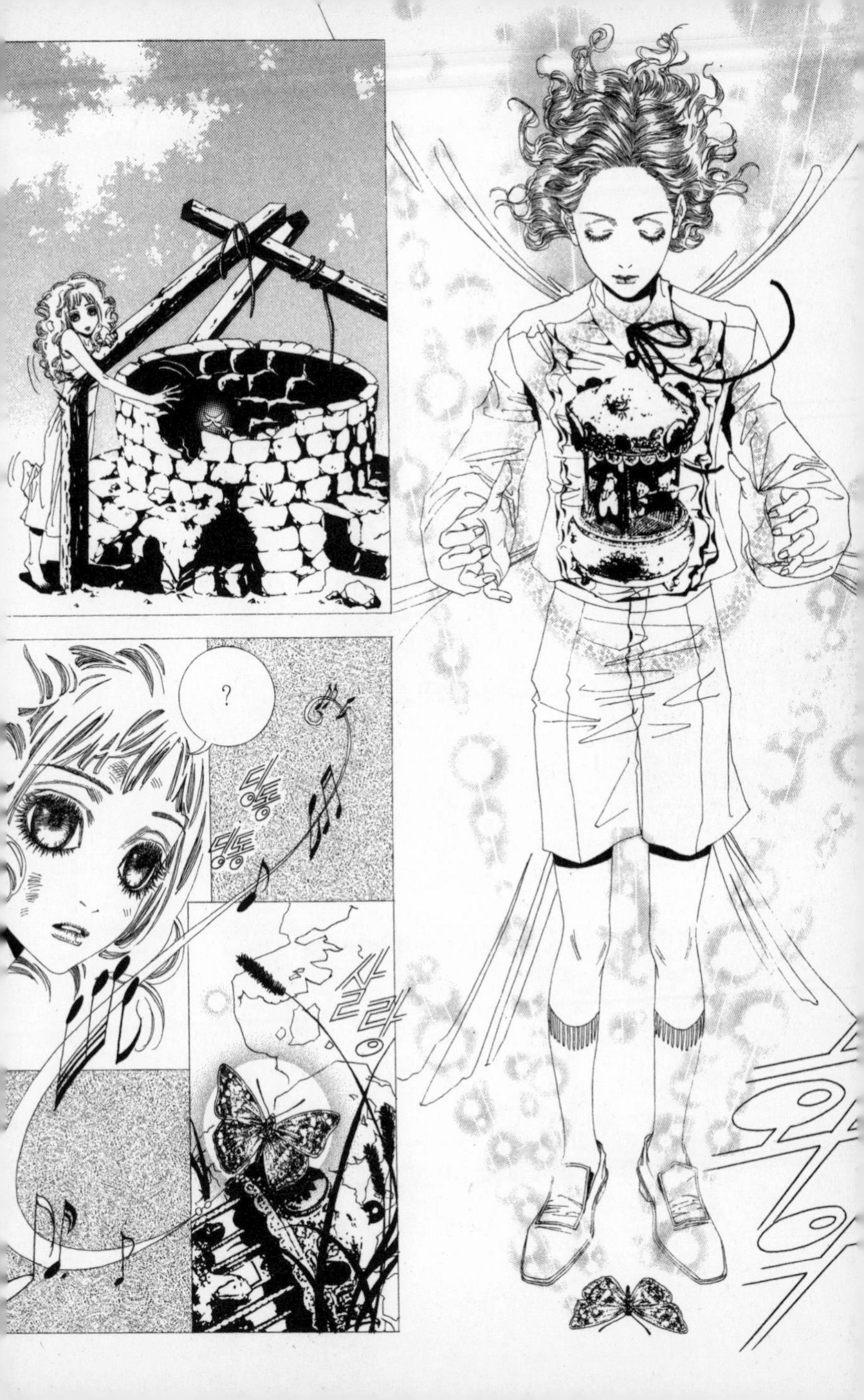
?
딩동
딩동
샤랄랑

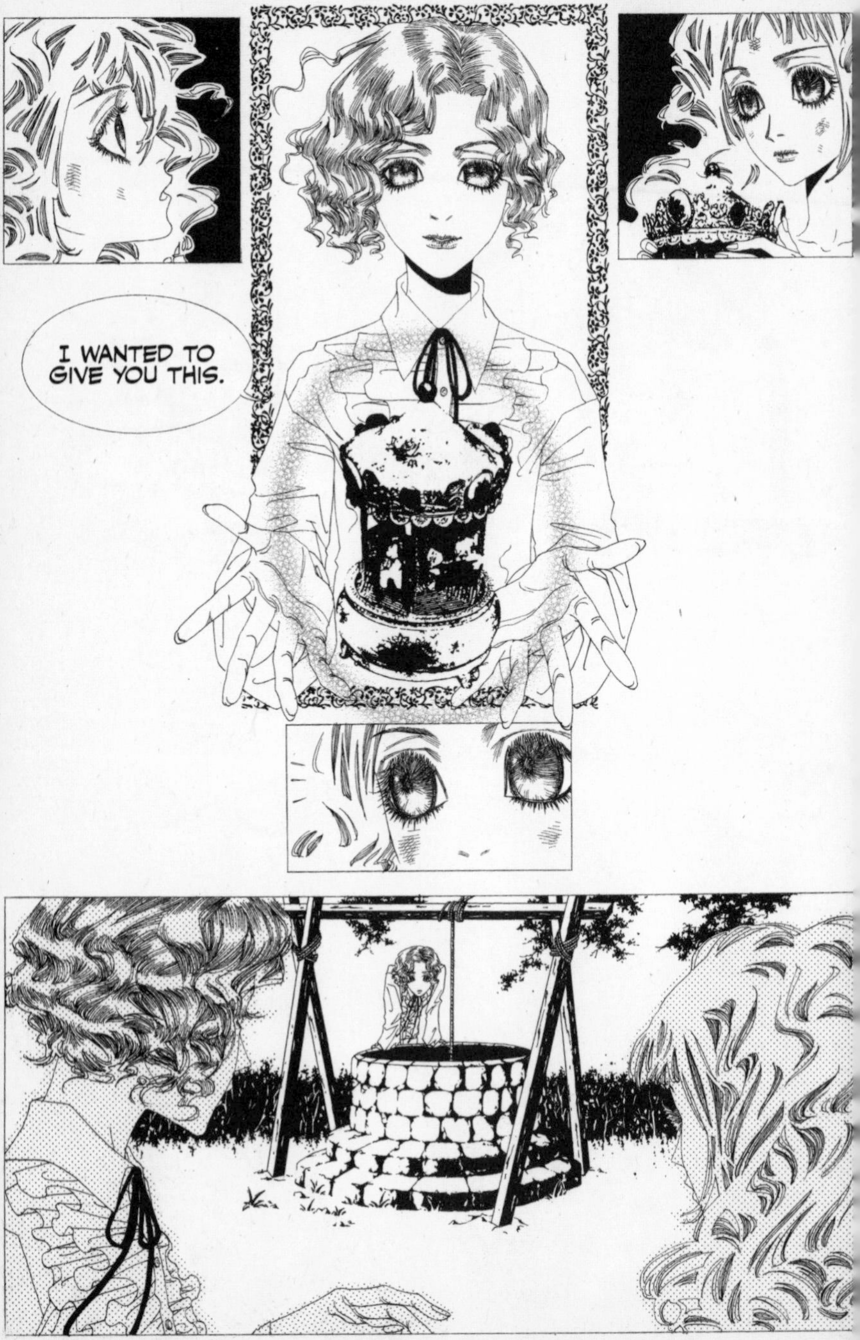
I WANTED TO GIVE YOU THIS.

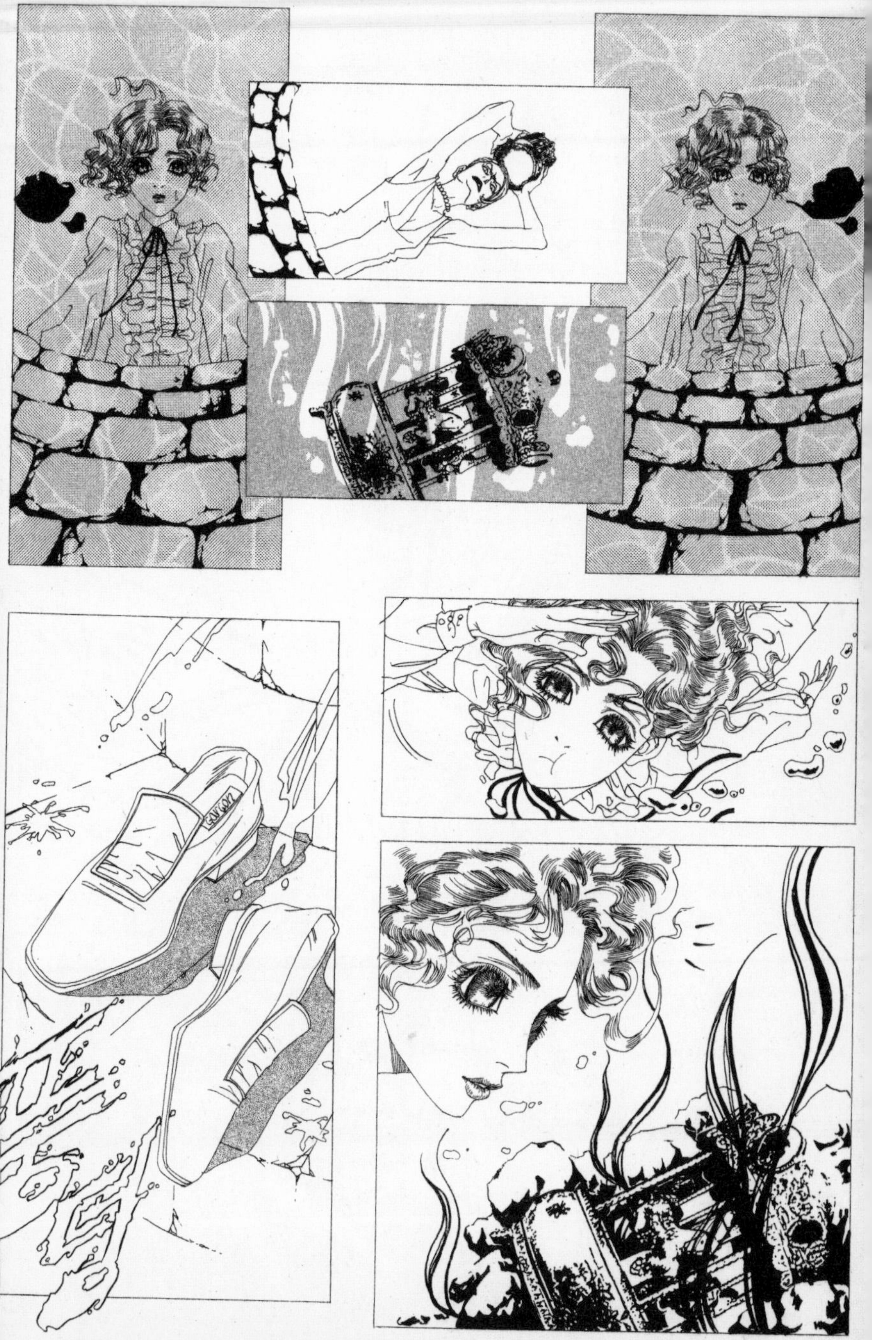
Garcon

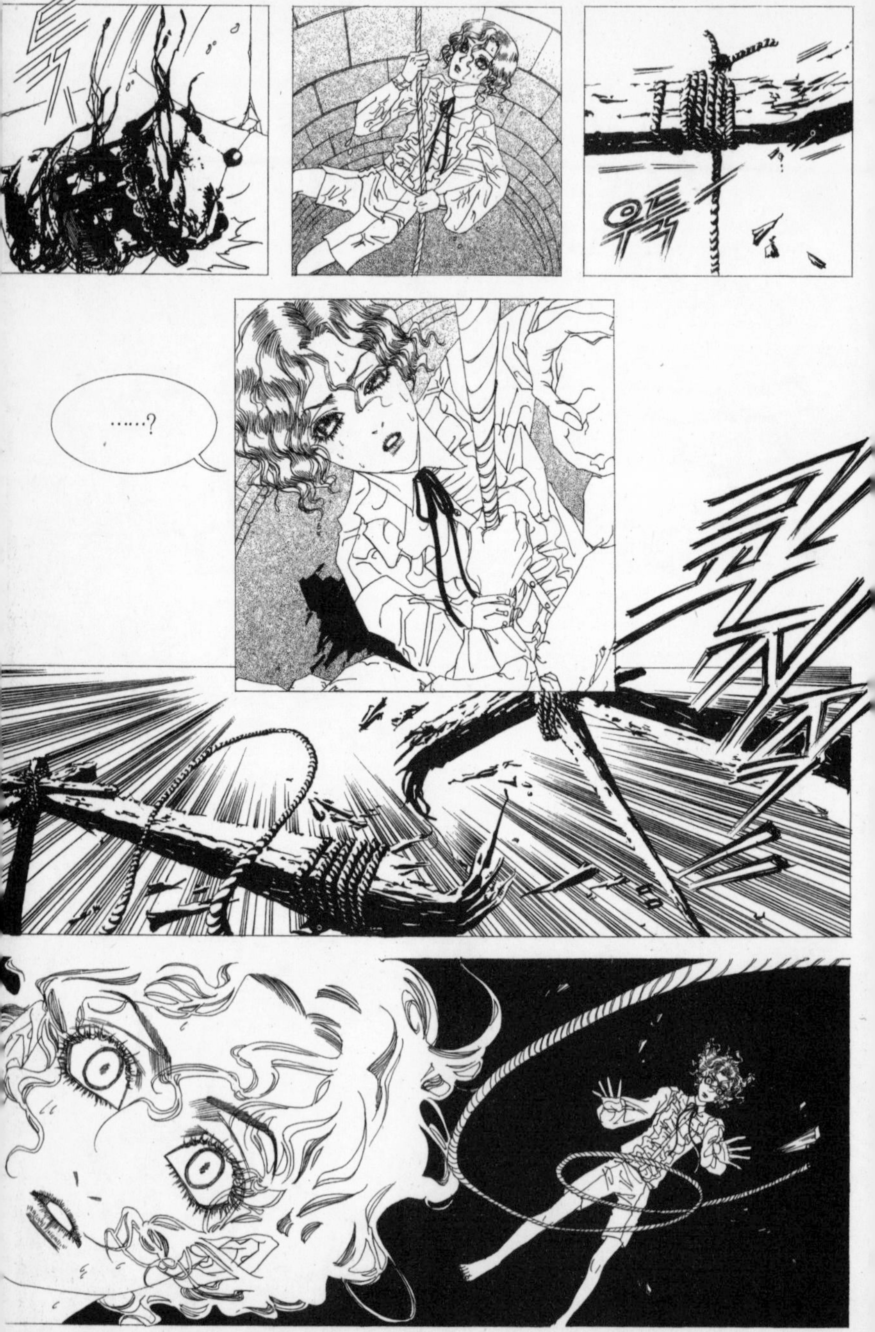
우득
......?

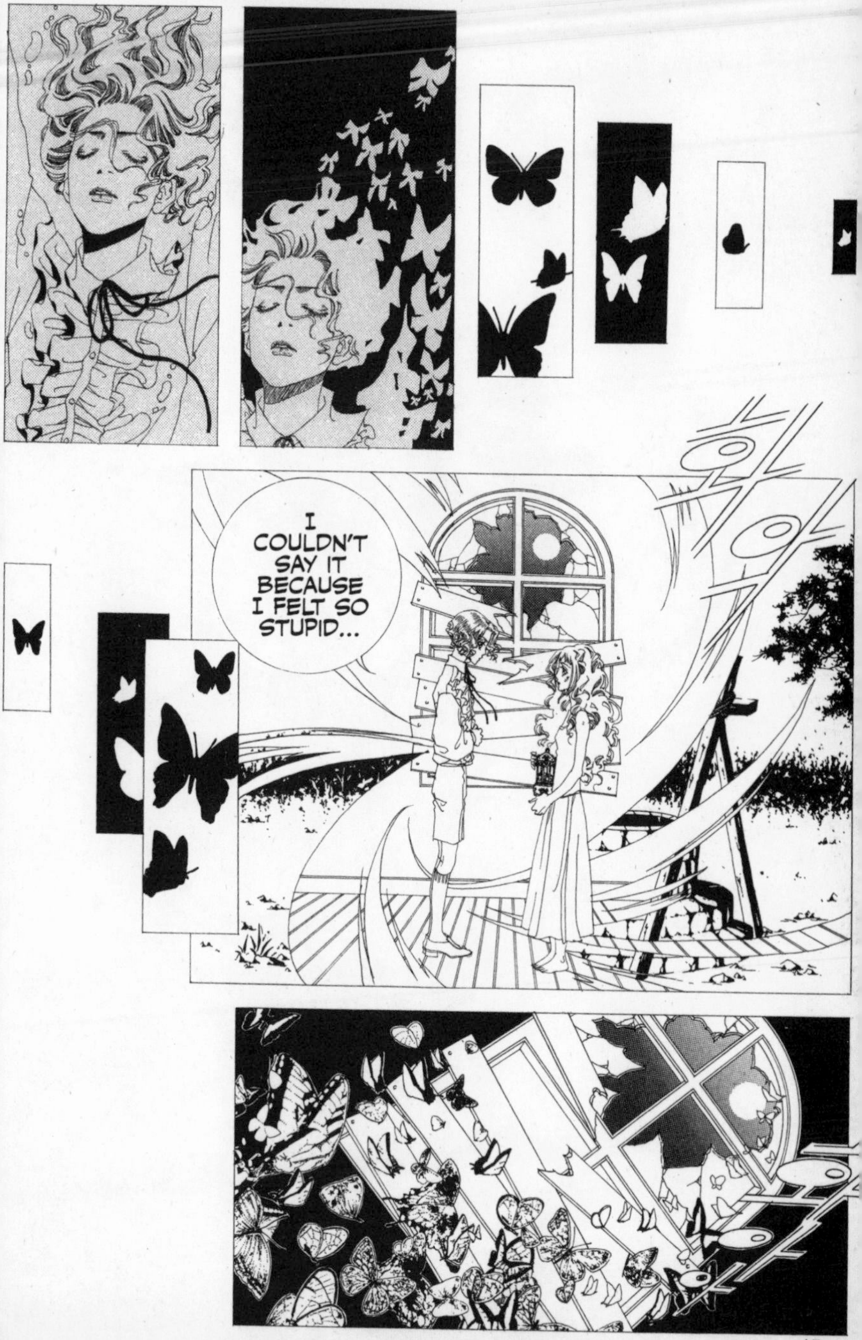
I COULDN'T SAY IT BECAUSE I FELT SO STUPID...

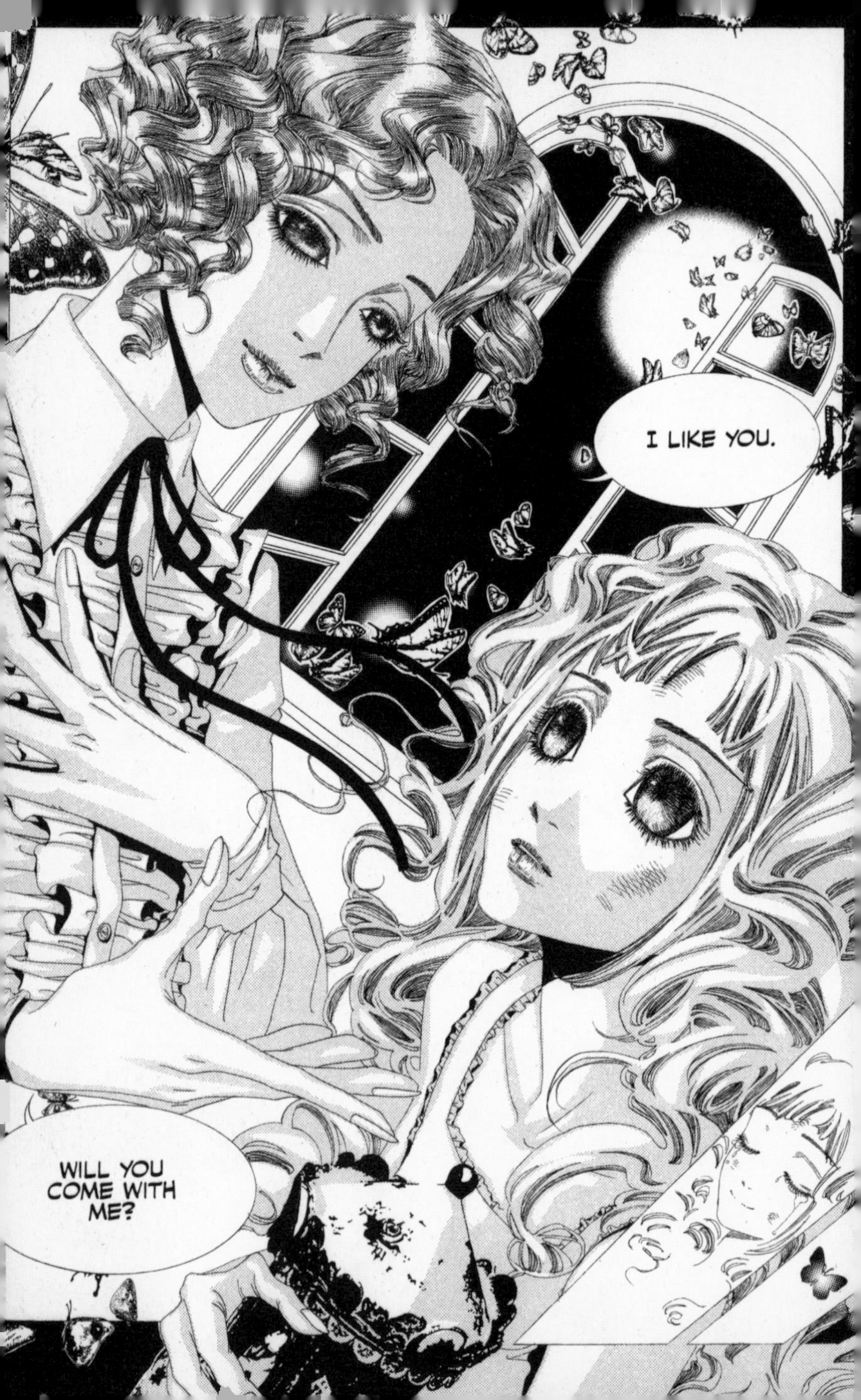
I LIKE YOU.
WILL YOU COME WITH ME?

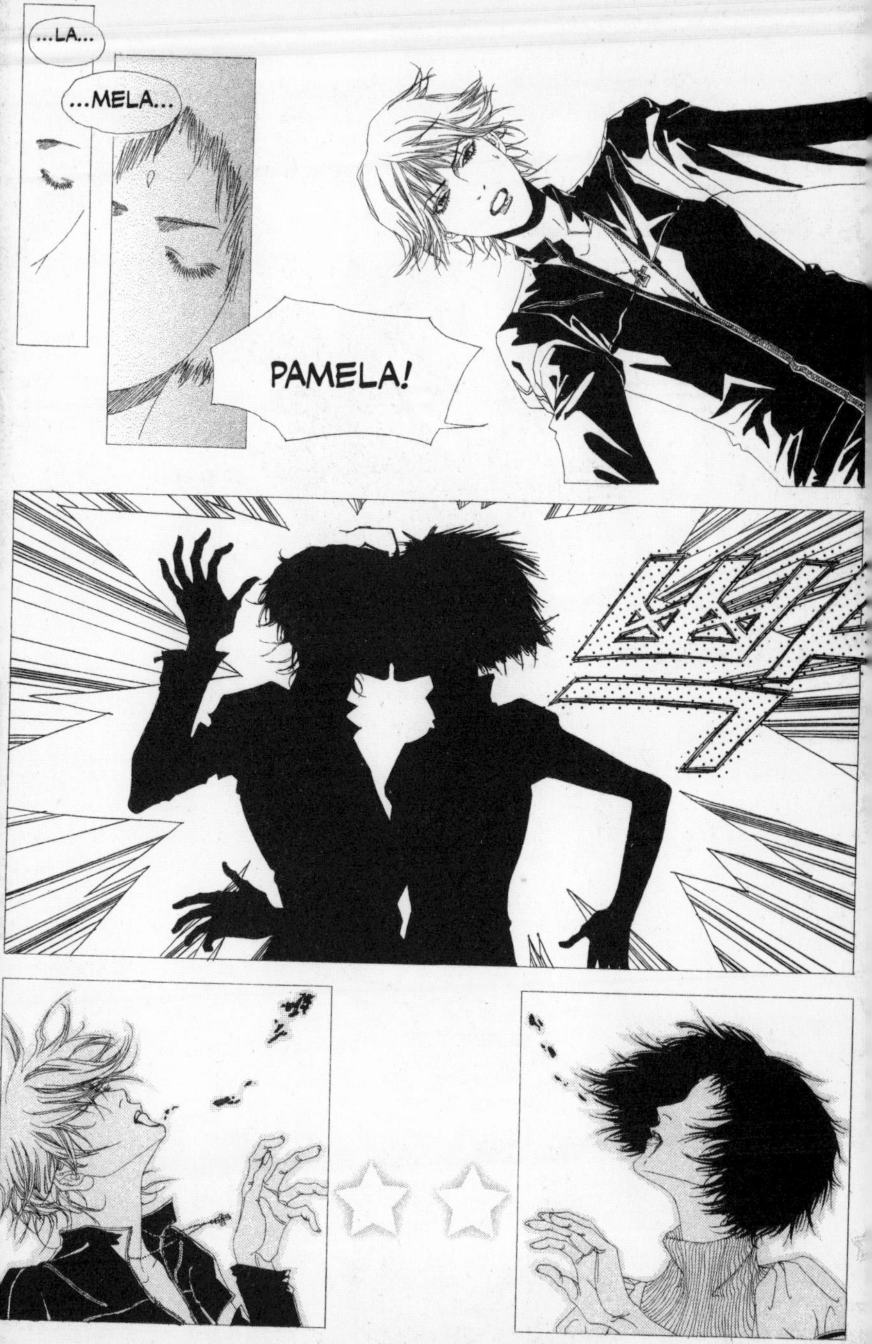
...LA...
...MELA...
PAMELA!

THAT WAS A POWERFUL KISS! IT NEARLY BROKE MY TEETH.

WHAT THE HELL ARE YOU TRYING TO DO?!

WHAT AM I TRYING TO DO? YOU'RE TOO MUCH!

PAMELA, YOU SLEPT FOR THREE DAYS STRAIGHT.

I SLEPT FOR *THREE DAYS*? WHAT HAPPENED TO THE BOY?

WHAT BOY? ARE YOU TALKING IN YOUR SLEEP OR SOMETHING?

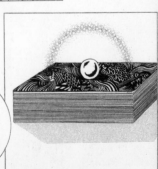

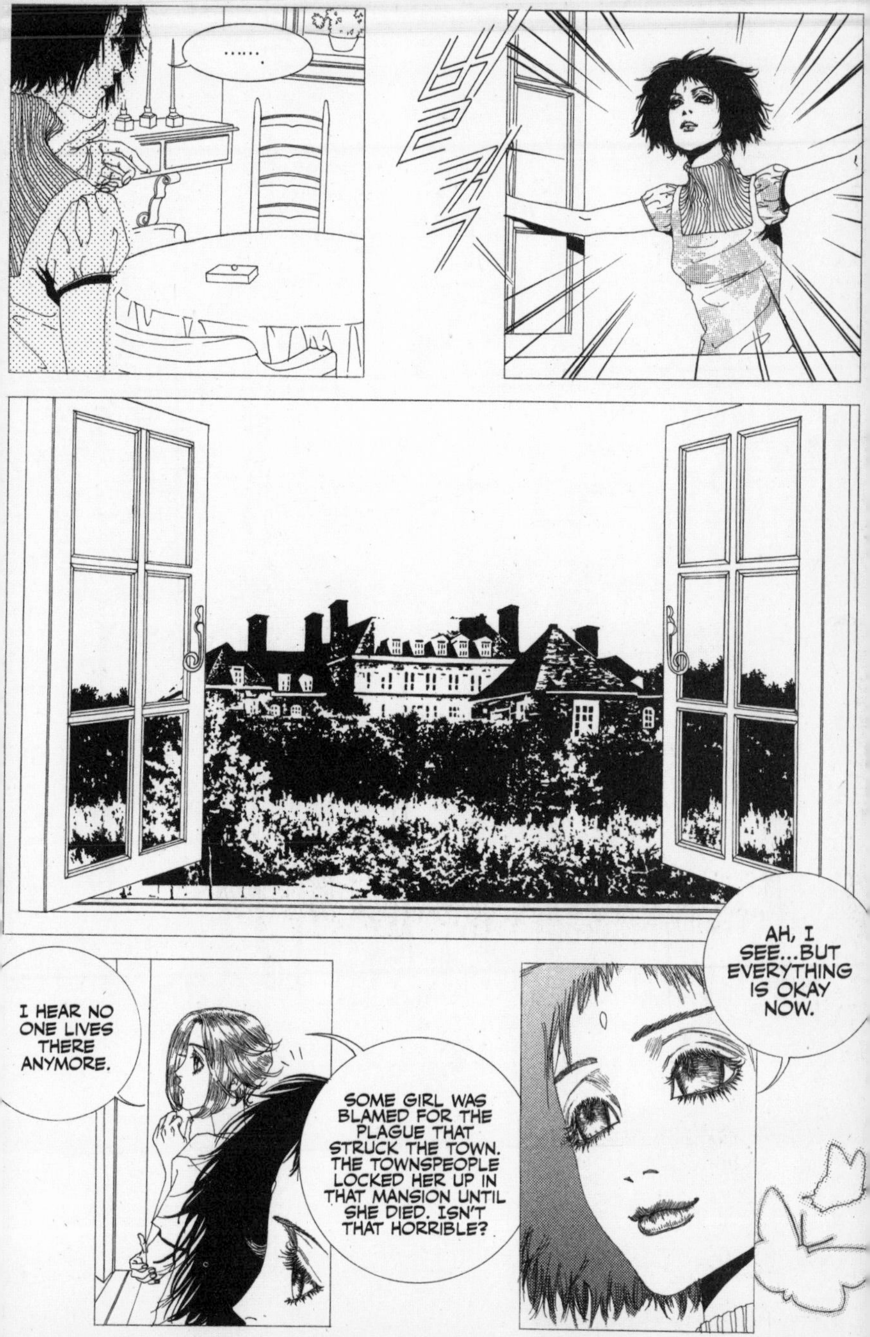
......
I HEAR NO ONE LIVES THERE ANYMORE.
SOME GIRL WAS BLAMED FOR THE PLAGUE THAT STRUCK THE TOWN. THE TOWNSPEOPLE LOCKED HER UP IN THAT MANSION UNTIL SHE DIED. ISN'T THAT HORRIBLE?
AH, I SEE...BUT EVERYTHING IS OKAY NOW.

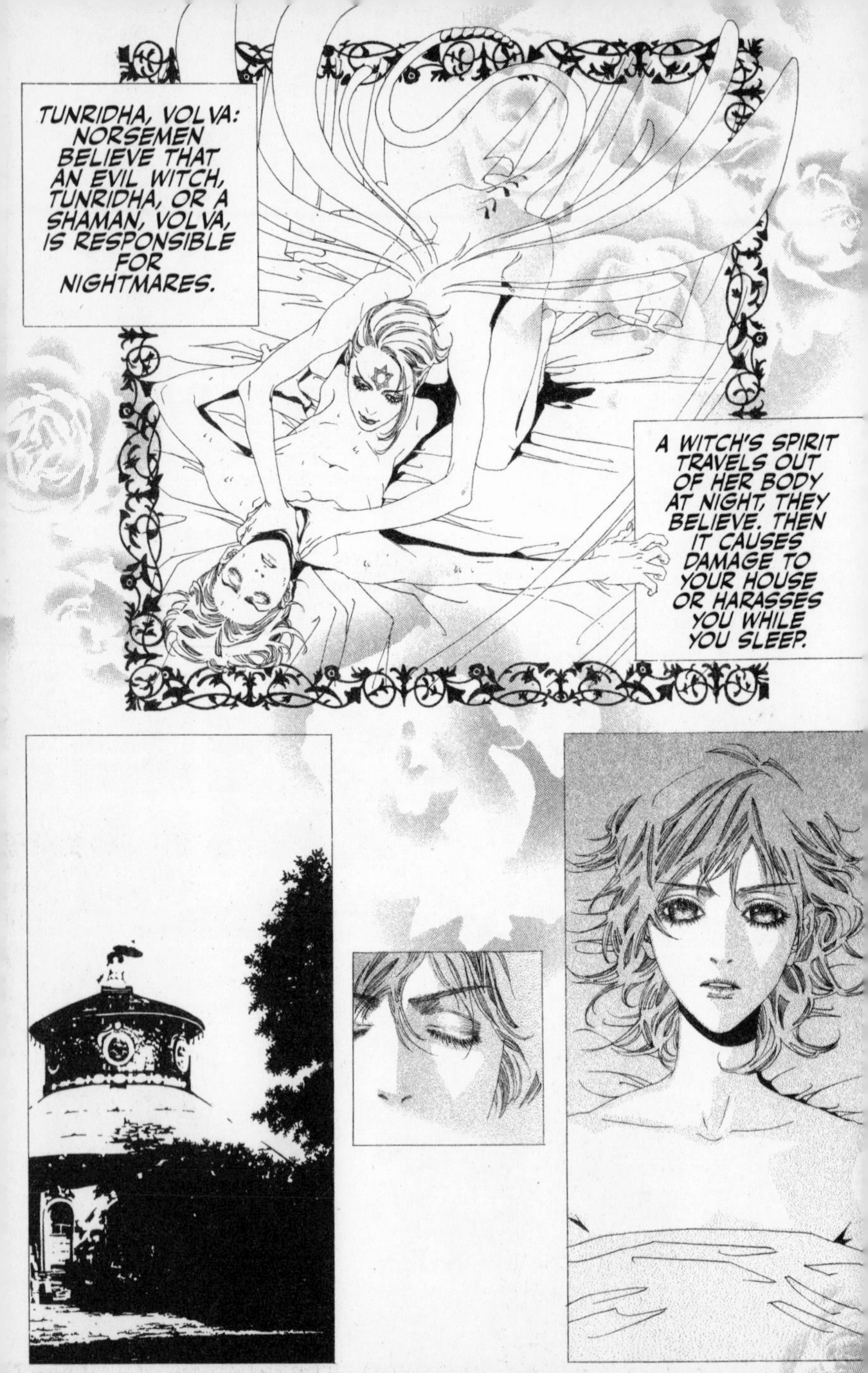
TUNRIDHA, VOLVA: NORSEMEN BELIEVE THAT AN EVIL WITCH, TUNRIDHA, OR A SHAMAN, VOLVA, IS RESPONSIBLE FOR NIGHTMARES.
A WITCH'S SPIRIT TRAVELS OUT OF HER BODY AT NIGHT, THEY BELIEVE. THEN IT CAUSES DAMAGE TO YOUR HOUSE OR HARASSES YOU WHILE YOU SLEEP.

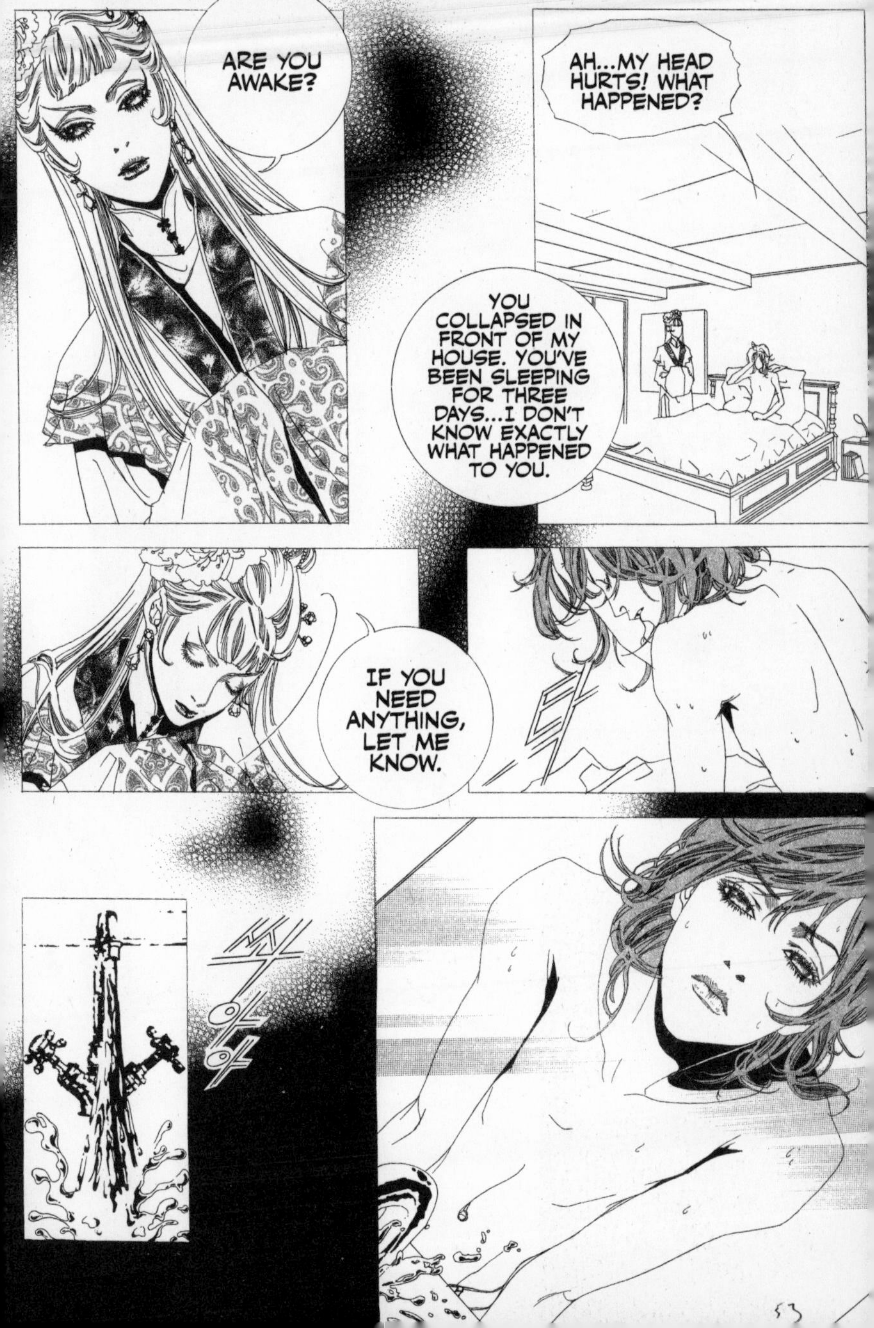
ARE YOU AWAKE?
AH...MY HEAD HURTS! WHAT HAPPENED?
YOU COLLAPSED IN FRONT OF MY HOUSE. YOU'VE BEEN SLEEPING FOR THREE DAYS...I DON'T KNOW EXACTLY WHAT HAPPENED TO YOU.
IF YOU NEED ANYTHING, LET ME KNOW.

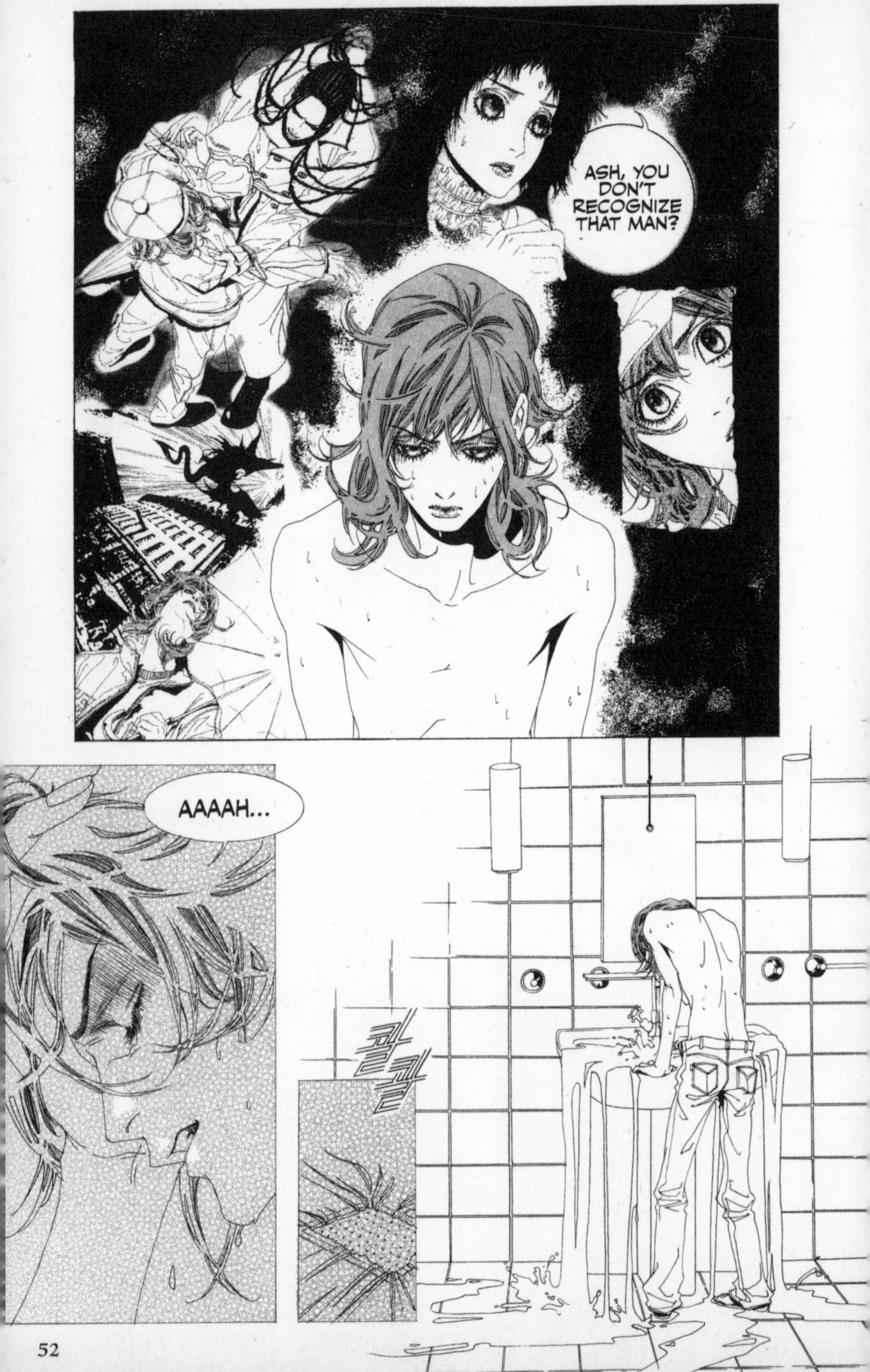
ASH, YOU DON'T RECOGNIZE THAT MAN?
AAAAH...

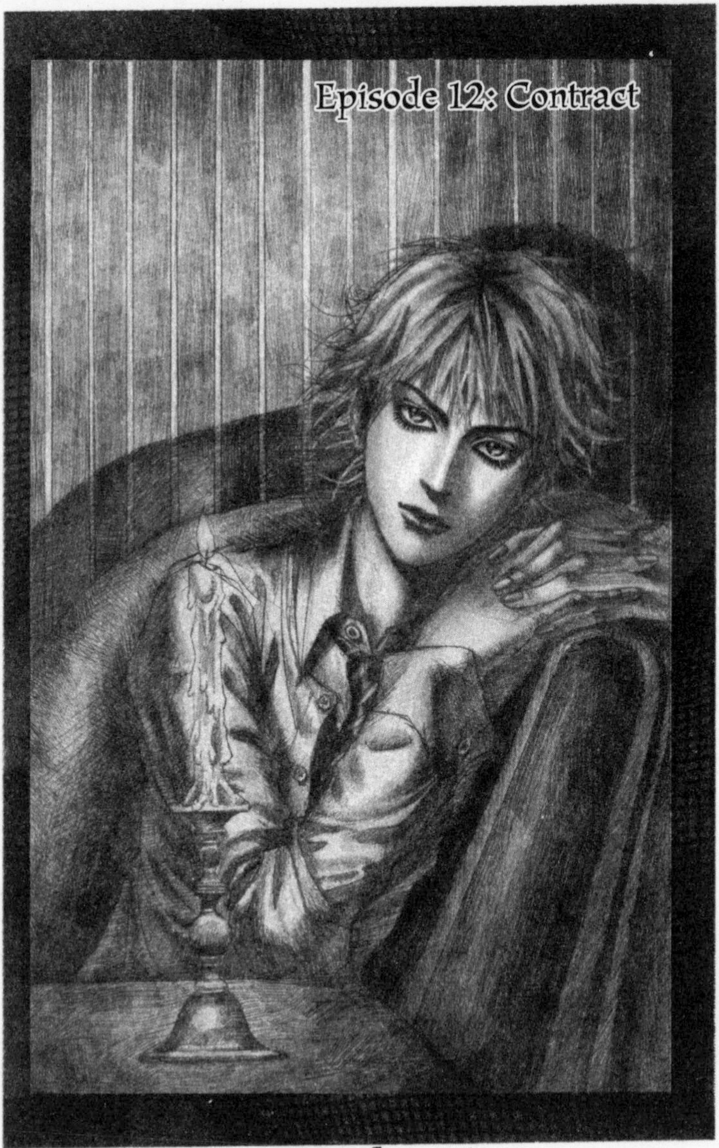
Episode 12: Contract

ILLUSTRATION FROM MASTER TAROT

Wachet
On watch

Wachet on Watch: The attitude of a traveler who leaves everything behind and embarks on a journey; a volatile situation; the need to be wary of sudden disasters or hardships.

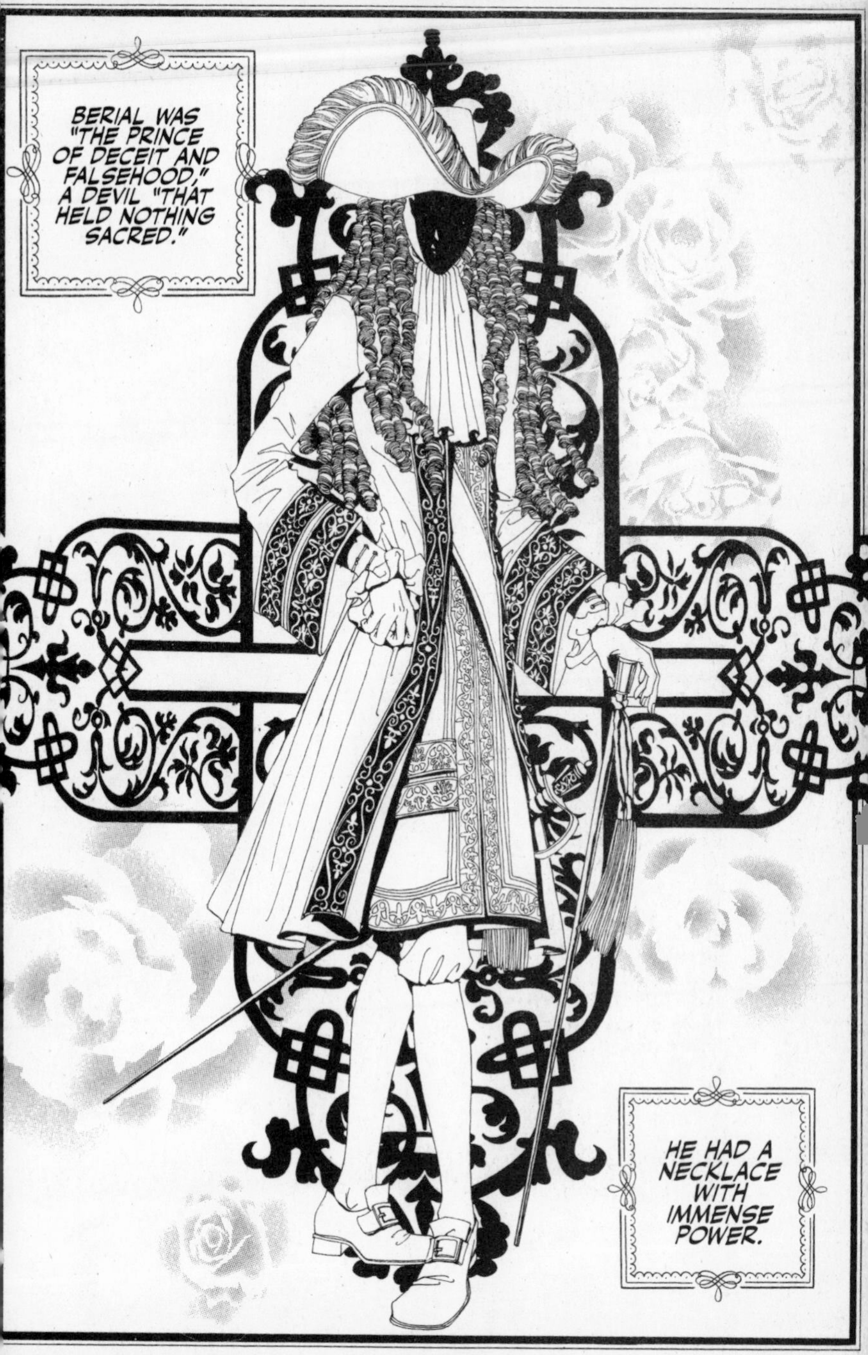
BERIAL WAS "THE PRINCE OF DECEIT AND FALSEHOOD," A DEVIL "THAT HELD NOTHING SACRED."
HE HAD A NECKLACE WITH IMMENSE POWER.

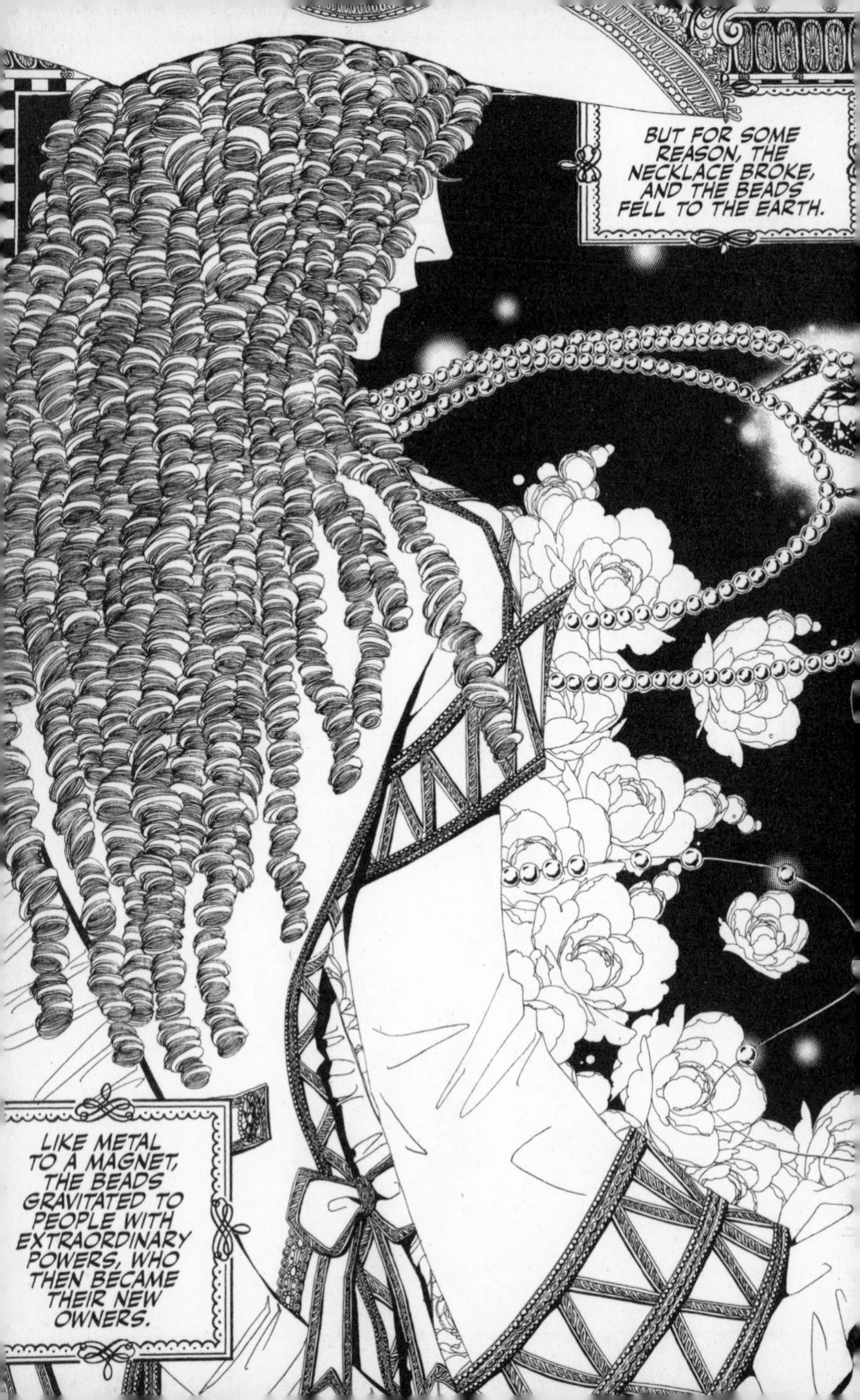
BUT FOR SOME REASON, THE NECKLACE BROKE, AND THE BEADS FELL TO THE EARTH.
LIKE METAL TO A MAGNET, THE BEADS GRAVITATED TO PEOPLE WITH EXTRAORDINARY POWERS, WHO THEN BECAME THEIR NEW OWNERS.

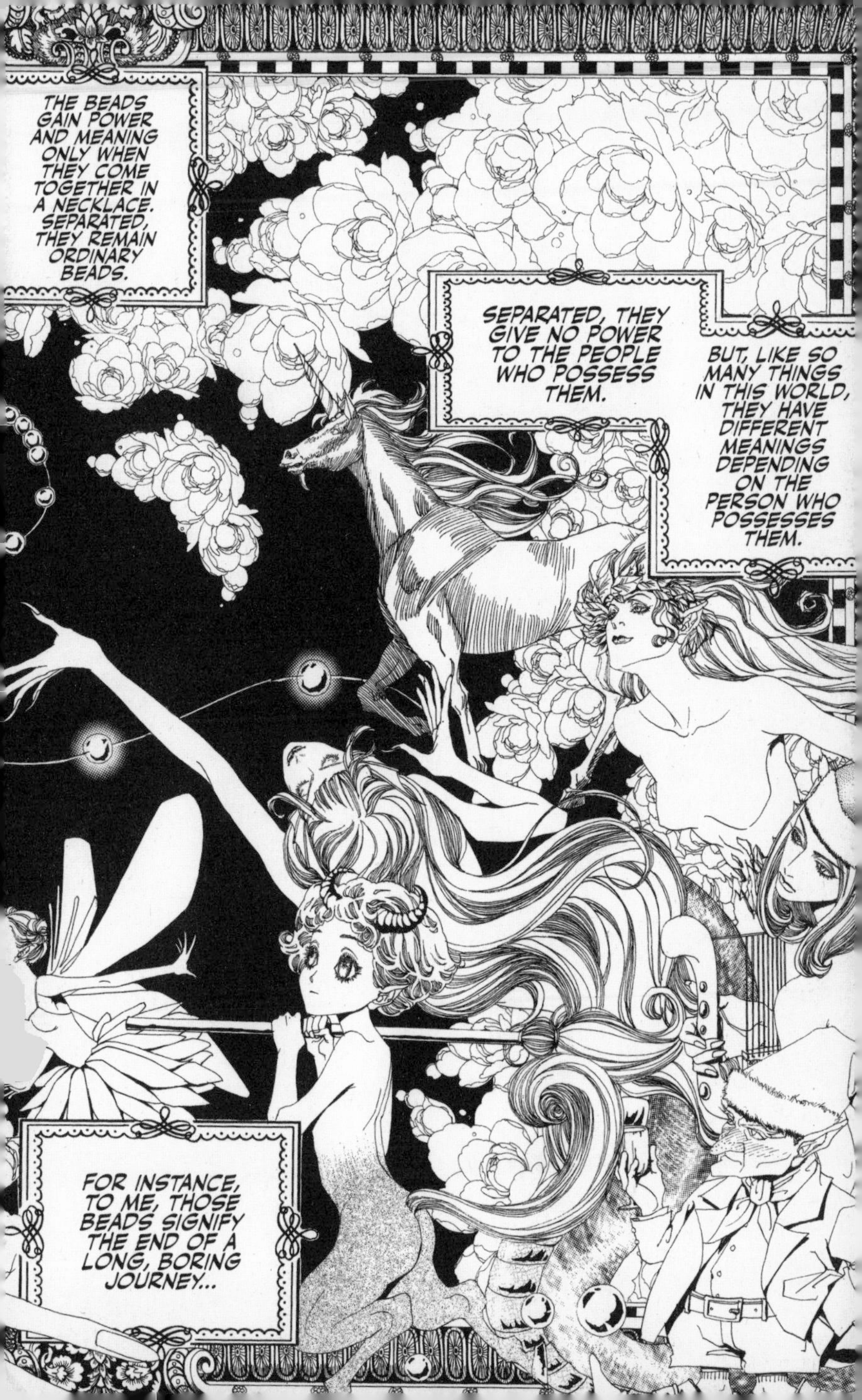
THE BEADS GAIN POWER AND MEANING ONLY WHEN THEY COME TOGETHER IN A NECKLACE. SEPARATED, THEY REMAIN ORDINARY BEADS.
SEPARATED, THEY GIVE NO POWER TO THE PEOPLE WHO POSSESS THEM.
BUT, LIKE SO MANY THINGS IN THIS WORLD, THEY HAVE DIFFERENT MEANINGS DEPENDING ON THE PERSON WHO POSSESSES THEM.
FOR INSTANCE, TO ME, THOSE BEADS SIGNIFY THE END OF A LONG, BORING JOURNEY...

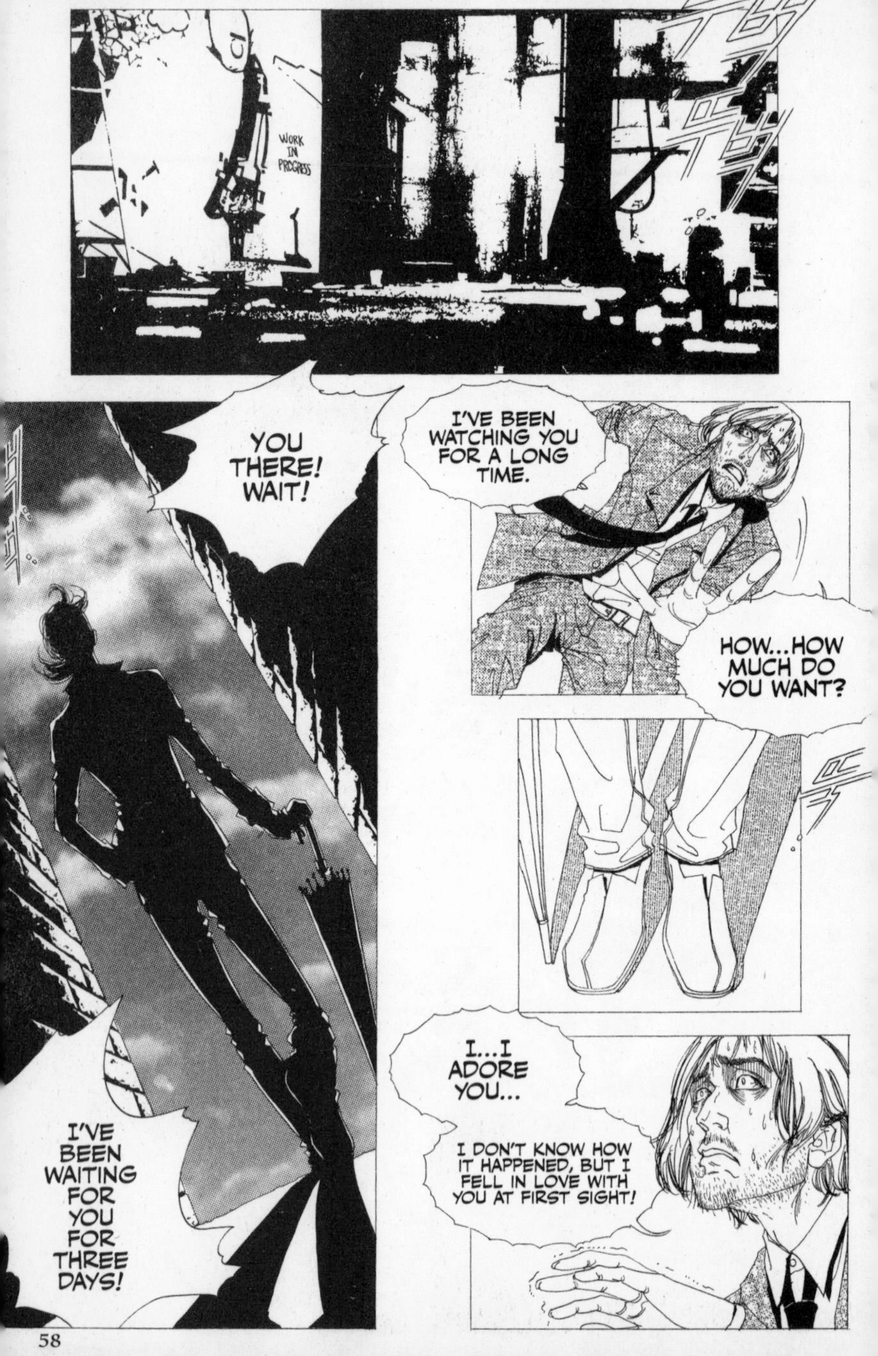
WORK IN PROGRESS
YOU THERE! WAIT!
I'VE BEEN WAITING FOR YOU FOR THREE DAYS!
I'VE BEEN WATCHING YOU FOR A LONG TIME.
HOW...HOW MUCH DO YOU WANT?
I...I ADORE YOU...
I DON'T KNOW HOW IT HAPPENED, BUT I FELL IN LOVE WITH YOU AT FIRST SIGHT!

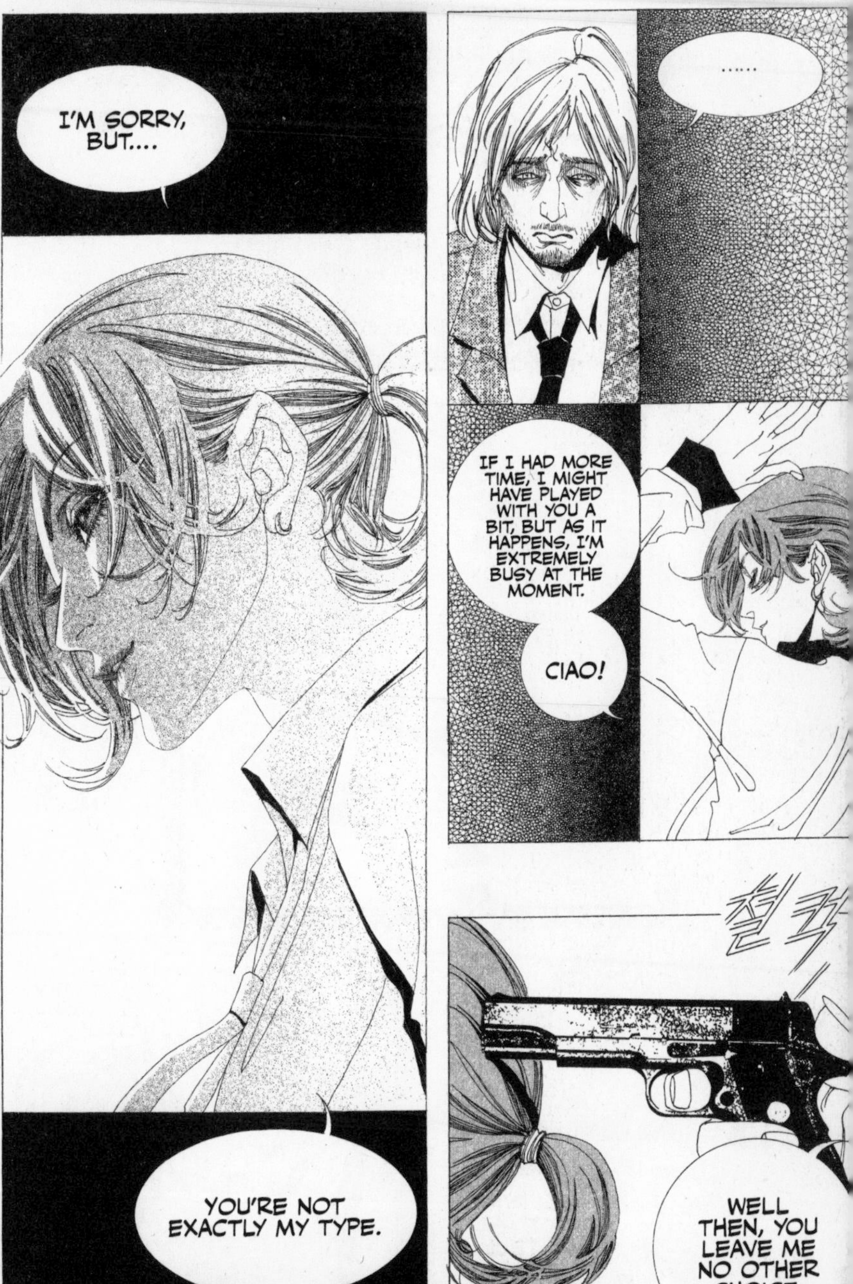
I'M SORRY, BUT....
YOU'RE NOT EXACTLY MY TYPE.
......
IF I HAD MORE TIME, I MIGHT HAVE PLAYED WITH YOU A BIT, BUT AS IT HAPPENS, I'M EXTREMELY BUSY AT THE MOMENT.
CIAO!
철컥
WELL THEN, YOU LEAVE ME NO OTHER CHOICE.

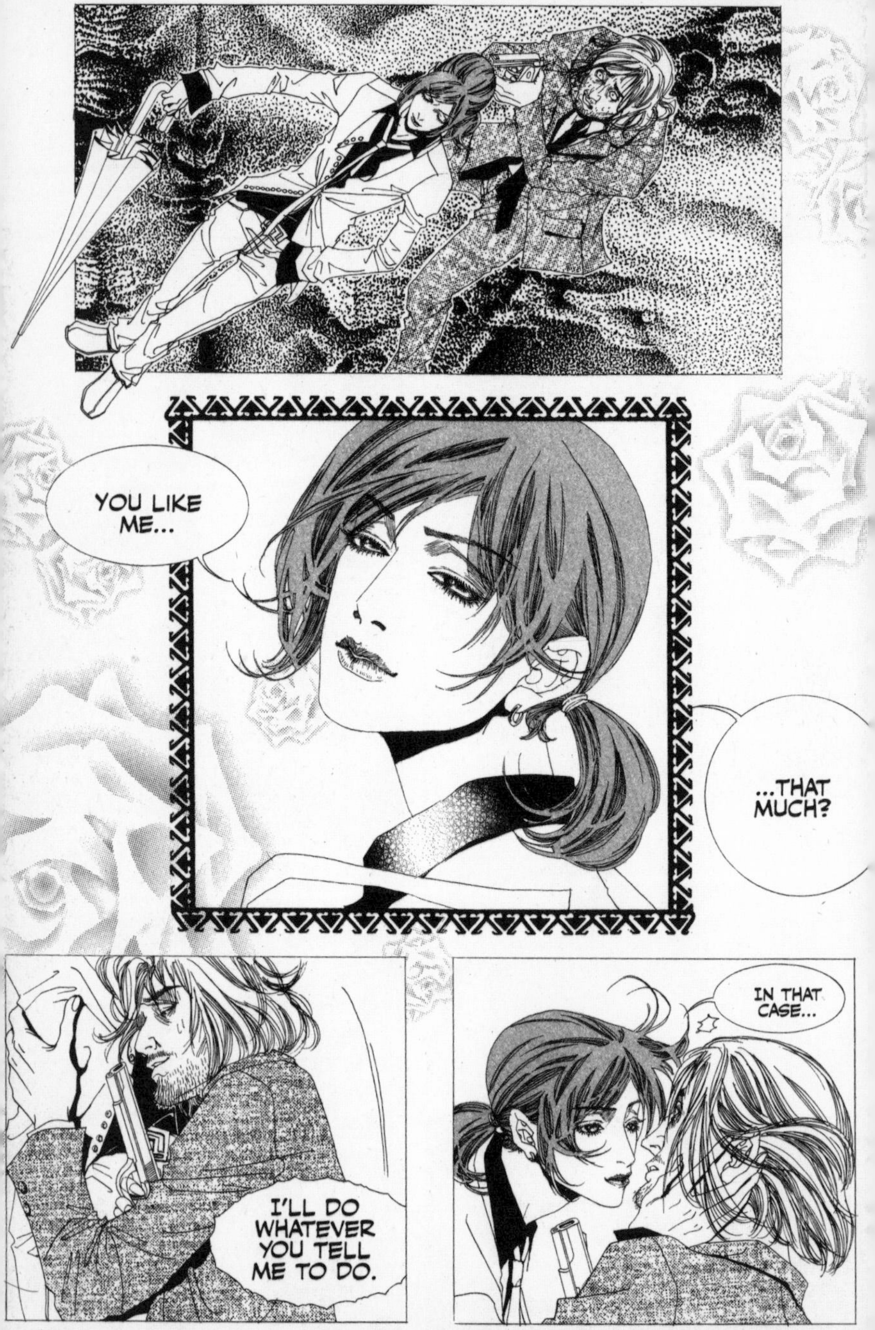
YOU LIKE ME...
...THAT MUCH?
I'LL DO WHATEVER YOU TELL ME TO DO.
IN THAT CASE...

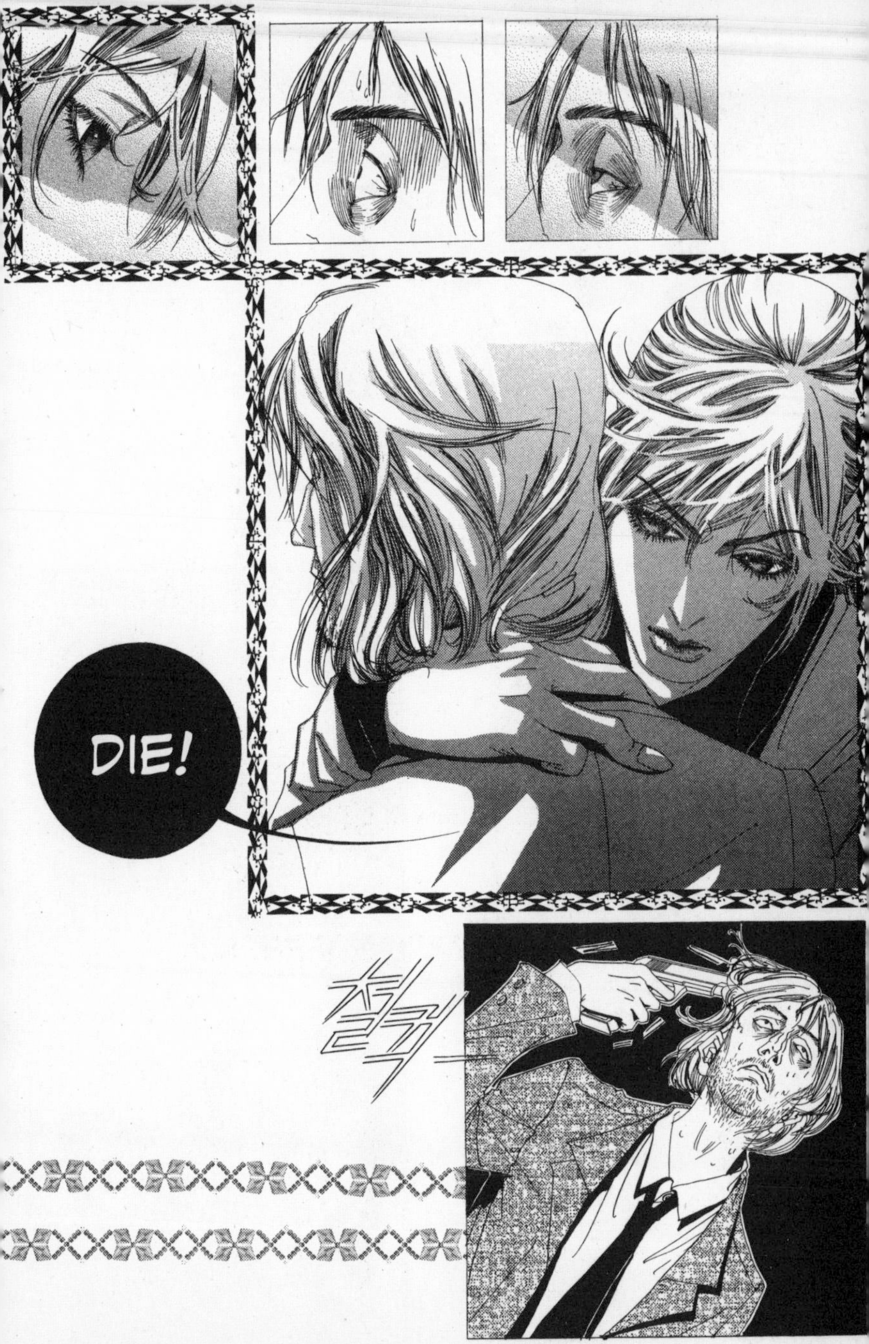
DIE!

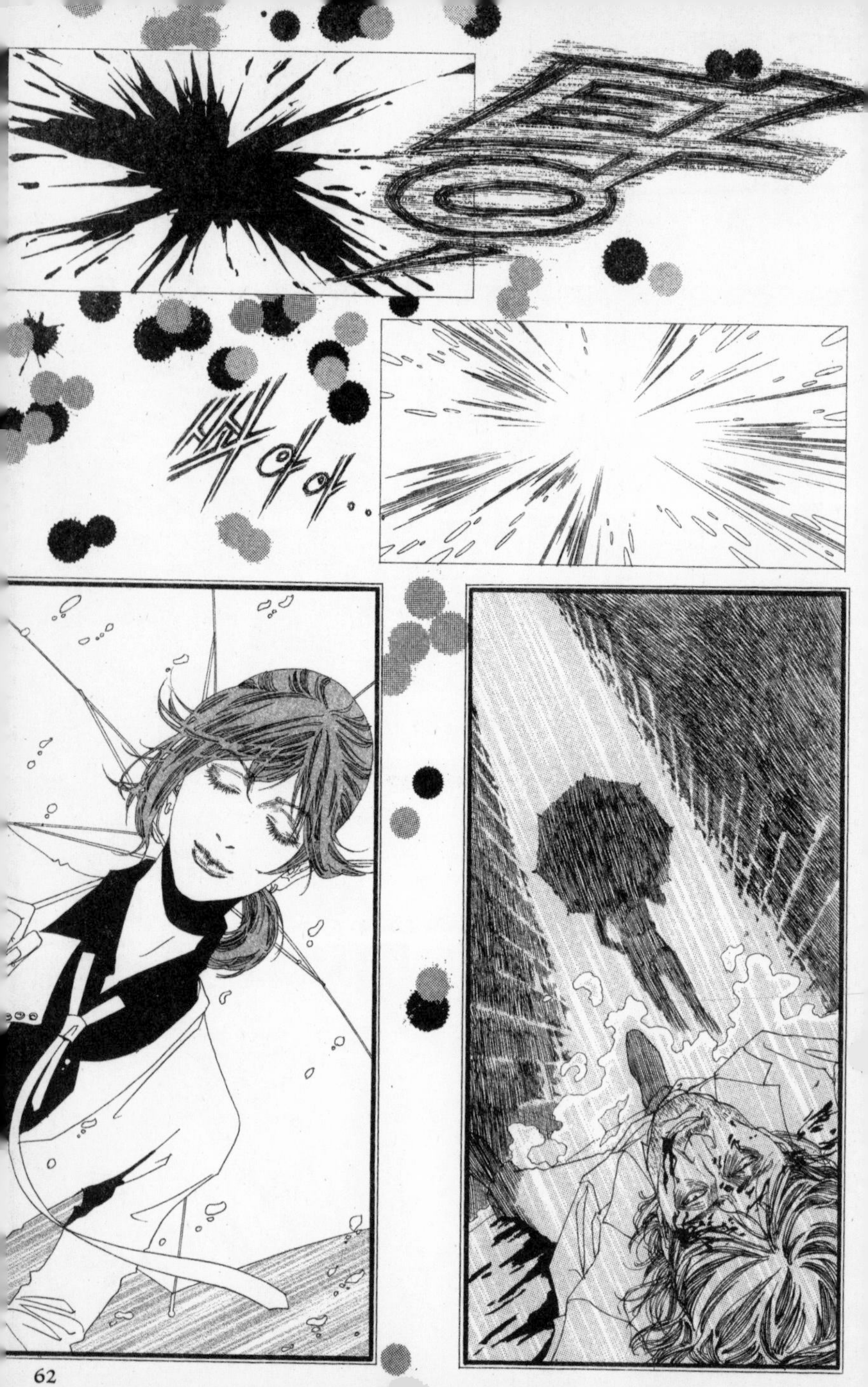
탕
쌔아아..

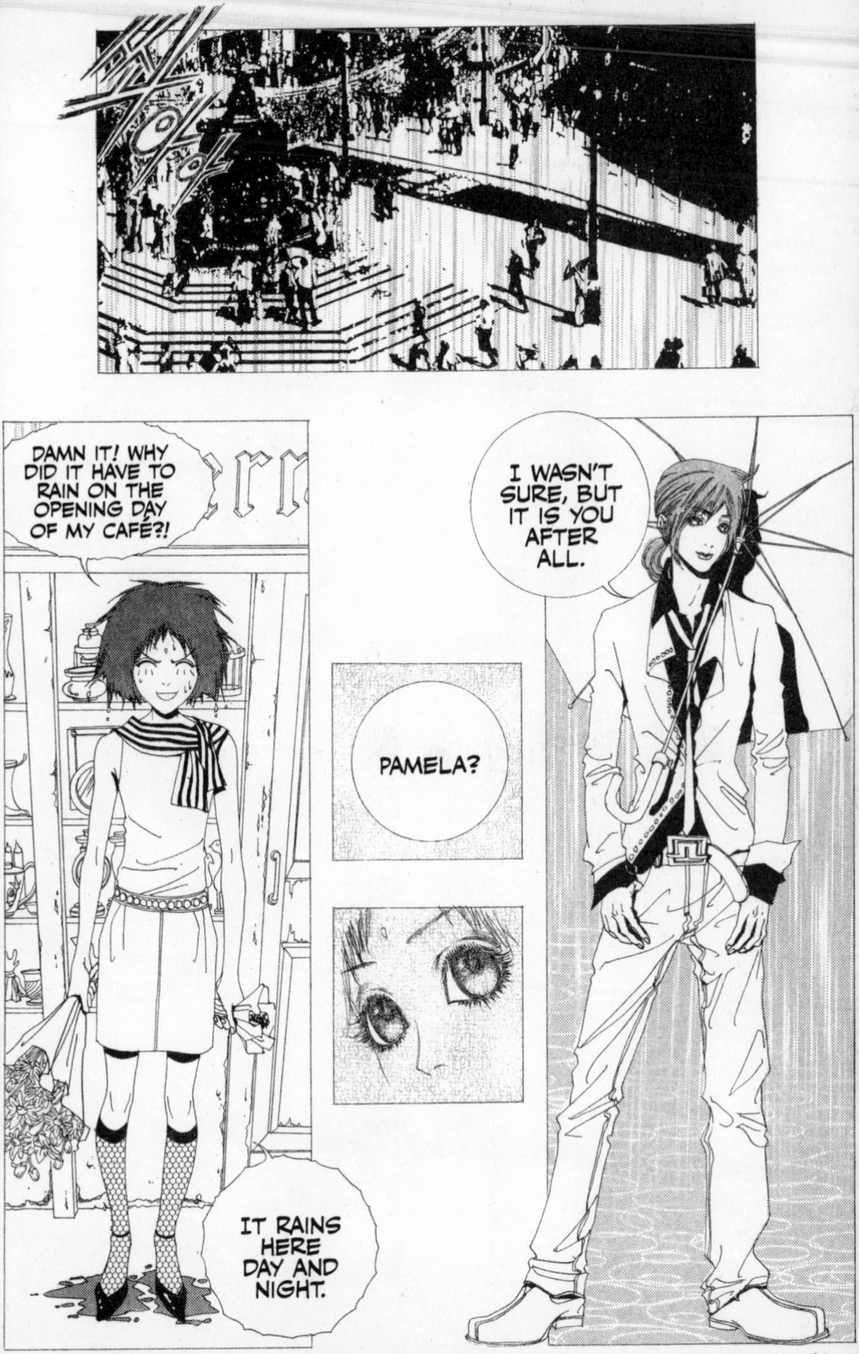
DAMN IT! WHY DID IT HAVE TO RAIN ON THE OPENING DAY OF MY CAFÉ?!
IT RAINS HERE DAY AND NIGHT.
PAMELA?
I WASN'T SURE, BUT IT IS YOU AFTER ALL.

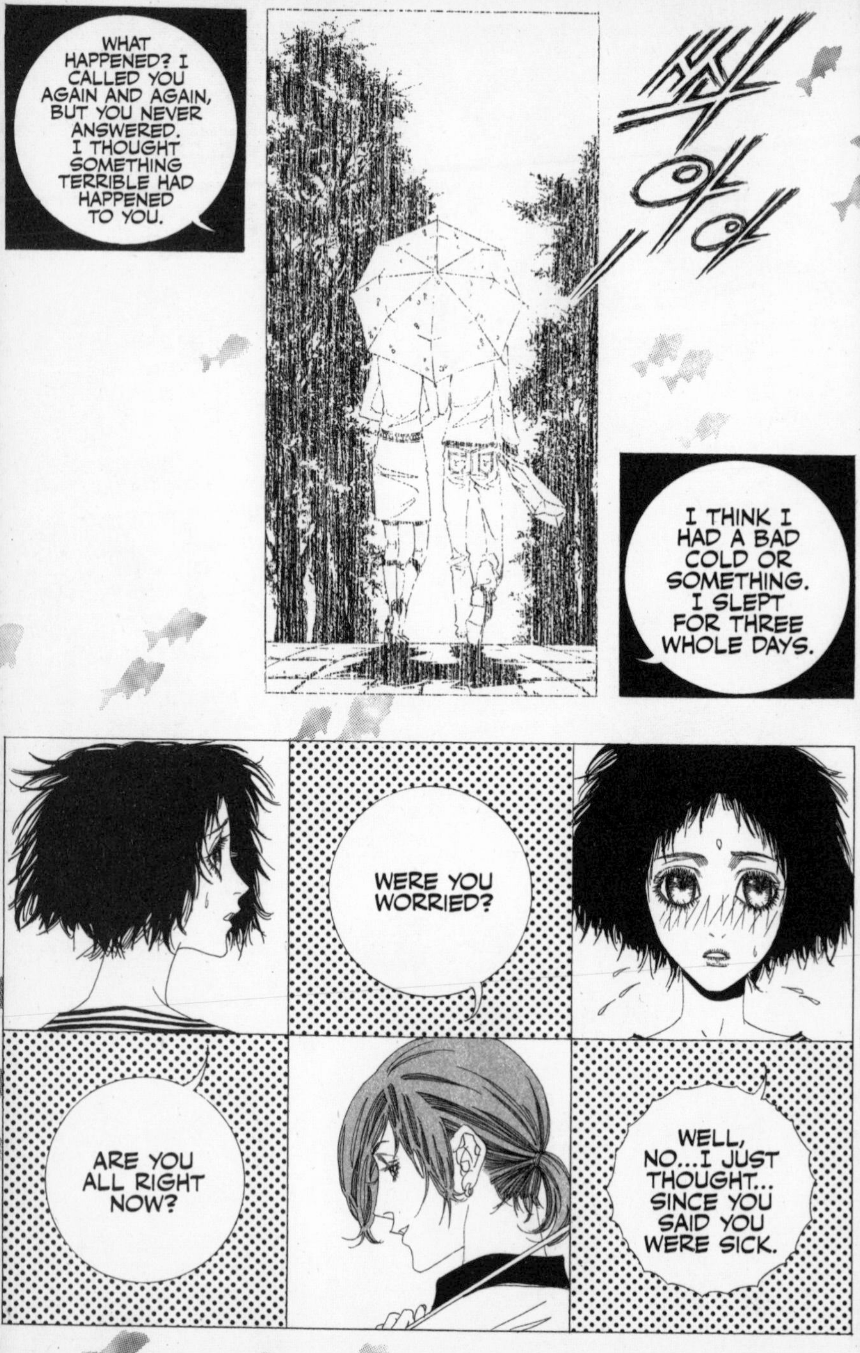
WHAT HAPPENED? I CALLED YOU AGAIN AND AGAIN, BUT YOU NEVER ANSWERED. I THOUGHT SOMETHING TERRIBLE HAD HAPPENED TO YOU.
쏴아아
I THINK I HAD A BAD COLD OR SOMETHING. I SLEPT FOR THREE WHOLE DAYS.
WERE YOU WORRIED?
ARE YOU ALL RIGHT NOW?
WELL, NO...I JUST THOUGHT... SINCE YOU SAID YOU WERE SICK.

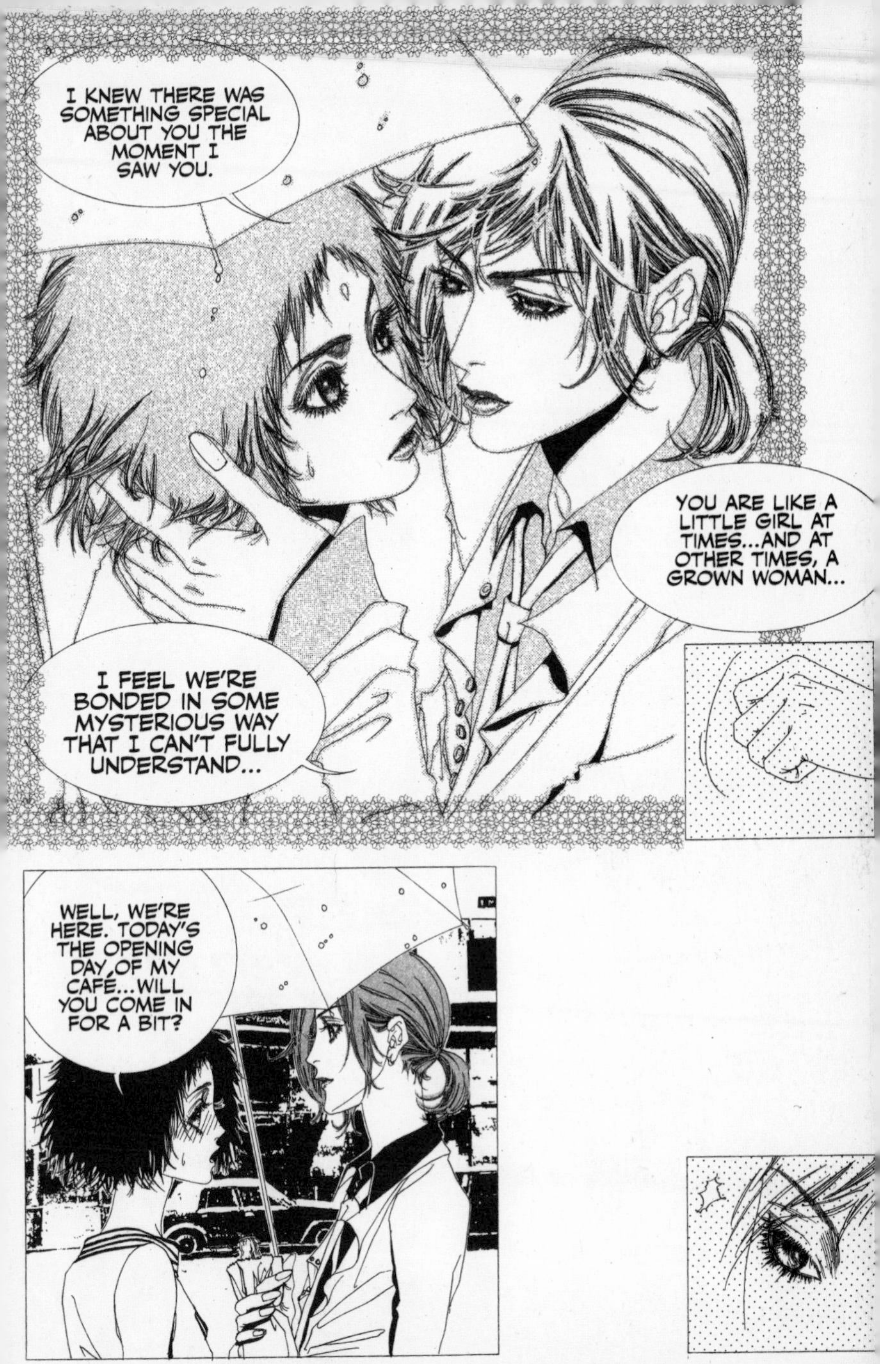
I KNEW THERE WAS SOMETHING SPECIAL ABOUT YOU THE MOMENT I SAW YOU.
YOU ARE LIKE A LITTLE GIRL AT TIMES...AND AT OTHER TIMES, A GROWN WOMAN...
I FEEL WE'RE BONDED IN SOME MYSTERIOUS WAY THAT I CAN'T FULLY UNDERSTAND...
WELL, WE'RE HERE. TODAY'S THE OPENING DAY OF MY CAFÉ...WILL YOU COME IN FOR A BIT?

I'M SORRY. I'LL STOP BY NEXT TIME. I HAVE TO GO NOW.

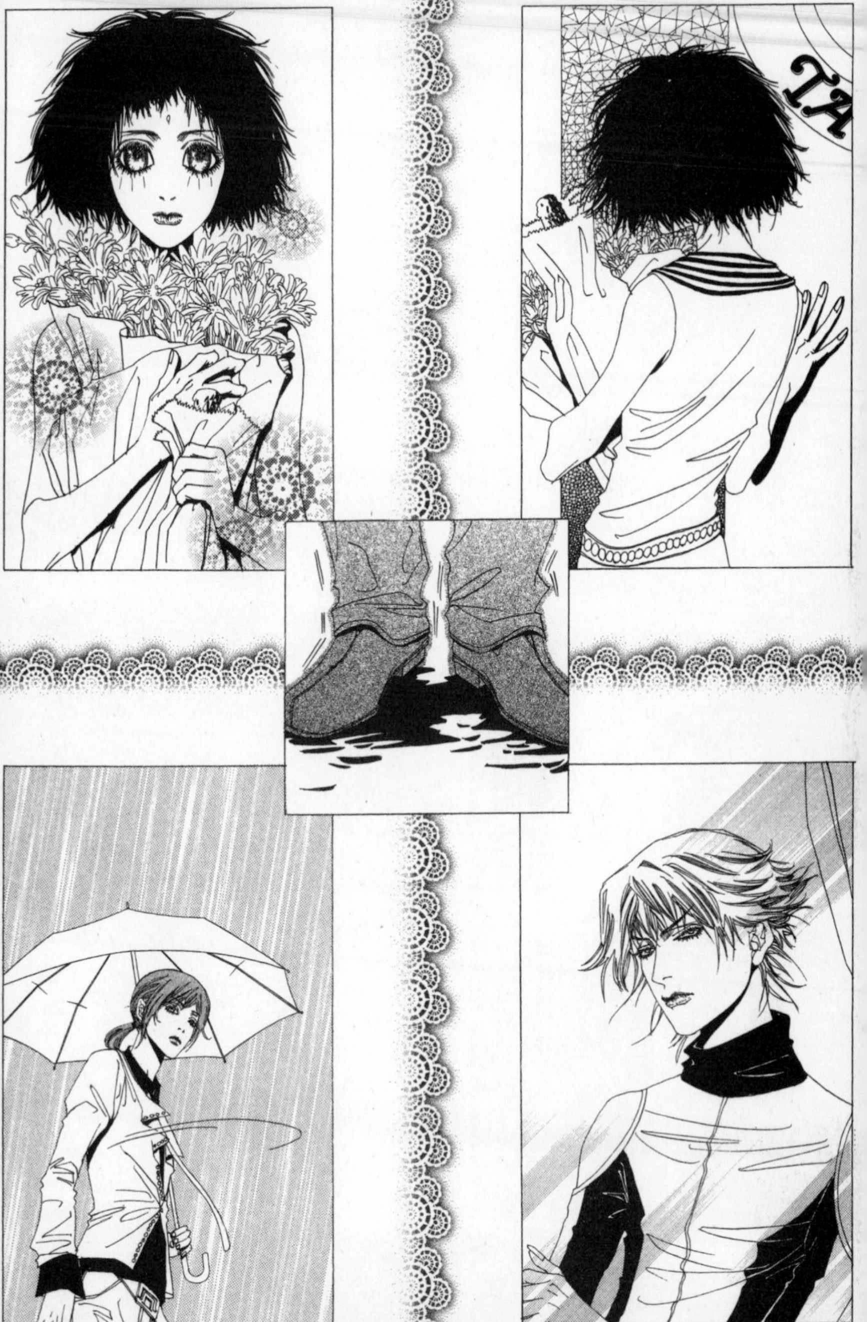
TA

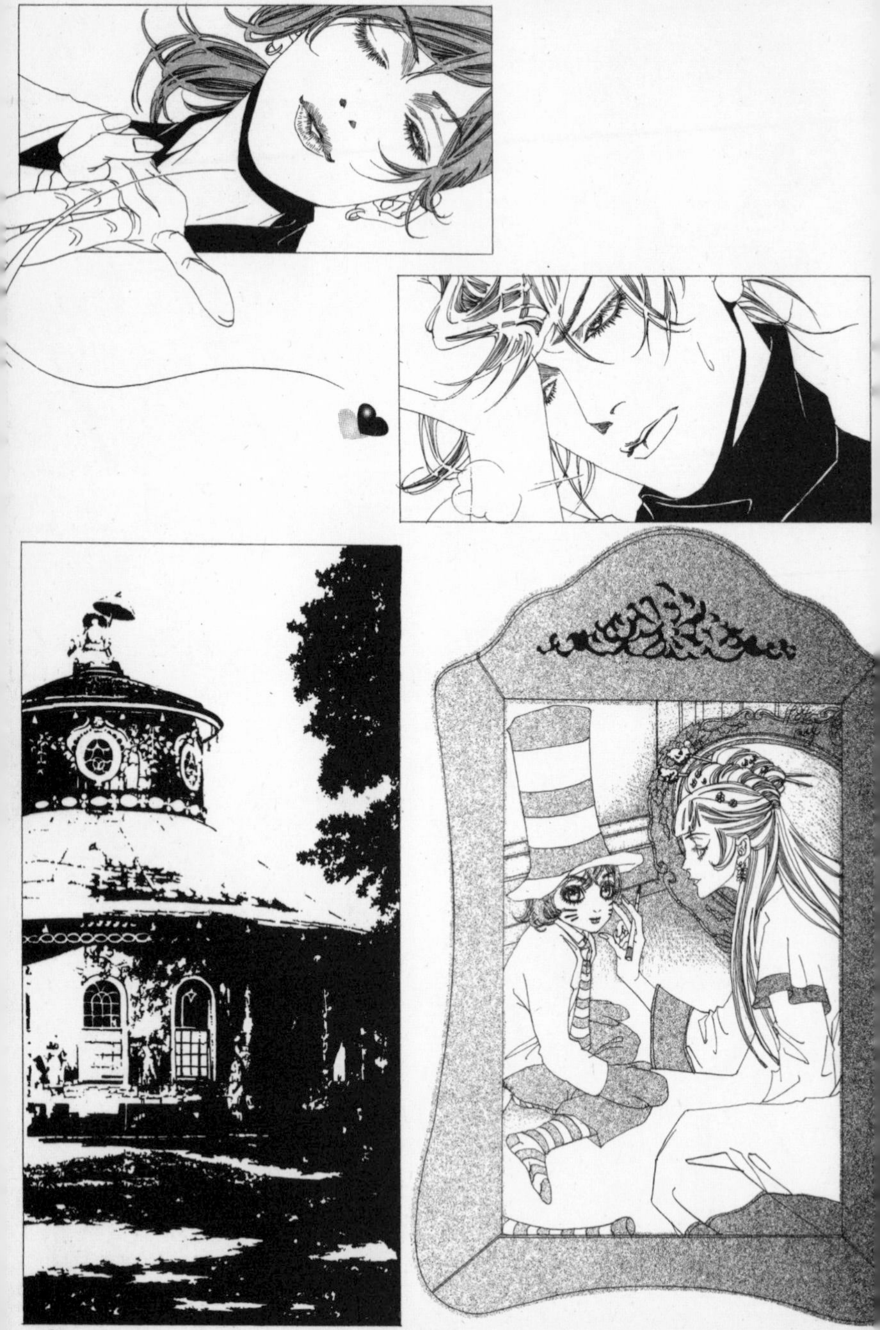

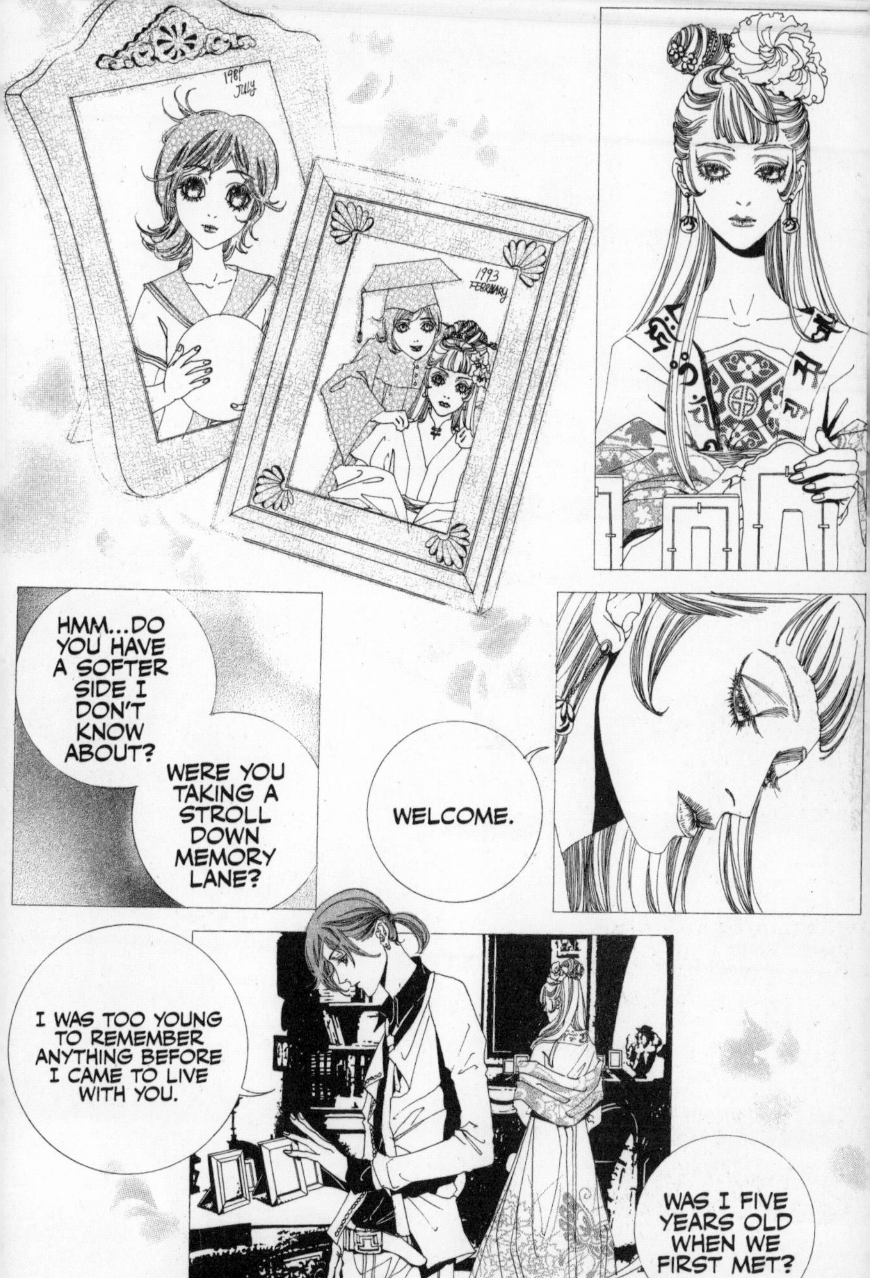
1981 JULY
1993 FEBRUARY
HMM...DO YOU HAVE A SOFTER SIDE I DON'T KNOW ABOUT?
WERE YOU TAKING A STROLL DOWN MEMORY LANE?
WELCOME.
I WAS TOO YOUNG TO REMEMBER ANYTHING BEFORE I CAME TO LIVE WITH YOU.
WAS I FIVE YEARS OLD WHEN WE FIRST MET?

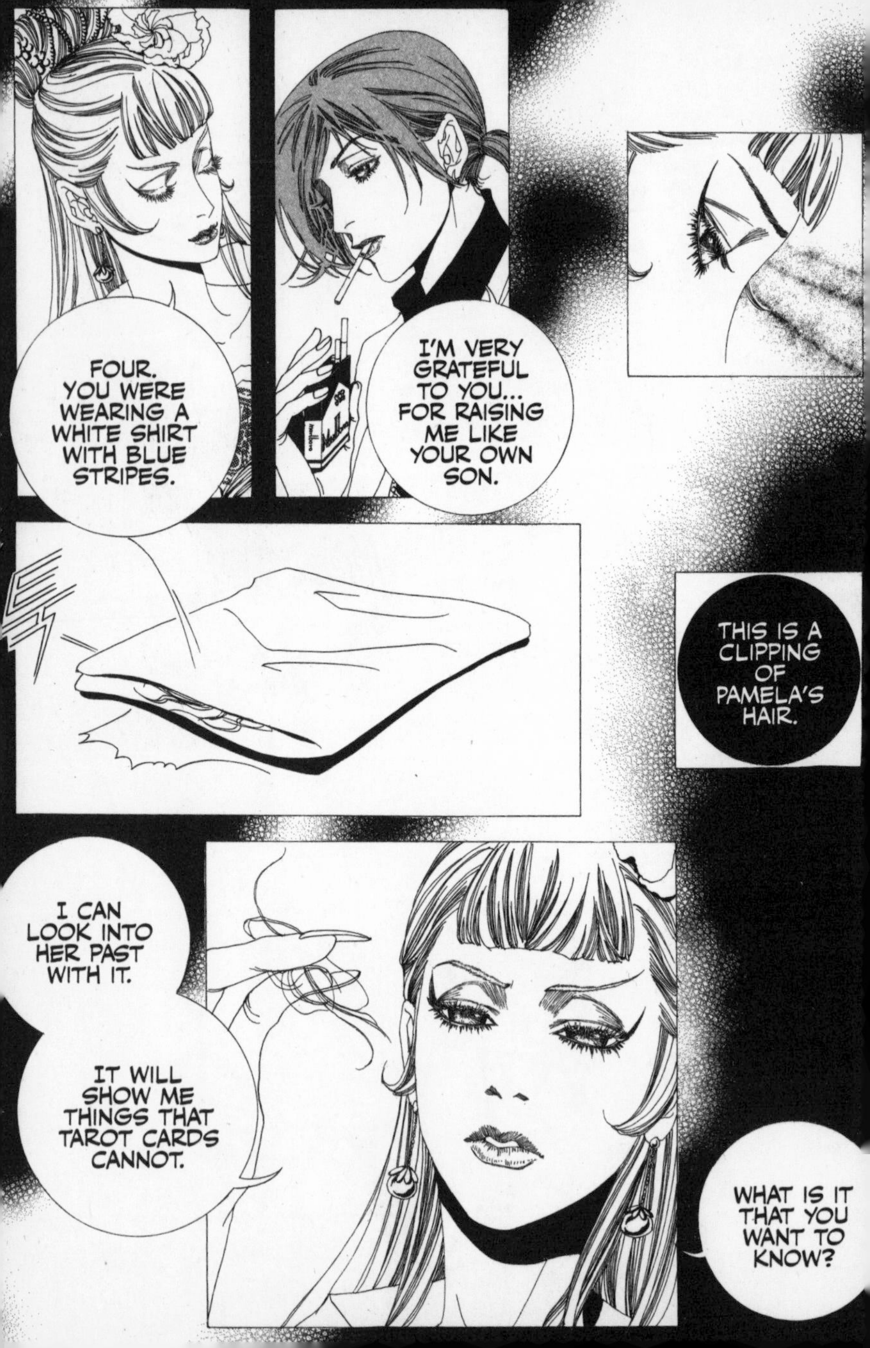
FOUR. YOU WERE WEARING A WHITE SHIRT WITH BLUE STRIPES.
I'M VERY GRATEFUL TO YOU... FOR RAISING ME LIKE YOUR OWN SON.
THIS IS A CLIPPING OF PAMELA'S HAIR.
I CAN LOOK INTO HER PAST WITH IT.
IT WILL SHOW ME THINGS THAT TAROT CARDS CANNOT.
WHAT IS IT THAT YOU WANT TO KNOW?

I CAN'T SHOW YOU EVERYTHING.

THERE'S A LIMIT TO HOW MUCH I CAN SEE.

I WANT TO KNOW HOW PAMELA AND BELUS MET.

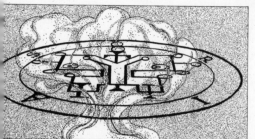

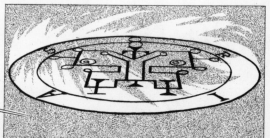

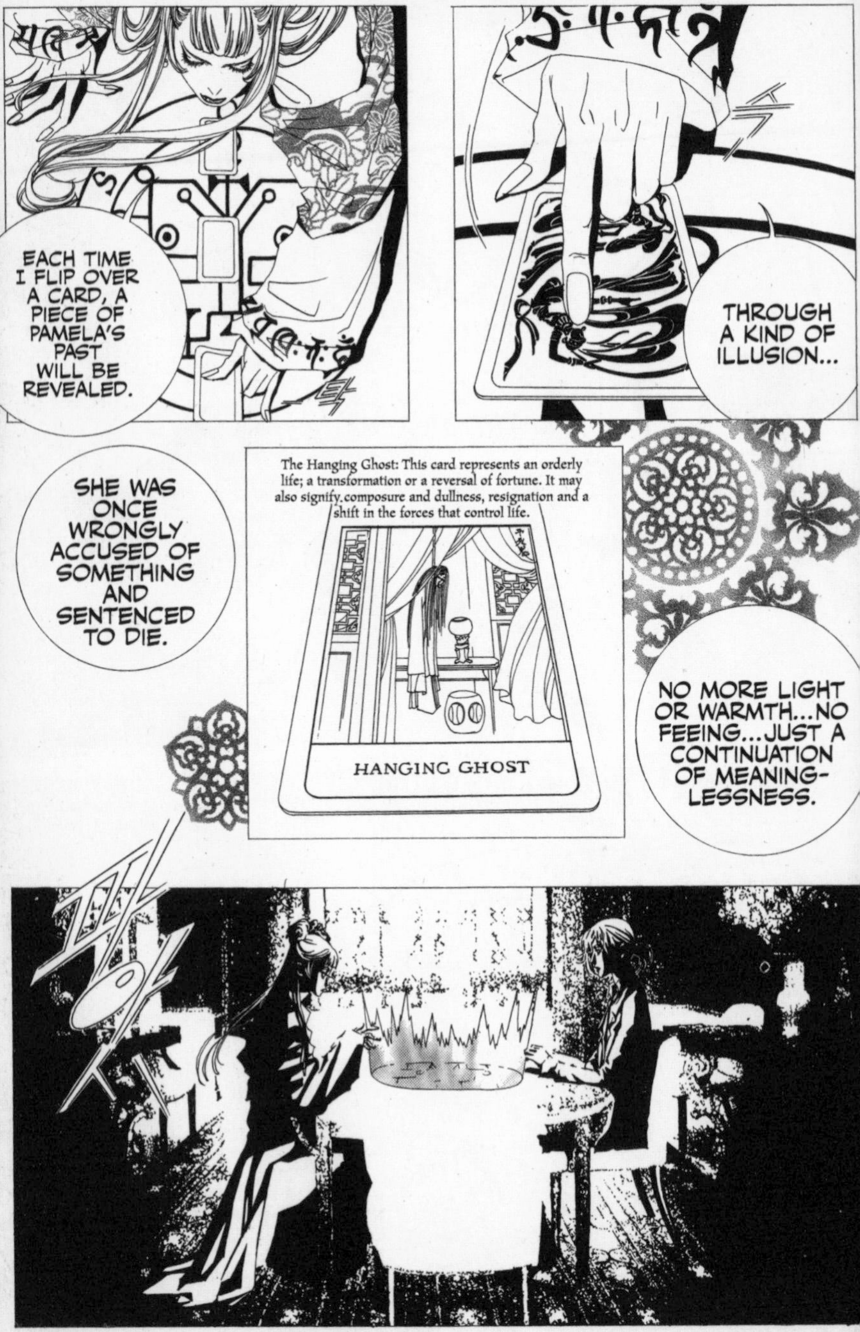
EACH TIME I FLIP OVER A CARD, A PIECE OF PAMELA'S PAST WILL BE REVEALED.
THROUGH A KIND OF ILLUSION...
SHE WAS ONCE WRONGLY ACCUSED OF SOMETHING AND SENTENCED TO DIE.
The Hanging Ghost: This card represents an orderly life; a transformation or a reversal of fortune. It may also signify composure and dullness, resignation and a shift in the forces that control life.
HANGING GHOST
NO MORE LIGHT OR WARMTH...NO FEEING...JUST A CONTINUATION OF MEANING-LESSNESS.

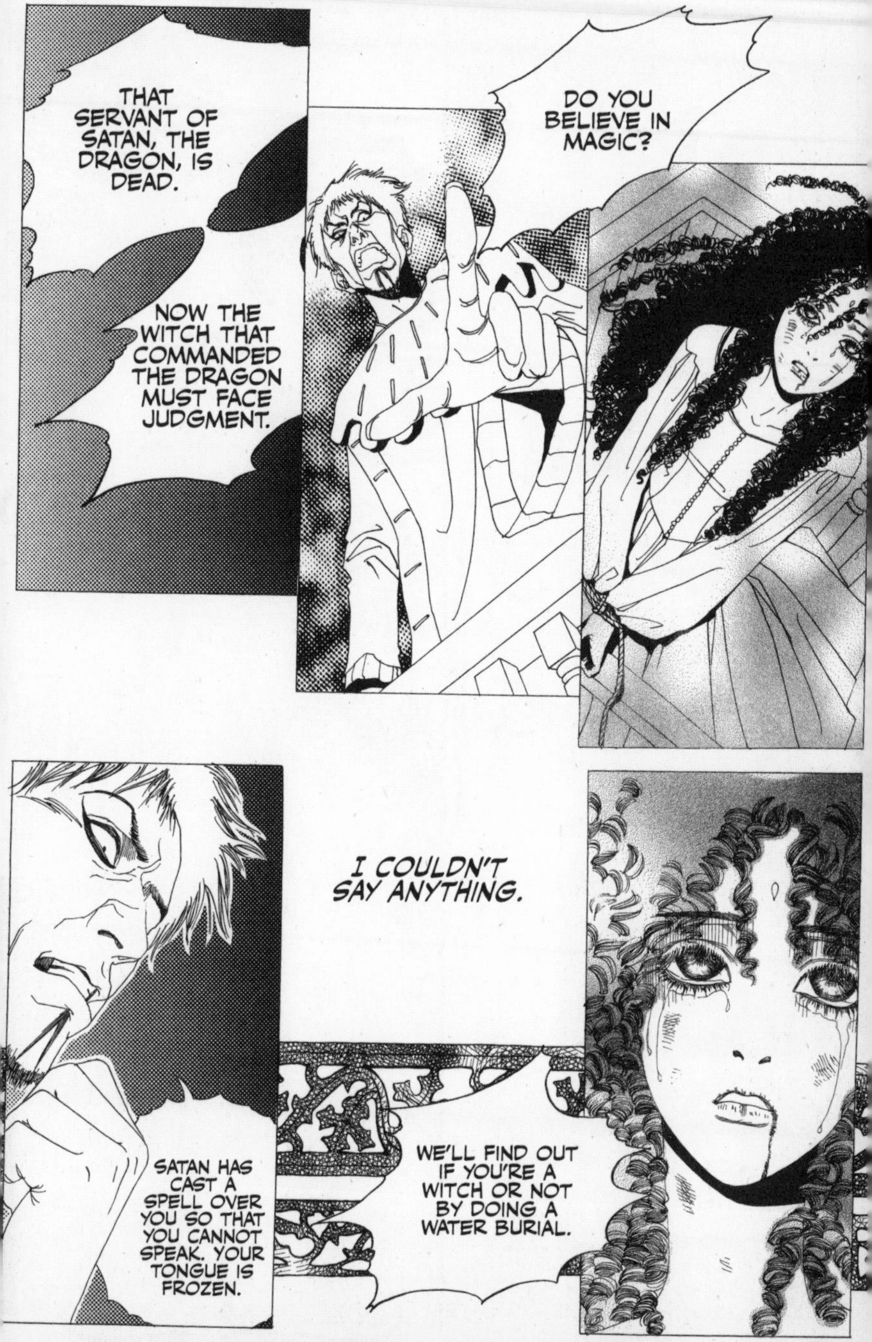
THAT SERVANT OF SATAN, THE DRAGON, IS DEAD.
NOW THE WITCH THAT COMMANDED THE DRAGON MUST FACE JUDGMENT.
DO YOU BELIEVE IN MAGIC?
SATAN HAS CAST A SPELL OVER YOU SO THAT YOU CANNOT SPEAK. YOUR TONGUE IS FROZEN.
I COULDN'T SAY ANYTHING.
WE'LL FIND OUT IF YOU'RE A WITCH OR NOT BY DOING A WATER BURIAL.

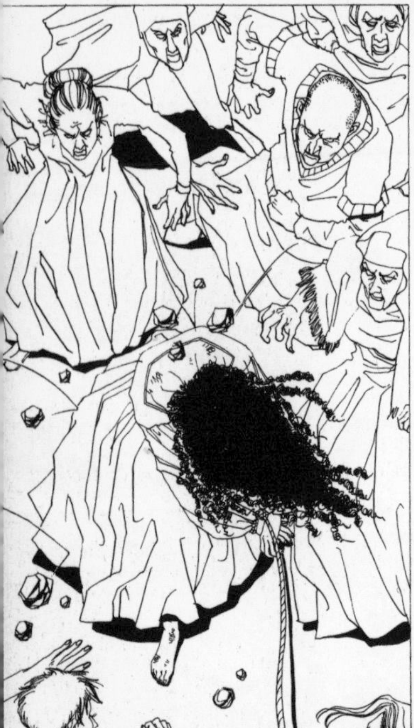

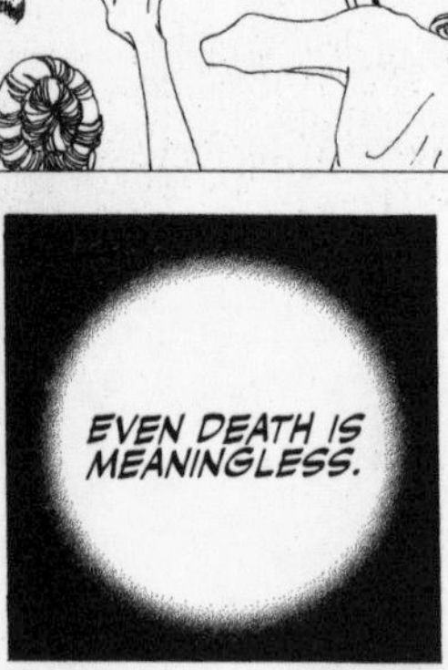
EVEN DEATH IS MEANINGLESS.

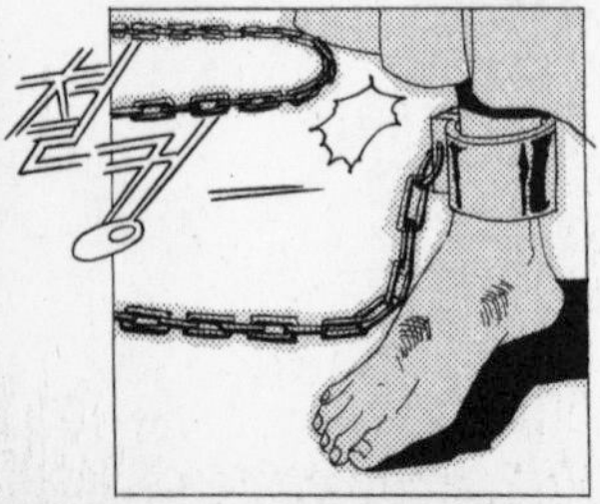
철컹

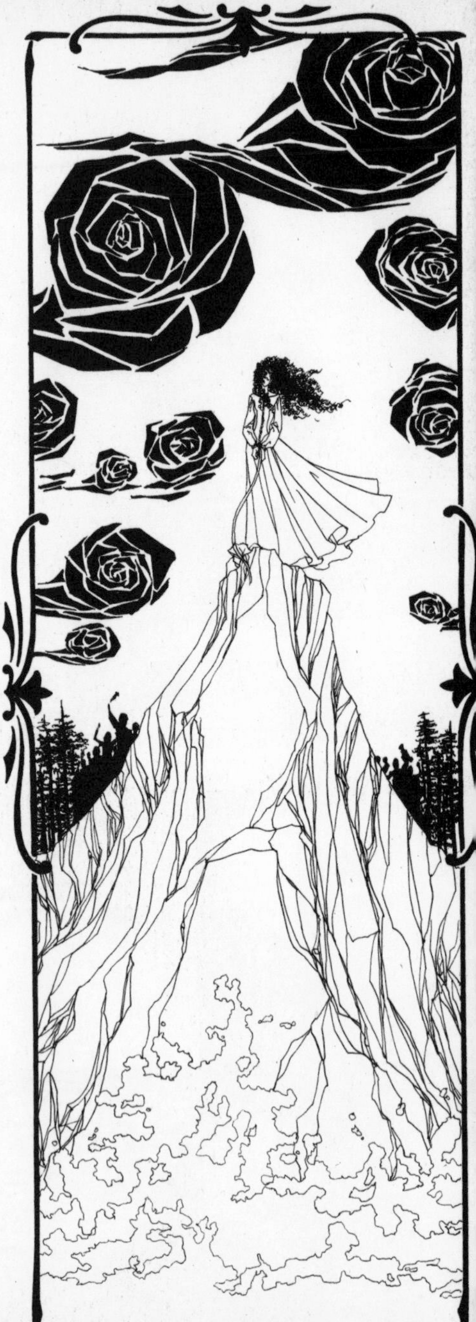

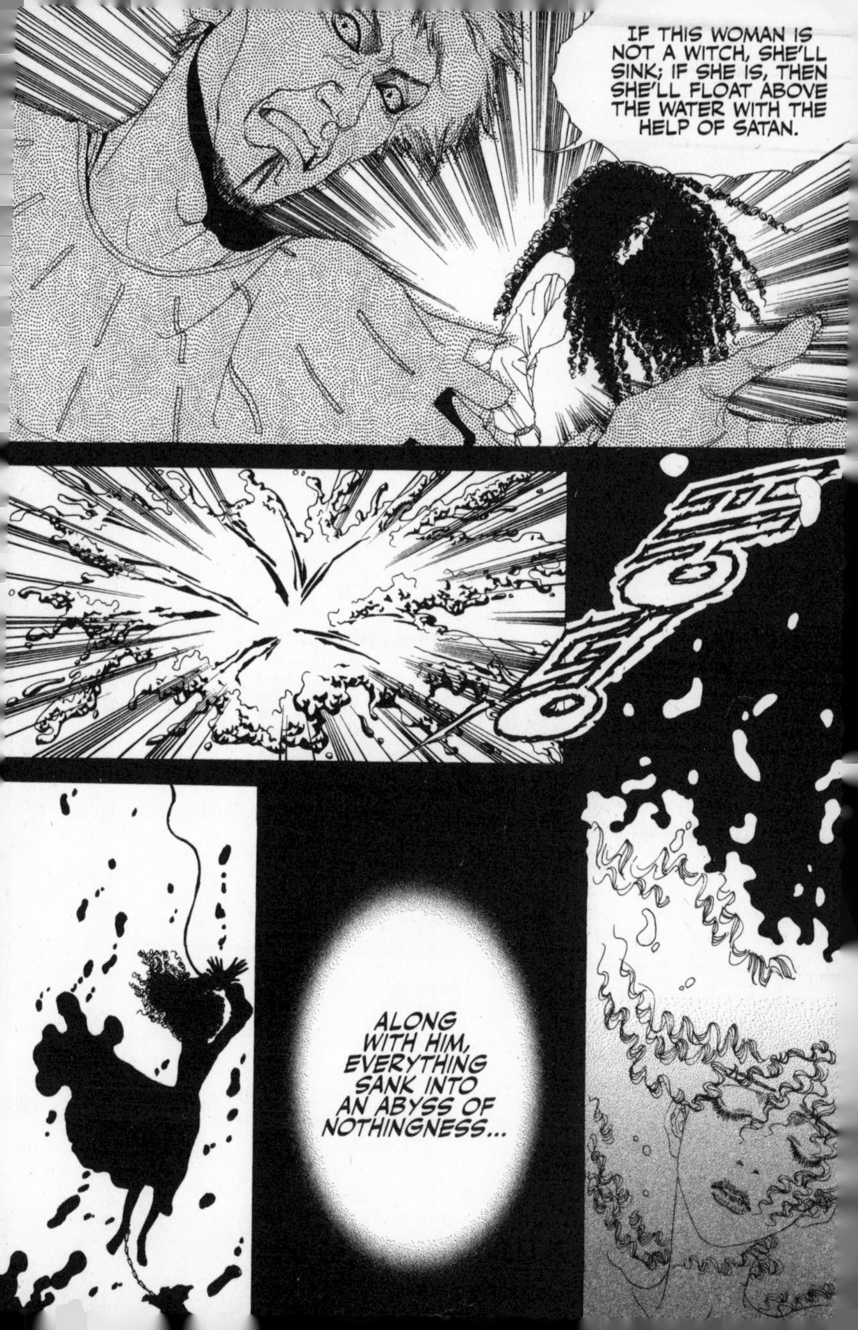
IF THIS WOMAN IS NOT A WITCH, SHE'LL SINK; IF SHE IS, THEN SHE'LL FLOAT ABOVE THE WATER WITH THE HELP OF SATAN.
ALONG WITH HIM, EVERYTHING SANK INTO AN ABYSS OF NOTHINGNESS...

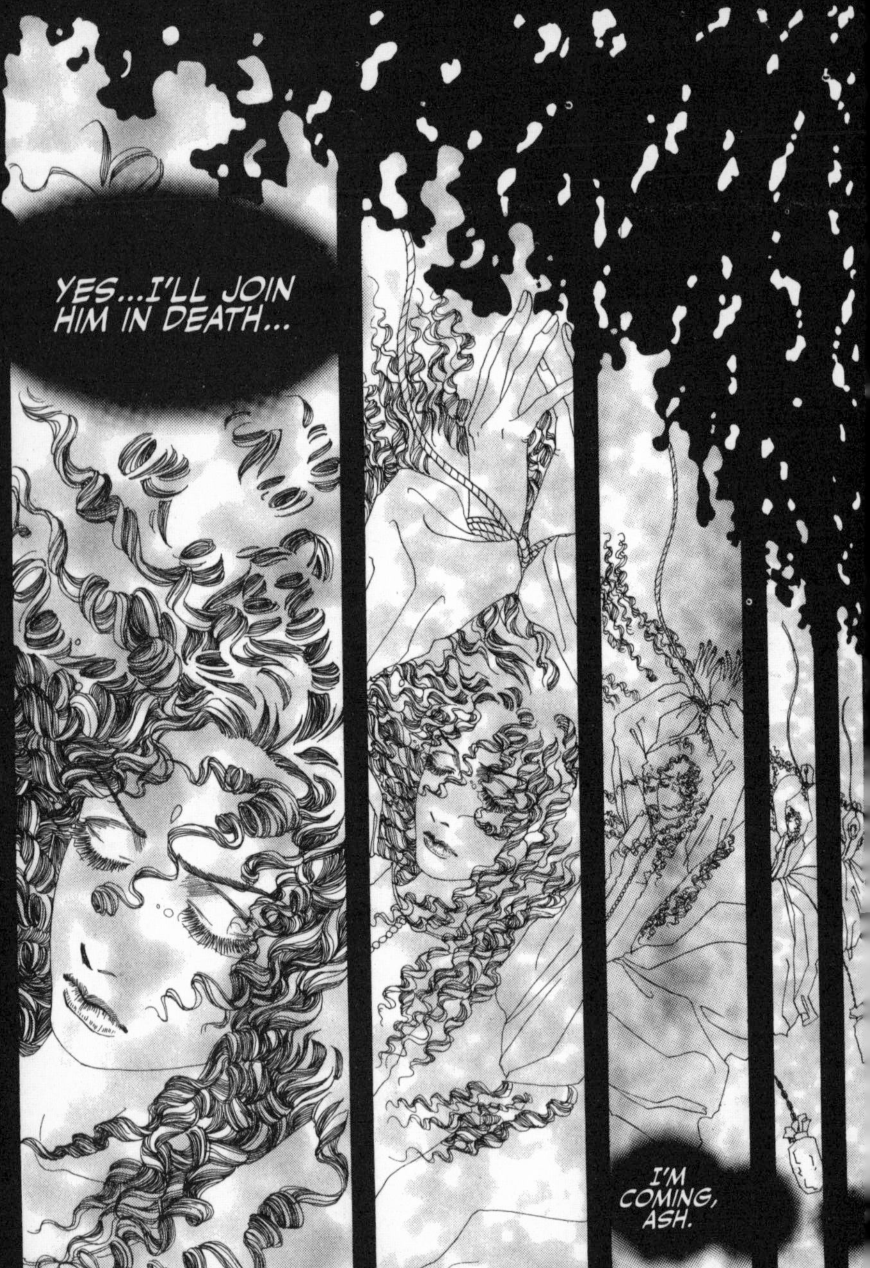
YES...I'LL JOIN HIM IN DEATH...
I'M COMING, ASH.

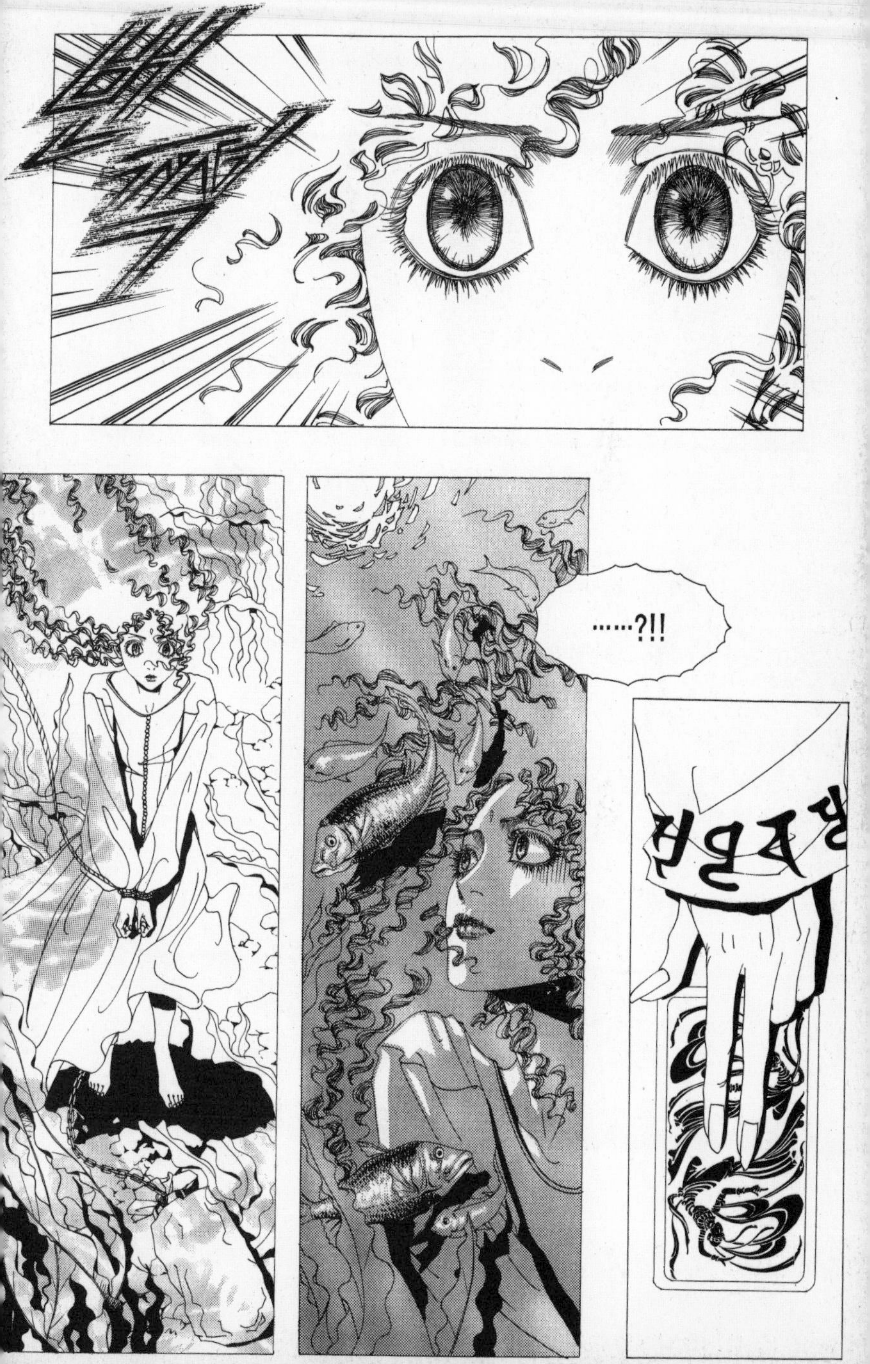
......?!!

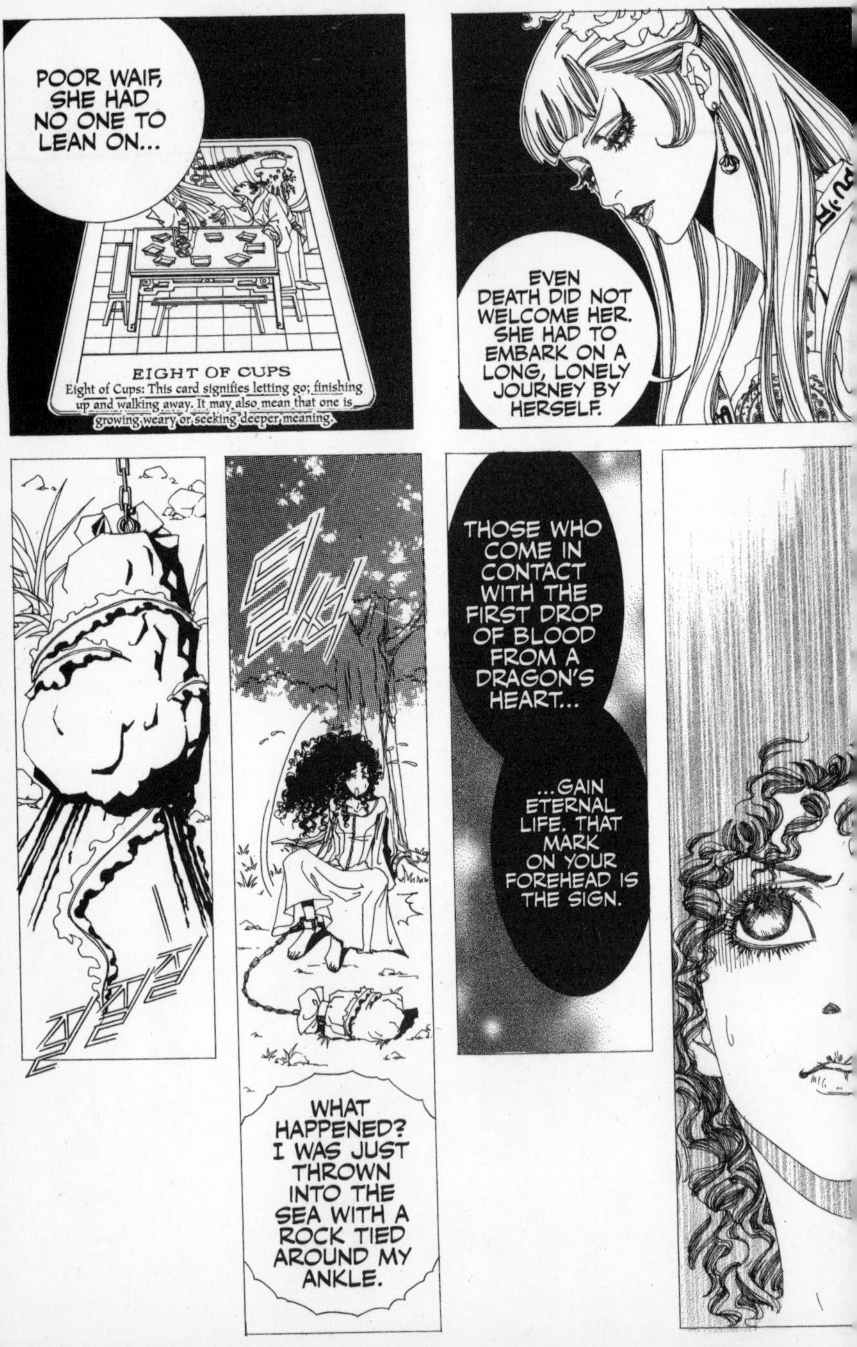
POOR WAIF, SHE HAD NO ONE TO LEAN ON...
EIGHT OF CUPS
Eight of Cups: This card signifies letting go; finishing up and walking away. It may also mean that one is growing weary or seeking deeper meaning.
EVEN DEATH DID NOT WELCOME HER. SHE HAD TO EMBARK ON A LONG, LONELY JOURNEY BY HERSELF.
WHAT HAPPENED? I WAS JUST THROWN INTO THE SEA WITH A ROCK TIED AROUND MY ANKLE.
THOSE WHO COME IN CONTACT WITH THE FIRST DROP OF BLOOD FROM A DRAGON'S HEART...
...GAIN ETERNAL LIFE. THAT MARK ON YOUR FOREHEAD IS THE SIGN.

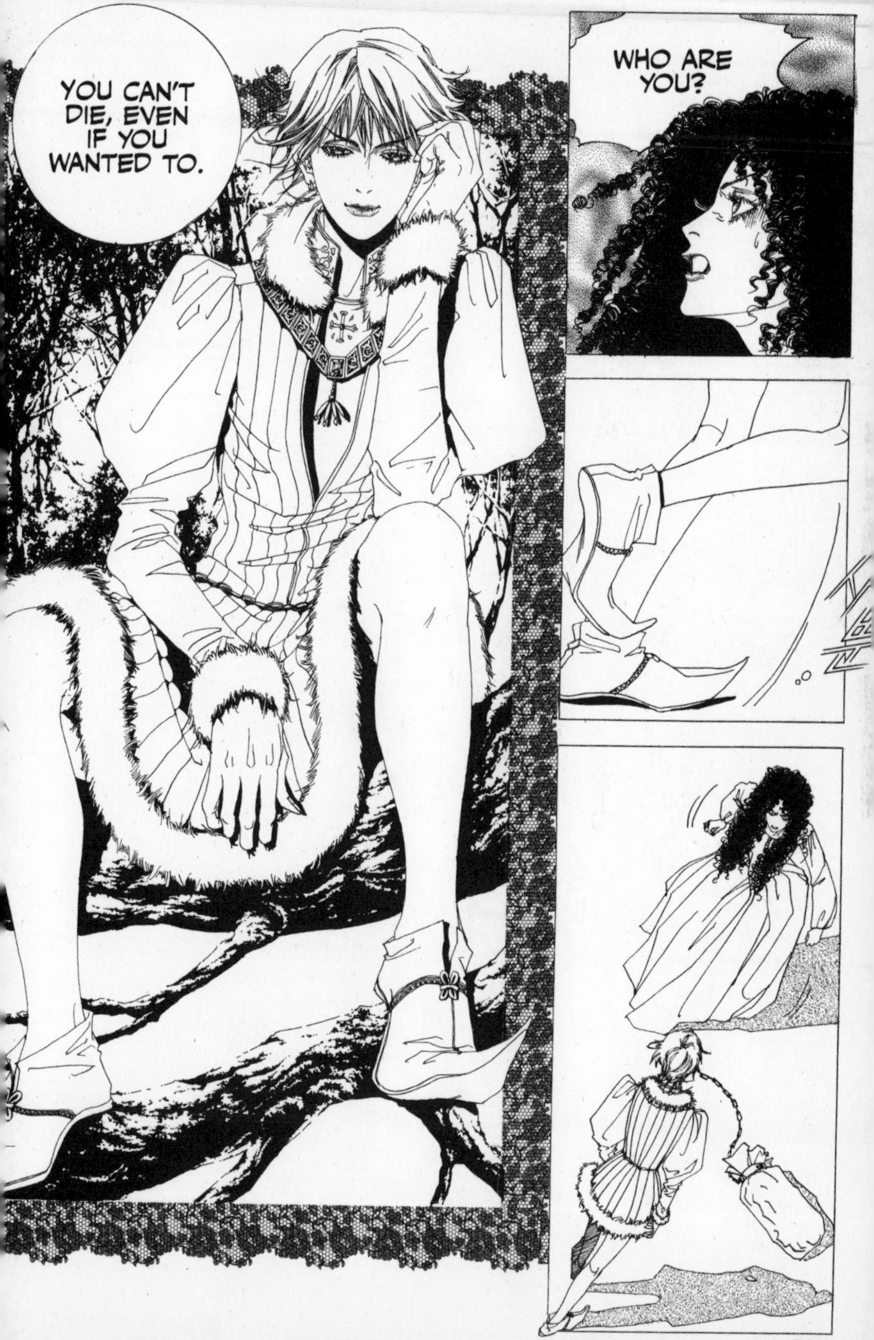
YOU CAN'T DIE, EVEN IF YOU WANTED TO.
WHO ARE YOU?

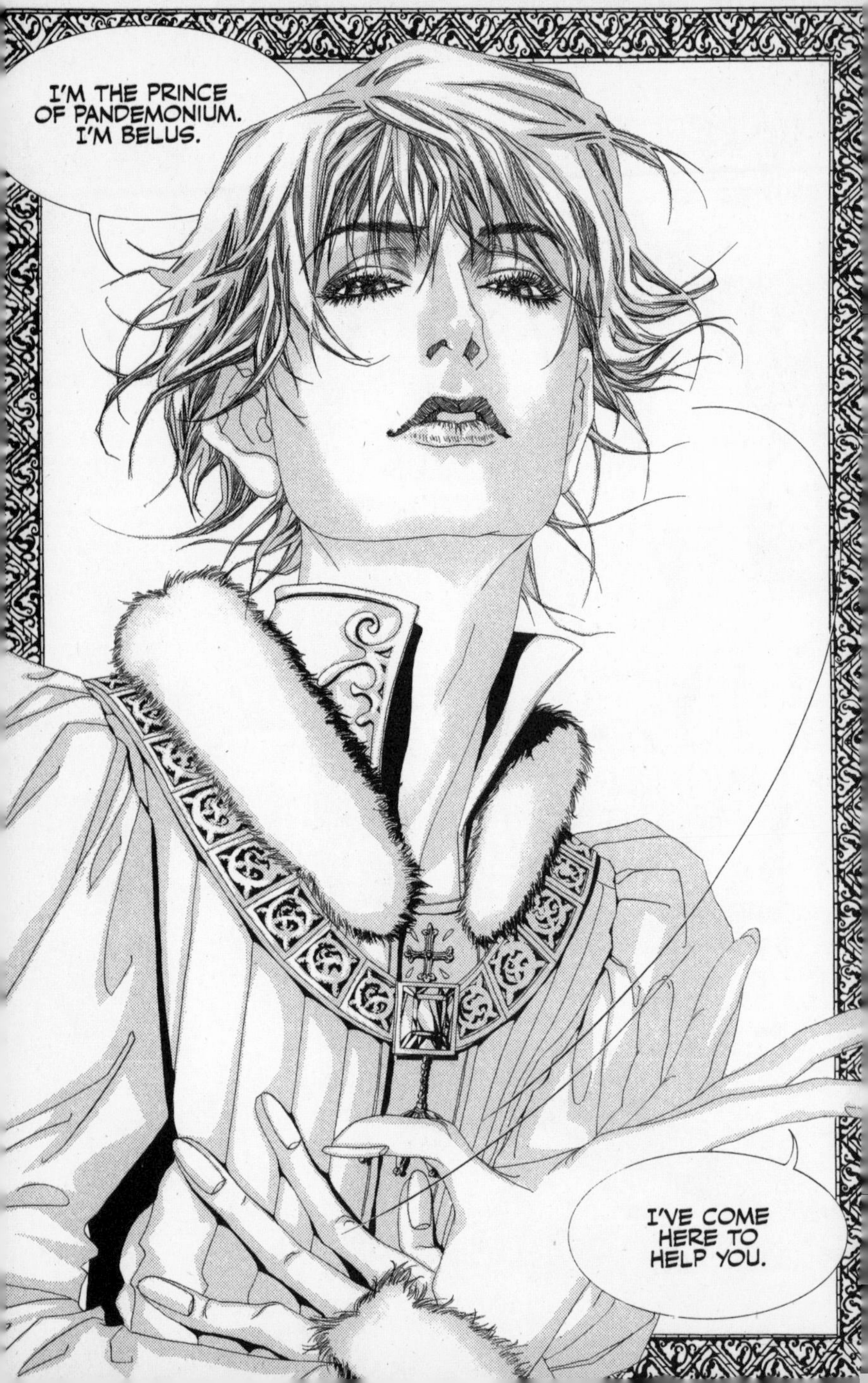
I'M THE PRINCE OF PANDEMONIUM. I'M BELUS.
I'VE COME HERE TO HELP YOU.

XI

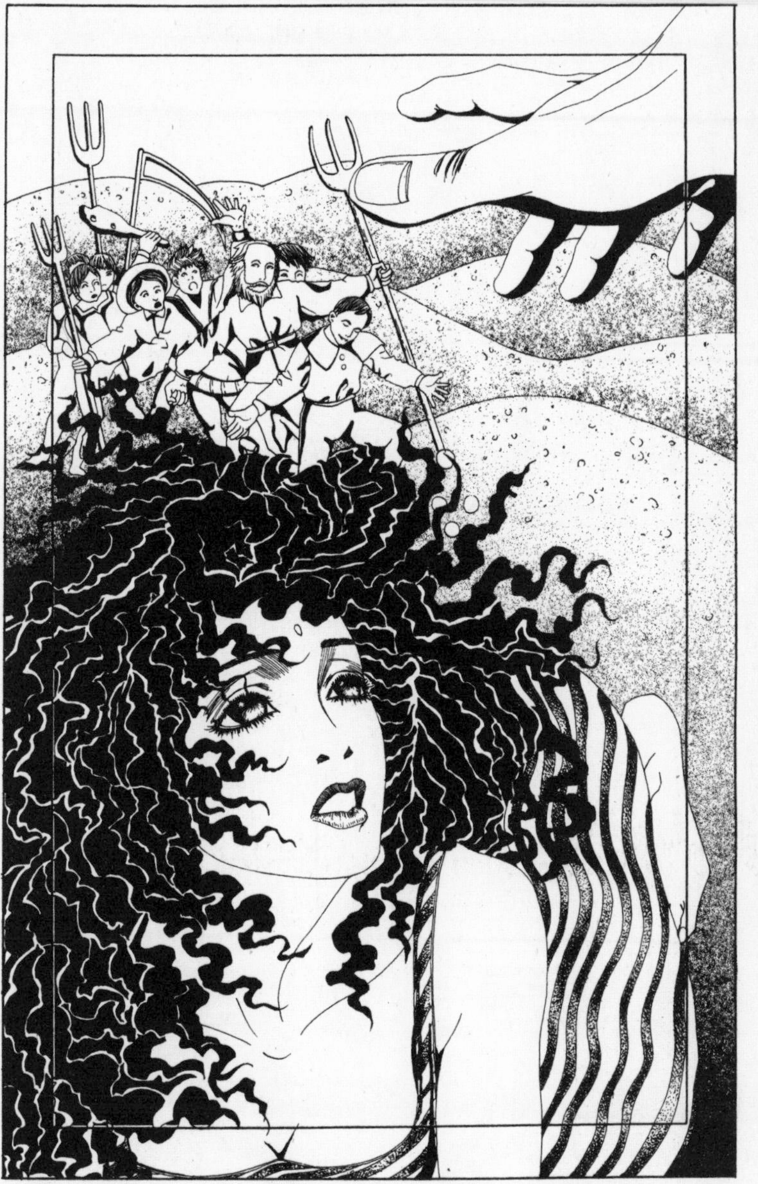

ILLUSTRATION FROM MASTER TAROT

Vergebung
Forgiving

Forgiving: The ability to overcome one's sins by forgiving others.

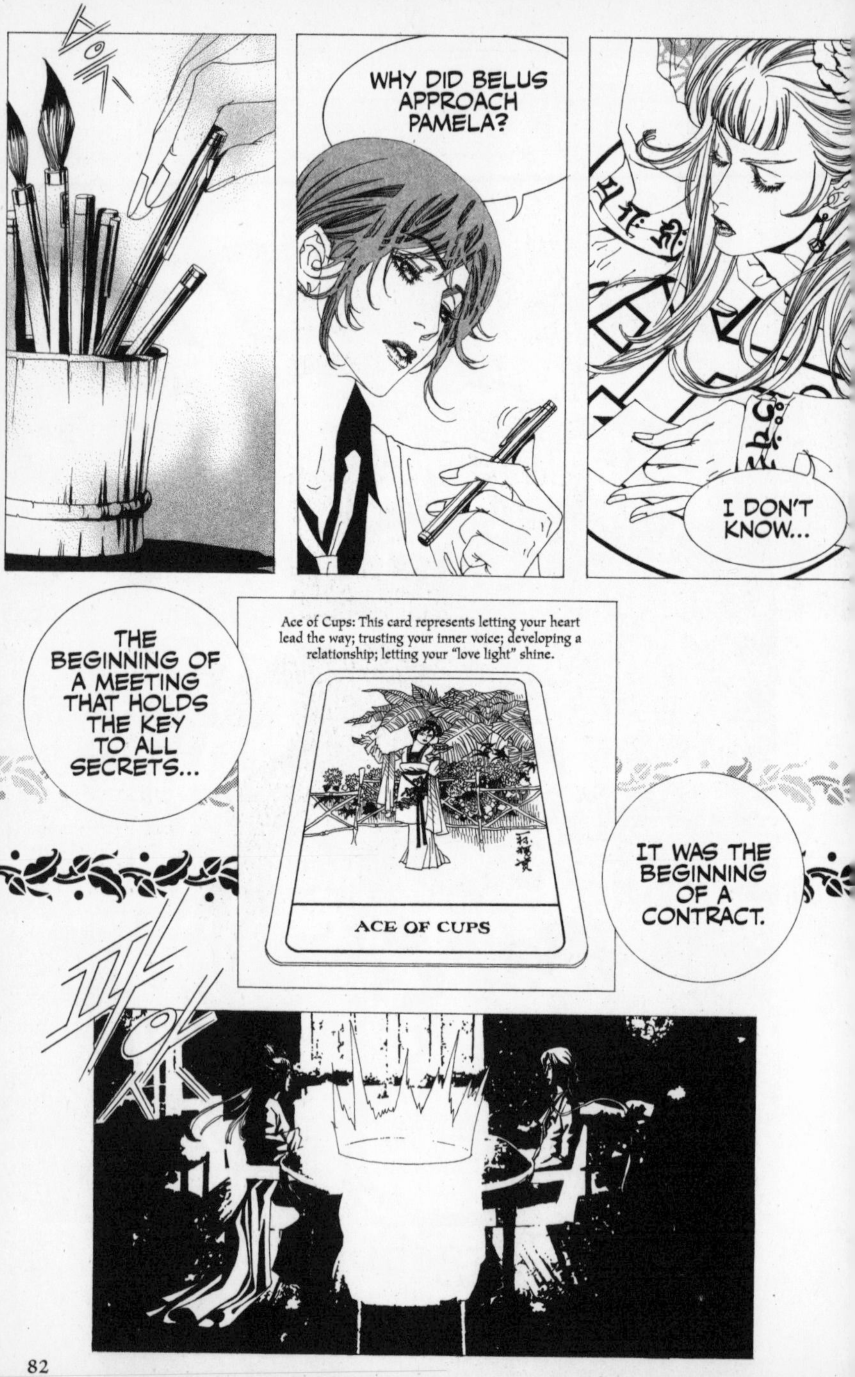
WHY DID BELUS APPROACH PAMELA?
I DON'T KNOW...
THE BEGINNING OF A MEETING THAT HOLDS THE KEY TO ALL SECRETS...
Ace of Cups: This card represents letting your heart lead the way; trusting your inner voice; developing a relationship; letting your "love light" shine.
ACE OF CUPS
IT WAS THE BEGINNING OF A CONTRACT.

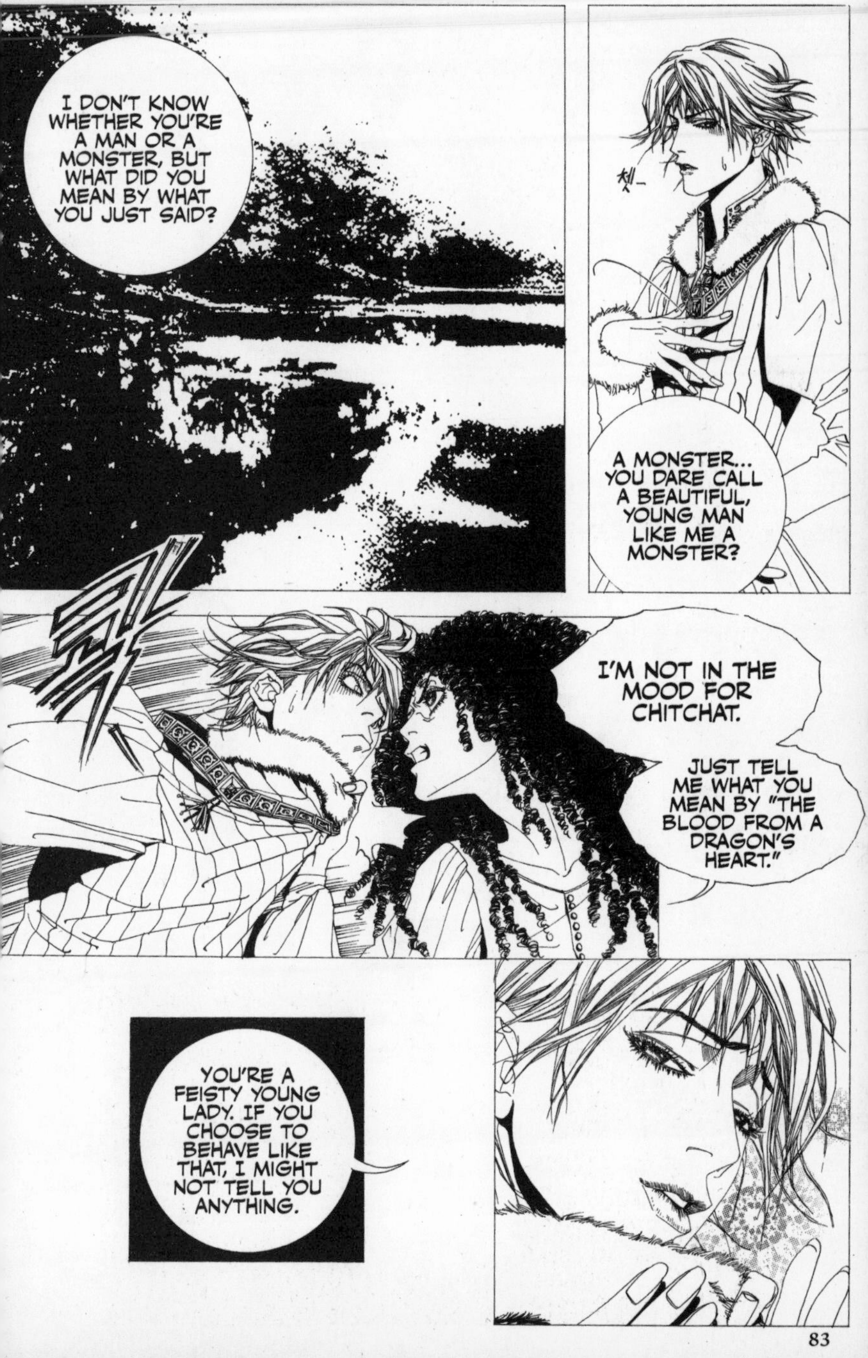
I DON'T KNOW WHETHER YOU'RE A MAN OR A MONSTER, BUT WHAT DID YOU MEAN BY WHAT YOU JUST SAID?
A MONSTER... YOU DARE CALL A BEAUTIFUL, YOUNG MAN LIKE ME A MONSTER?
I'M NOT IN THE MOOD FOR CHITCHAT.
JUST TELL ME WHAT YOU MEAN BY "THE BLOOD FROM A DRAGON'S HEART."
YOU'RE A FEISTY YOUNG LADY. IF YOU CHOOSE TO BEHAVE LIKE THAT, I MIGHT NOT TELL YOU ANYTHING.

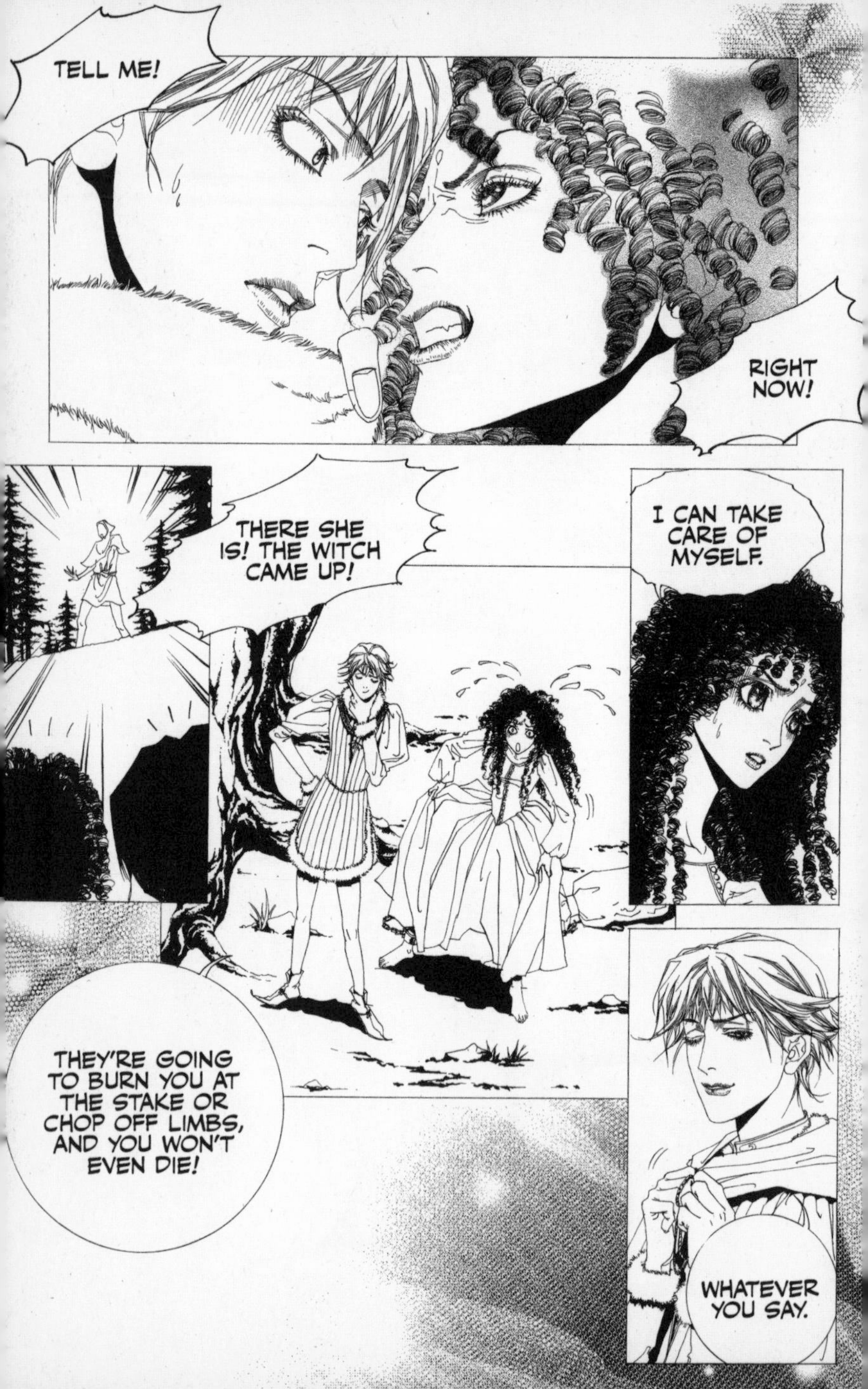

TELL ME!
RIGHT NOW!
THERE SHE IS! THE WITCH CAME UP!
I CAN TAKE CARE OF MYSELF.
THEY'RE GOING TO BURN YOU AT THE STAKE OR CHOP OFF LIMBS, AND YOU WON'T EVEN DIE!
WHATEVER YOU SAY.

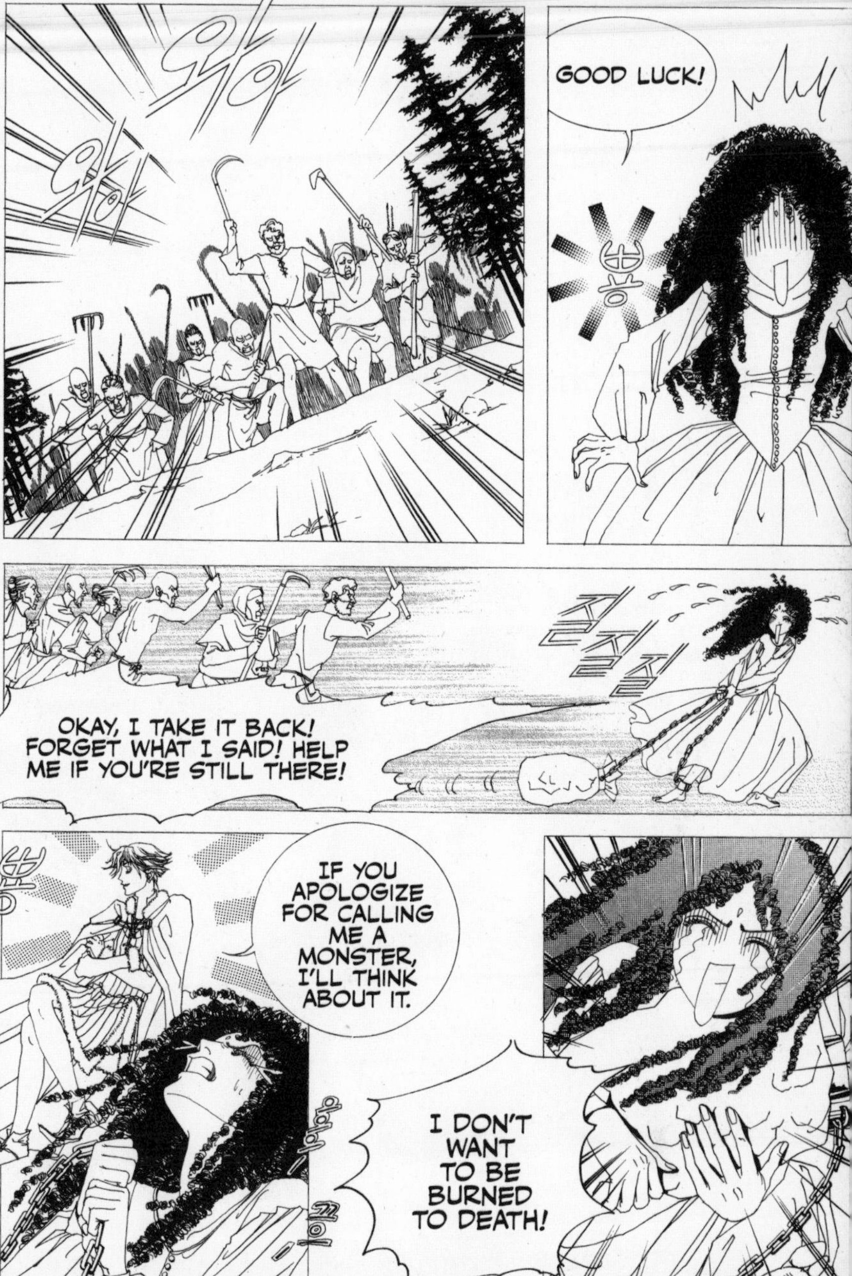
GOOD LUCK!
OKAY, I TAKE IT BACK! FORGET WHAT I SAID! HELP ME IF YOU'RE STILL THERE!
IF YOU APOLOGIZE FOR CALLING ME A MONSTER, I'LL THINK ABOUT IT.
I DON'T WANT TO BE BURNED TO DEATH!

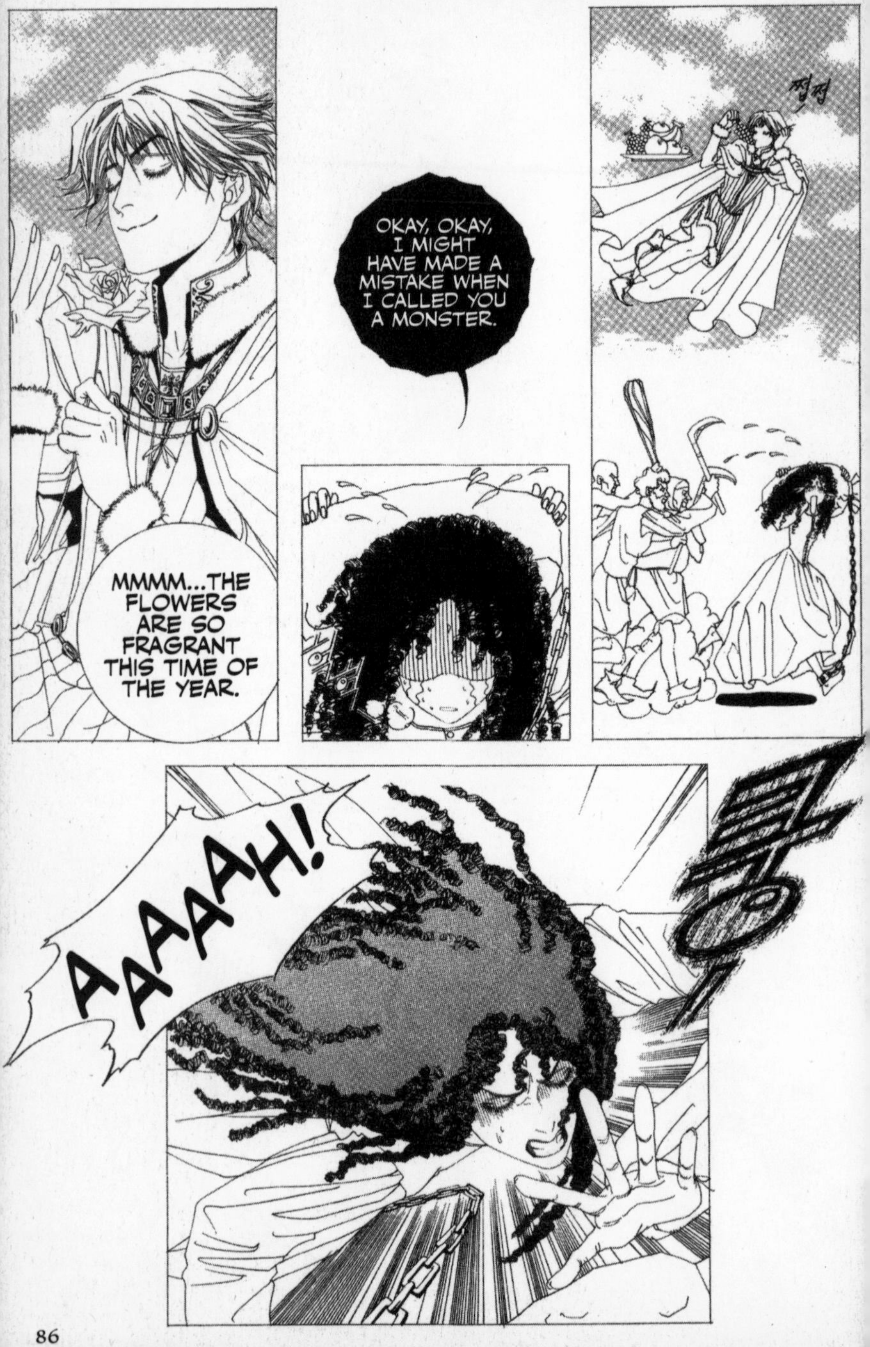
MMMM...THE FLOWERS ARE SO FRAGRANT THIS TIME OF THE YEAR.
OKAY, OKAY, I MIGHT HAVE MADE A MISTAKE WHEN I CALLED YOU A MONSTER.
쩝쩝
AAAAH!

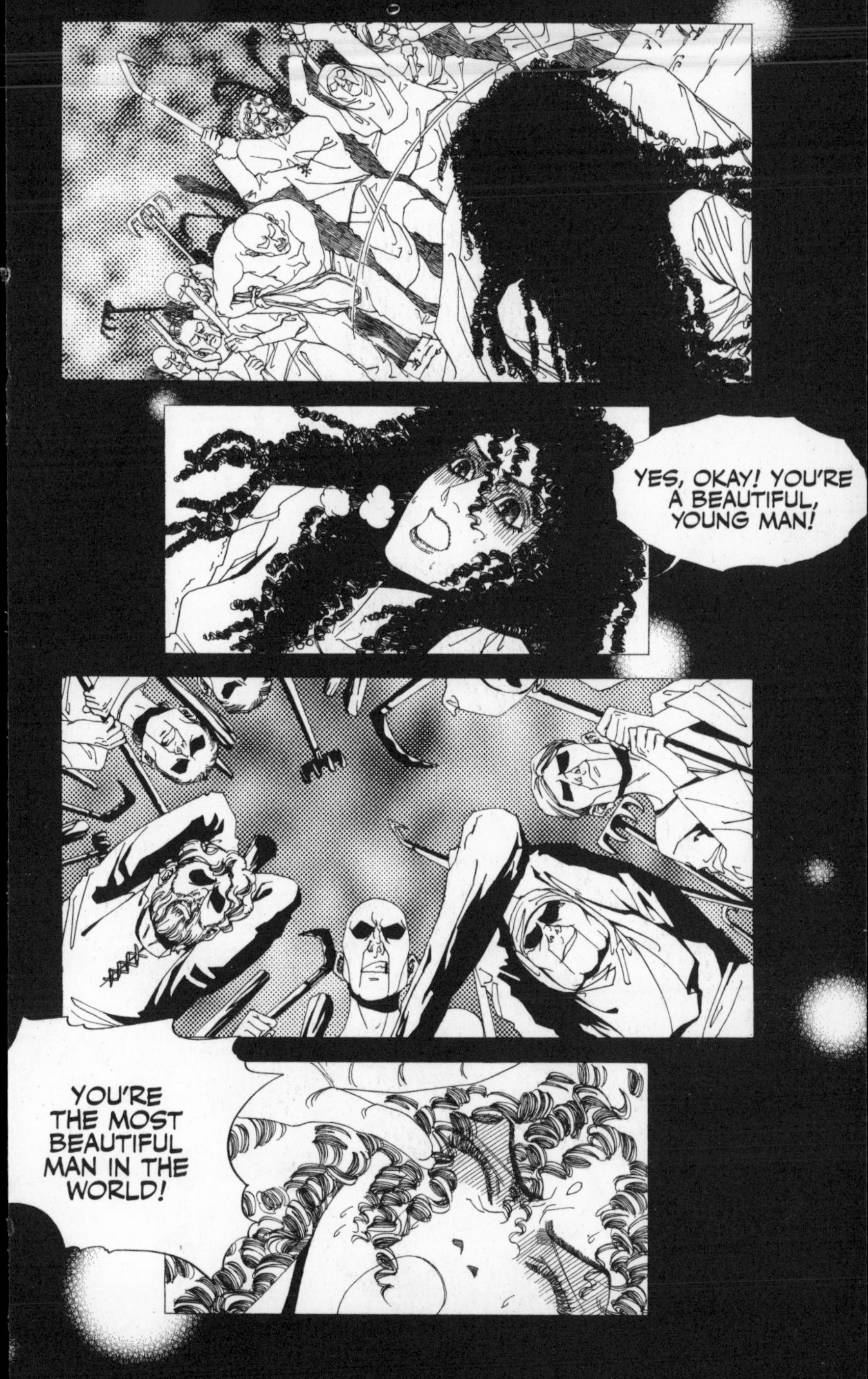
YES, OKAY! YOU'RE A BEAUTIFUL, YOUNG MAN!
YOU'RE THE MOST BEAUTIFUL MAN IN THE WORLD!

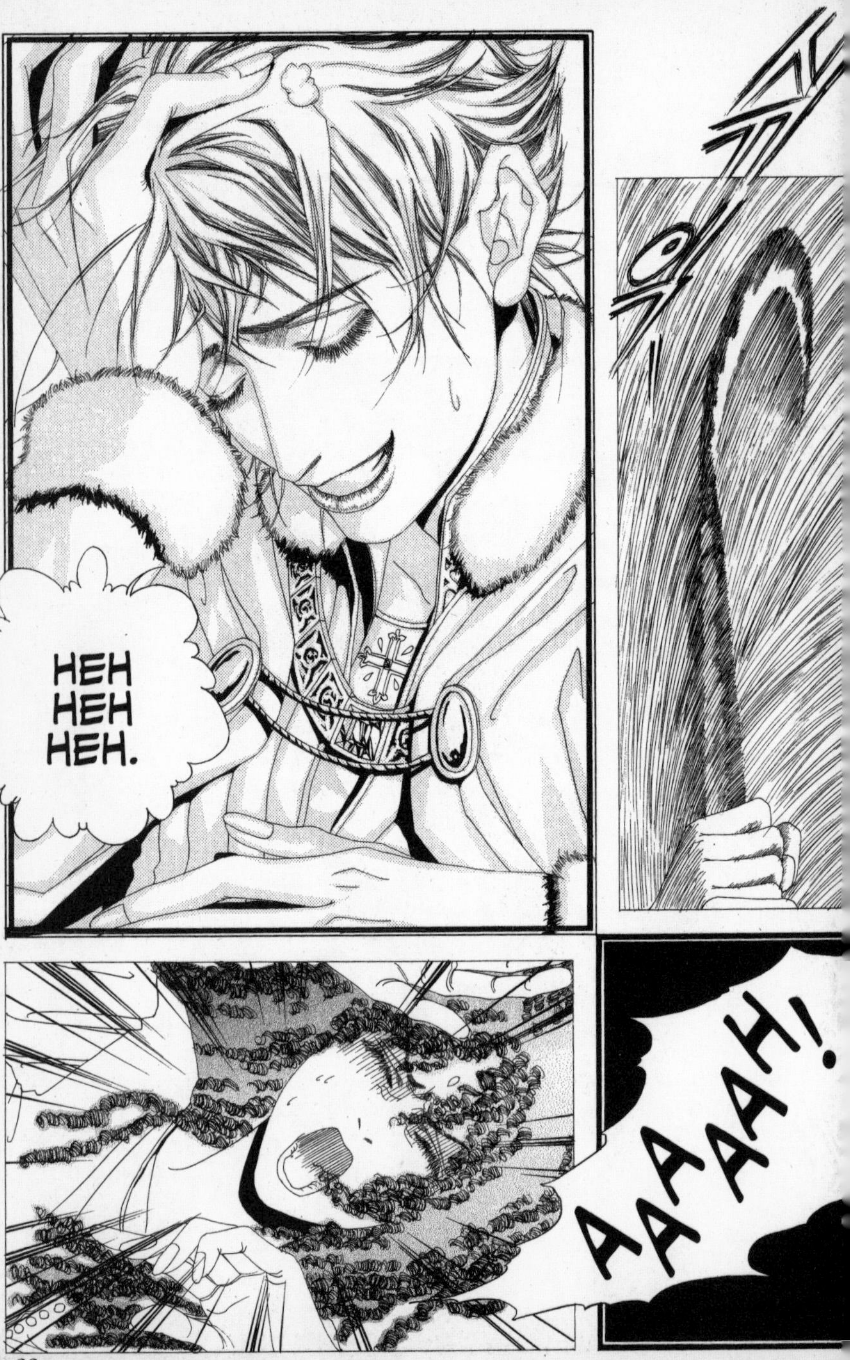
HEH HEH HEH.
AAAAAH!

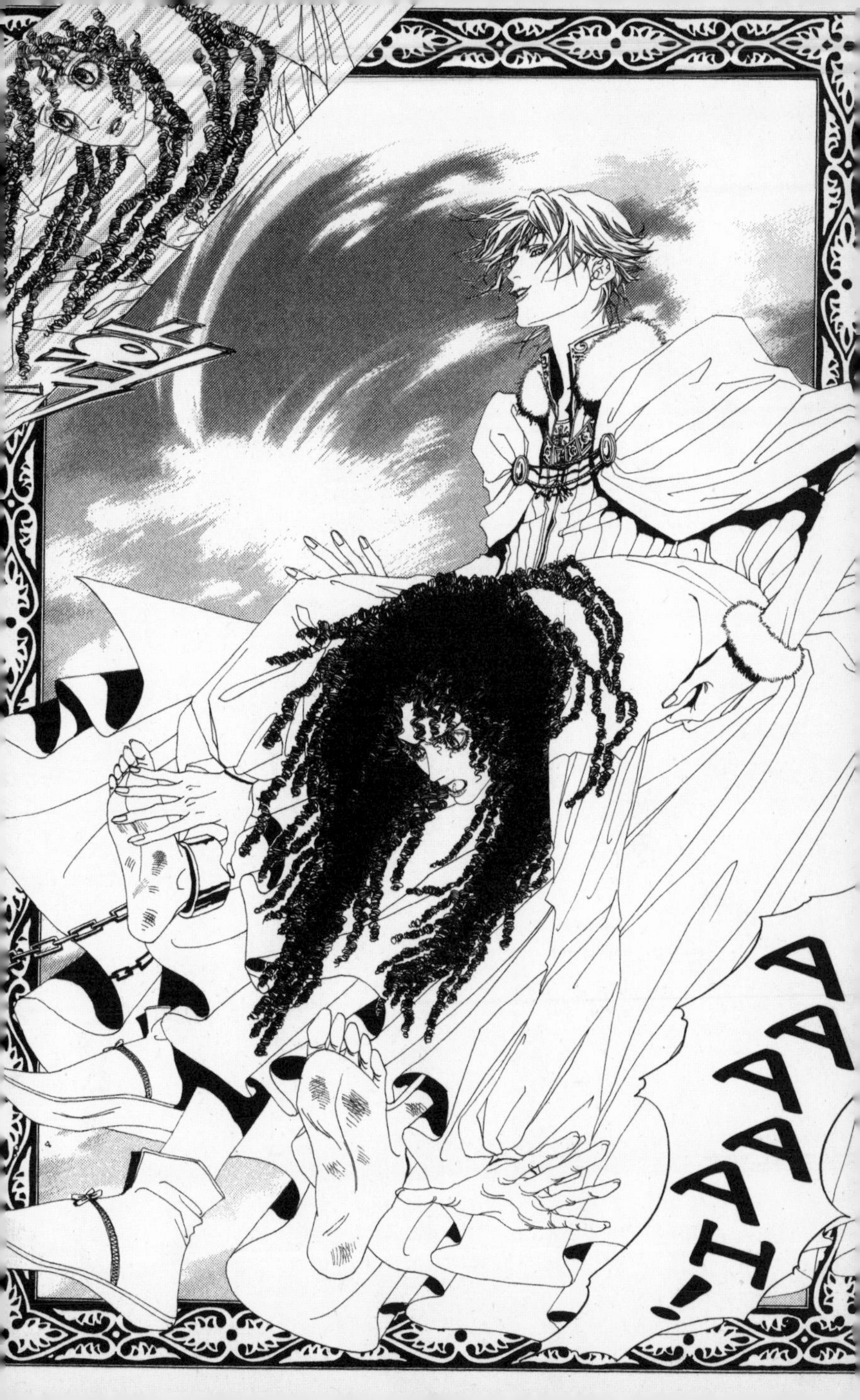
AAAAAH!

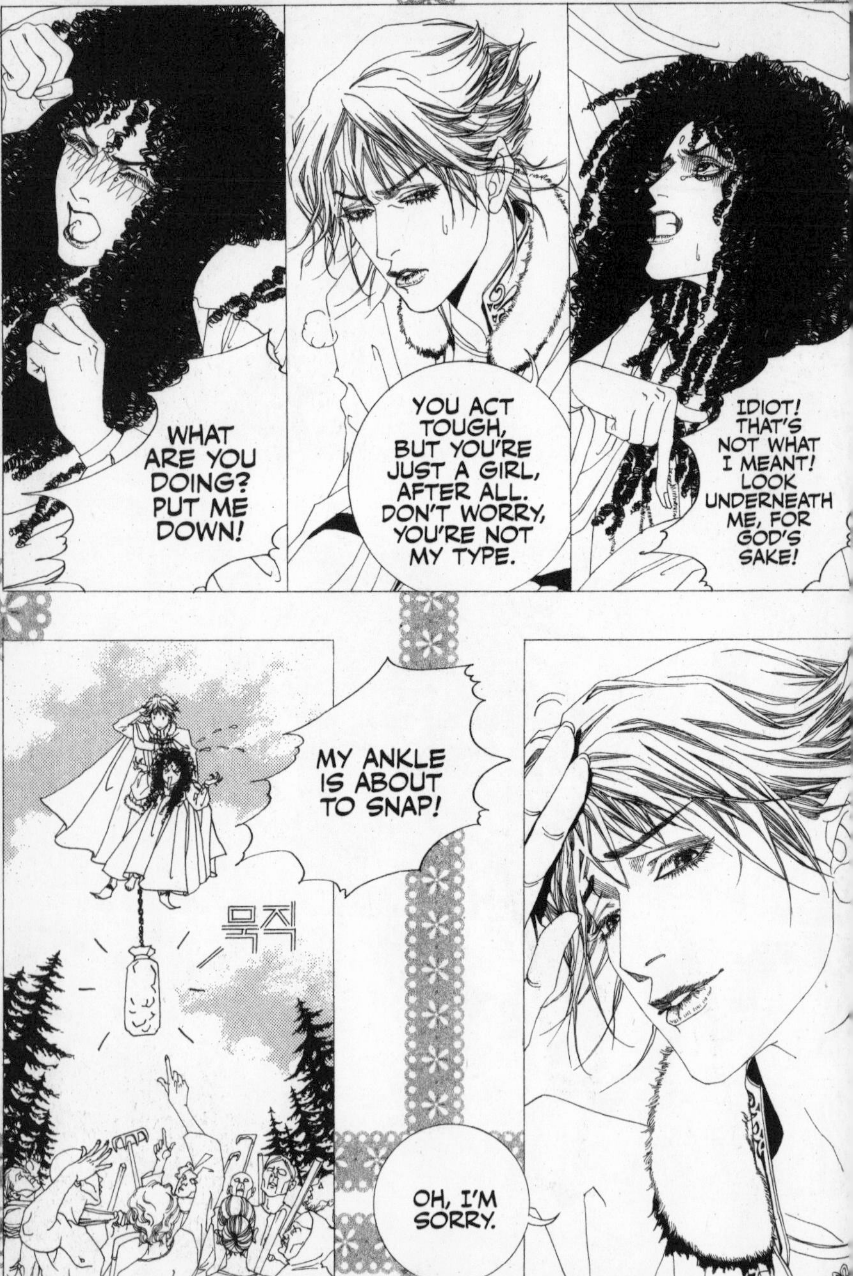
WHAT ARE YOU DOING? PUT ME DOWN!
YOU ACT TOUGH, BUT YOU'RE JUST A GIRL, AFTER ALL. DON'T WORRY, YOU'RE NOT MY TYPE.
IDIOT! THAT'S NOT WHAT I MEANT! LOOK UNDERNEATH ME, FOR GOD'S SAKE!
묵직
MY ANKLE IS ABOUT TO SNAP!
OH, I'M SORRY.

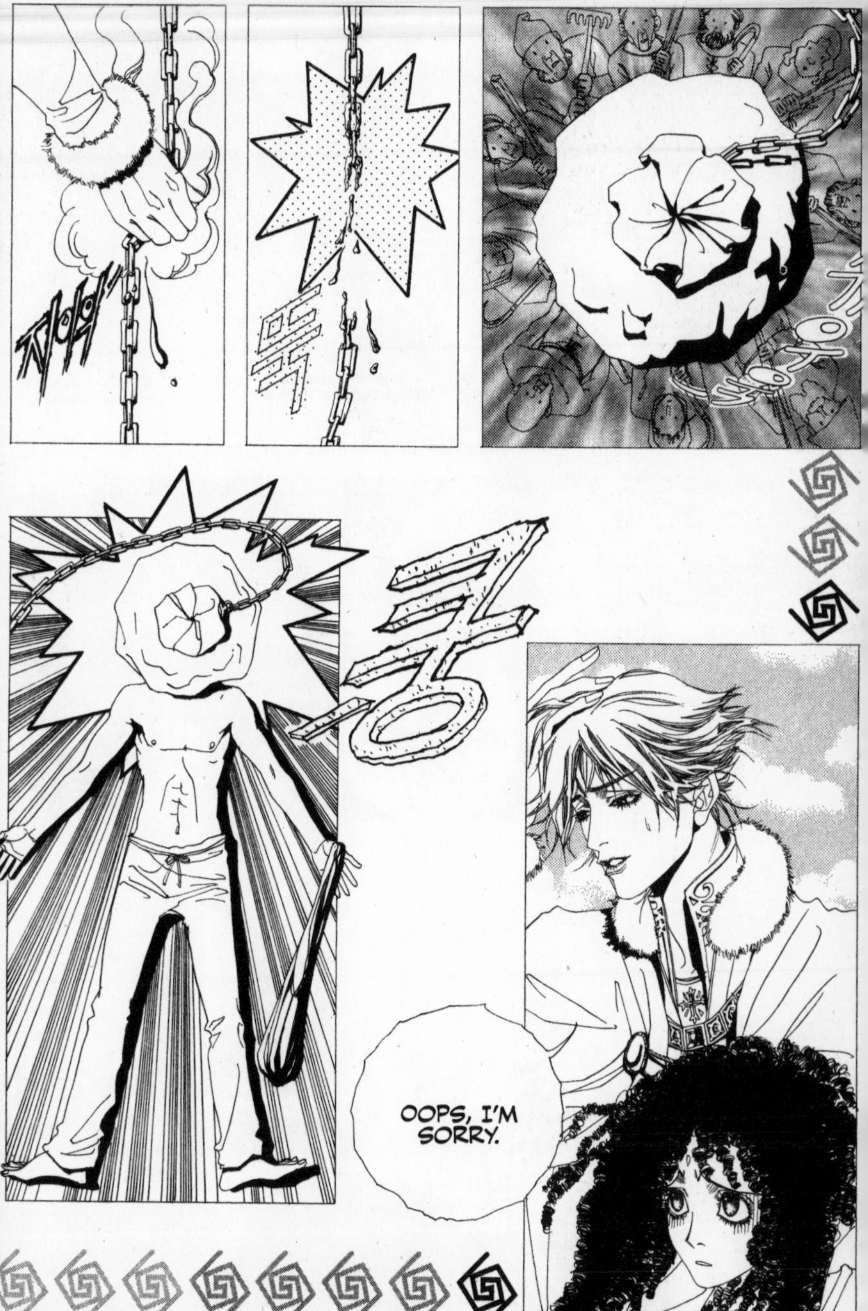
OOPS, I'M SORRY.

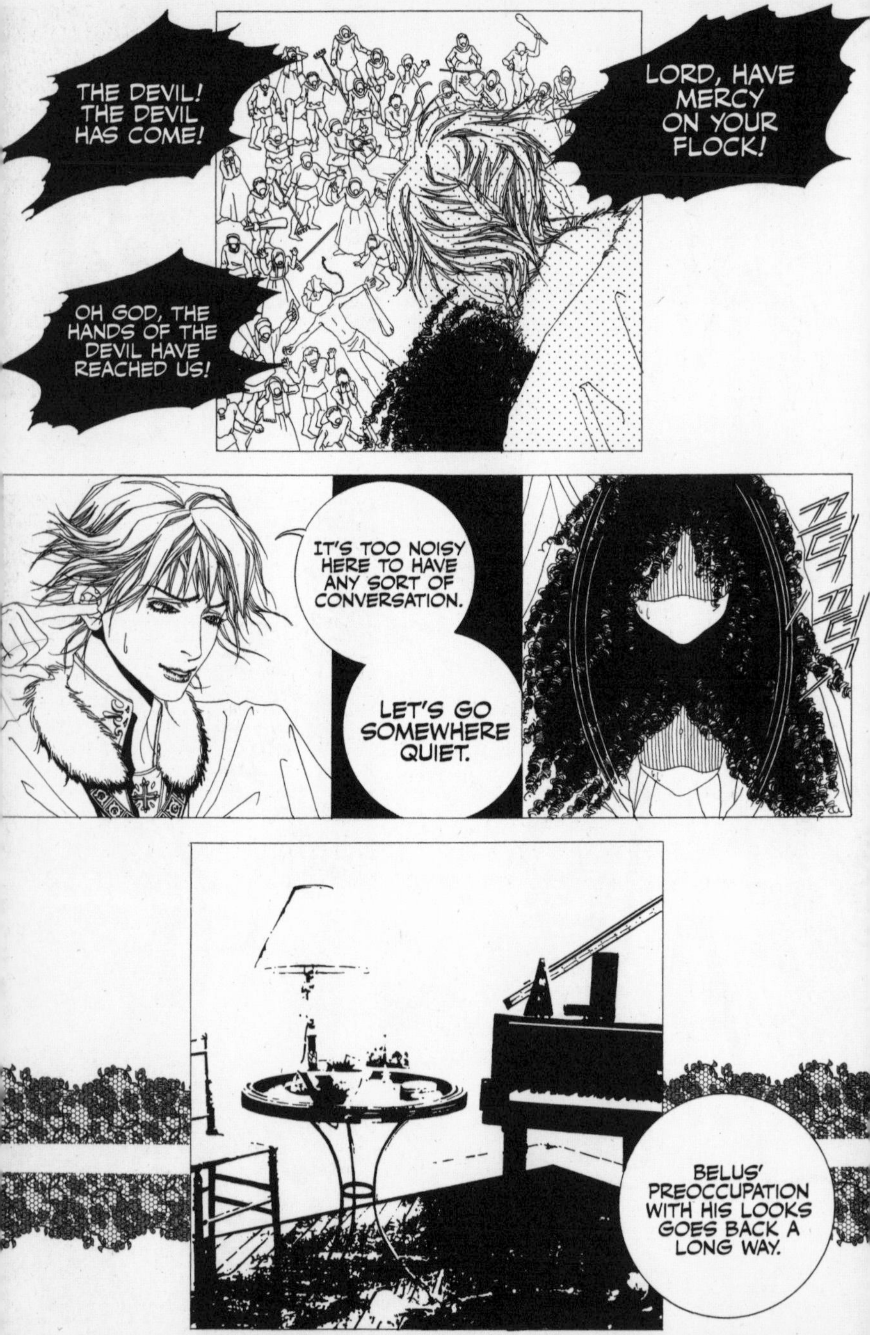
THE DEVIL! THE DEVIL HAS COME!
LORD, HAVE MERCY ON YOUR FLOCK!
OH GOD, THE HANDS OF THE DEVIL HAVE REACHED US!
IT'S TOO NOISY HERE TO HAVE ANY SORT OF CONVERSATION.
LET'S GO SOMEWHERE QUIET.
BELUS' PREOCCUPATION WITH HIS LOOKS GOES BACK A LONG WAY.

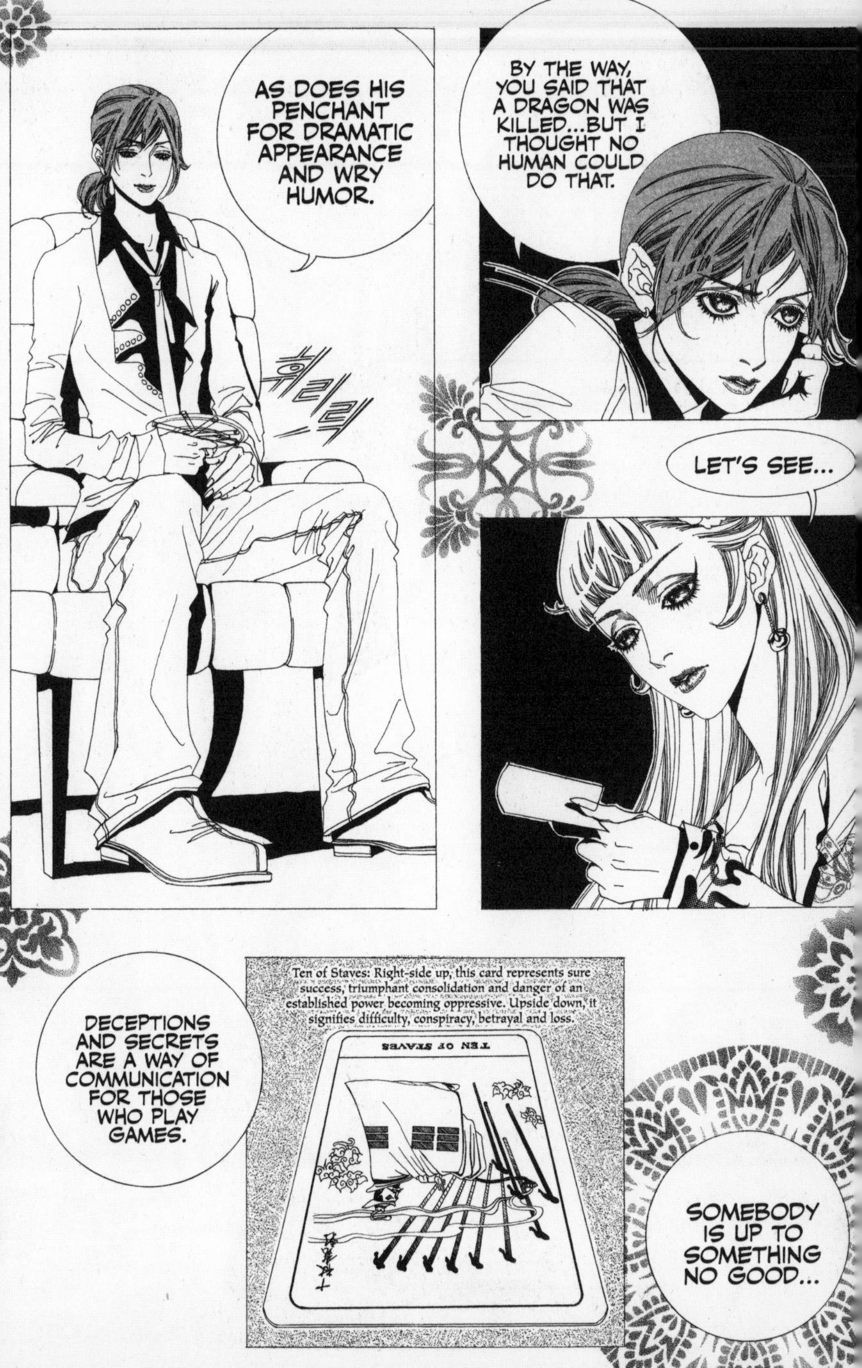
AS DOES HIS PENCHANT FOR DRAMATIC APPEARANCE AND WRY HUMOR.
휘리릭
BY THE WAY, YOU SAID THAT A DRAGON WAS KILLED...BUT I THOUGHT NO HUMAN COULD DO THAT.
LET'S SEE...
DECEPTIONS AND SECRETS ARE A WAY OF COMMUNICATION FOR THOSE WHO PLAY GAMES.
Ten of Staves: Right-side up, this card represents sure success, triumphant consolidation and danger of an established power becoming oppressive. Upside down, it signifies difficulty, conspiracy, betrayal and loss.
SOMEBODY IS UP TO SOMETHING NO GOOD...

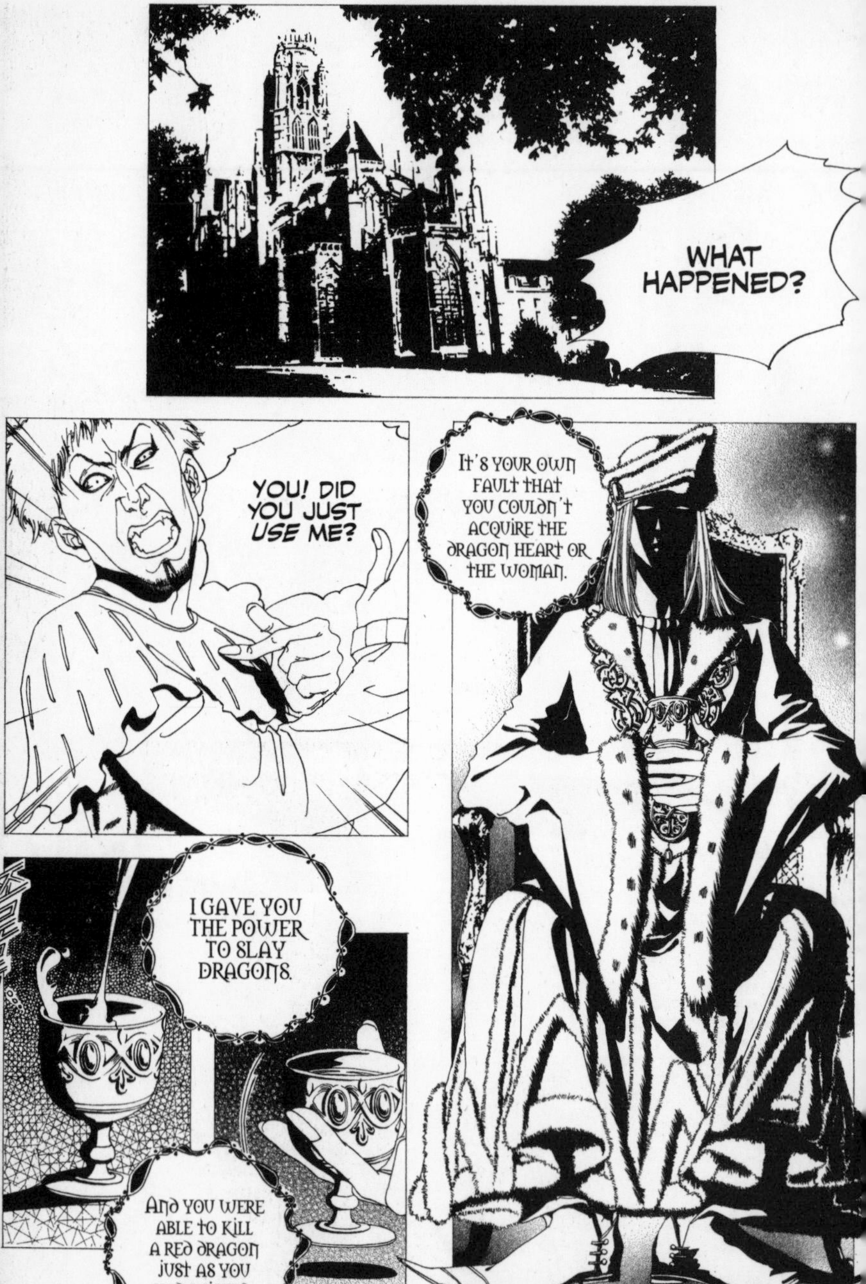
WHAT HAPPENED?
YOU! DID YOU JUST USE ME?
I GAVE YOU THE POWER TO SLAY DRAGONS.
AND YOU WERE ABLE TO KILL A RED DRAGON JUST AS YOU HAD WISHED.
IT'S YOUR OWN FAULT THAT YOU COULDN'T ACQUIRE THE DRAGON HEART OR THE WOMAN.

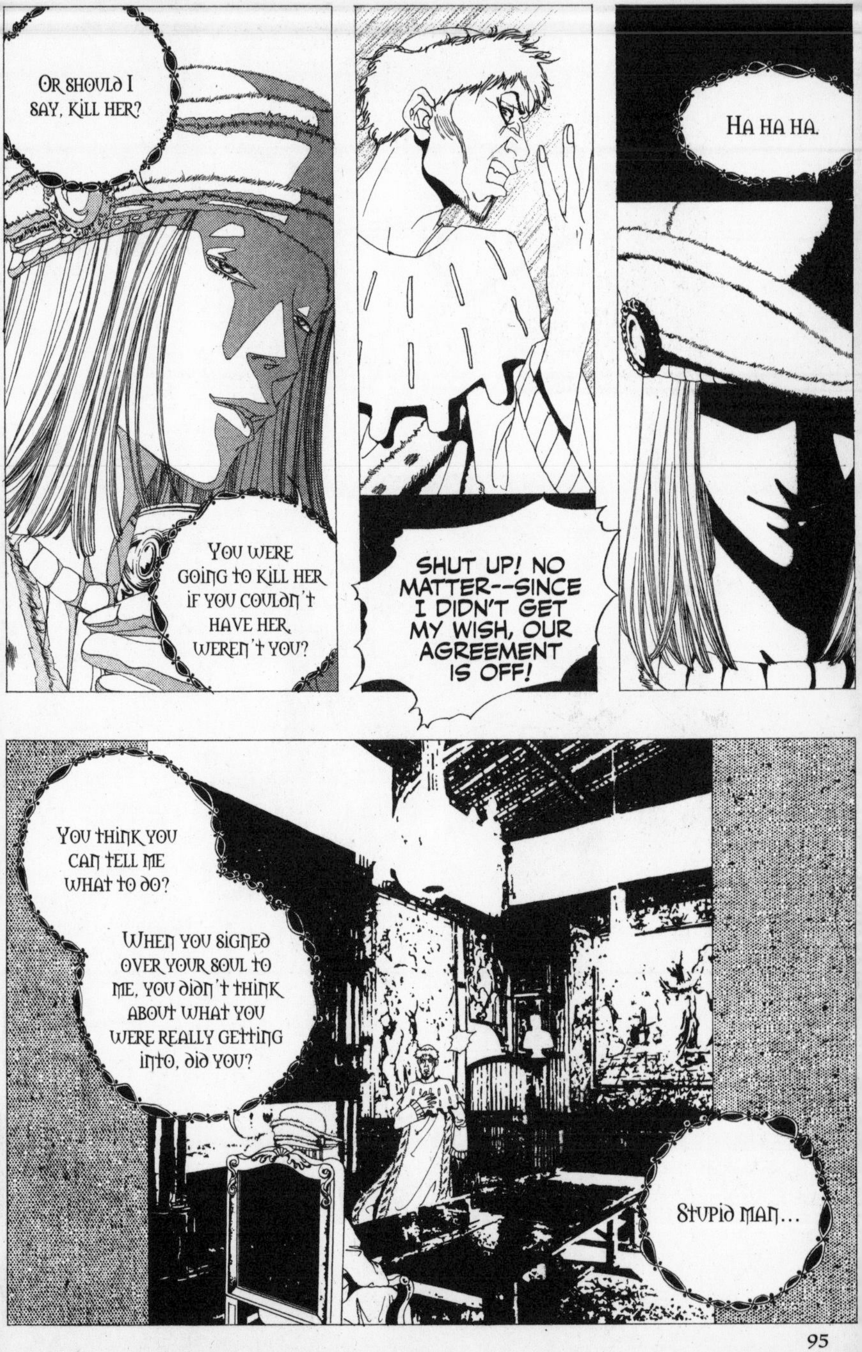
OR SHOULD I SAY, KILL HER?
YOU WERE GOING TO KILL HER IF YOU COULDN'T HAVE HER, WEREN'T YOU?
SHUT UP! NO MATTER--SINCE I DIDN'T GET MY WISH, OUR AGREEMENT IS OFF!
HA HA HA.
YOU THINK YOU CAN TELL ME WHAT TO DO?
WHEN YOU SIGNED OVER YOUR SOUL TO ME, YOU DIDN'T THINK ABOUT WHAT YOU WERE REALLY GETTING INTO, DID YOU?
STUPID MAN...

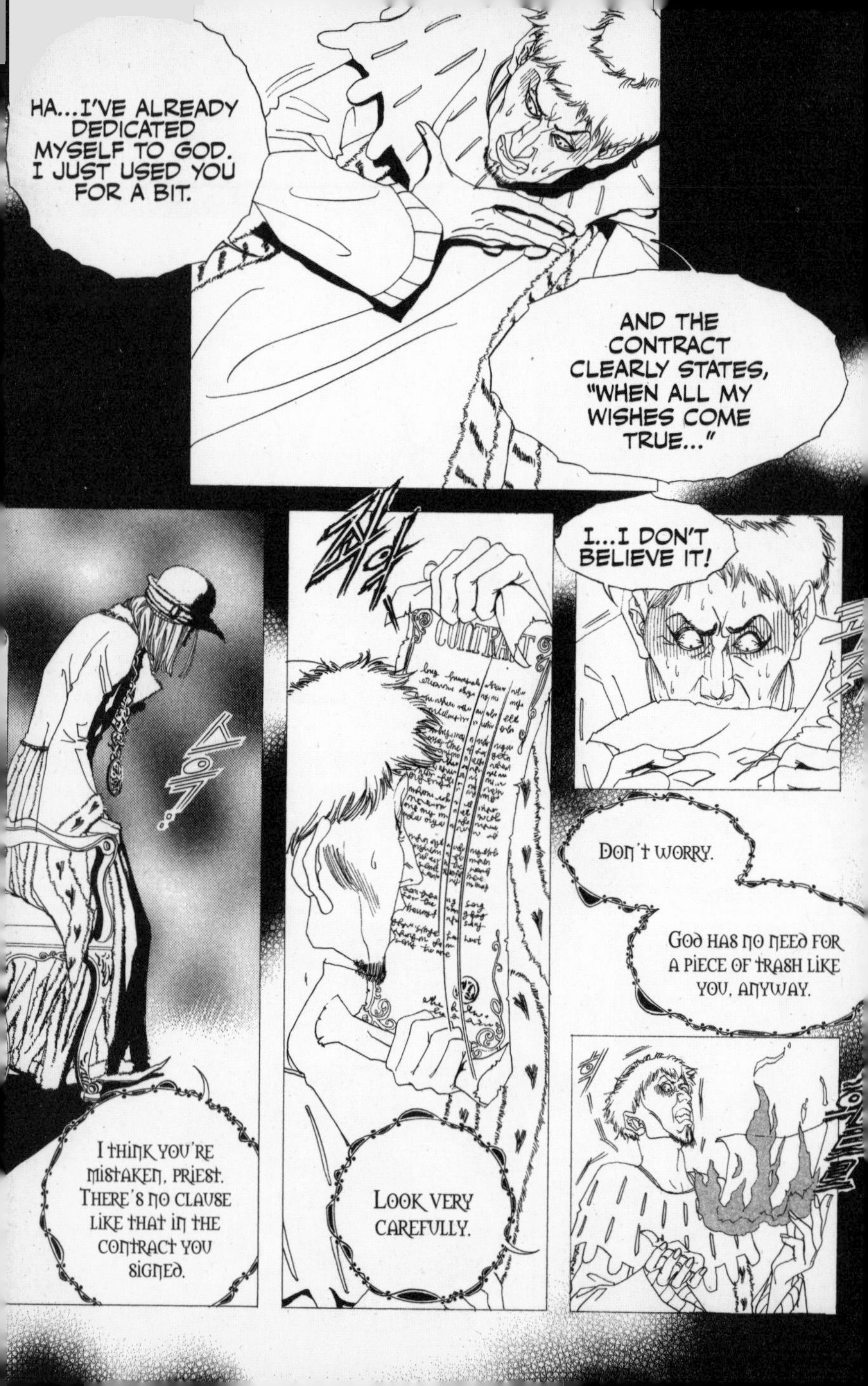
HA...I'VE ALREADY DEDICATED MYSELF TO GOD. I JUST USED YOU FOR A BIT.
AND THE CONTRACT CLEARLY STATES, "WHEN ALL MY WISHES COME TRUE..."
I think you're mistaken, priest. There's no clause like that in the contract you signed.
Look very carefully.
I...I DON'T BELIEVE IT!
Don't worry.
God has no need for a piece of trash like you, anyway.

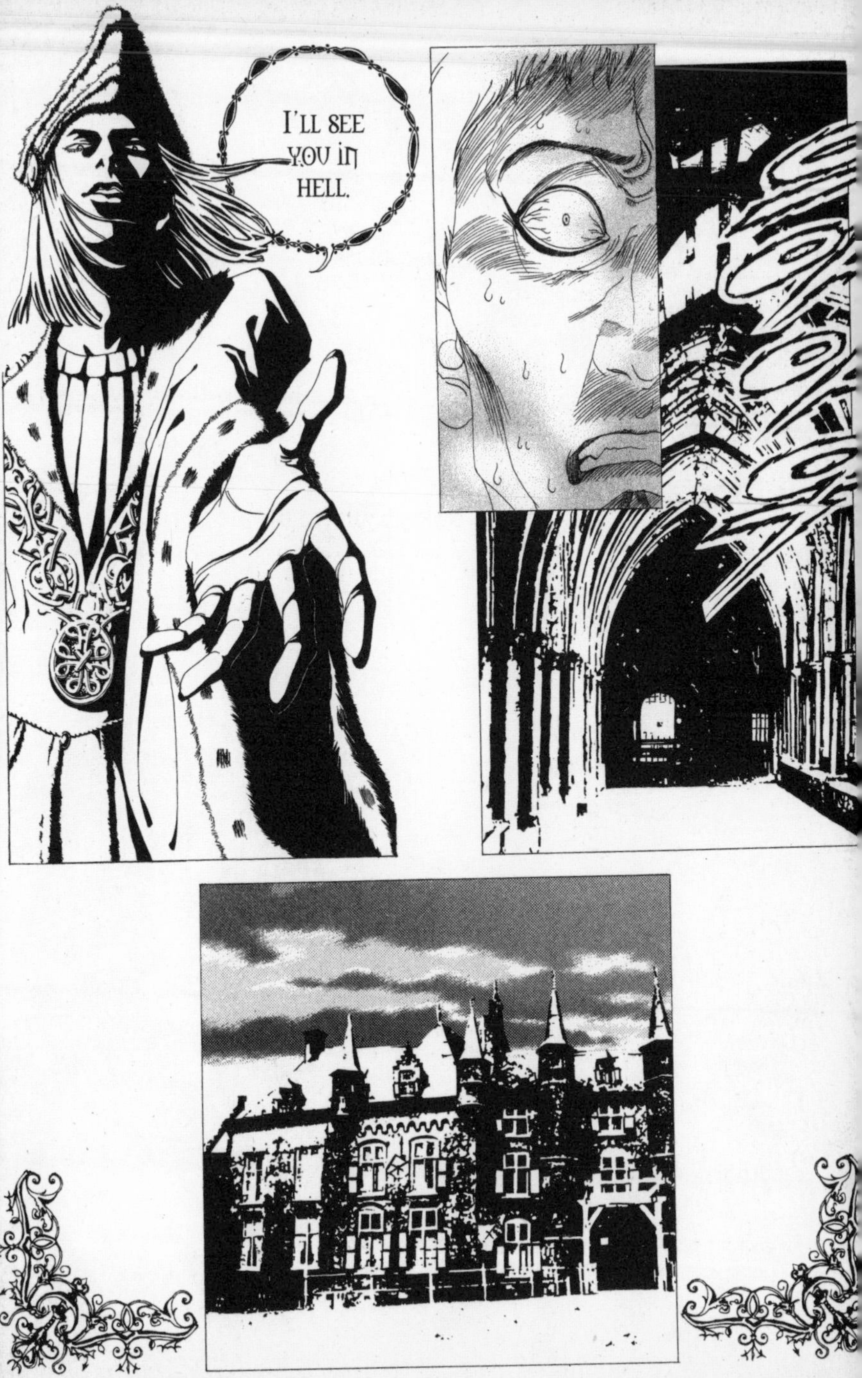
I'LL SEE YOU IN HELL.

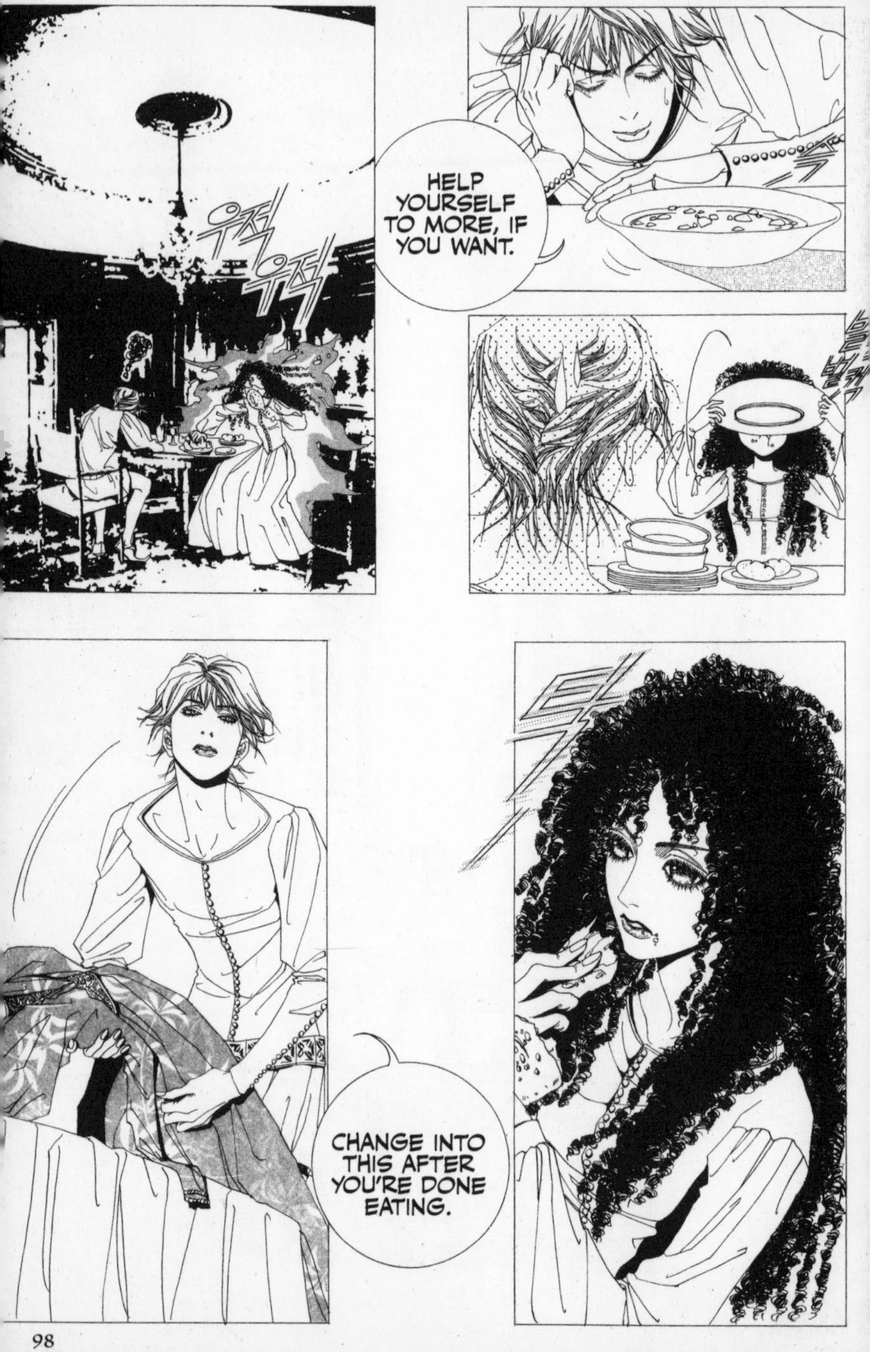
HELP YOURSELF TO MORE, IF YOU WANT.
CHANGE INTO THIS AFTER YOU'RE DONE EATING.

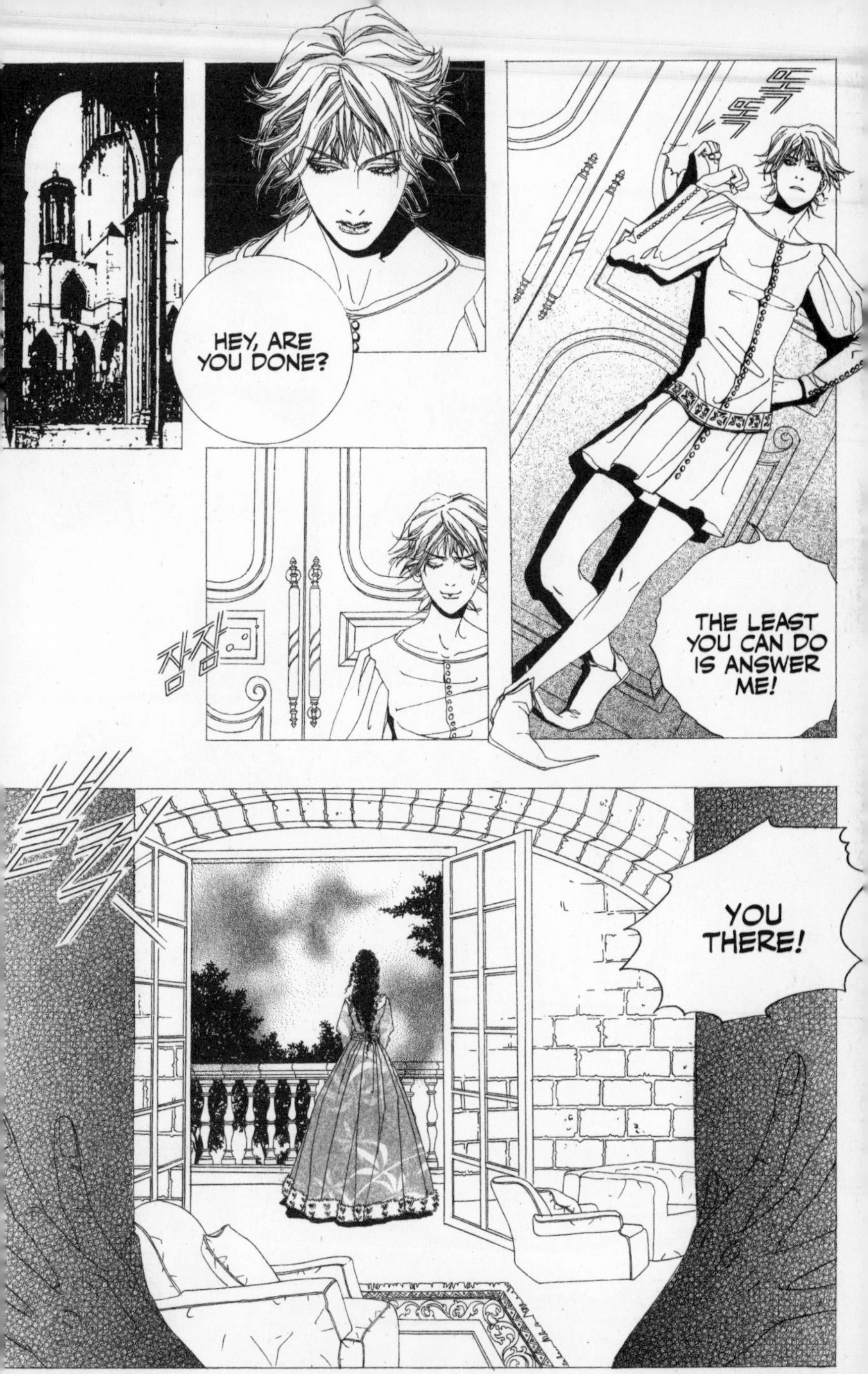
HEY, ARE YOU DONE?
잠잠...
똑 똑
THE LEAST YOU CAN DO IS ANSWER ME!
벌컥
YOU THERE!

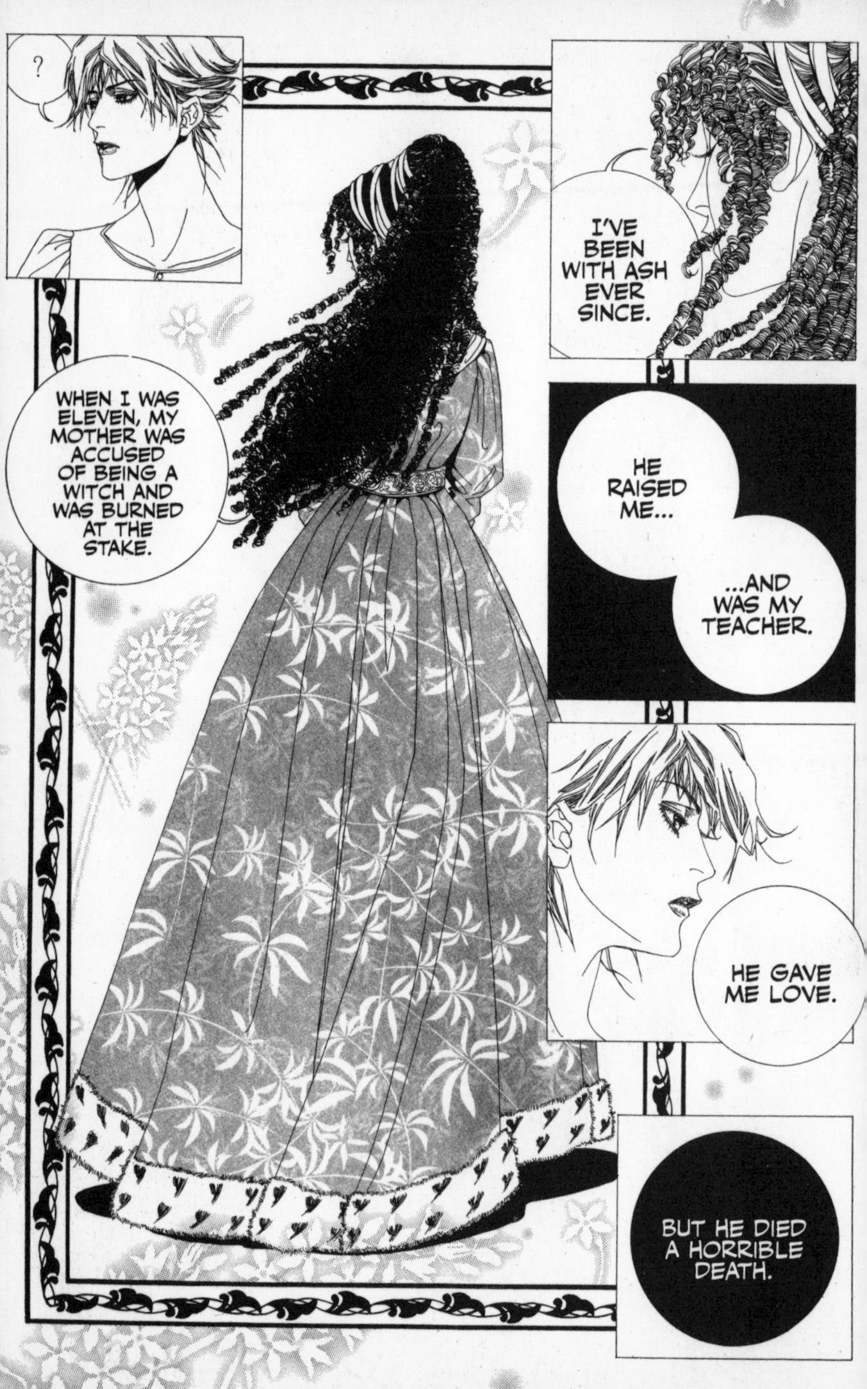
?
I'VE BEEN WITH ASH EVER SINCE.
WHEN I WAS ELEVEN, MY MOTHER WAS ACCUSED OF BEING A WITCH AND WAS BURNED AT THE STAKE.
HE RAISED ME...
...AND WAS MY TEACHER.
HE GAVE ME LOVE.
BUT HE DIED A HORRIBLE DEATH.

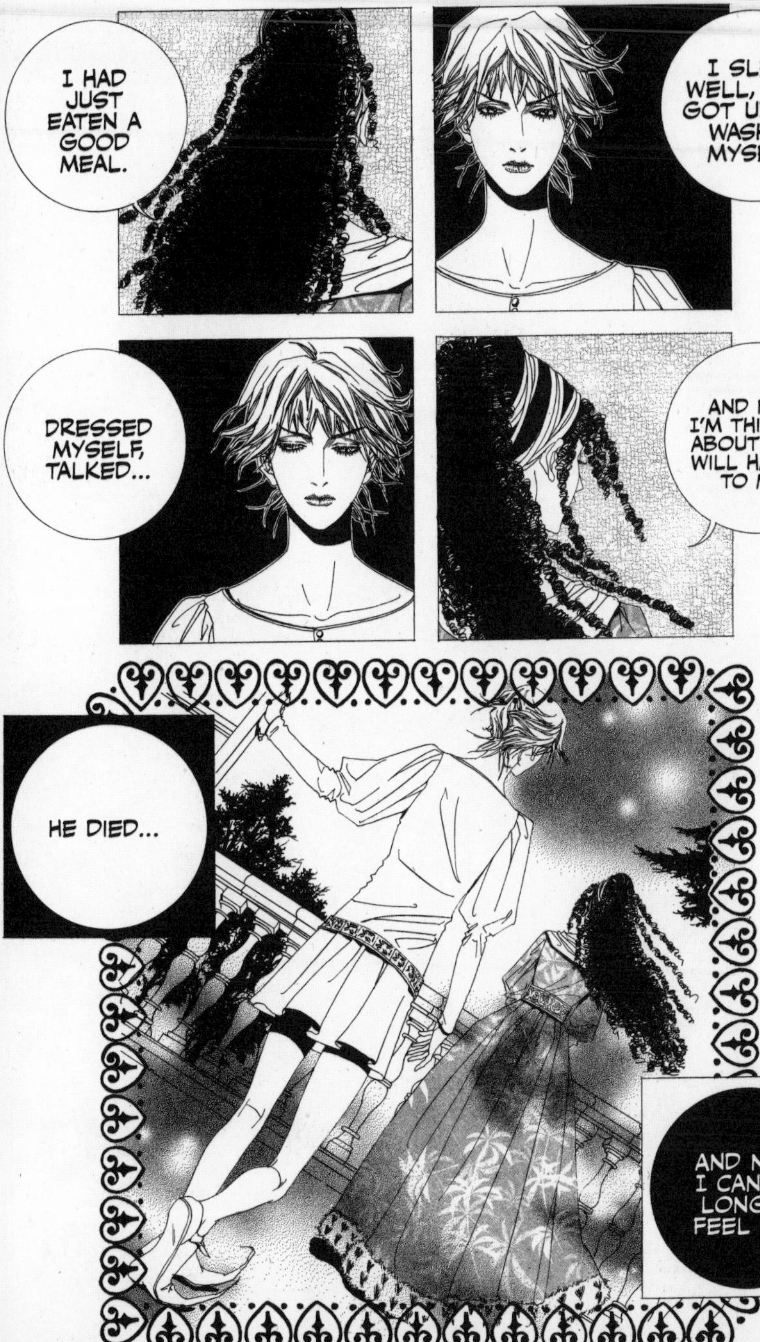
I HAD JUST EATEN A GOOD MEAL.
I SLEPT WELL, THEN GOT UP AND WASHED MYSELF.
DRESSED MYSELF, TALKED...
AND NOW I'M THINKING ABOUT WHAT WILL HAPPEN TO ME.
HE DIED...
AND NOW I CAN NO LONGER FEEL HIM.

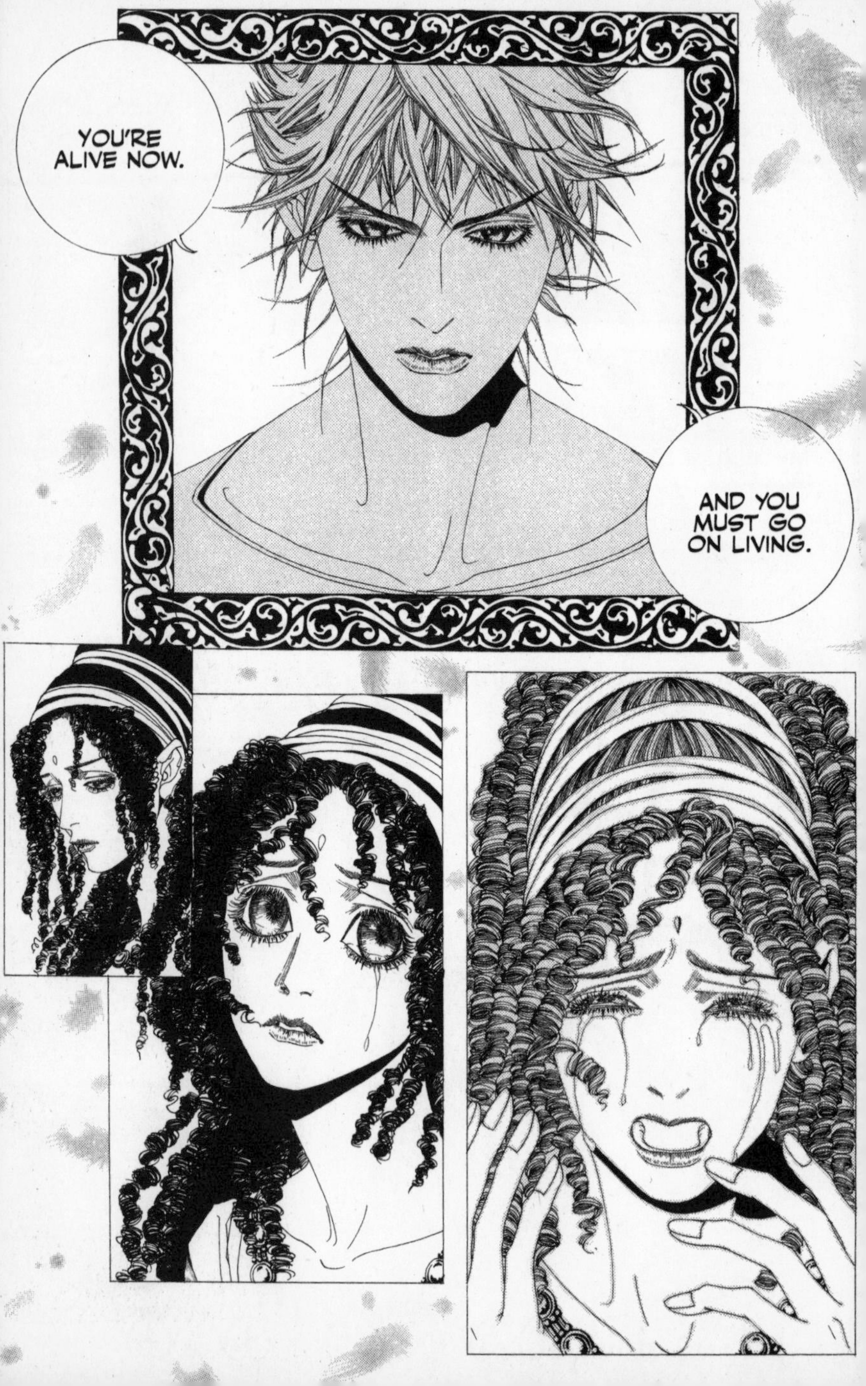
YOU'RE ALIVE NOW.
AND YOU MUST GO ON LIVING.

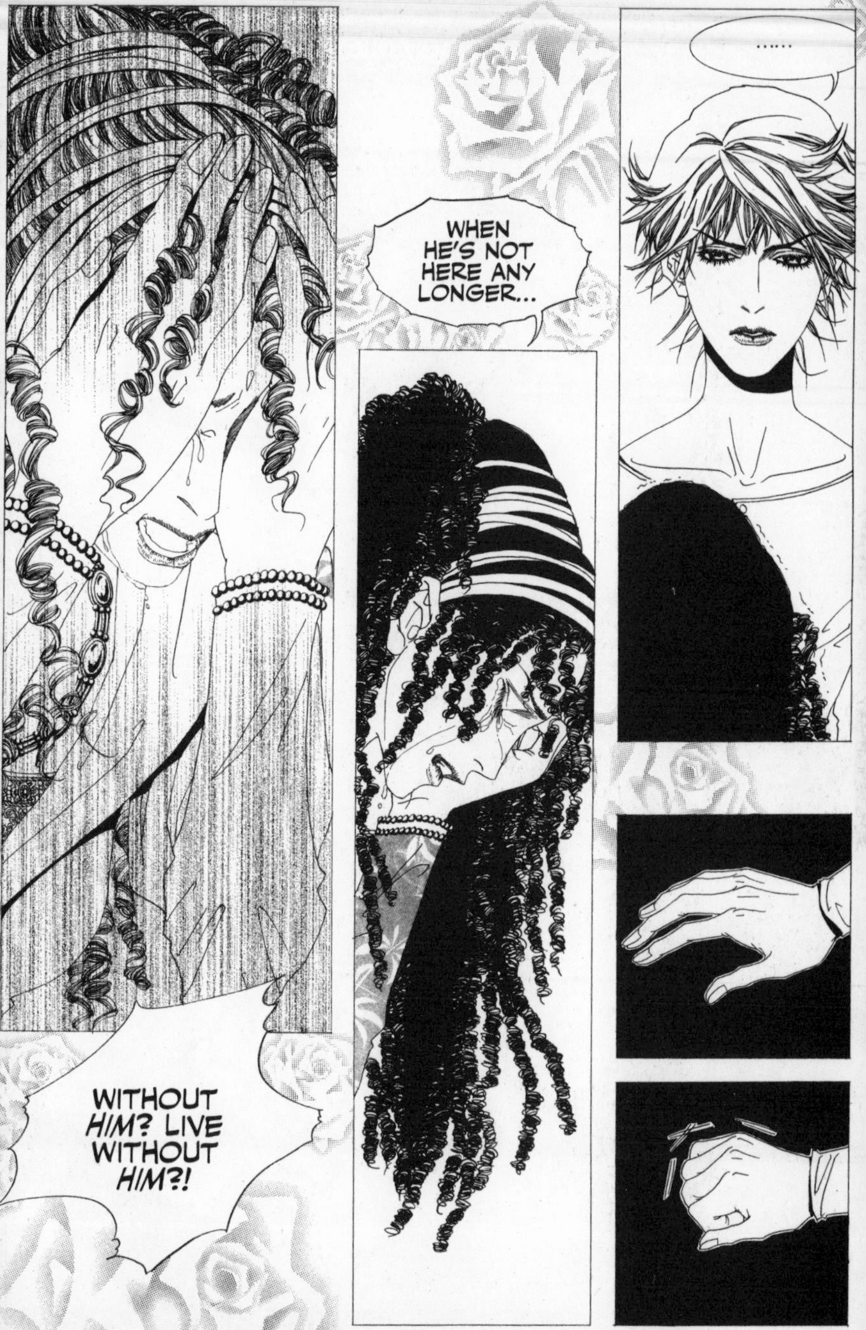
WITHOUT *HIM*? LIVE WITHOUT *HIM*?!
WHEN HE'S NOT HERE ANY LONGER...
......

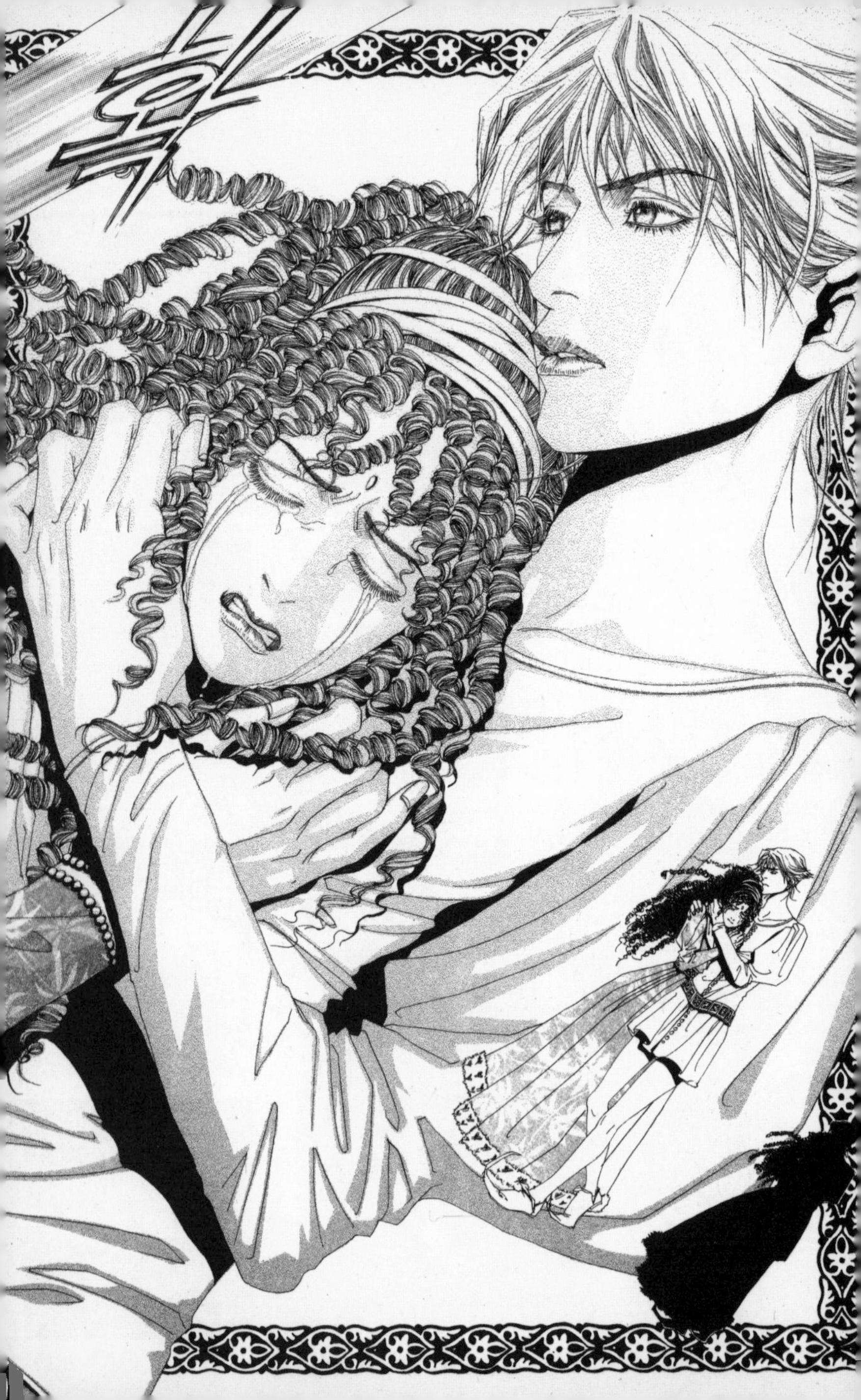

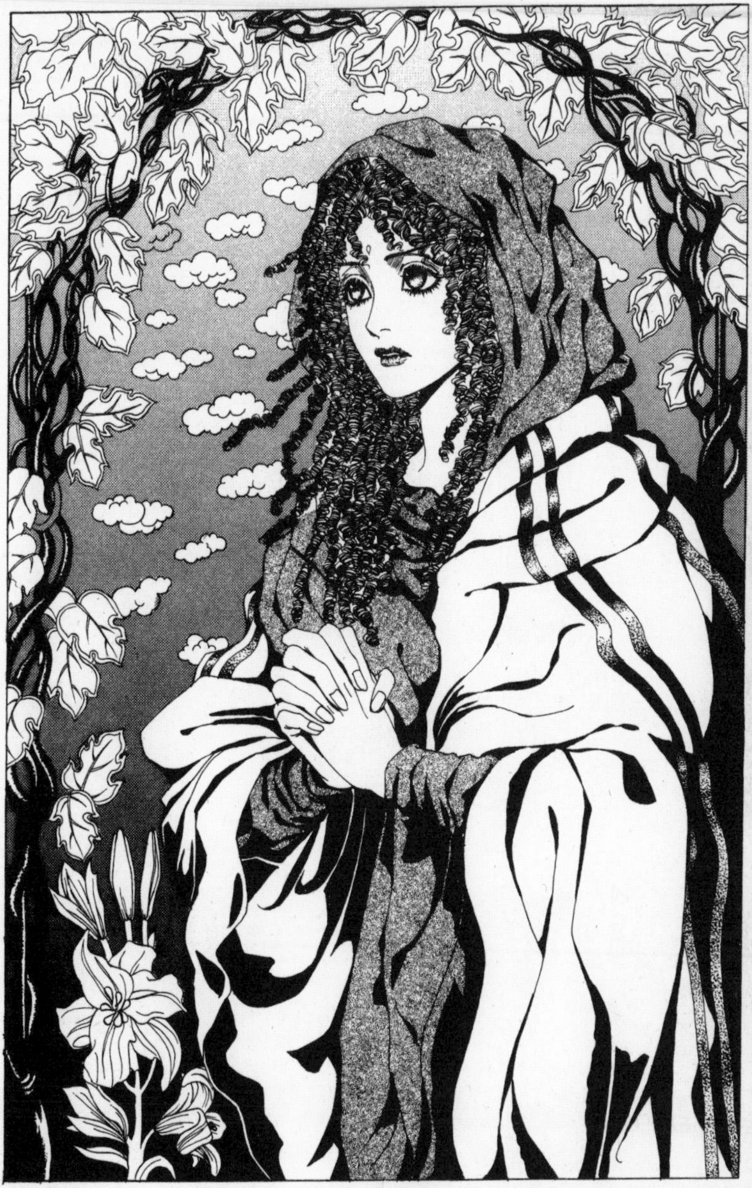

ILLUSTRATION FROM MASTER TAROT

Die Verehrerin
The Devotee

The Devotee: Joyfully and willingly entrusting someone else with the task of making your wishes come true.

THE MOST IMPORTANT PART STILL REMAINS.

THE CONTRACT IS THE BEGINNING OF A JOURNEY.

Knight of Staves: Right-side up, this card signifies travel or progressing toward unknown territory. Upside down, it means unexpected change, skirmish, separation or dismissal.

KNIGHT OF STAVES

SHE WHO HAD LOWERED HER ANCHOR INTO THE SEA OF HER PAST MEMORIES...

...SHE CUT HERSELF LOOSE AND BEGAN A JOURNEY TOWARD A MYSTERIOUS FUTURE...

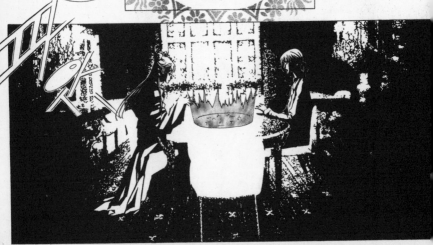

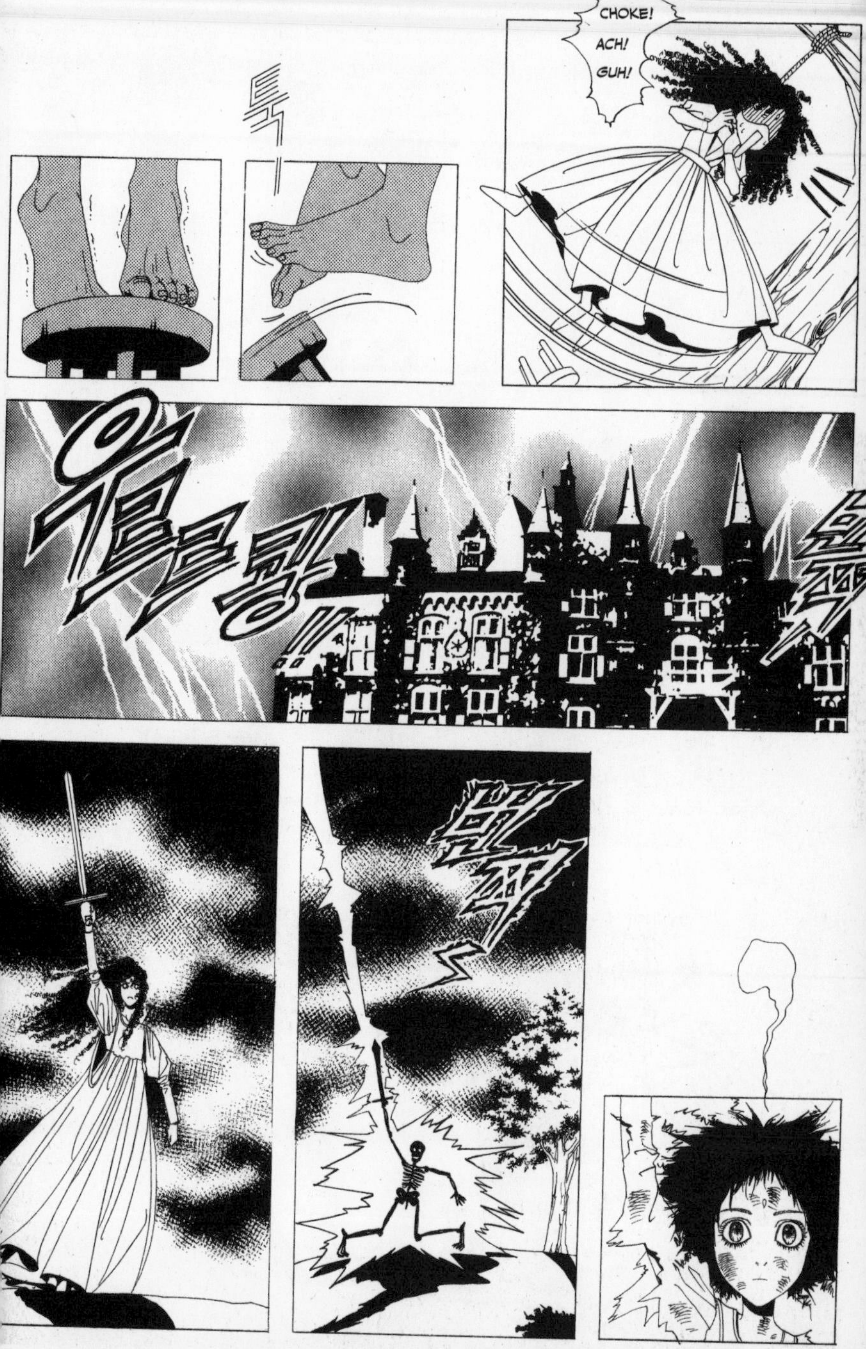
툭
CHOKE!
ACH!
GUH!
우르르쾅!!
번쩍

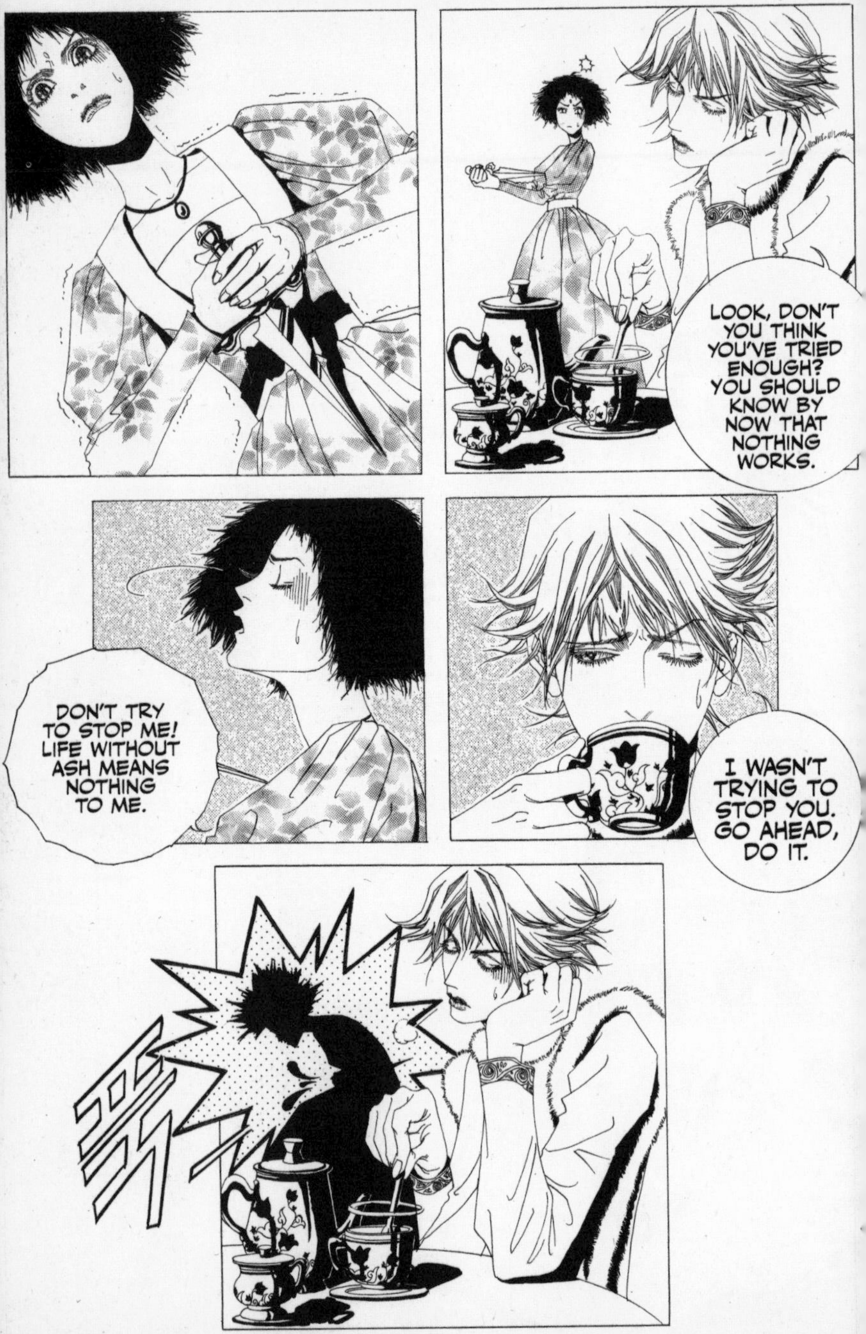
LOOK, DON'T YOU THINK YOU'VE TRIED ENOUGH? YOU SHOULD KNOW BY NOW THAT NOTHING WORKS.
DON'T TRY TO STOP ME! LIFE WITHOUT ASH MEANS NOTHING TO ME.
I WASN'T TRYING TO STOP YOU. GO AHEAD, DO IT.

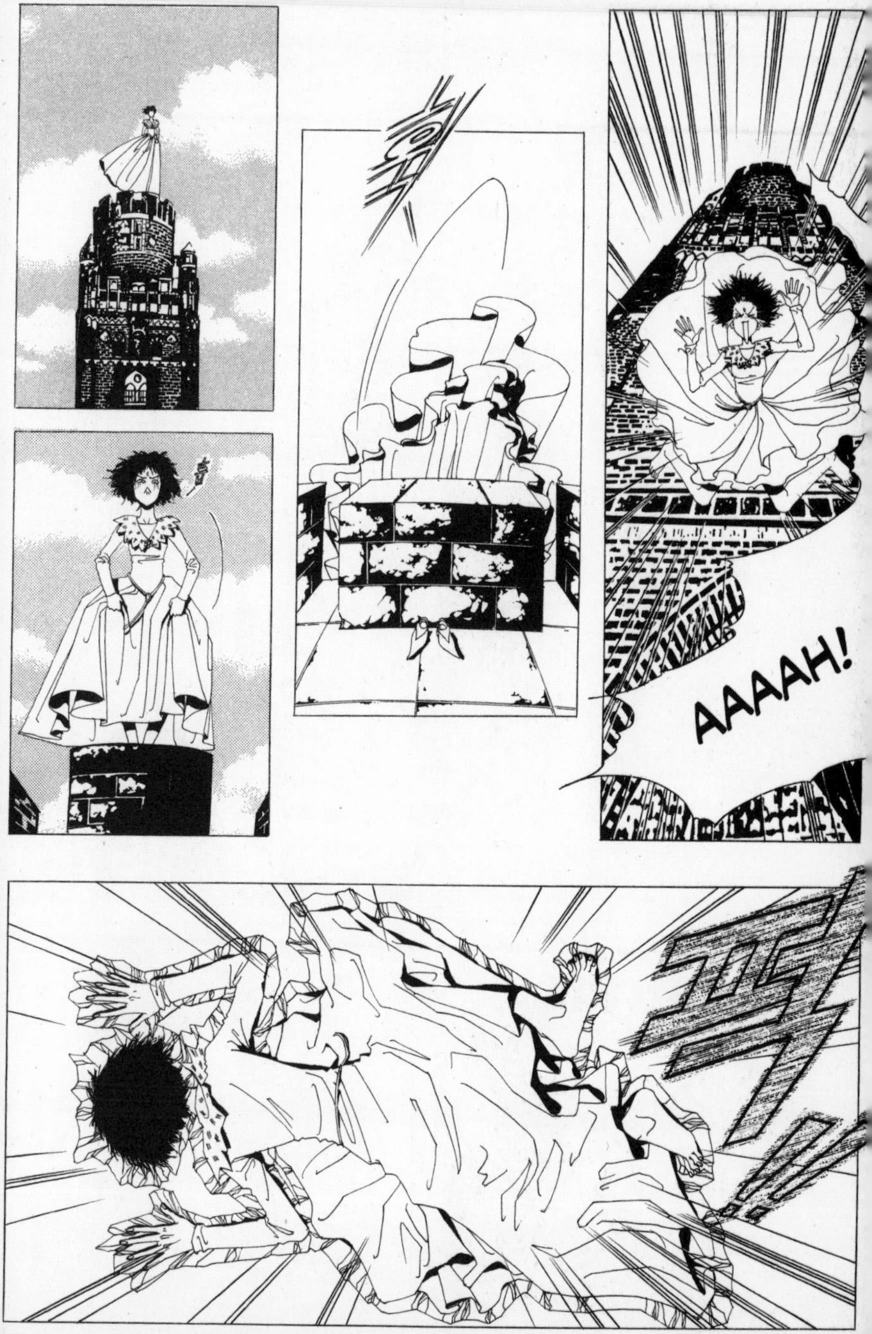
AAAAH!

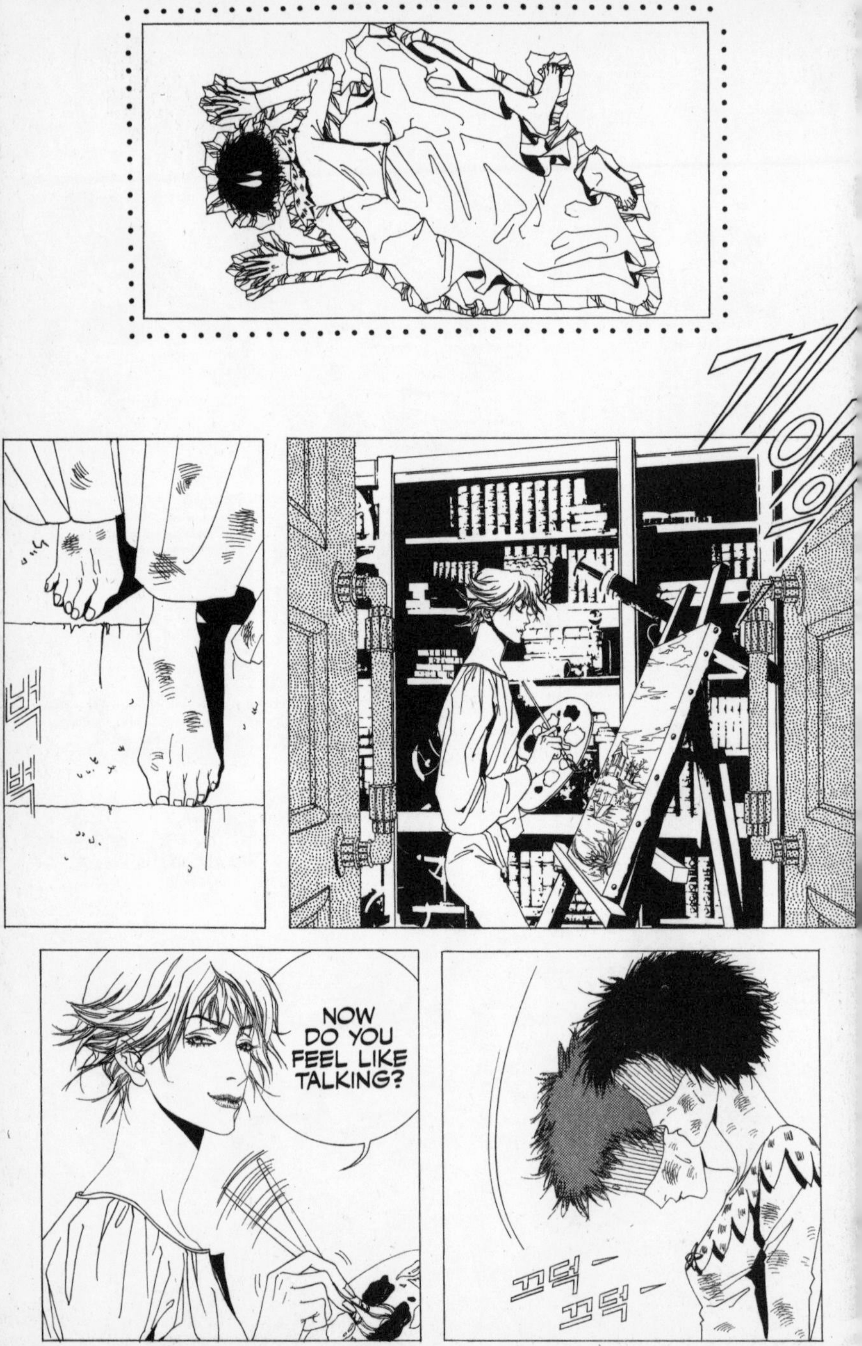
벅
벅
NOW DO YOU FEEL LIKE TALKING?
끄덕 -
끄덕 -

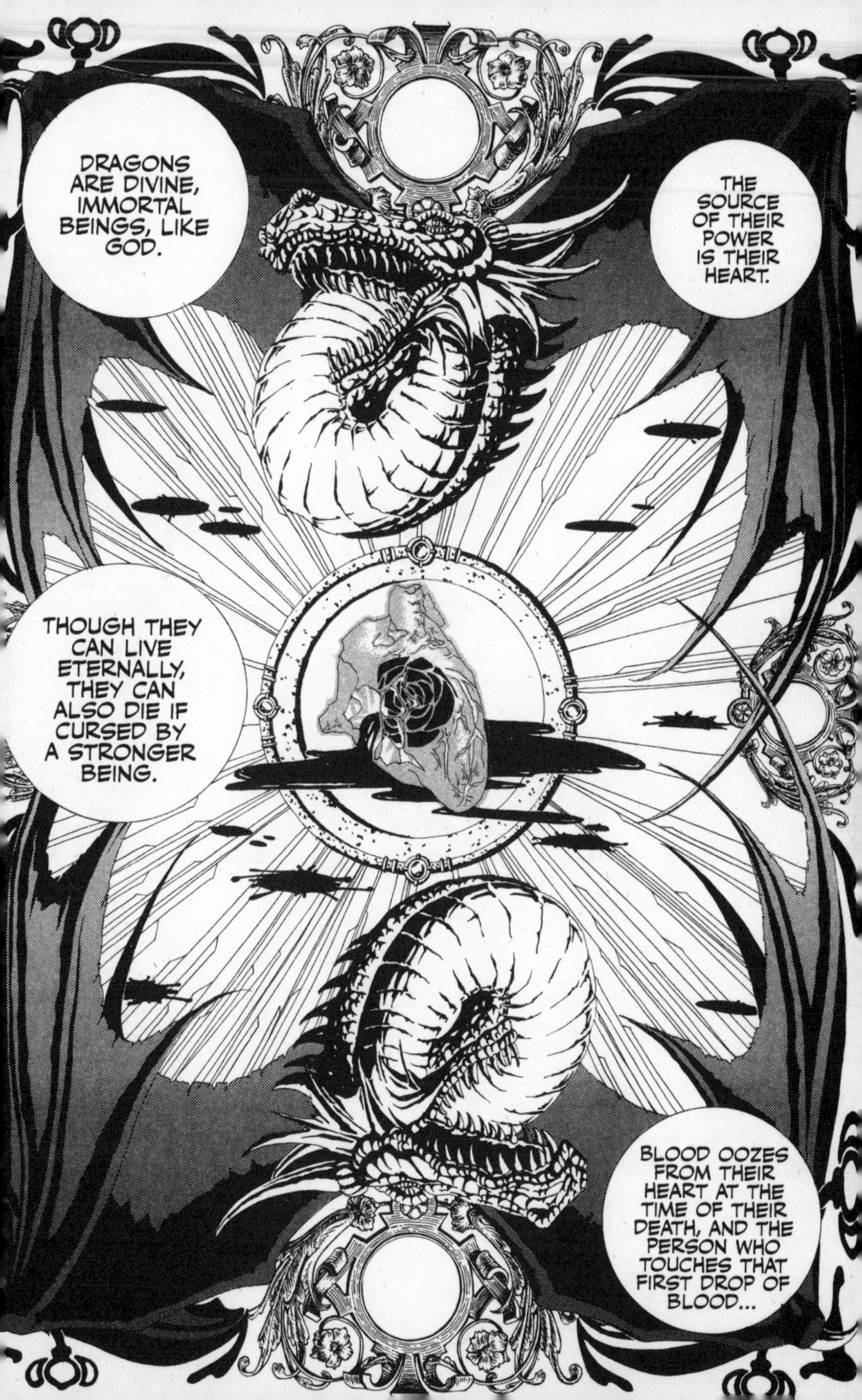
DRAGONS ARE DIVINE, IMMORTAL BEINGS, LIKE GOD.
THE SOURCE OF THEIR POWER IS THEIR HEART.
THOUGH THEY CAN LIVE ETERNALLY, THEY CAN ALSO DIE IF CURSED BY A STRONGER BEING.
BLOOD OOZES FROM THEIR HEART AT THE TIME OF THEIR DEATH, AND THE PERSON WHO TOUCHES THAT FIRST DROP OF BLOOD...

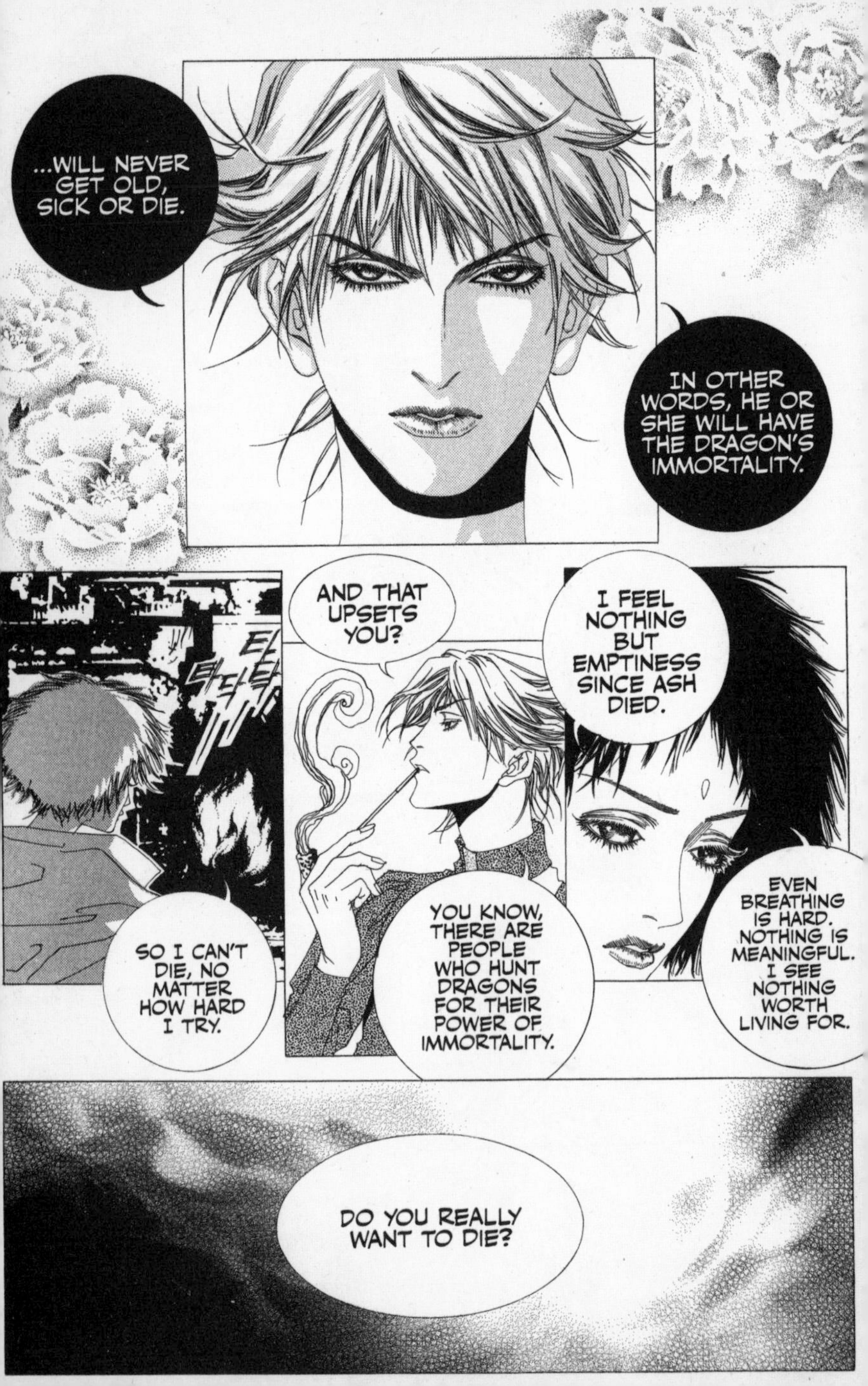
...WILL NEVER GET OLD, SICK OR DIE.
IN OTHER WORDS, HE OR SHE WILL HAVE THE DRAGON'S IMMORTALITY.
SO I CAN'T DIE, NO MATTER HOW HARD I TRY.
AND THAT UPSETS YOU?
YOU KNOW, THERE ARE PEOPLE WHO HUNT DRAGONS FOR THEIR POWER OF IMMORTALITY.
I FEEL NOTHING BUT EMPTINESS SINCE ASH DIED.
EVEN BREATHING IS HARD. NOTHING IS MEANINGFUL. I SEE NOTHING WORTH LIVING FOR.
DO YOU REALLY WANT TO DIE?

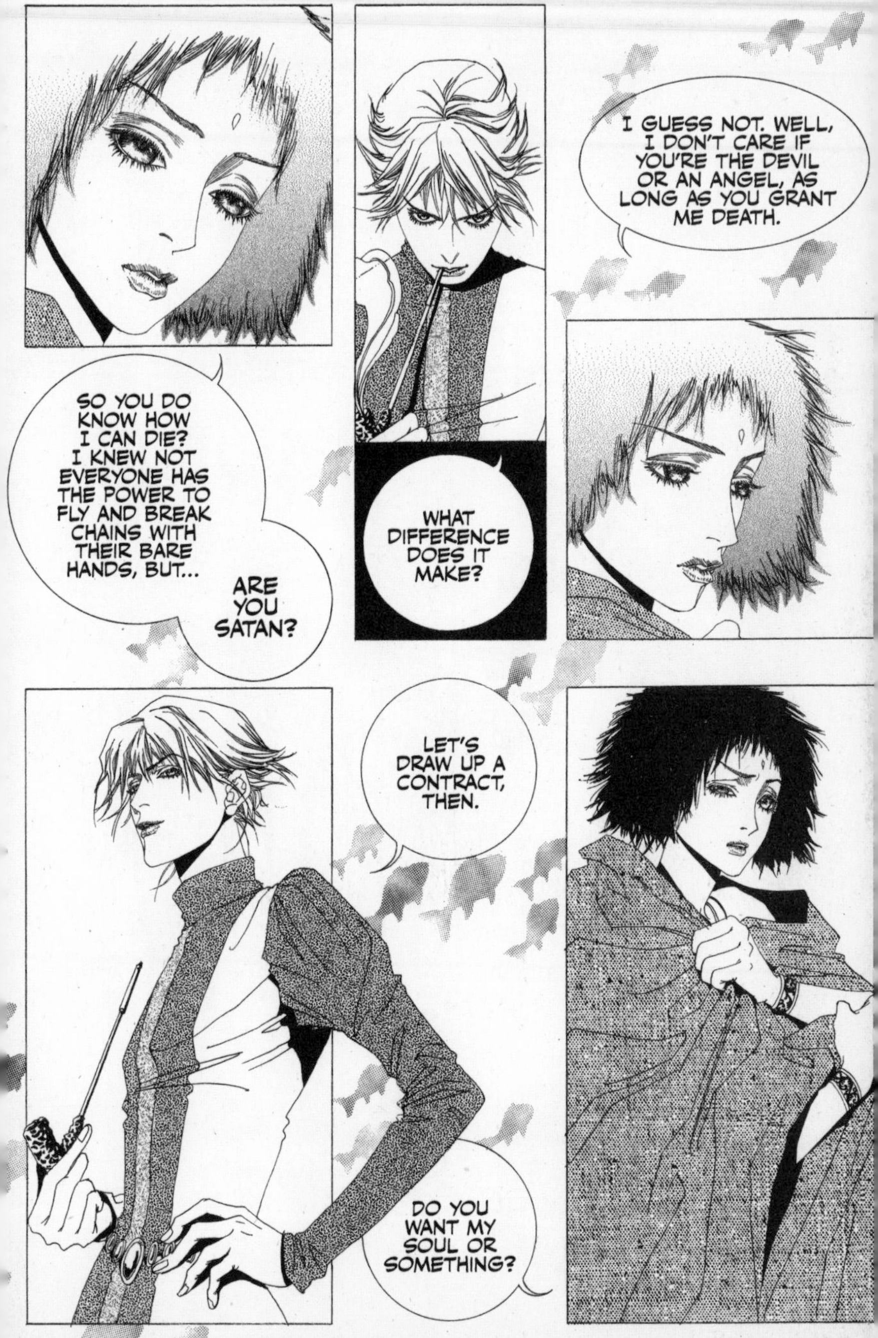
I GUESS NOT. WELL, I DON'T CARE IF YOU'RE THE DEVIL OR AN ANGEL, AS LONG AS YOU GRANT ME DEATH.
SO YOU DO KNOW HOW I CAN DIE? I KNEW NOT EVERYONE HAS THE POWER TO FLY AND BREAK CHAINS WITH THEIR BARE HANDS, BUT...
ARE YOU SATAN?
WHAT DIFFERENCE DOES IT MAKE?
LET'S DRAW UP A CONTRACT, THEN.
DO YOU WANT MY SOUL OR SOMETHING?

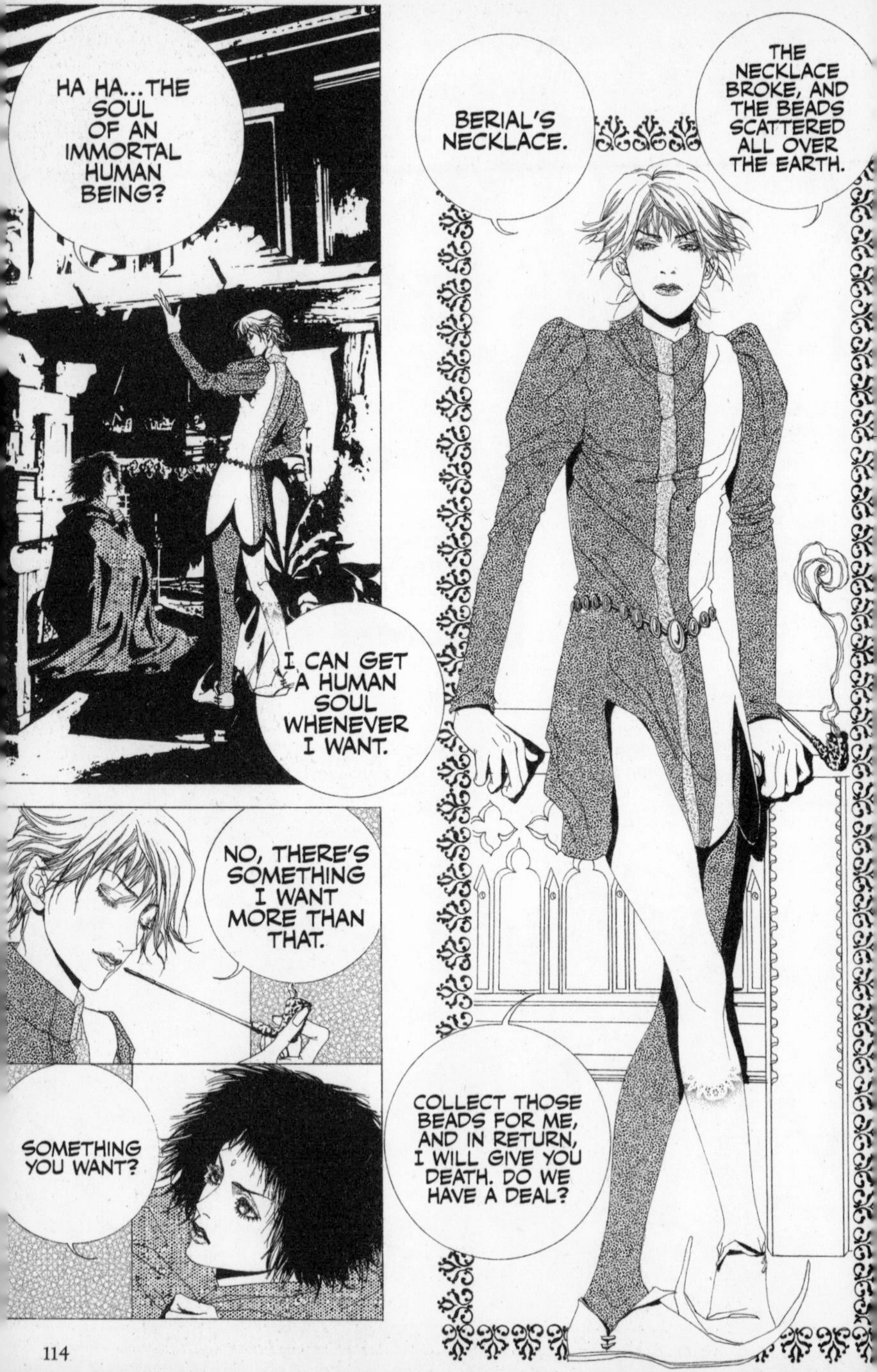
HA HA...THE SOUL OF AN IMMORTAL HUMAN BEING?
I CAN GET A HUMAN SOUL WHENEVER I WANT.
NO, THERE'S SOMETHING I WANT MORE THAN THAT.
SOMETHING YOU WANT?
BERIAL'S NECKLACE.
THE NECKLACE BROKE, AND THE BEADS SCATTERED ALL OVER THE EARTH.
COLLECT THOSE BEADS FOR ME, AND IN RETURN, I WILL GIVE YOU DEATH. DO WE HAVE A DEAL?

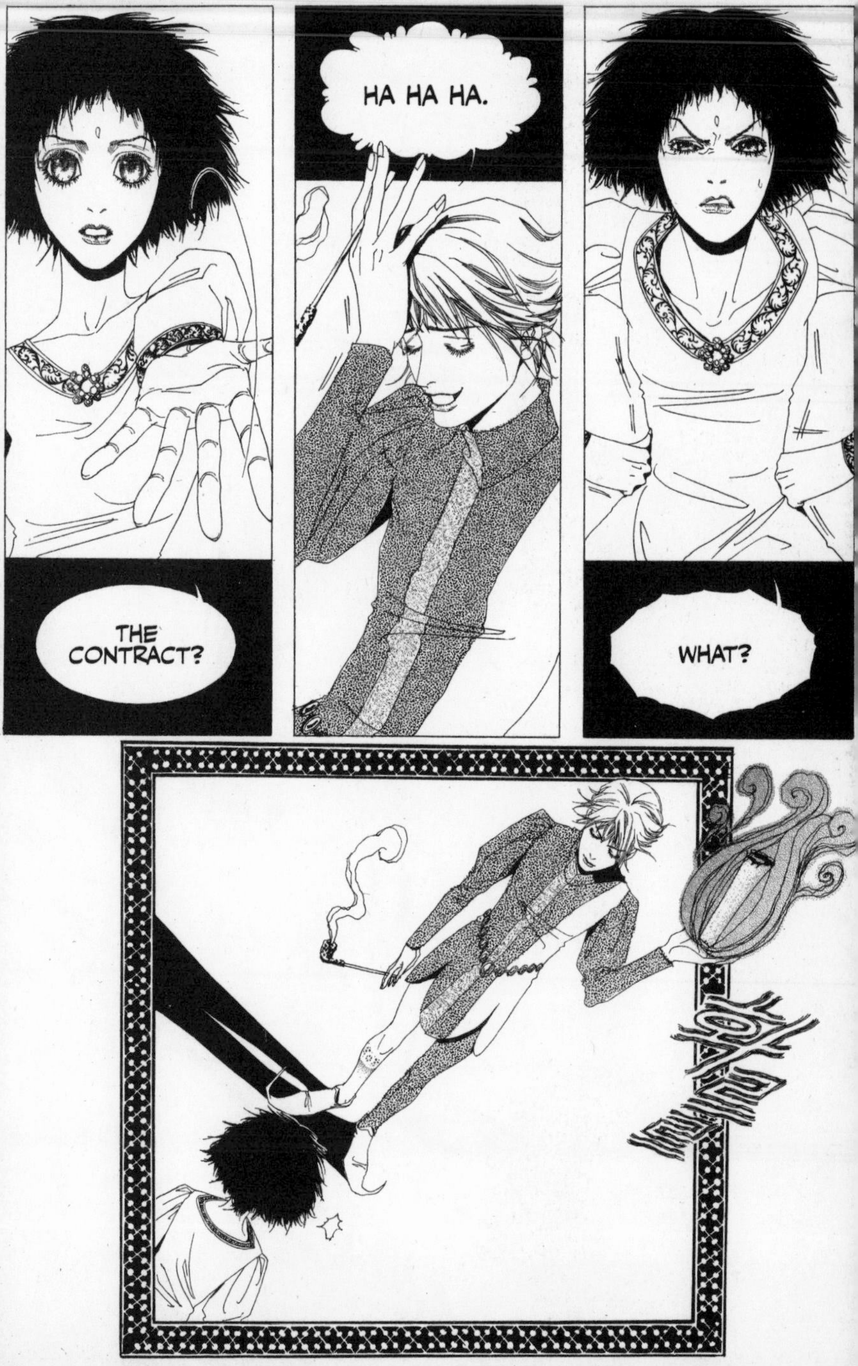
THE CONTRACT?
HA HA HA.
WHAT?

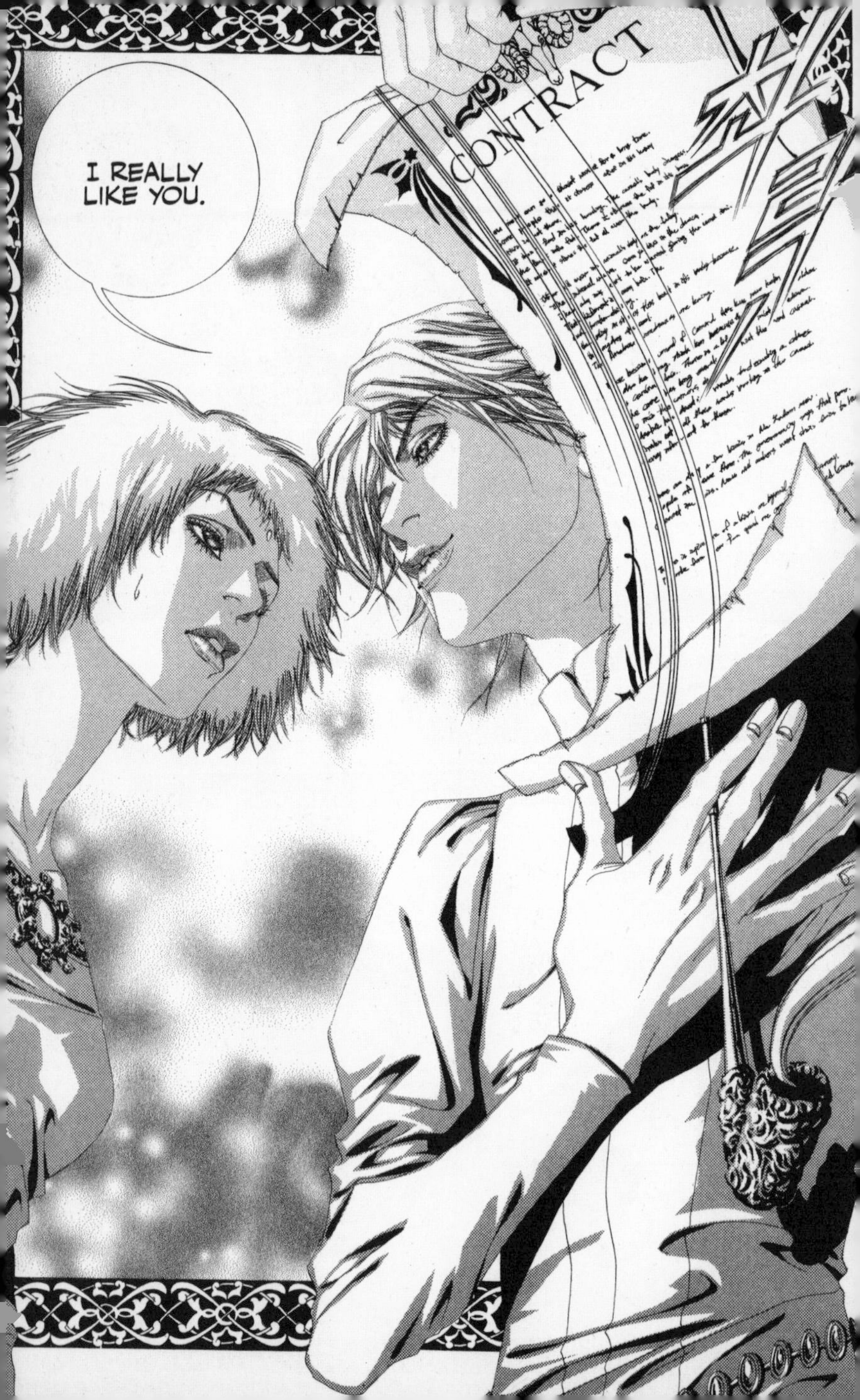
I REALLY LIKE YOU.
CONTRACT

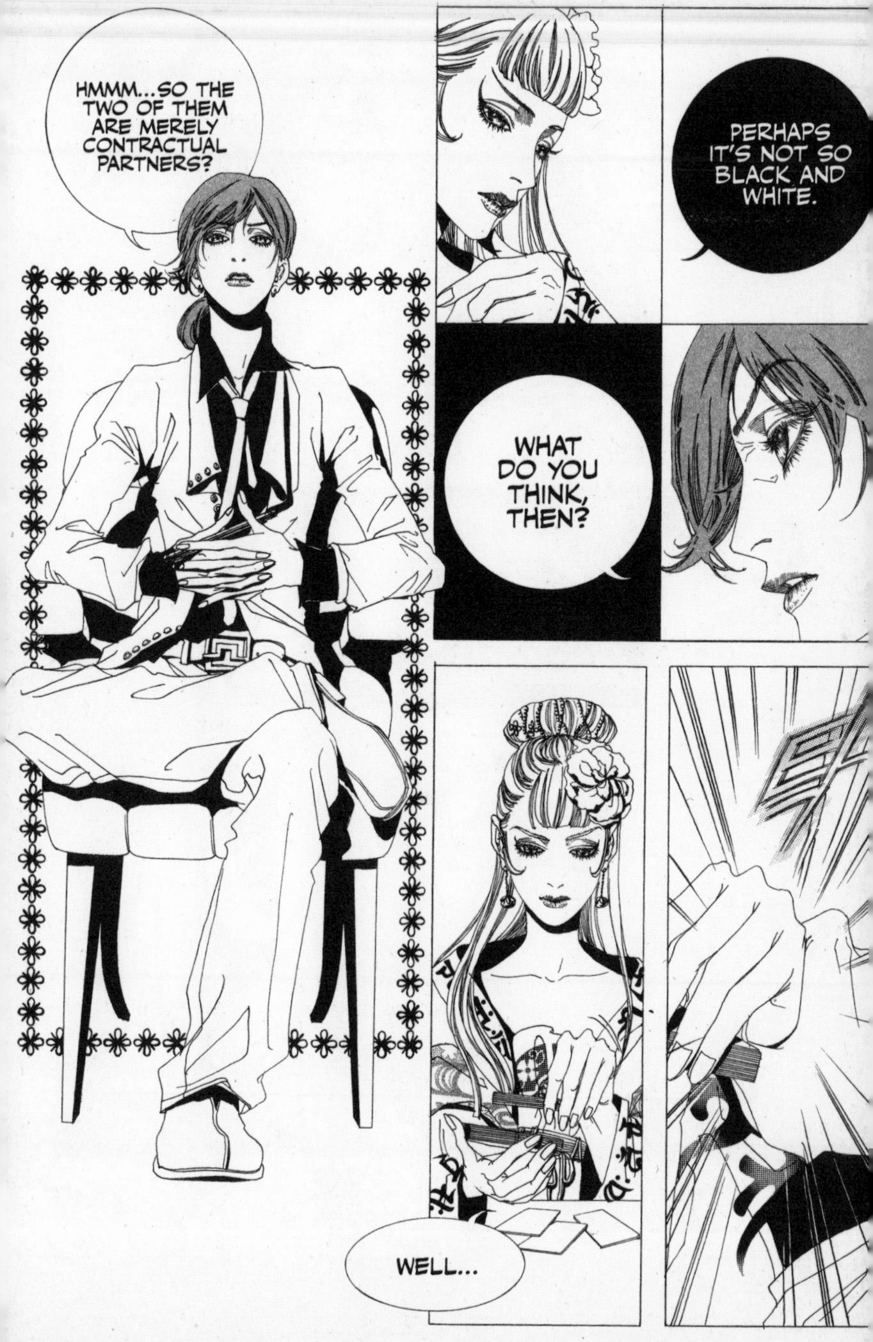
HMMM...SO THE TWO OF THEM ARE MERELY CONTRACTUAL PARTNERS?
PERHAPS IT'S NOT SO BLACK AND WHITE.
WHAT DO YOU THINK, THEN?
WELL...

SHOW ME HOW PAMELA FEELS ABOUT BELUS.

SHE DID SOMETHING NO ONE ELSE WAS ABLE TO DO. THAT WAS THE REASON BELUS NOTICED HER.

INTEREST, GAZE, GOODWILL-- IT IS CERTAIN THAT BELUS LIKES PAMELA.

The Tower: This card represents unexpected disaster or an abrupt change in lifestyle that can lead to new realizations; change of opinion.

XVI

THE TOWER

The Universe: This card represents perfection, completion, positive change, and achievement.

XVI

THE

I DON'T KNOW IF THAT AFFECTION IS PLATONIC OR ROMANTIC.

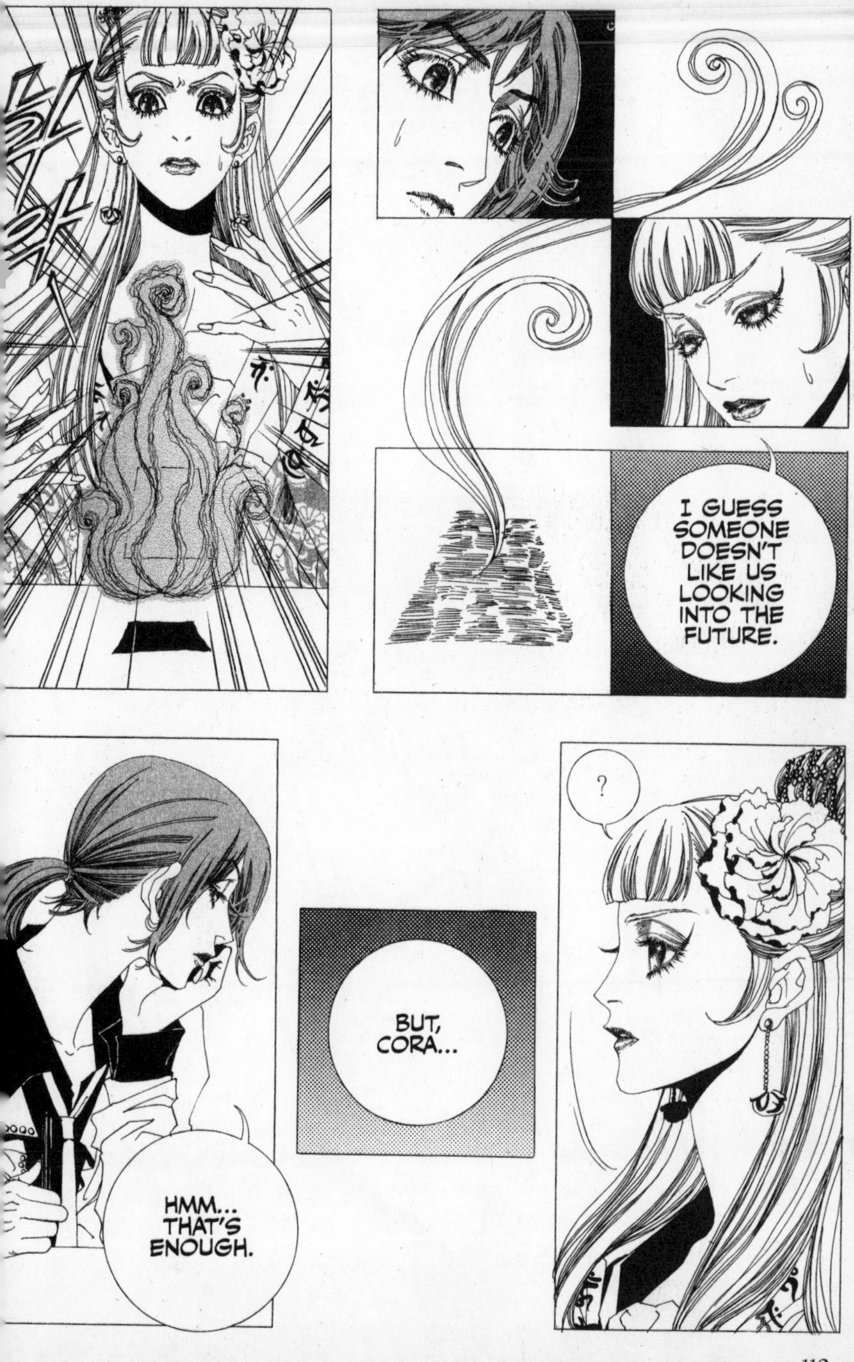
I GUESS SOMEONE DOESN'T LIKE US LOOKING INTO THE FUTURE.
HMM... THAT'S ENOUGH.
BUT, CORA...
?

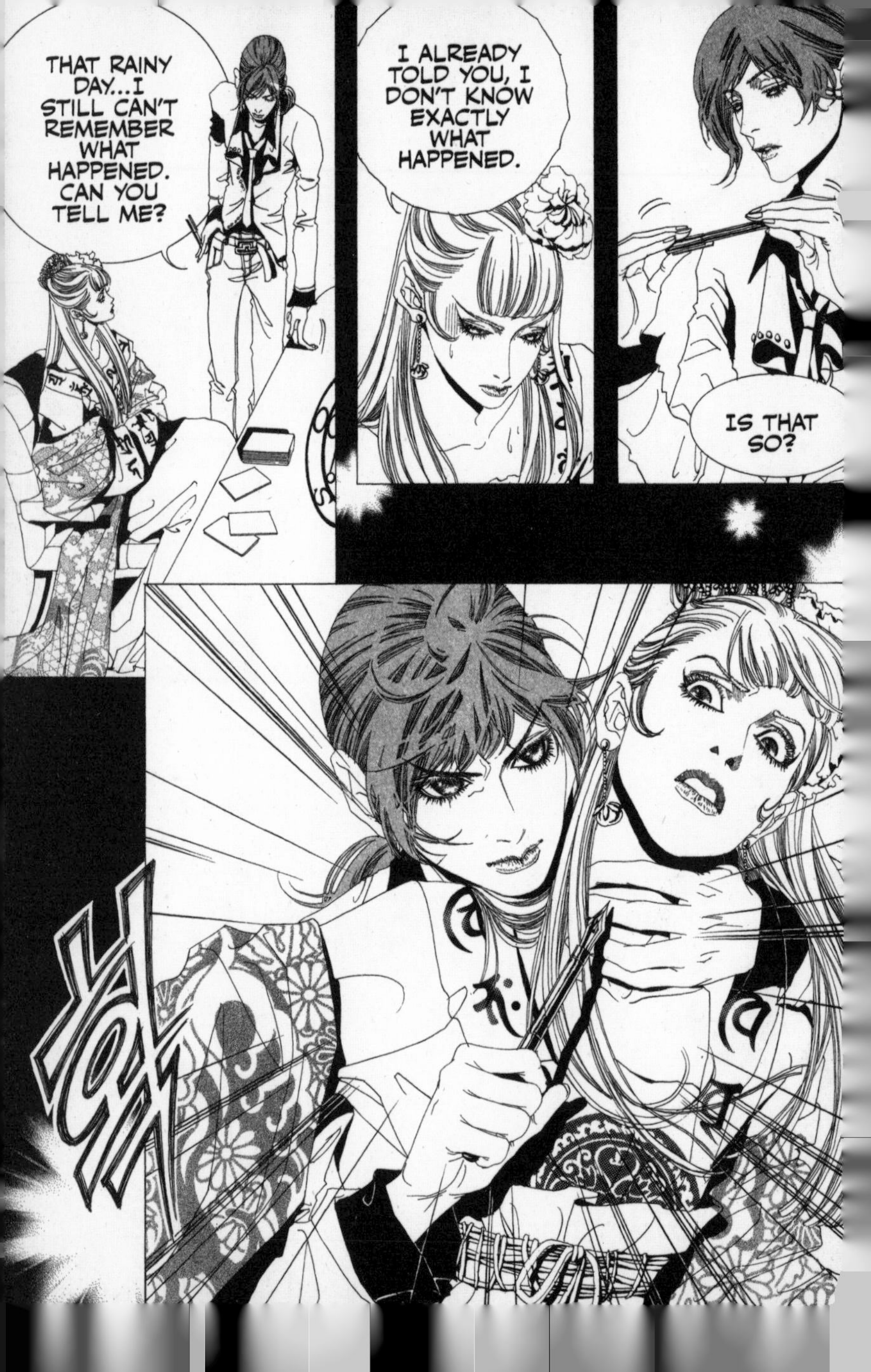
THAT RAINY DAY...I STILL CAN'T REMEMBER WHAT HAPPENED. CAN YOU TELL ME?
I ALREADY TOLD YOU, I DON'T KNOW EXACTLY WHAT HAPPENED.
IS THAT SO?

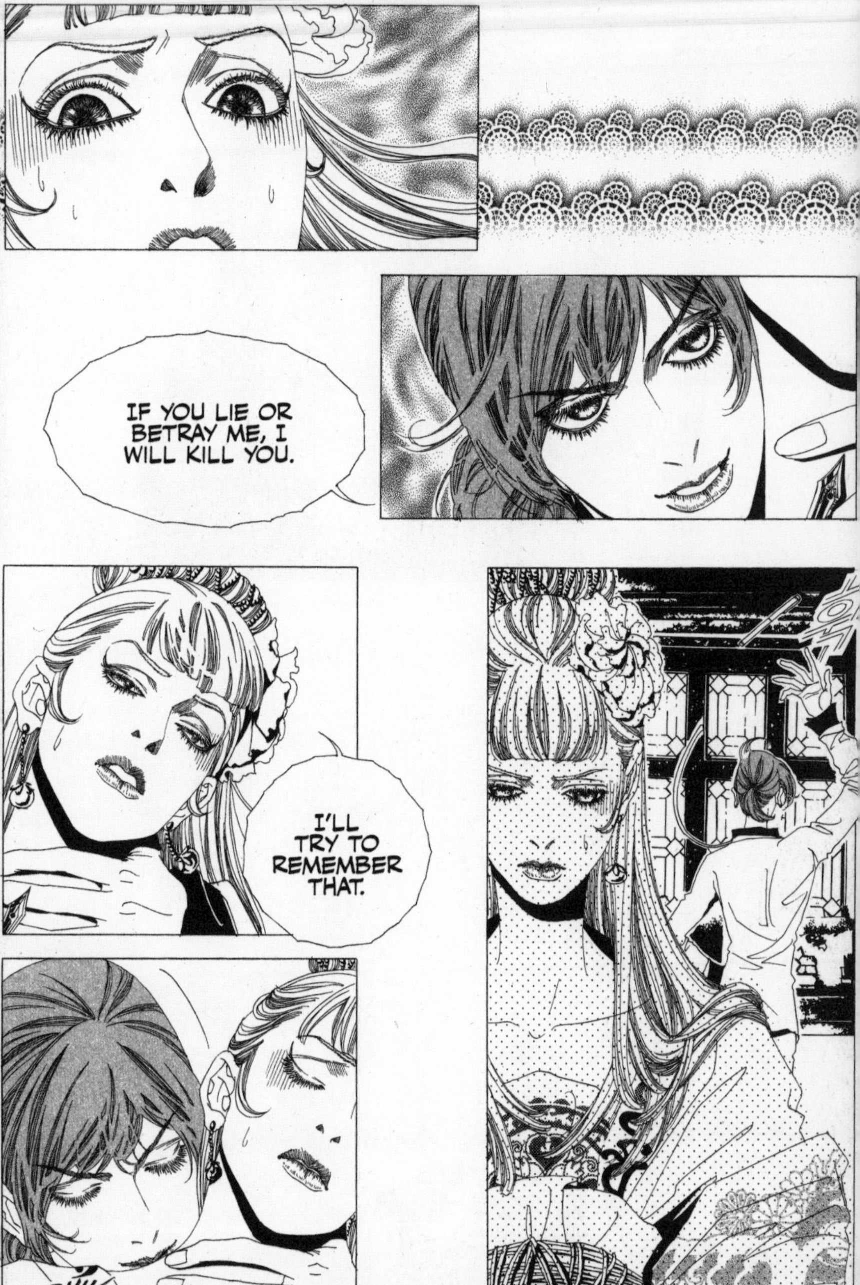
IF YOU LIE OR BETRAY ME, I WILL KILL YOU.
I'LL TRY TO REMEMBER THAT.
CHU

YOU REALLY WANT TO KNOW?

WHAT?

NOTHING. LET'S PARTY!

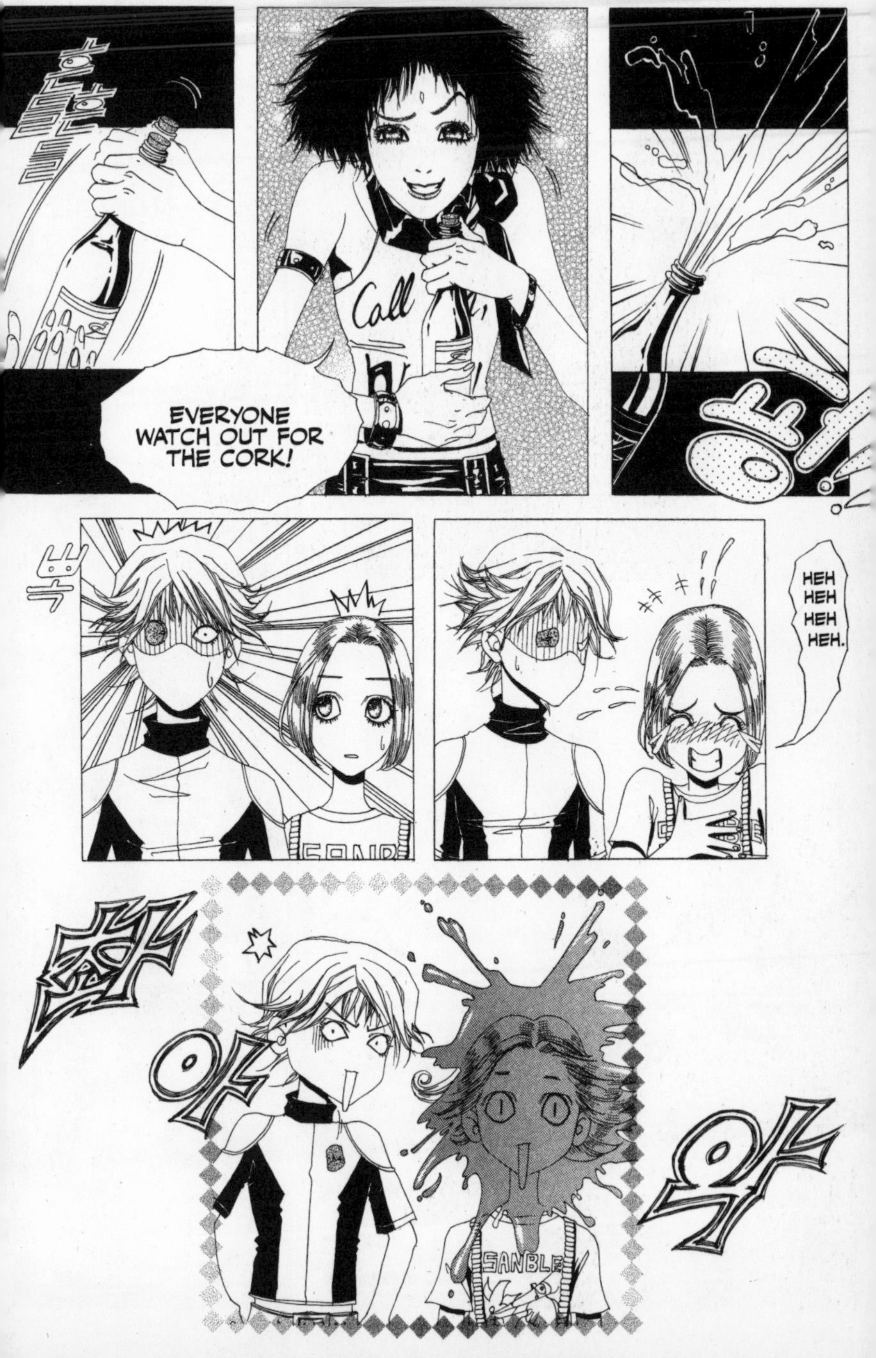
EVERYONE WATCH OUT FOR THE CORK!
HEH HEH HEH HEH.

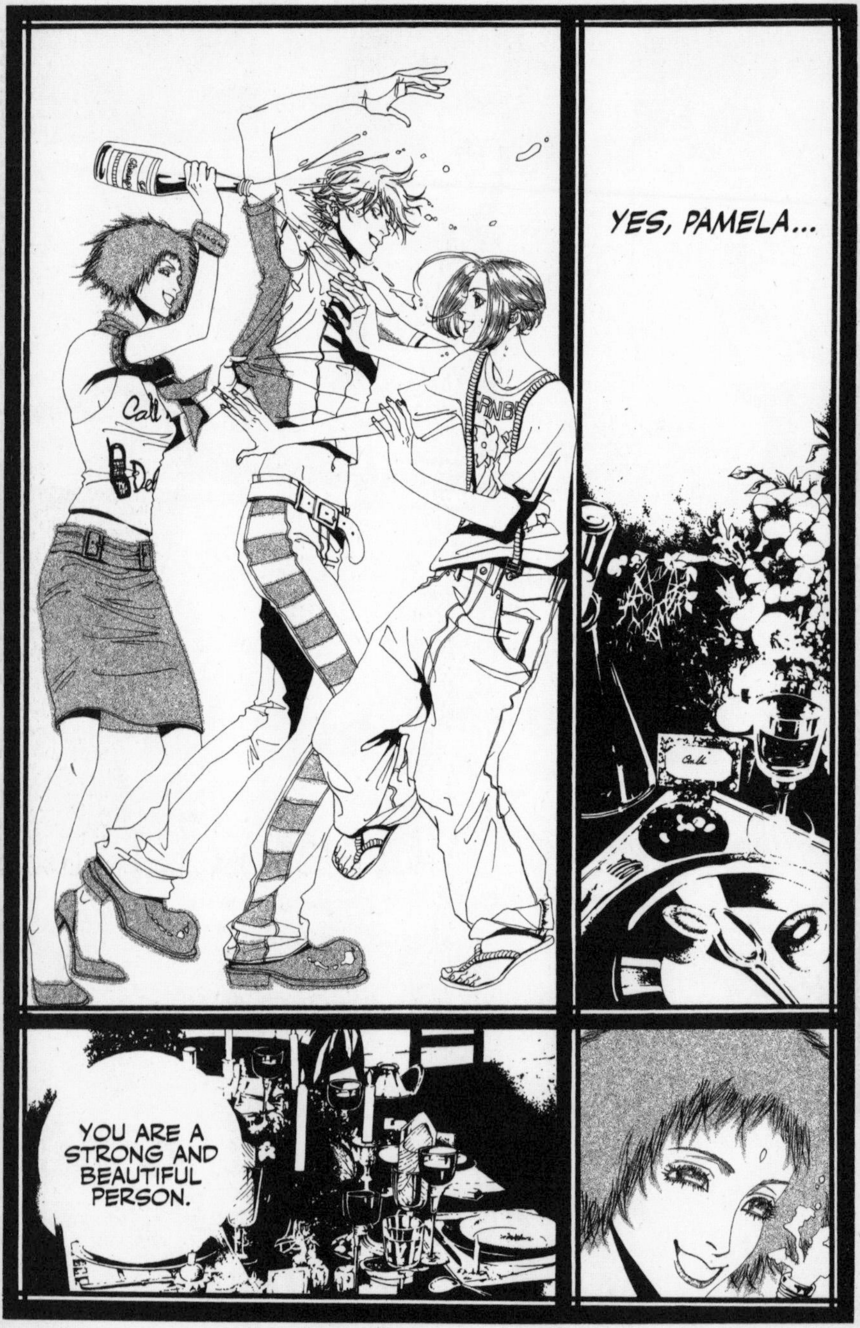
YES, PAMELA...
YOU ARE A STRONG AND BEAUTIFUL PERSON.

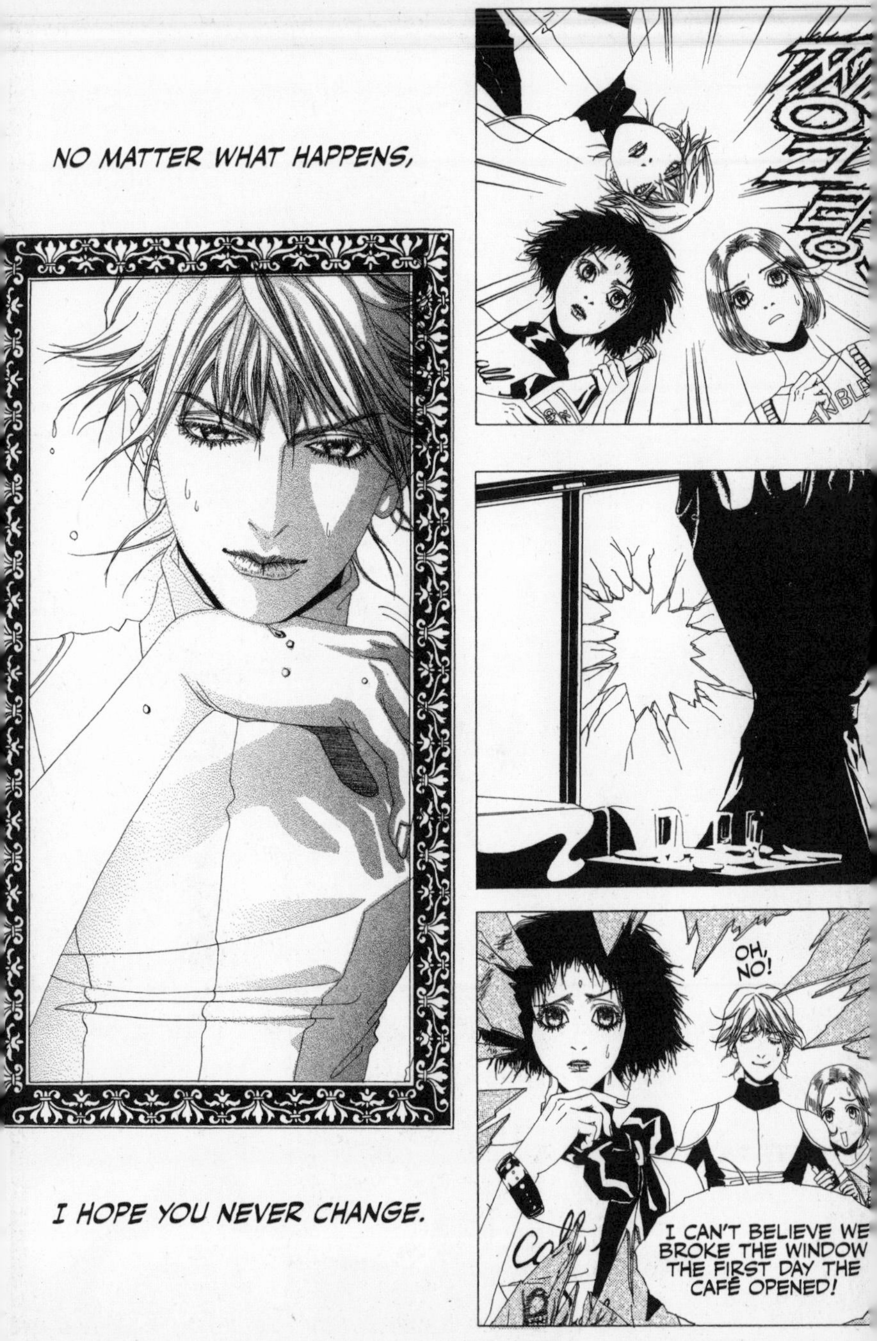
OH, NO!
I CAN'T BELIEVE WE BROKE THE WINDOW THE FIRST DAY THE CAFÉ OPENED!
NO MATTER WHAT HAPPENS,
I HOPE YOU NEVER CHANGE.

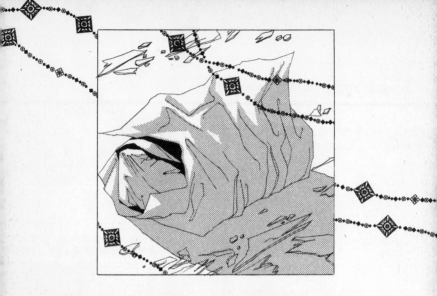

I WONDER WHO...

THAT'S STRANGE. THERE'S NO ONE OUTSIDE.

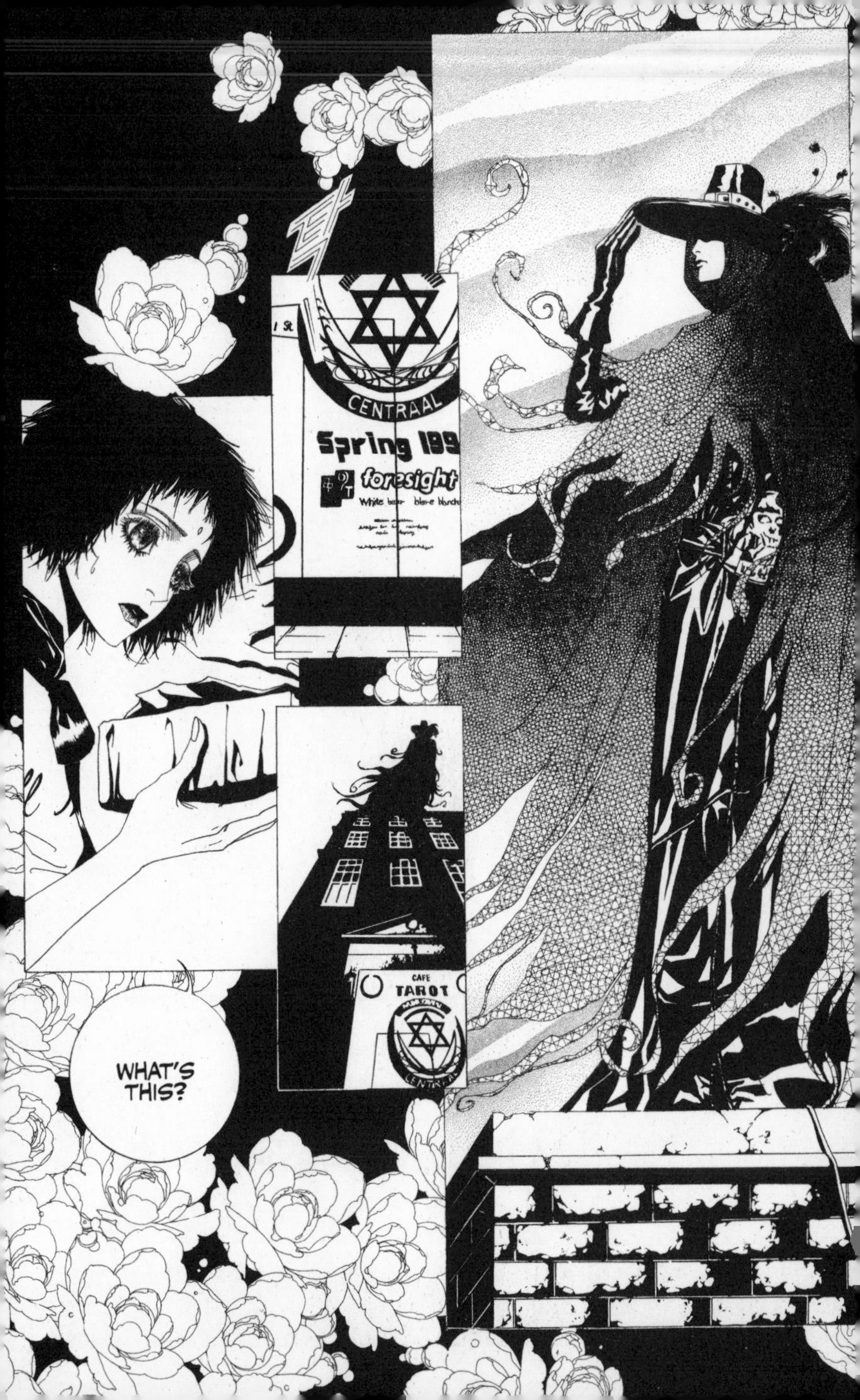
CENTRAAL
Spring 199
foresight
CAFE
TAROT
WHAT'S THIS?

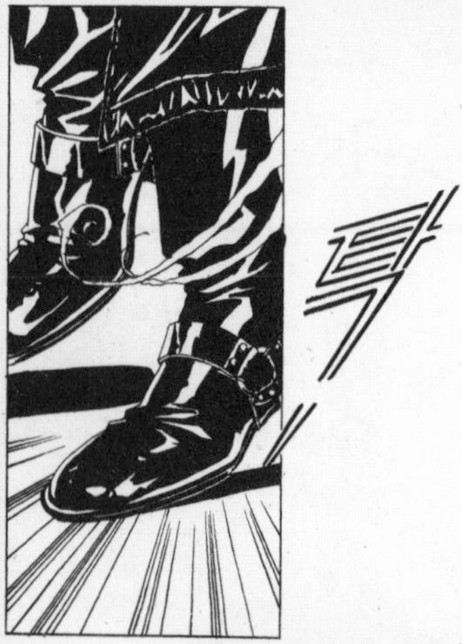
탁

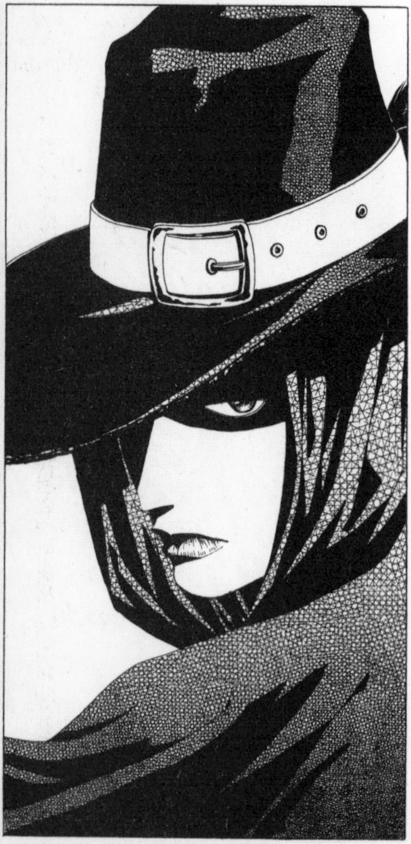

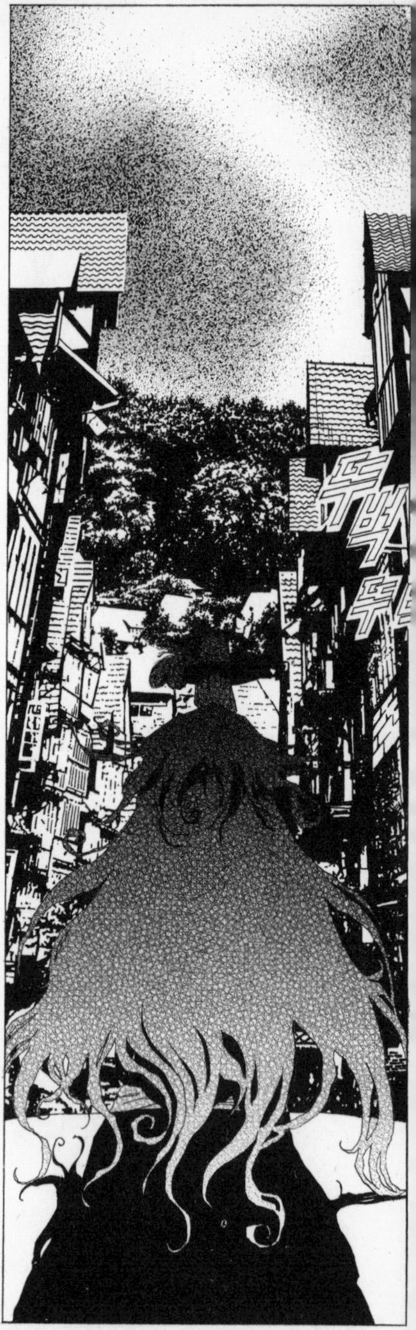
뚜벅
뚜

Episode 13: Leanan Sidhe (One)

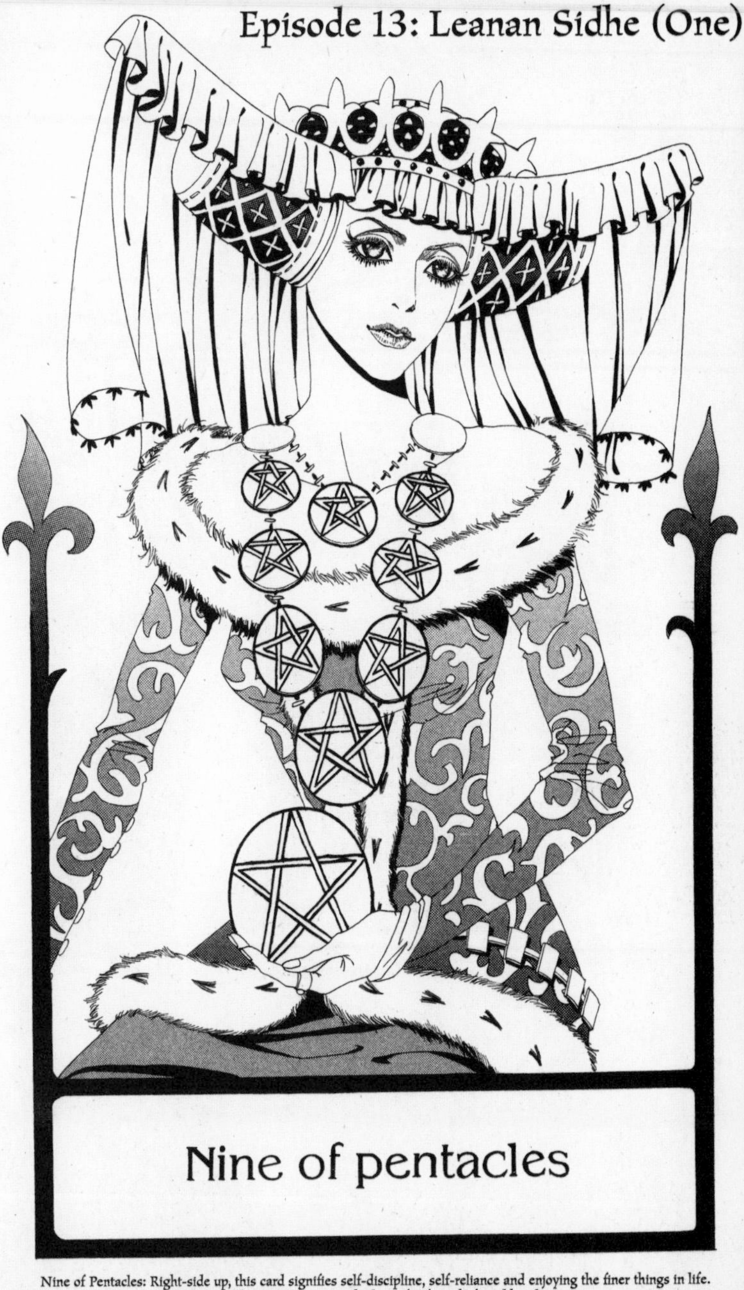
Nine of pentacles

Nine of Pentacles: Right-side up, this card signifies self-discipline, self-reliance and enjoying the finer things in life. Upside down, it represents the loss of safety, theft and breakup.

ILLUSTRATION FROM TAROT OF OLD PATH

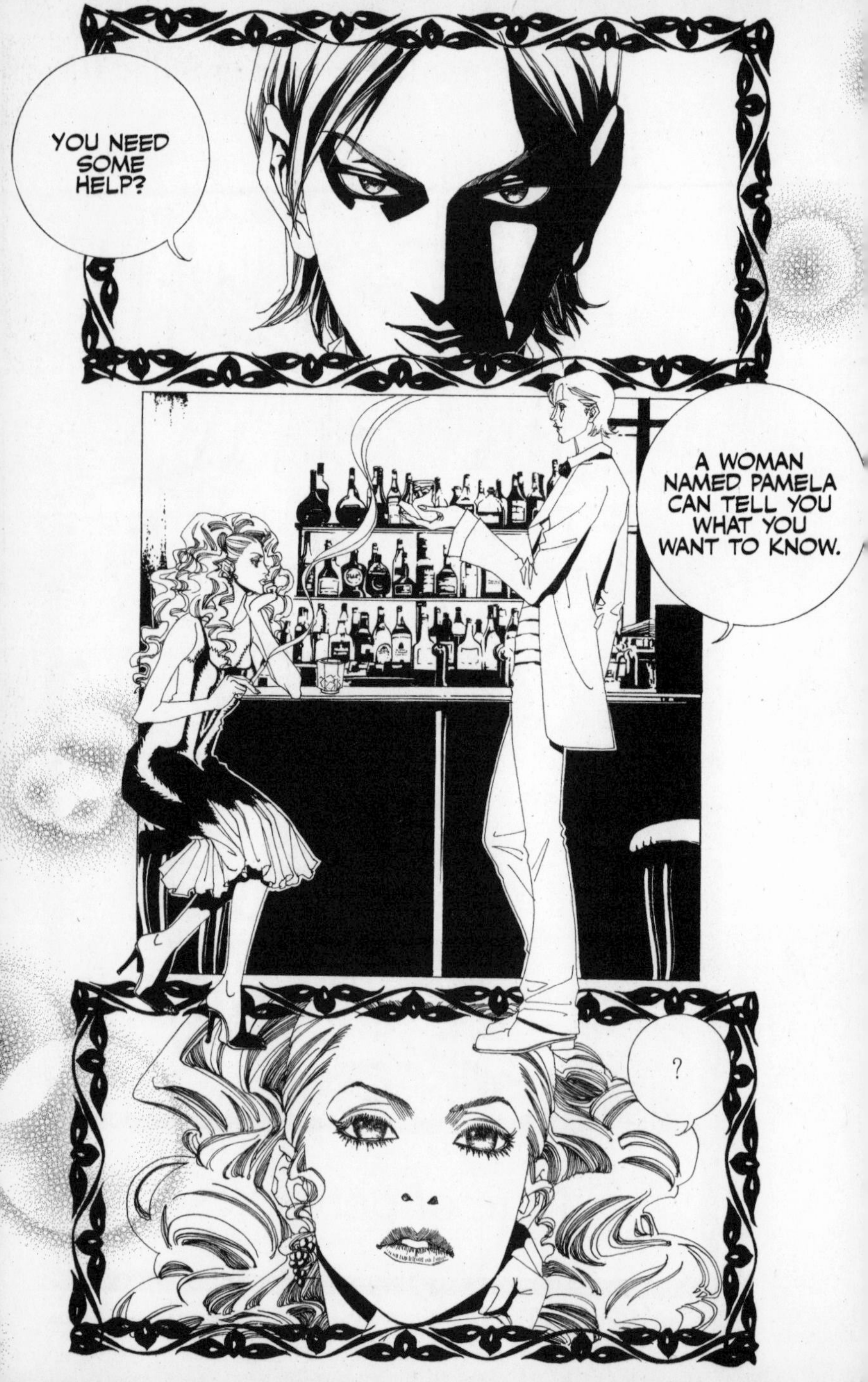
YOU NEED SOME HELP?
A WOMAN NAMED PAMELA CAN TELL YOU WHAT YOU WANT TO KNOW.
?

ON THE FIFTEENTH OF EACH MONTH, I LOSE CONTROL OF MYSELF AND I REMEMBER NOTHING.

IT'S BEEN LIKE THIS FOR A FULL YEAR.

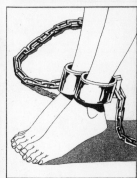

WHEN WILL I BE FREE OF THIS CURSE?

WHEN WILL I MEET NEBIROS AGAIN?

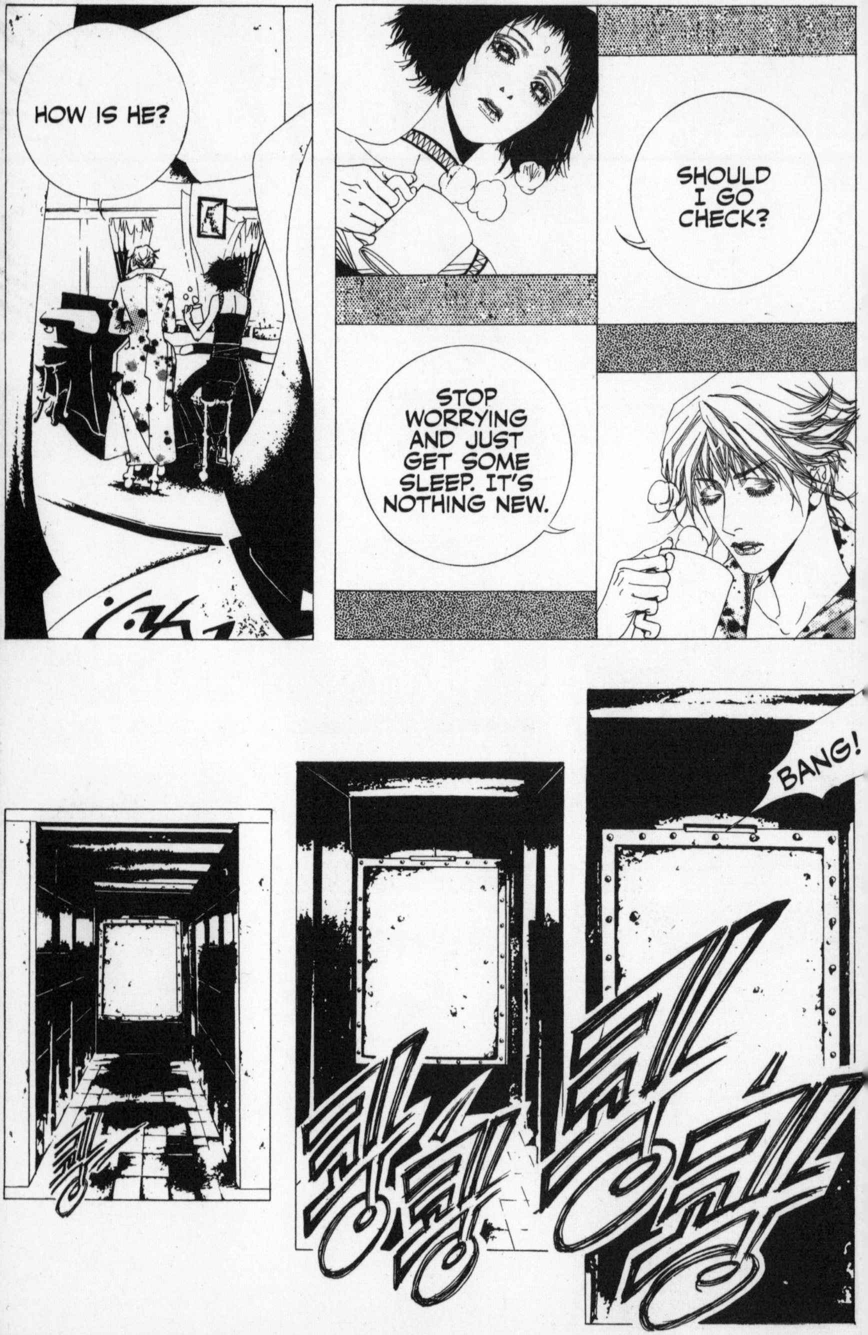
HOW IS HE?
SHOULD I GO CHECK?
STOP WORRYING AND JUST GET SOME SLEEP. IT'S NOTHING NEW.
BANG!

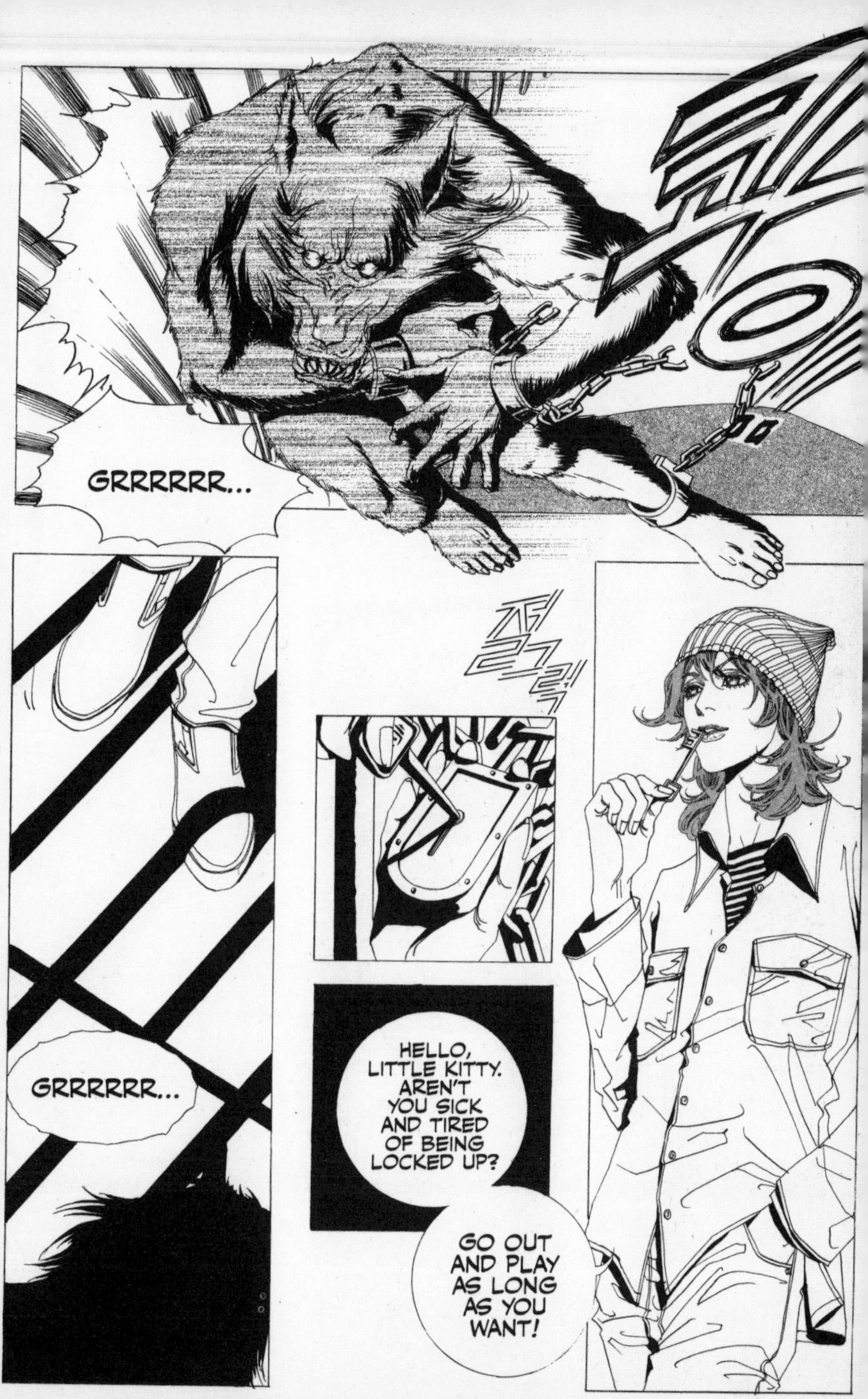
GRRRRRR...
GRRRRRR...
HELLO, LITTLE KITTY. AREN'T YOU SICK AND TIRED OF BEING LOCKED UP?
GO OUT AND PLAY AS LONG AS YOU WANT!

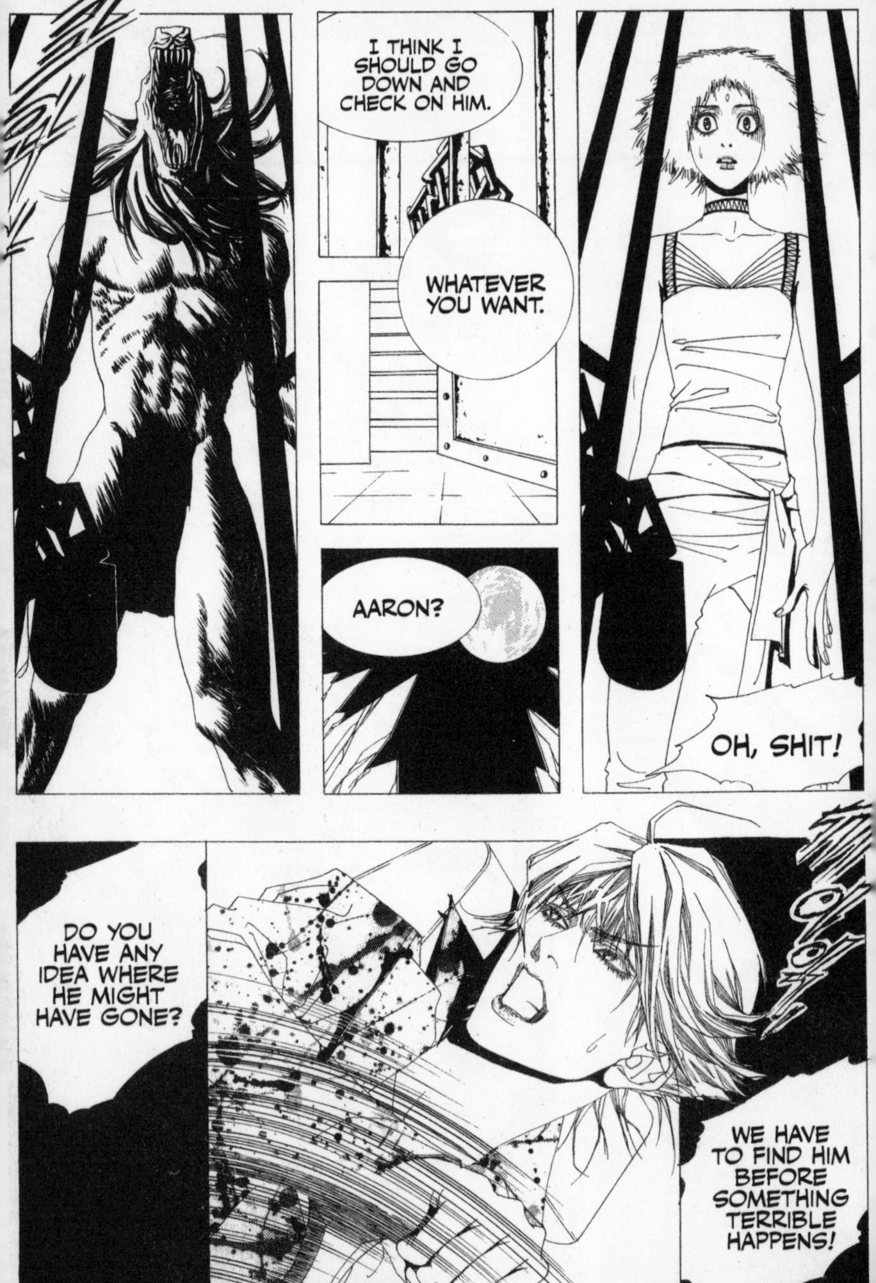
I THINK I SHOULD GO DOWN AND CHECK ON HIM.
WHATEVER YOU WANT.
AARON?
OH, SHIT!
DO YOU HAVE ANY IDEA WHERE HE MIGHT HAVE GONE?
WE HAVE TO FIND HIM BEFORE SOMETHING TERRIBLE HAPPENS!

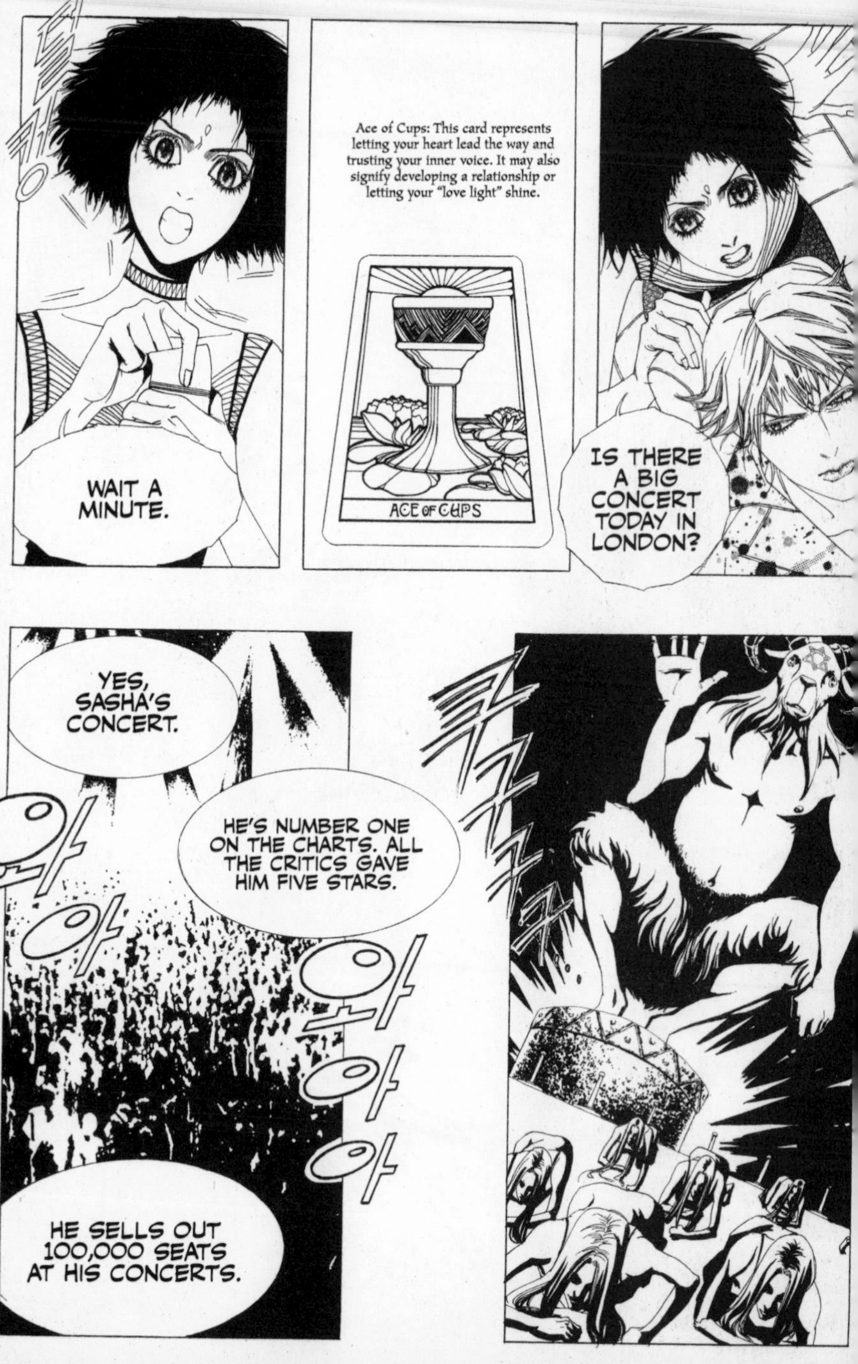
WAIT A MINUTE.
Ace of Cups: This card represents letting your heart lead the way and trusting your inner voice. It may also signify developing a relationship or letting your "love light" shine.
ACE OF CUPS
IS THERE A BIG CONCERT TODAY IN LONDON?
YES, SASHA'S CONCERT.
HE'S NUMBER ONE ON THE CHARTS. ALL THE CRITICS GAVE HIM FIVE STARS.
HE SELLS OUT 100,000 SEATS AT HIS CONCERTS.

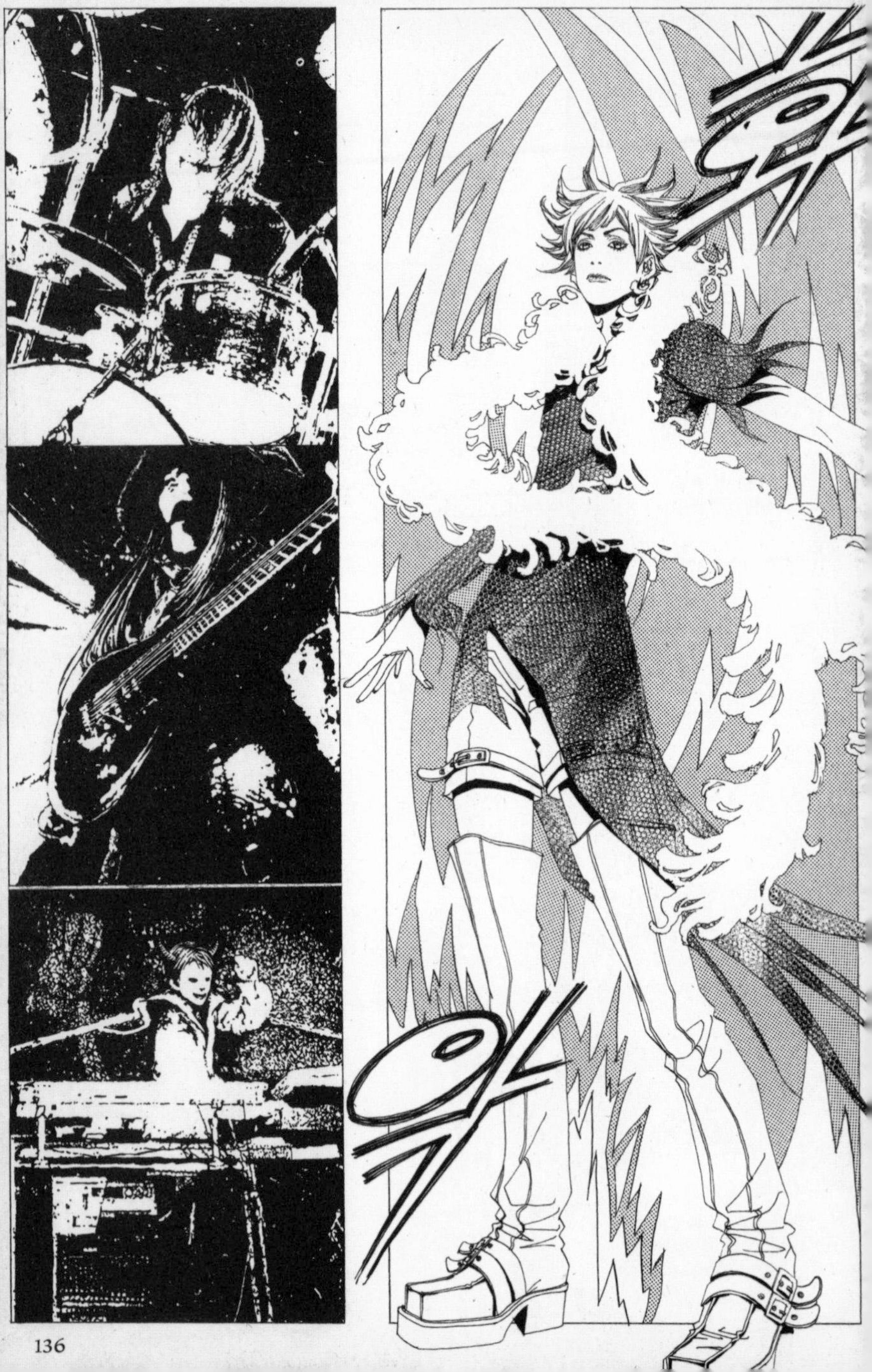

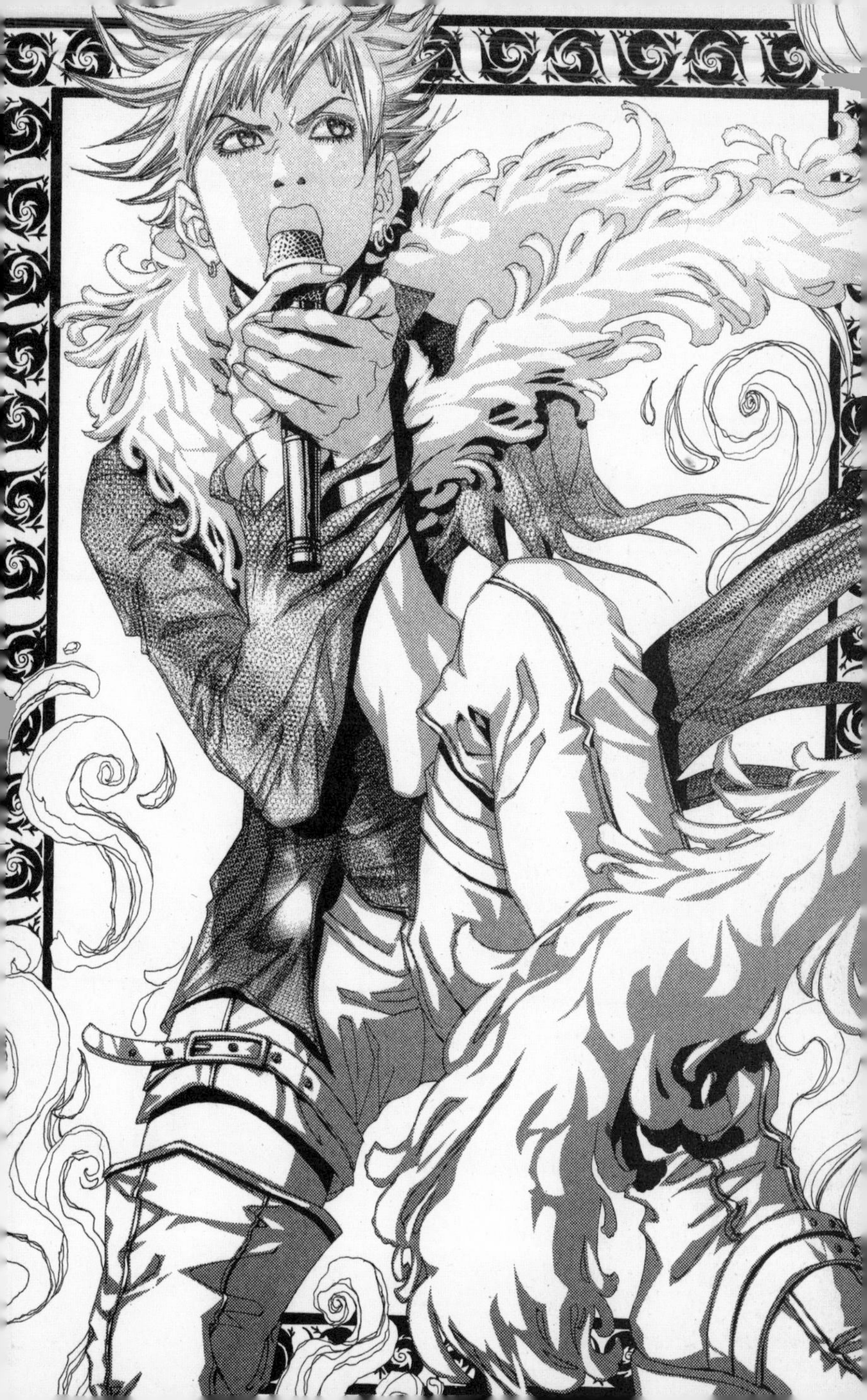

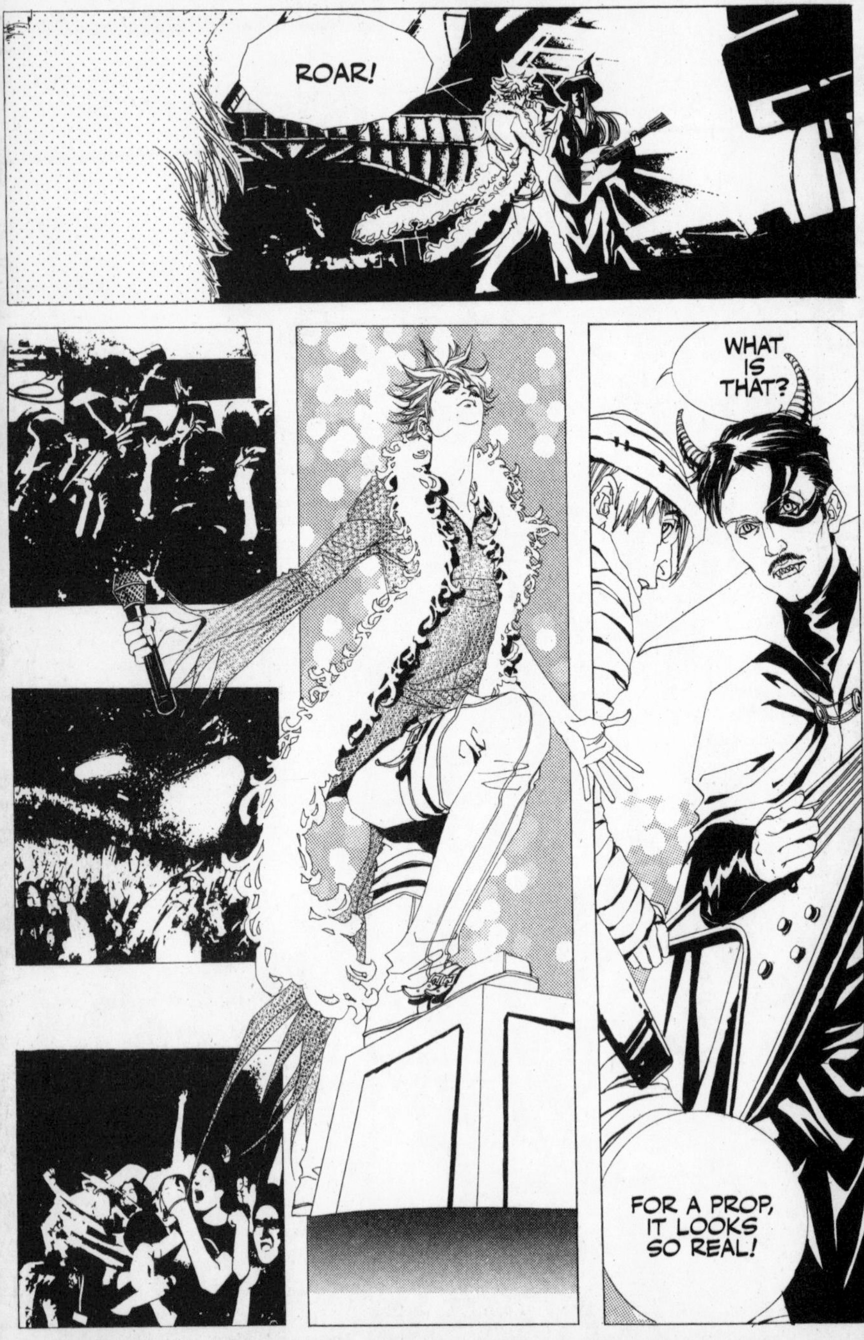
ROAR!
WHAT IS THAT?
FOR A PROP, IT LOOKS SO REAL!

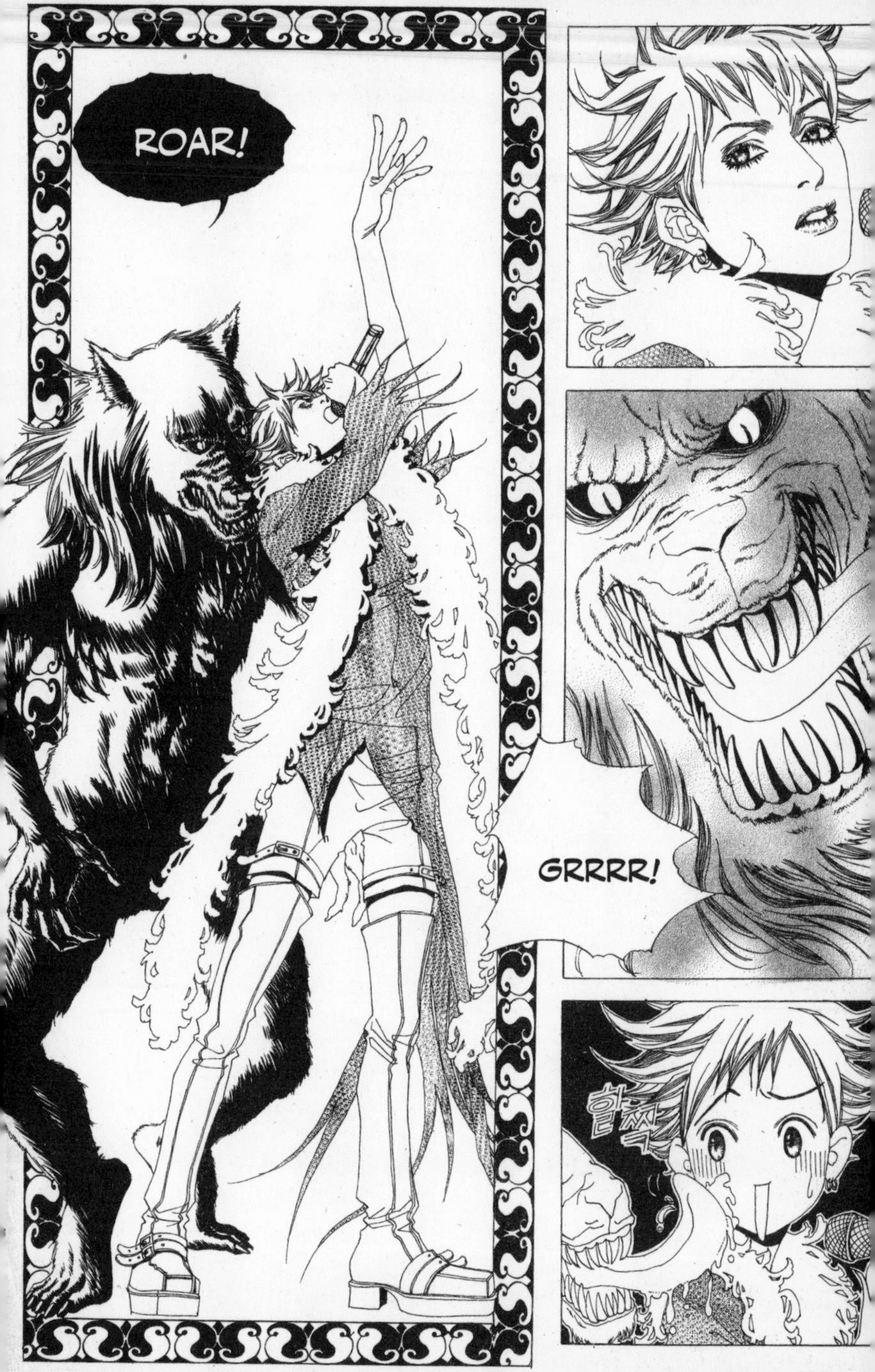
ROAR!
GRRRR!
할짝

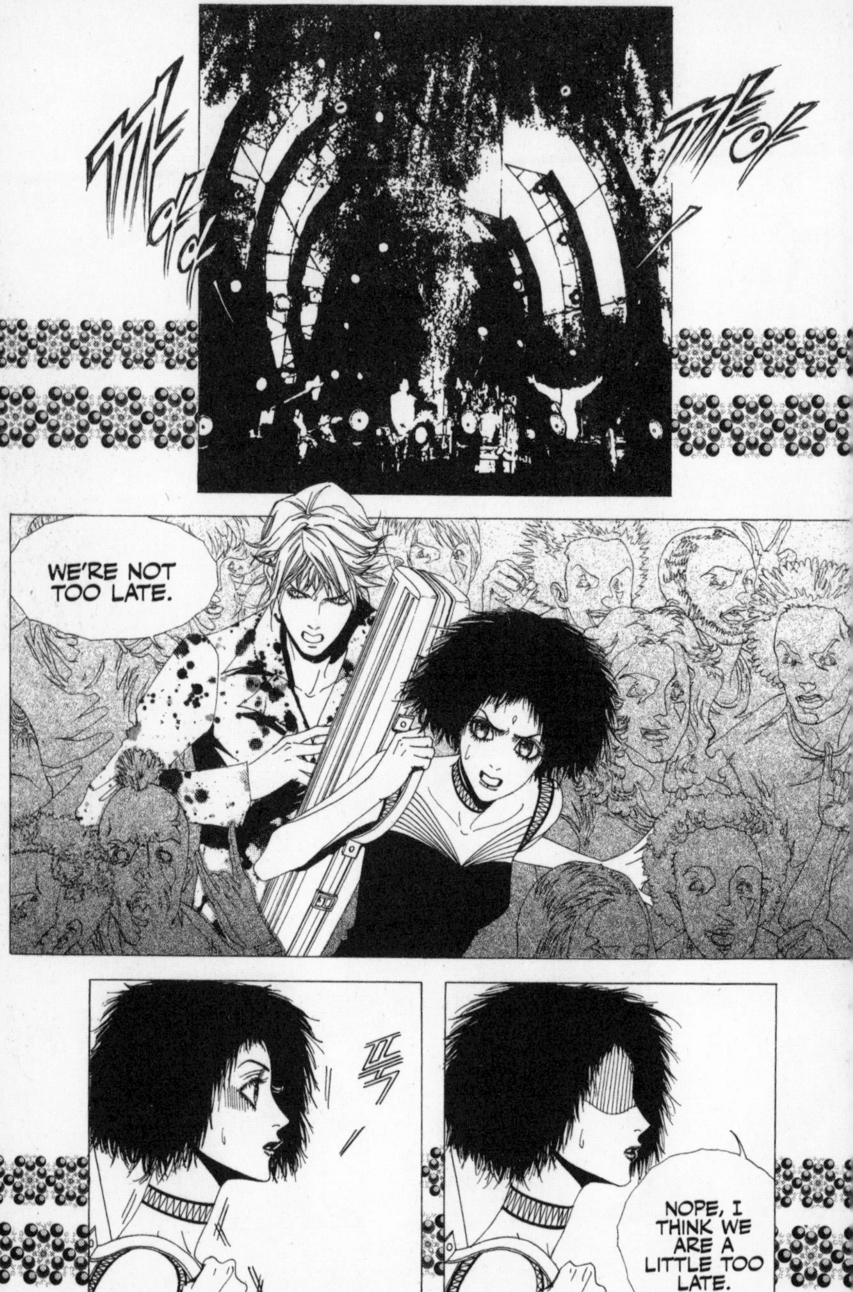
WE'RE NOT TOO LATE.
NOPE, I THINK WE ARE A LITTLE TOO LATE.

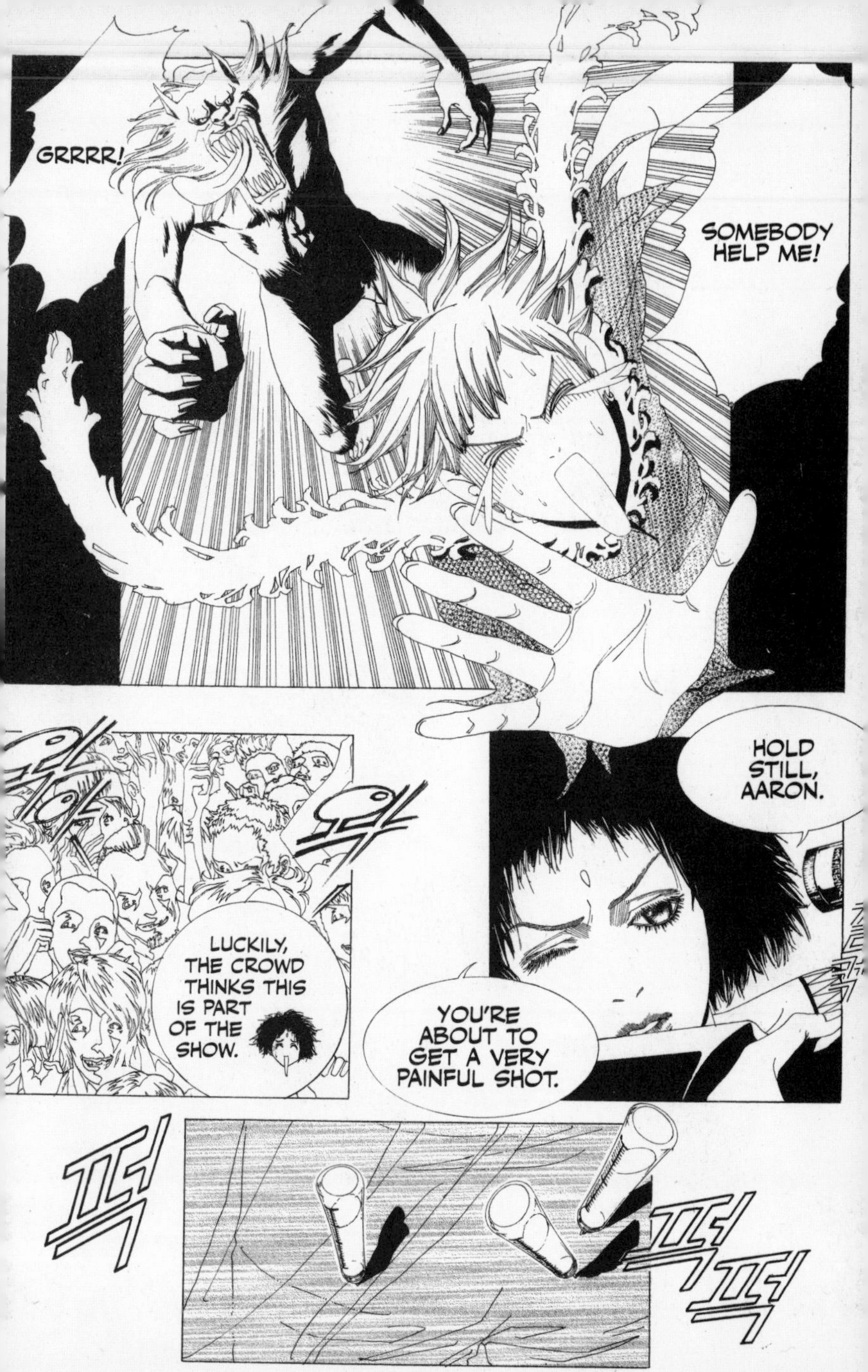
GRRRR!
SOMEBODY HELP ME!
LUCKILY, THE CROWD THINKS THIS IS PART OF THE SHOW.
HOLD STILL, AARON.
YOU'RE ABOUT TO GET A VERY PAINFUL SHOT.

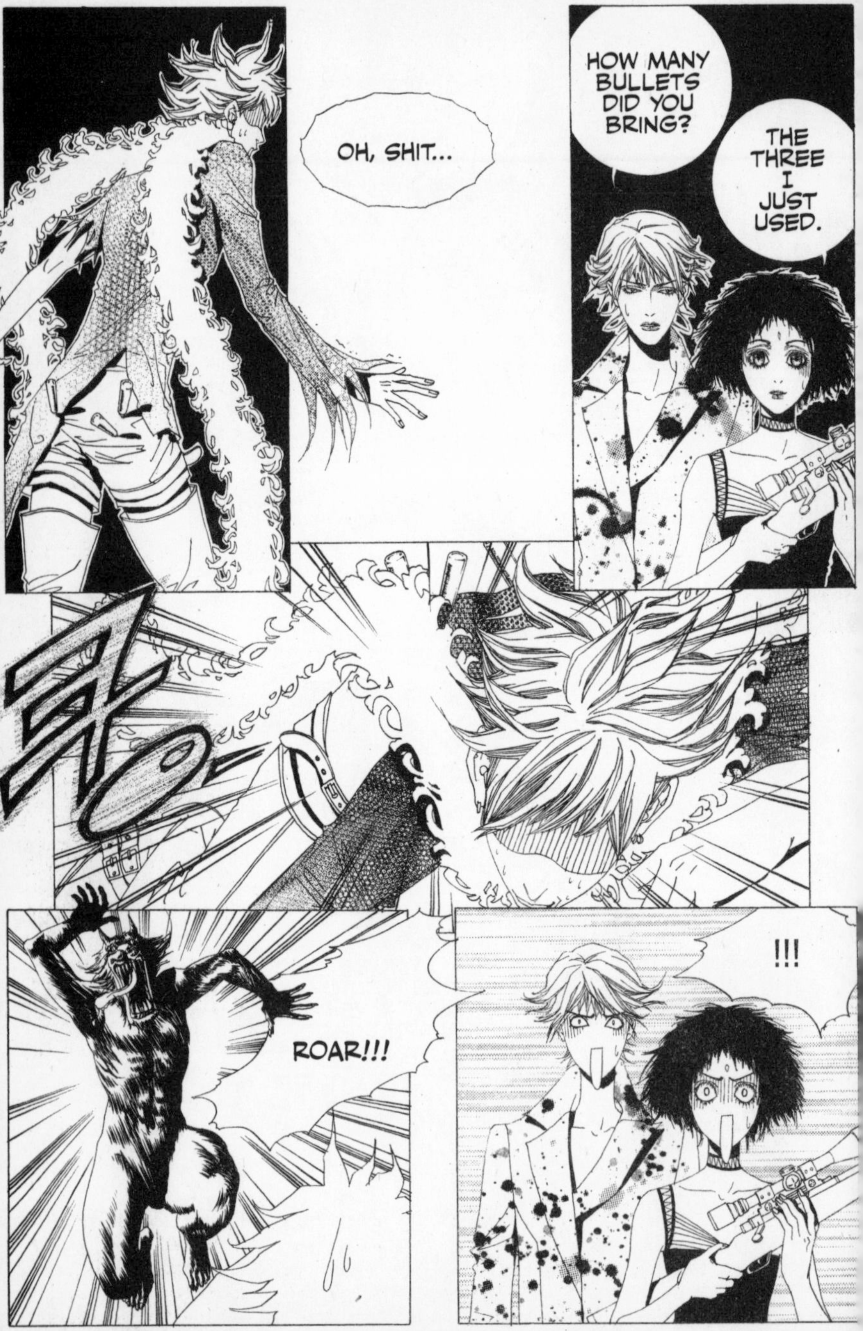
OH, SHIT...
HOW MANY BULLETS DID YOU BRING?
THE THREE I JUST USED.
ROAR!!!
!!!

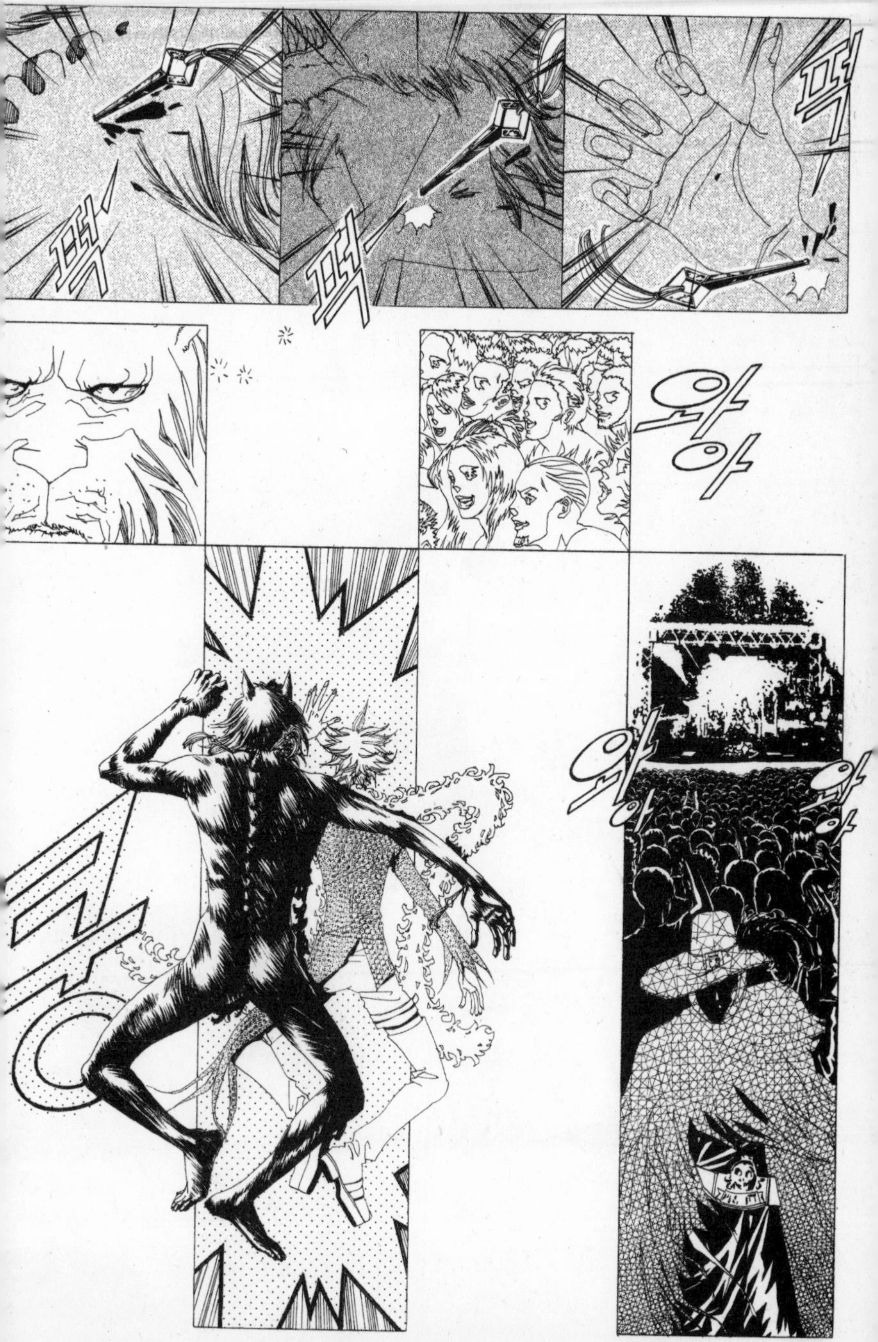
퍽
퍽
퍽
와아
와아
와아

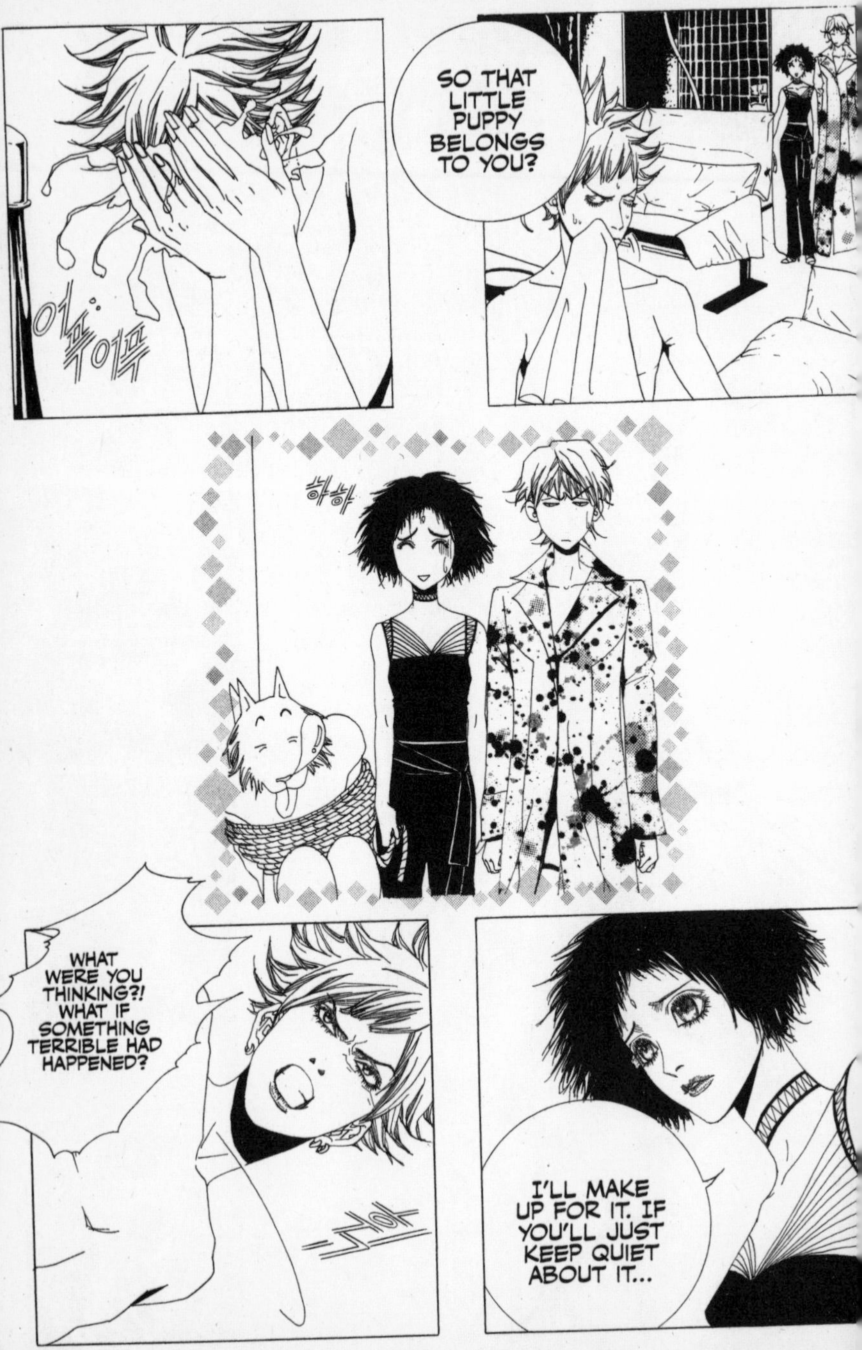
어푸어푸
SO THAT LITTLE PUPPY BELONGS TO YOU?
하하
WHAT WERE YOU THINKING?! WHAT IF SOMETHING TERRIBLE HAD HAPPENED?
I'LL MAKE UP FOR IT. IF YOU'LL JUST KEEP QUIET ABOUT IT...

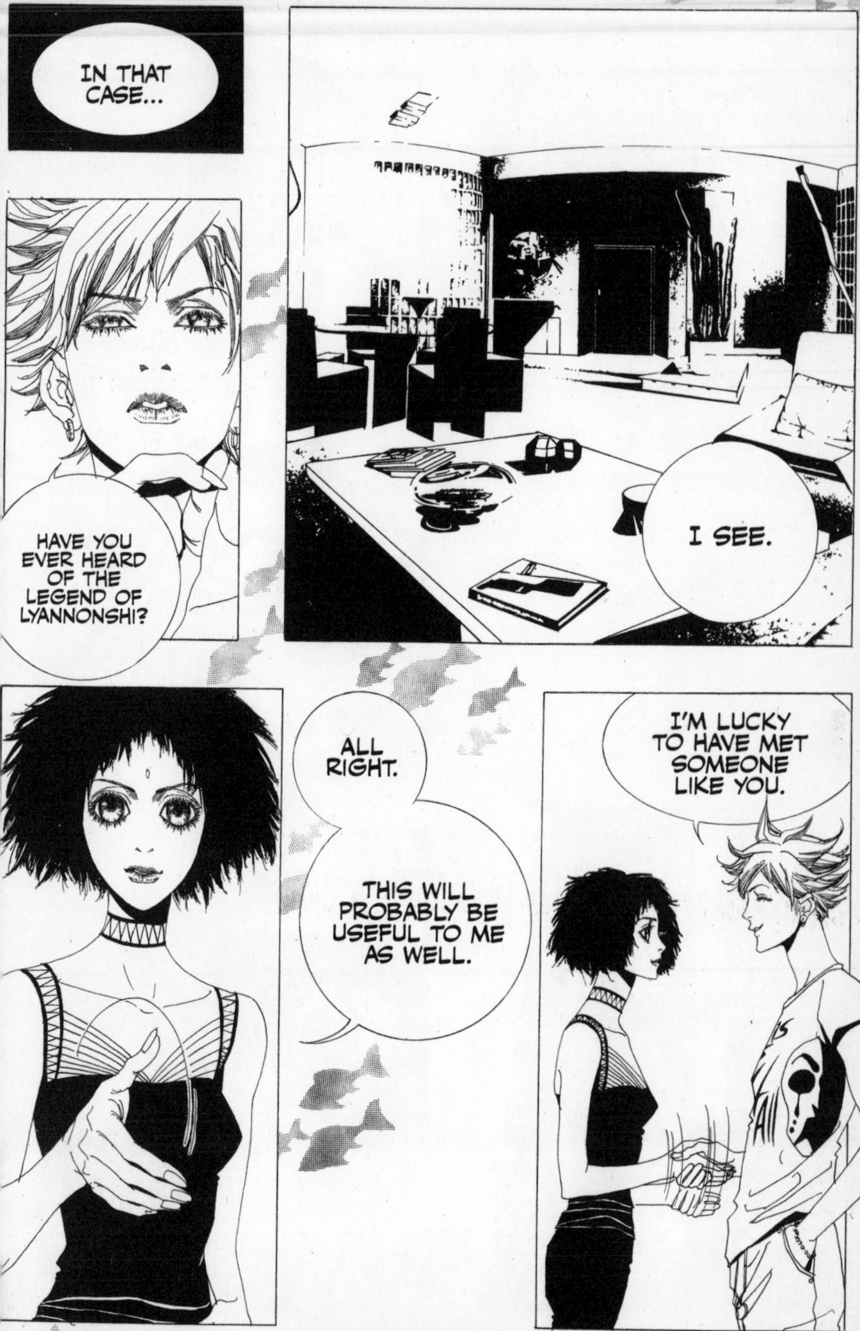
IN THAT CASE...
HAVE YOU EVER HEARD OF THE LEGEND OF LYANNONSHI?
I SEE.
ALL RIGHT.
THIS WILL PROBABLY BE USEFUL TO ME AS WELL.
I'M LUCKY TO HAVE MET SOMEONE LIKE YOU.

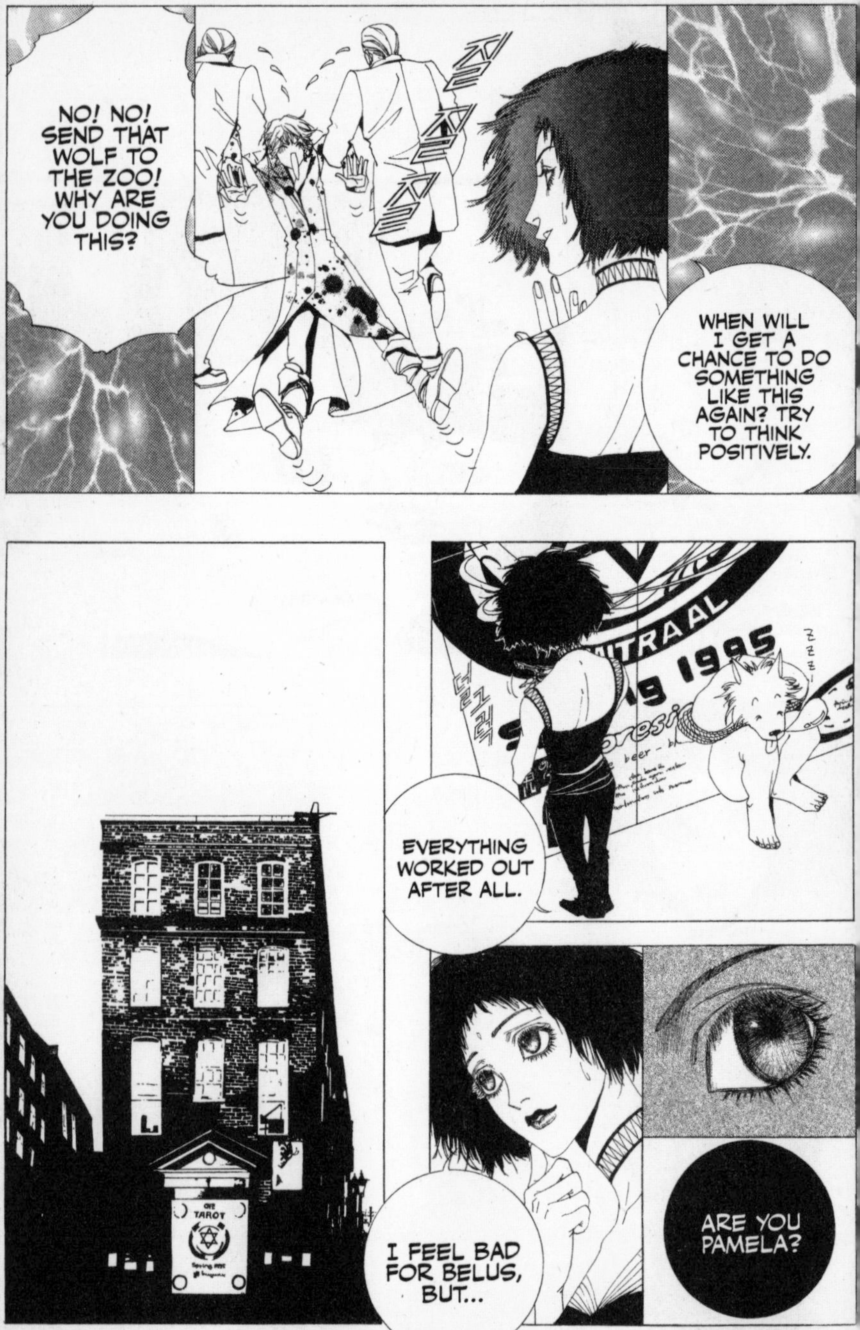
NO! NO! SEND THAT WOLF TO THE ZOO! WHY ARE YOU DOING THIS?
WHEN WILL I GET A CHANCE TO DO SOMETHING LIKE THIS AGAIN? TRY TO THINK POSITIVELY.
TAROT
EVERYTHING WORKED OUT AFTER ALL.
I FEEL BAD FOR BELUS, BUT...
ARE YOU PAMELA?

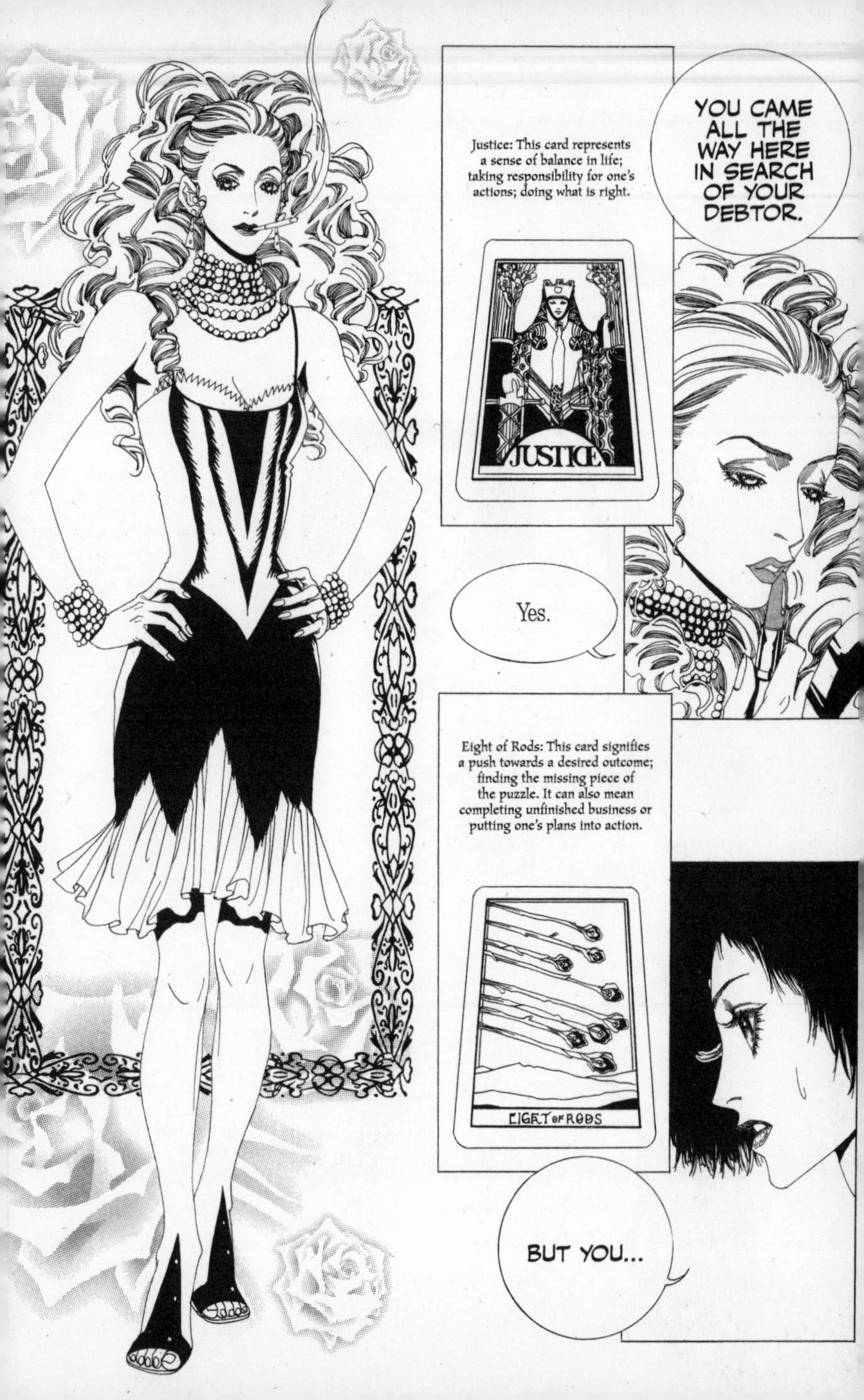

Justice: This card represents a sense of balance in life; taking responsibility for one's actions; doing what is right.
JUSTICE
YOU CAME ALL THE WAY HERE IN SEARCH OF YOUR DEBTOR.
Yes.
Eight of Rods: This card signifies a push towards a desired outcome; finding the missing piece of the puzzle. It can also mean completing unfinished business or putting one's plans into action.
EIGHT of RODS
BUT YOU...

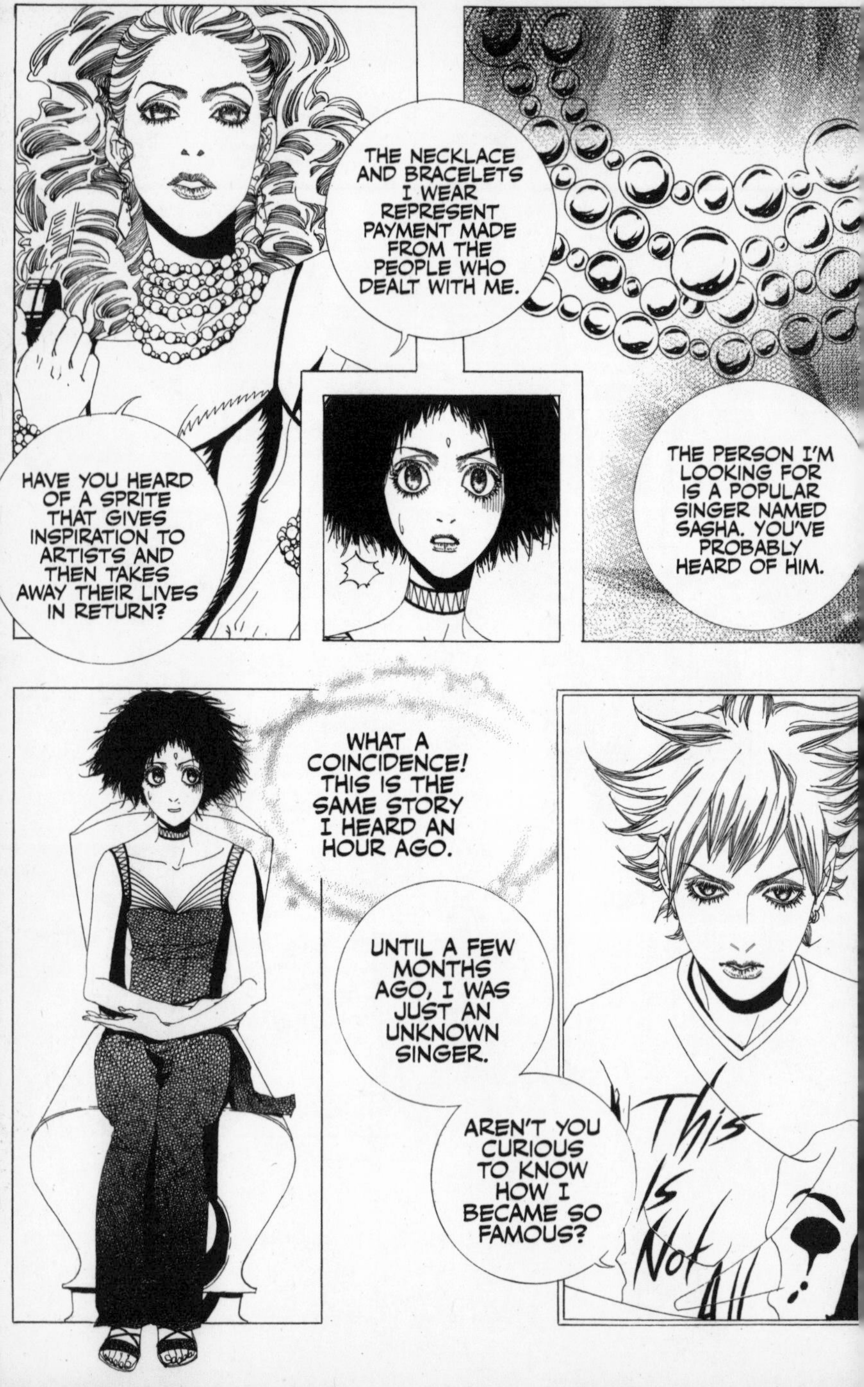
THE NECKLACE AND BRACELETS I WEAR REPRESENT PAYMENT MADE FROM THE PEOPLE WHO DEALT WITH ME.
HAVE YOU HEARD OF A SPRITE THAT GIVES INSPIRATION TO ARTISTS AND THEN TAKES AWAY THEIR LIVES IN RETURN?
THE PERSON I'M LOOKING FOR IS A POPULAR SINGER NAMED SASHA. YOU'VE PROBABLY HEARD OF HIM.
WHAT A COINCIDENCE! THIS IS THE SAME STORY I HEARD AN HOUR AGO.
UNTIL A FEW MONTHS AGO, I WAS JUST AN UNKNOWN SINGER.
AREN'T YOU CURIOUS TO KNOW HOW I BECAME SO FAMOUS?
This Is Not All

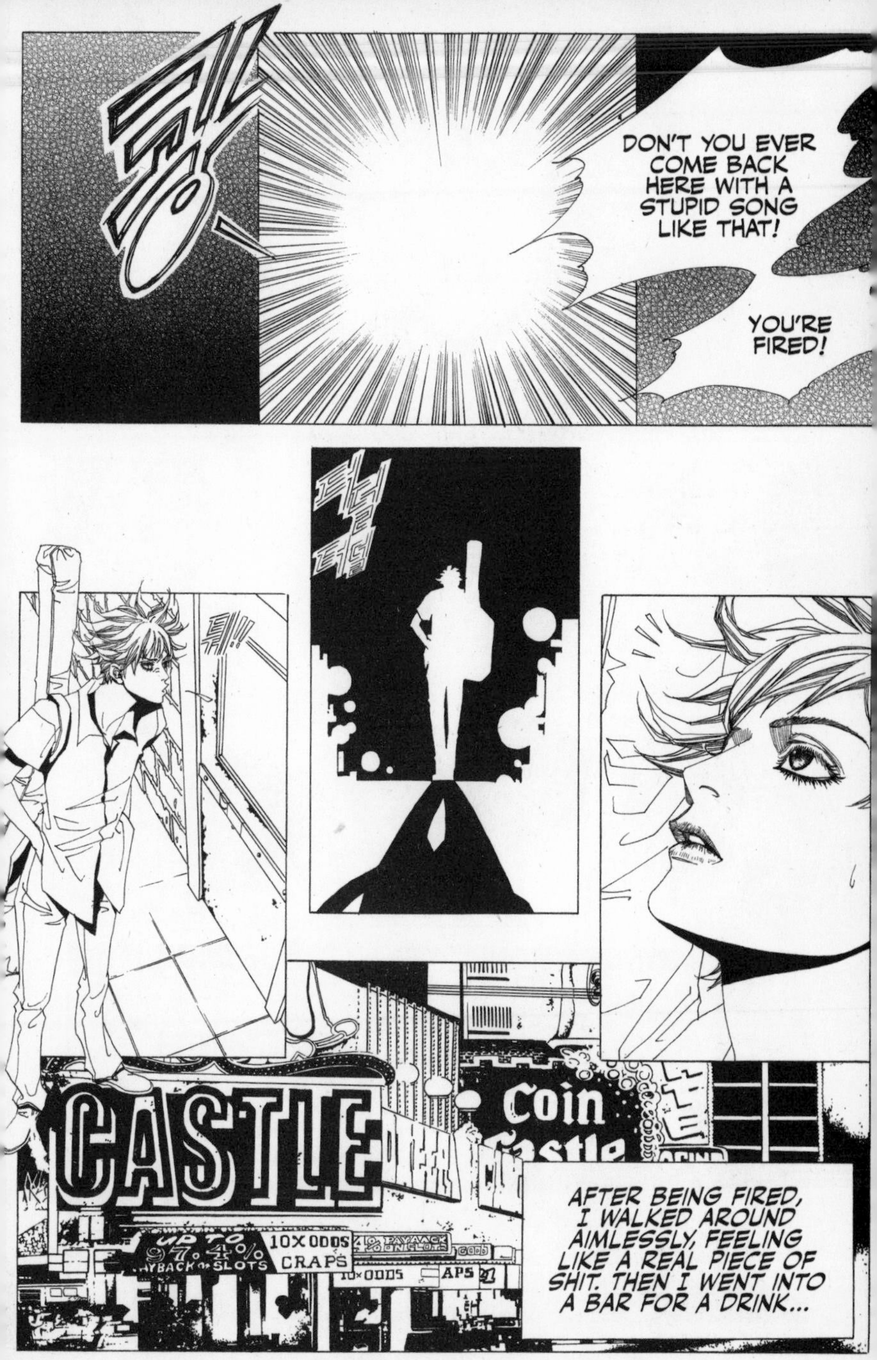

DON'T YOU EVER COME BACK HERE WITH A STUPID SONG LIKE THAT!
YOU'RE FIRED!
CASTLE
Coin Castle
UP TO 97.4% PAYBACK ON SLOTS
10X ODDS CRAPS
AFTER BEING FIRED, I WALKED AROUND AIMLESSLY, FEELING LIKE A REAL PIECE OF SHIT. THEN I WENT INTO A BAR FOR A DRINK...

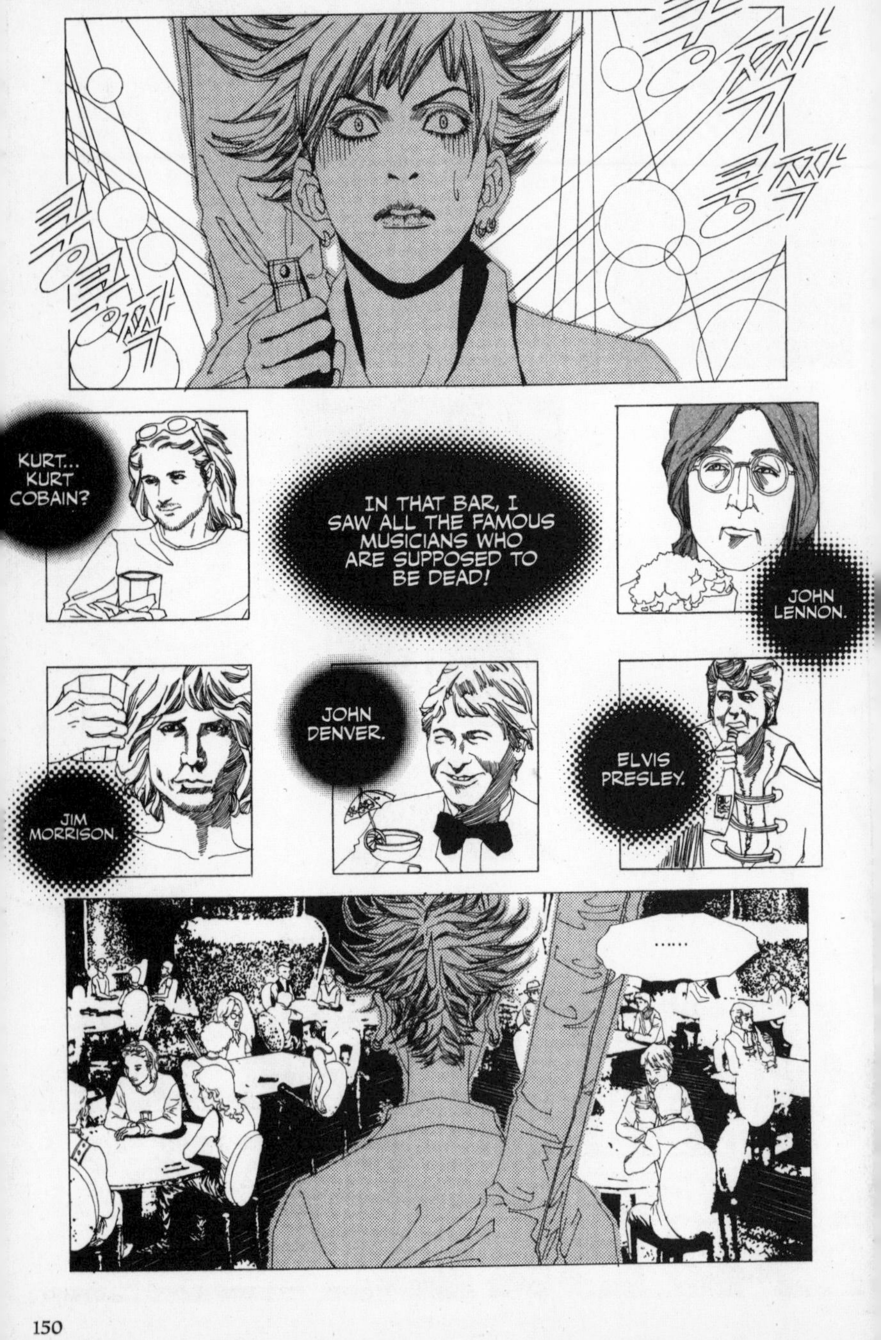
쿵 짝
KURT... KURT COBAIN?
IN THAT BAR, I SAW ALL THE FAMOUS MUSICIANS WHO ARE SUPPOSED TO BE DEAD!
JOHN LENNON.
JIM MORRISON.
JOHN DENVER.
ELVIS PRESLEY.
......

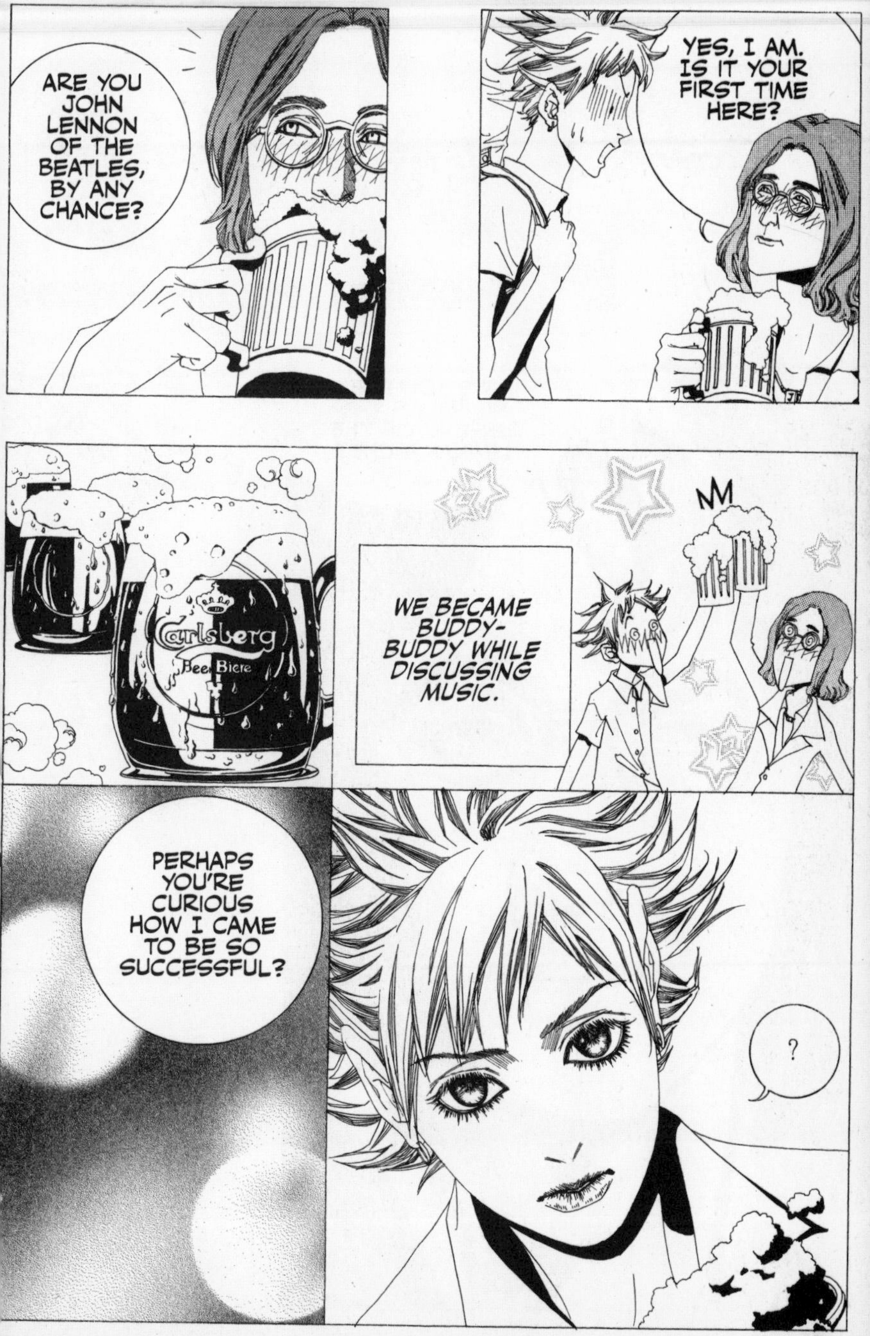
ARE YOU JOHN LENNON OF THE BEATLES, BY ANY CHANCE?
YES, I AM. IS IT YOUR FIRST TIME HERE?
Carlsberg
Beer Biere
WE BECAME BUDDY-BUDDY WHILE DISCUSSING MUSIC.
PERHAPS YOU'RE CURIOUS HOW I CAME TO BE SO SUCCESSFUL?
?

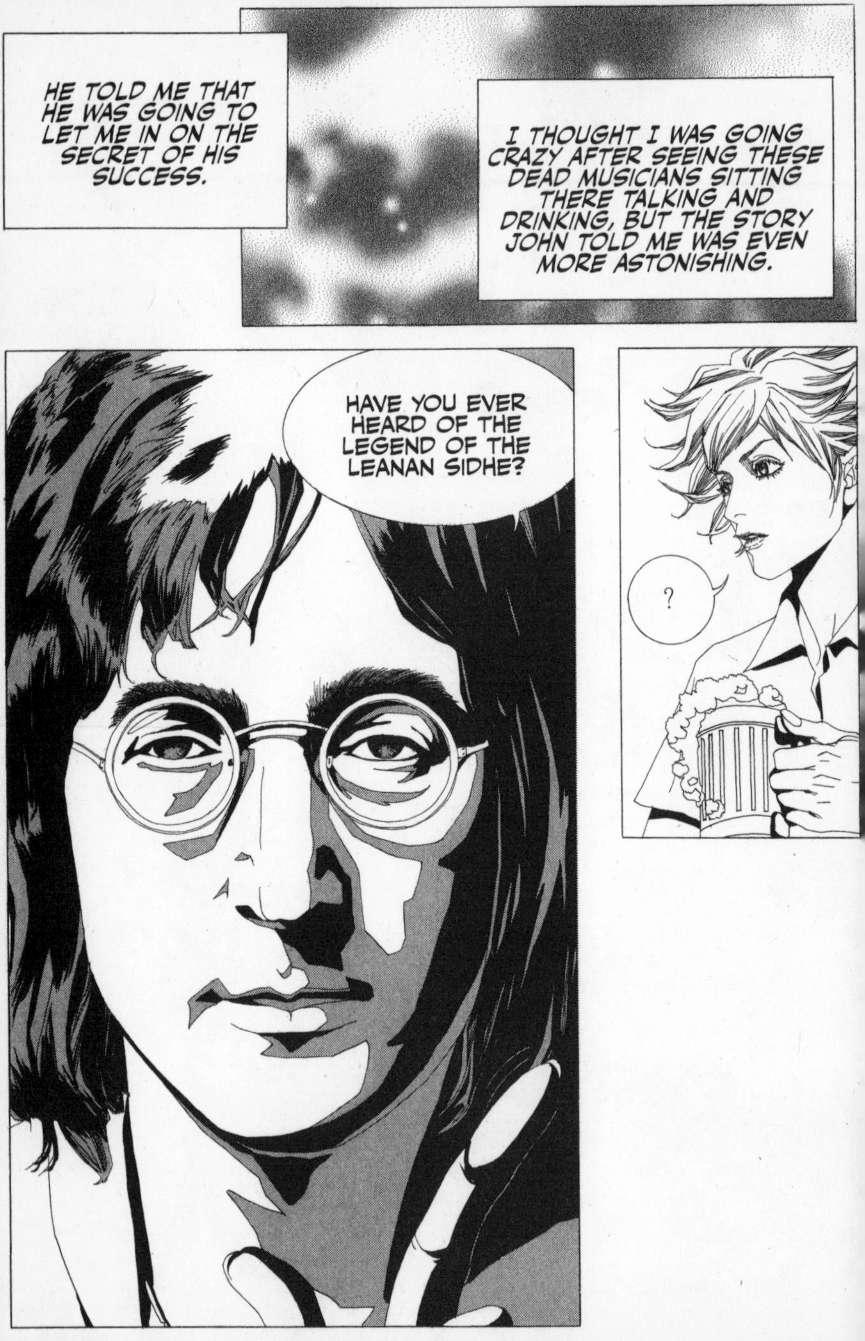
HE TOLD ME THAT HE WAS GOING TO LET ME IN ON THE SECRET OF HIS SUCCESS.
I THOUGHT I WAS GOING CRAZY AFTER SEEING THESE DEAD MUSICIANS SITTING THERE TALKING AND DRINKING, BUT THE STORY JOHN TOLD ME WAS EVEN MORE ASTONISHING.
HAVE YOU EVER HEARD OF THE LEGEND OF THE LEANAN SIDHE?
?

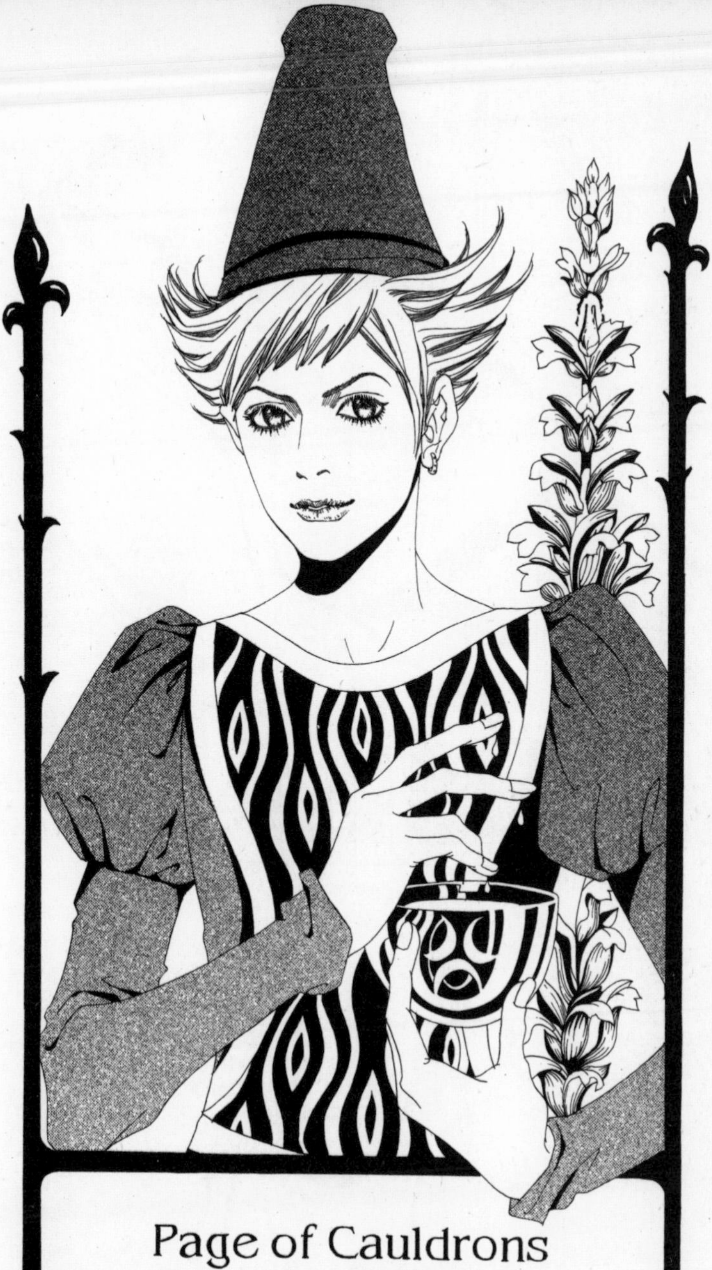
Page of Cauldrons

ILLUSTRATION FROM TAROT OF OLD PATH

Page of Cauldrons: Right-side up, this card represents someone with an artistic gift; someone prone to contemplation. Upside down, it represents a girl or a boy with light brown hair; a youth with extreme intelligence.

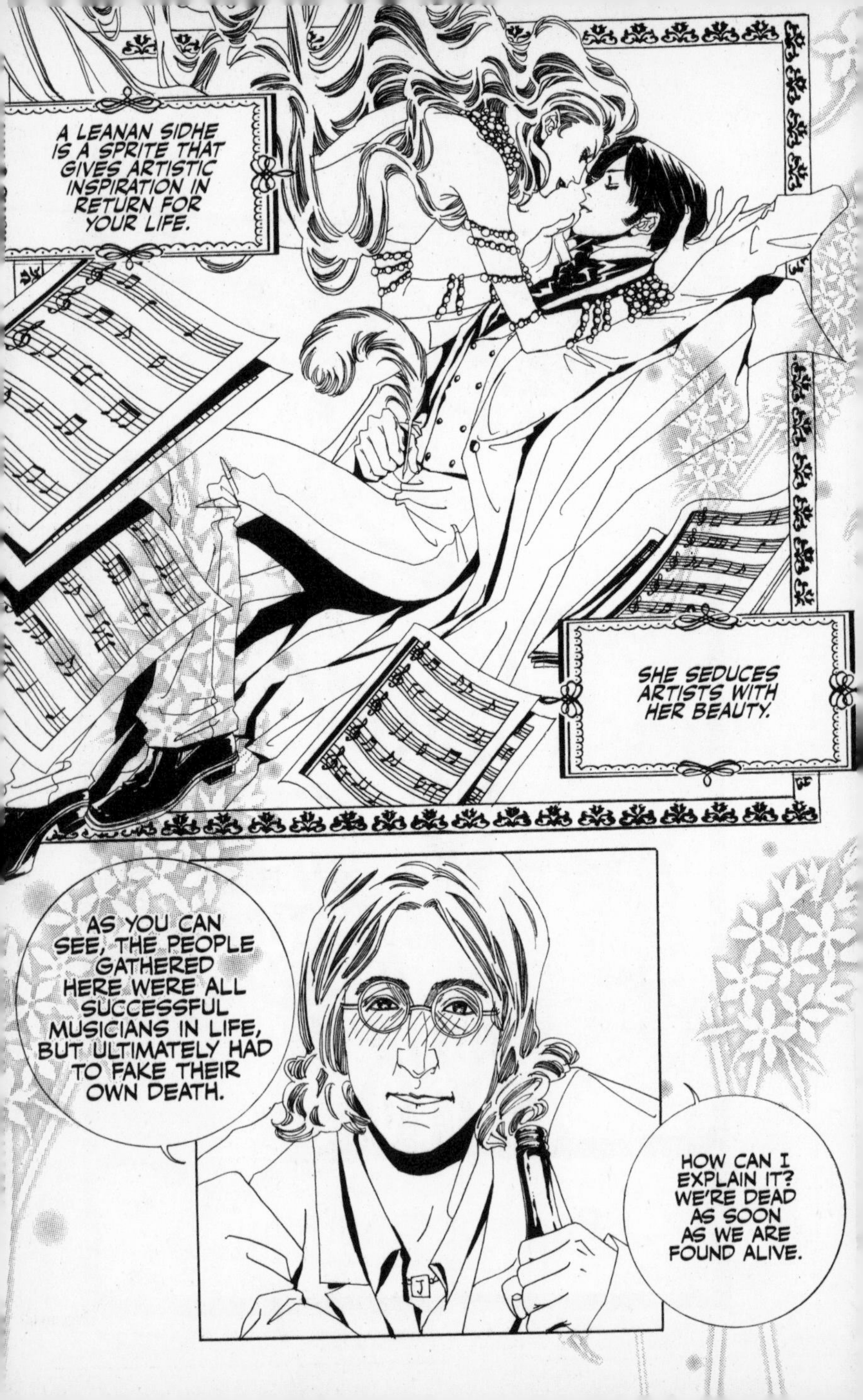
A LEANAN SIDHE IS A SPRITE THAT GIVES ARTISTIC INSPIRATION IN RETURN FOR YOUR LIFE.
SHE SEDUCES ARTISTS WITH HER BEAUTY.
AS YOU CAN SEE, THE PEOPLE GATHERED HERE WERE ALL SUCCESSFUL MUSICIANS IN LIFE, BUT ULTIMATELY HAD TO FAKE THEIR OWN DEATH.
HOW CAN I EXPLAIN IT? WE'RE DEAD AS SOON AS WE ARE FOUND ALIVE.

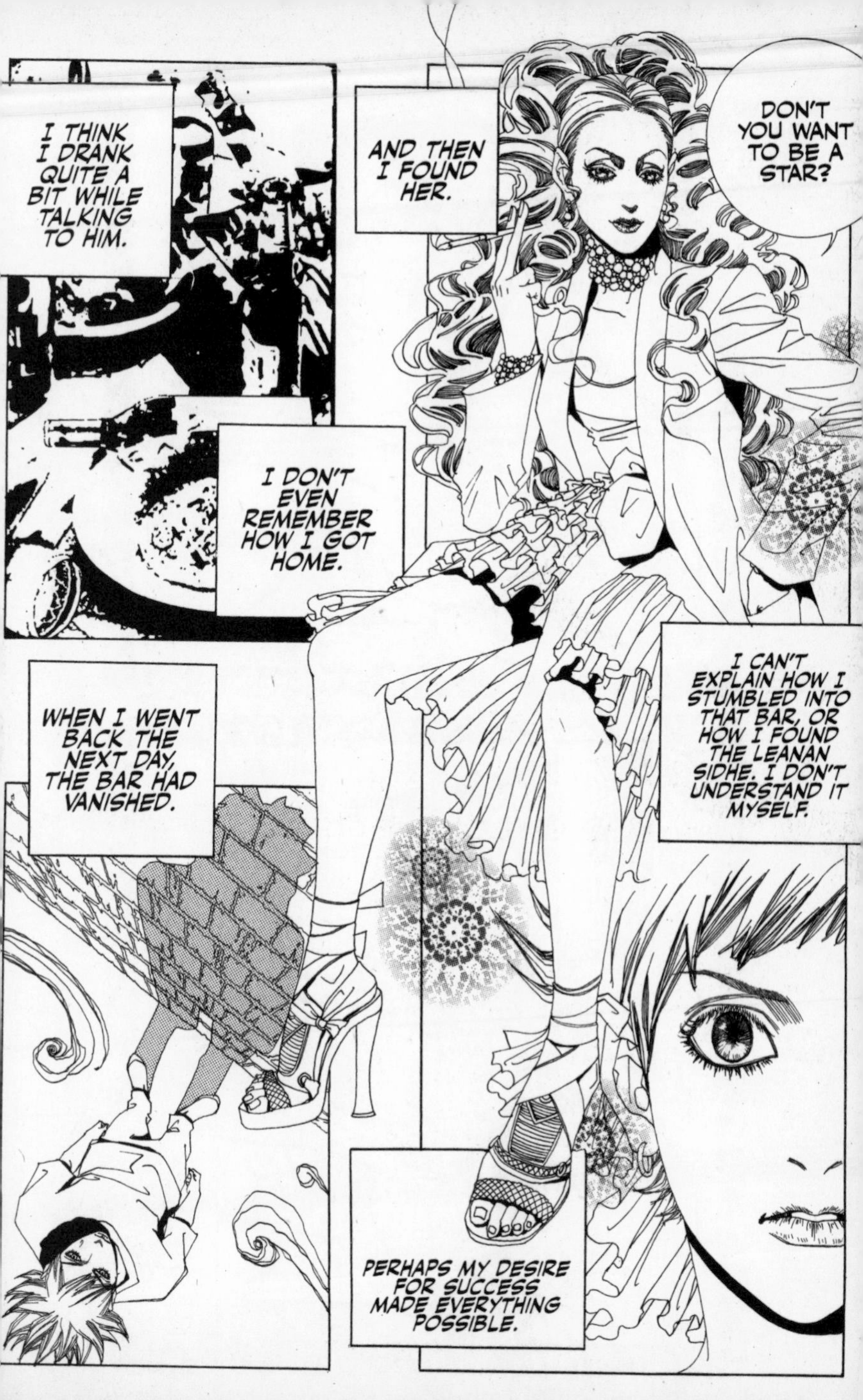
I THINK I DRANK QUITE A BIT WHILE TALKING TO HIM.
I DON'T EVEN REMEMBER HOW I GOT HOME.
WHEN I WENT BACK THE NEXT DAY, THE BAR HAD VANISHED.
AND THEN I FOUND HER.
DON'T YOU WANT TO BE A STAR?
I CAN'T EXPLAIN HOW I STUMBLED INTO THAT BAR, OR HOW I FOUND THE LEANAN SIDHE. I DON'T UNDERSTAND IT MYSELF.
PERHAPS MY DESIRE FOR SUCCESS MADE EVERYTHING POSSIBLE.

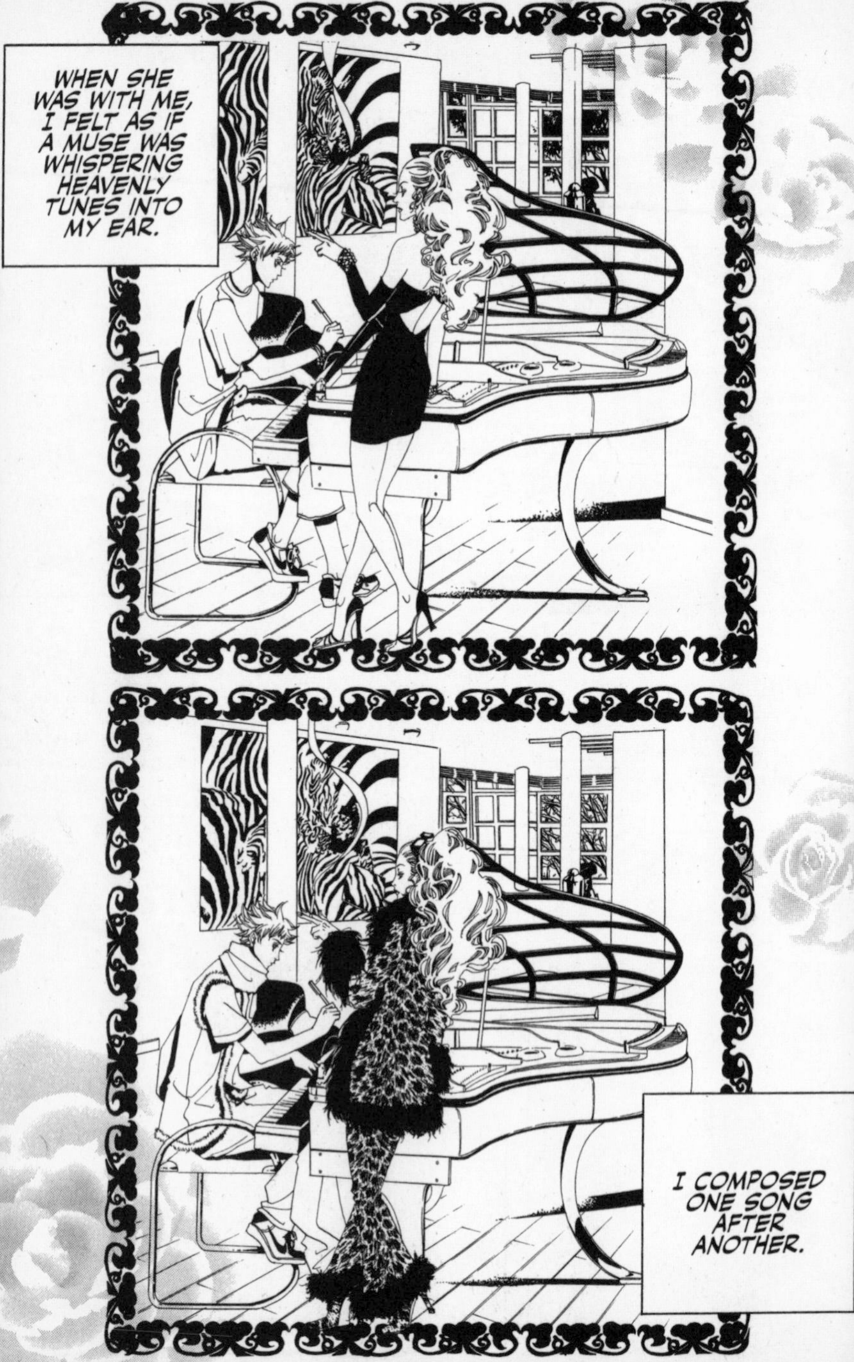
WHEN SHE WAS WITH ME, I FELT AS IF A MUSE WAS WHISPERING HEAVENLY TUNES INTO MY EAR.
I COMPOSED ONE SONG AFTER ANOTHER.

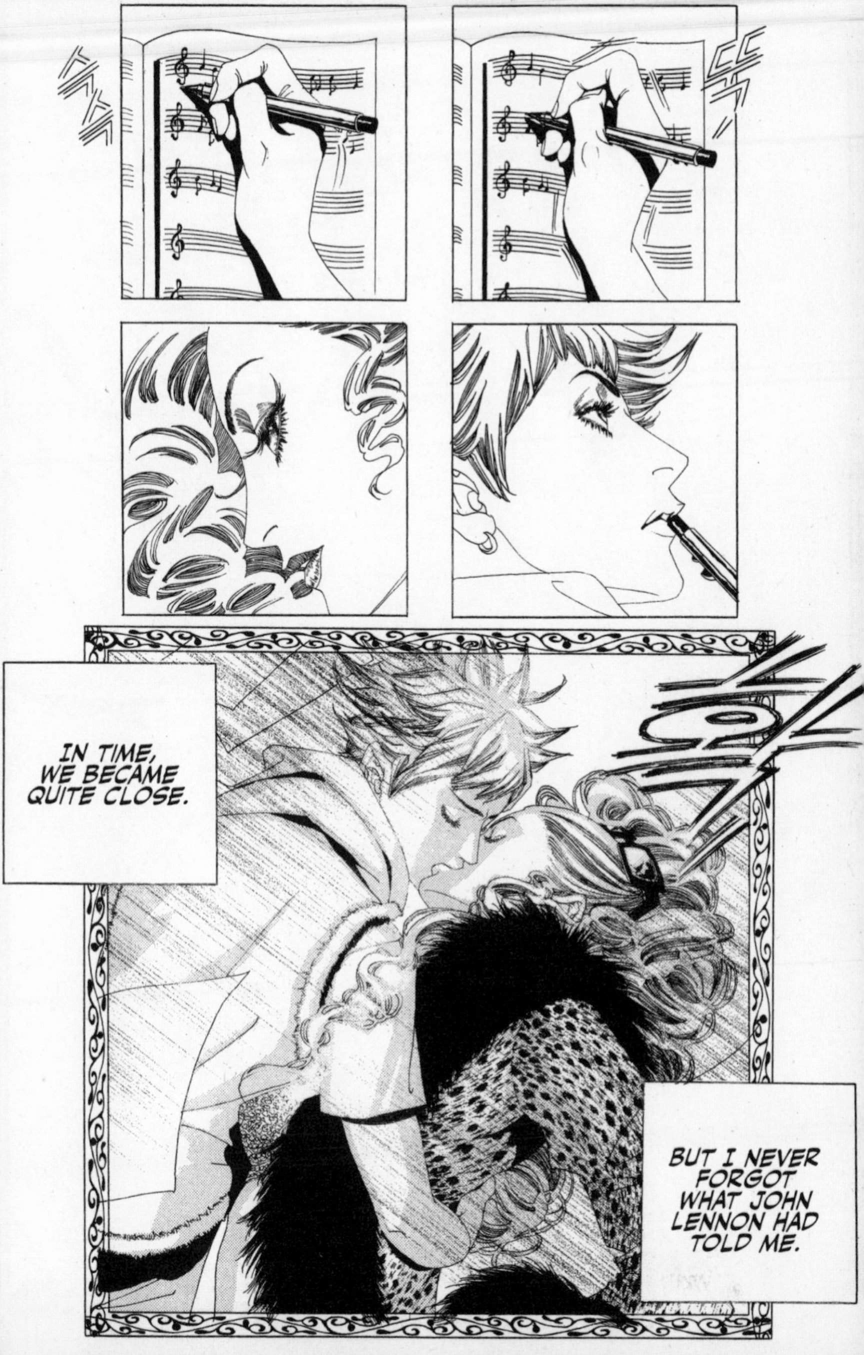
IN TIME, WE BECAME QUITE CLOSE.
BUT I NEVER FORGOT WHAT JOHN LENNON HAD TOLD ME.

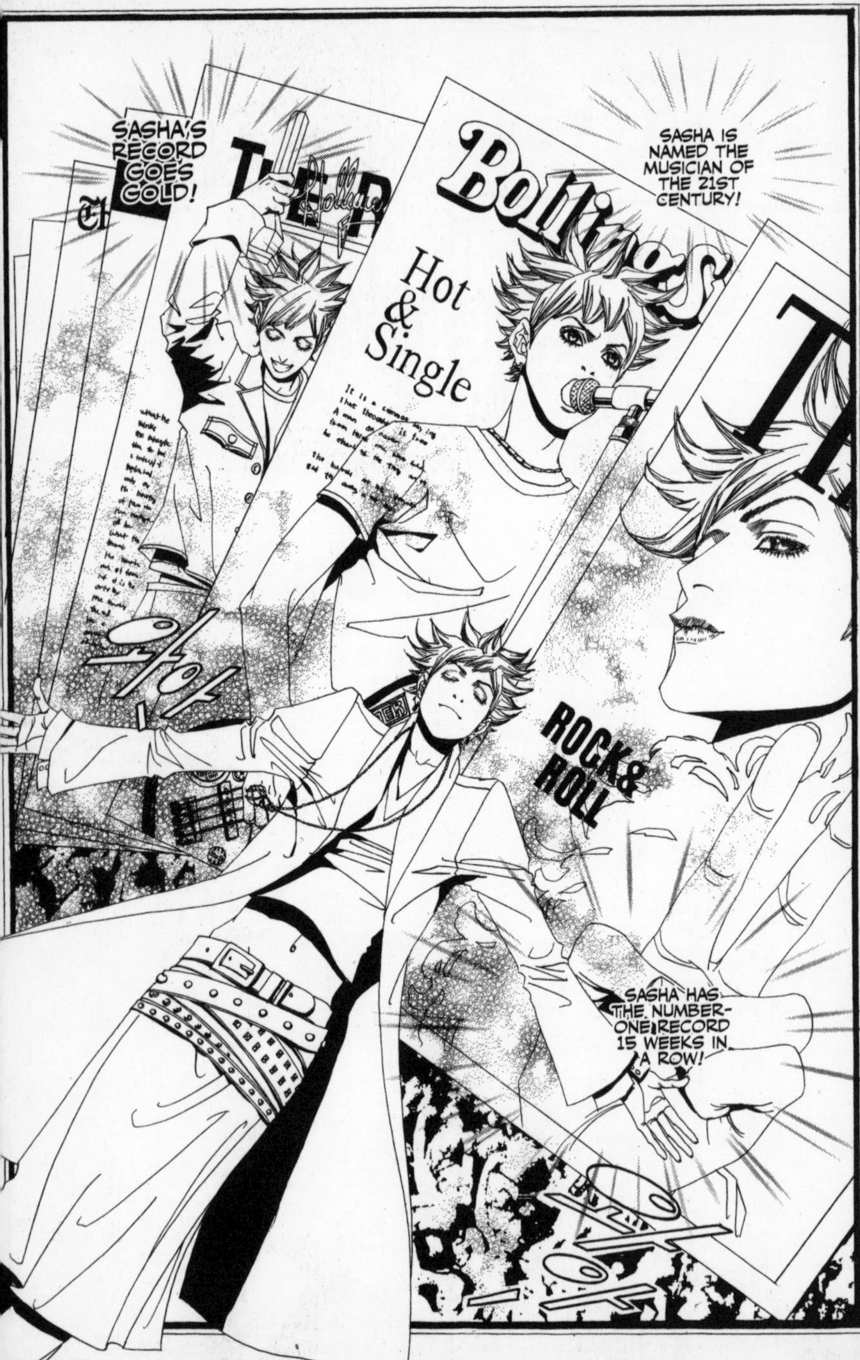
SASHA'S RECORD GOES GOLD!
SASHA IS NAMED THE MUSICIAN OF THE 21ST CENTURY!
Hot & Single
ROCK& ROLL
SASHA HAS THE NUMBER-ONE RECORD 15 WEEKS IN A ROW!

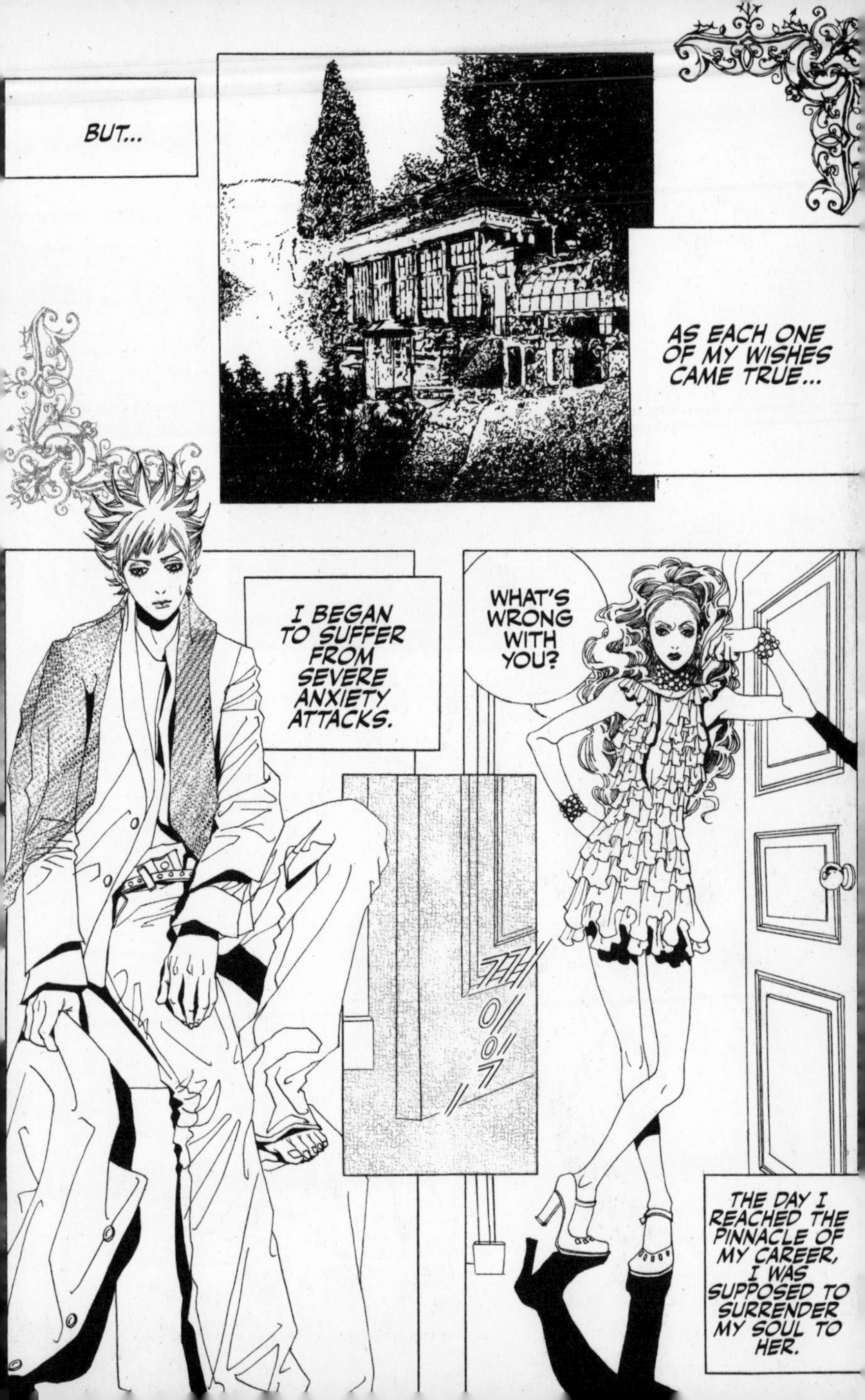
BUT...
AS EACH ONE OF MY WISHES CAME TRUE...
I BEGAN TO SUFFER FROM SEVERE ANXIETY ATTACKS.
WHAT'S WRONG WITH YOU?
THE DAY I REACHED THE PINNACLE OF MY CAREER, I WAS SUPPOSED TO SURRENDER MY SOUL TO HER.

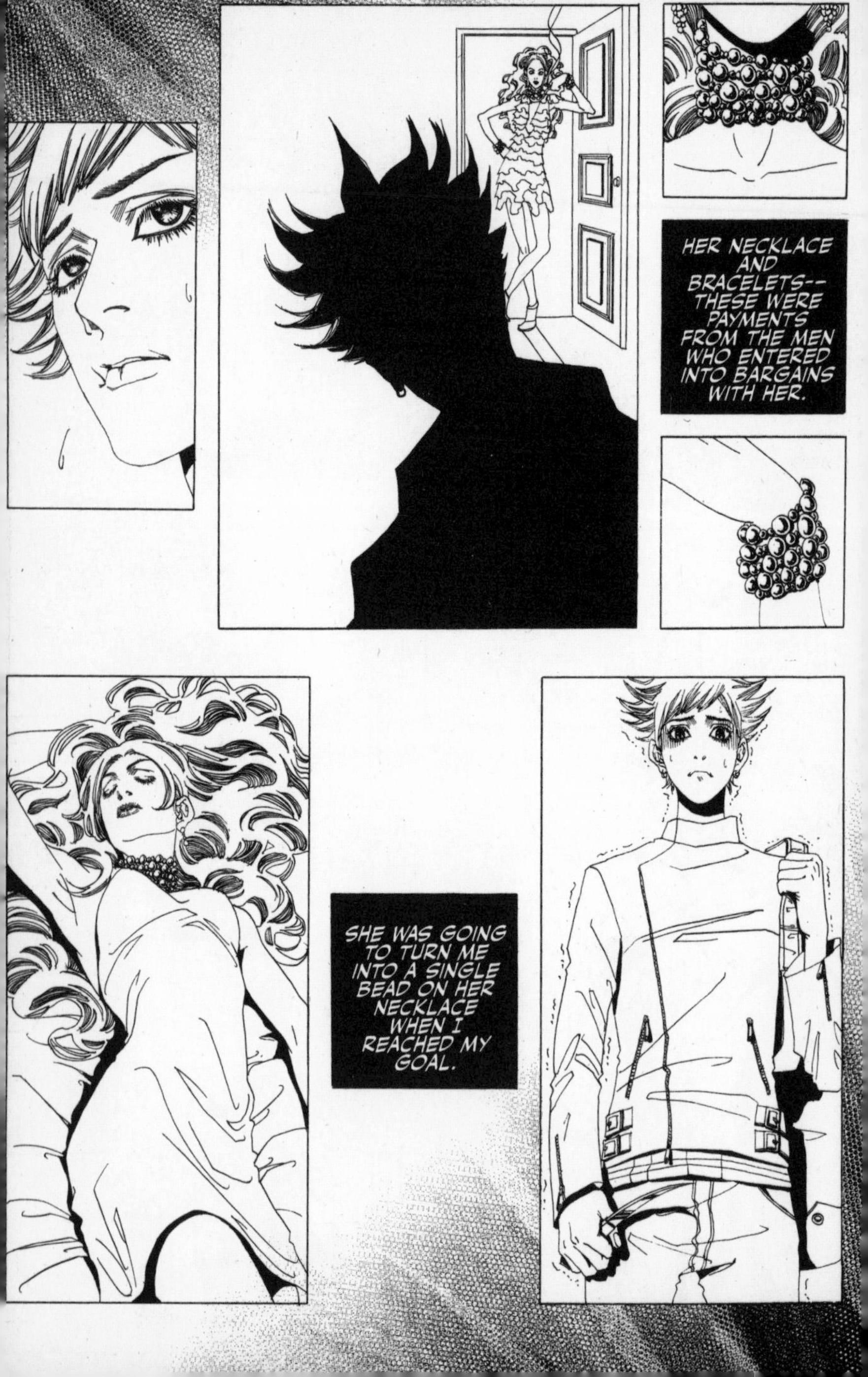
HER NECKLACE AND BRACELETS-- THESE WERE PAYMENTS FROM THE MEN WHO ENTERED INTO BARGAINS WITH HER.
SHE WAS GOING TO TURN ME INTO A SINGLE BEAD ON HER NECKLACE WHEN I REACHED MY GOAL.

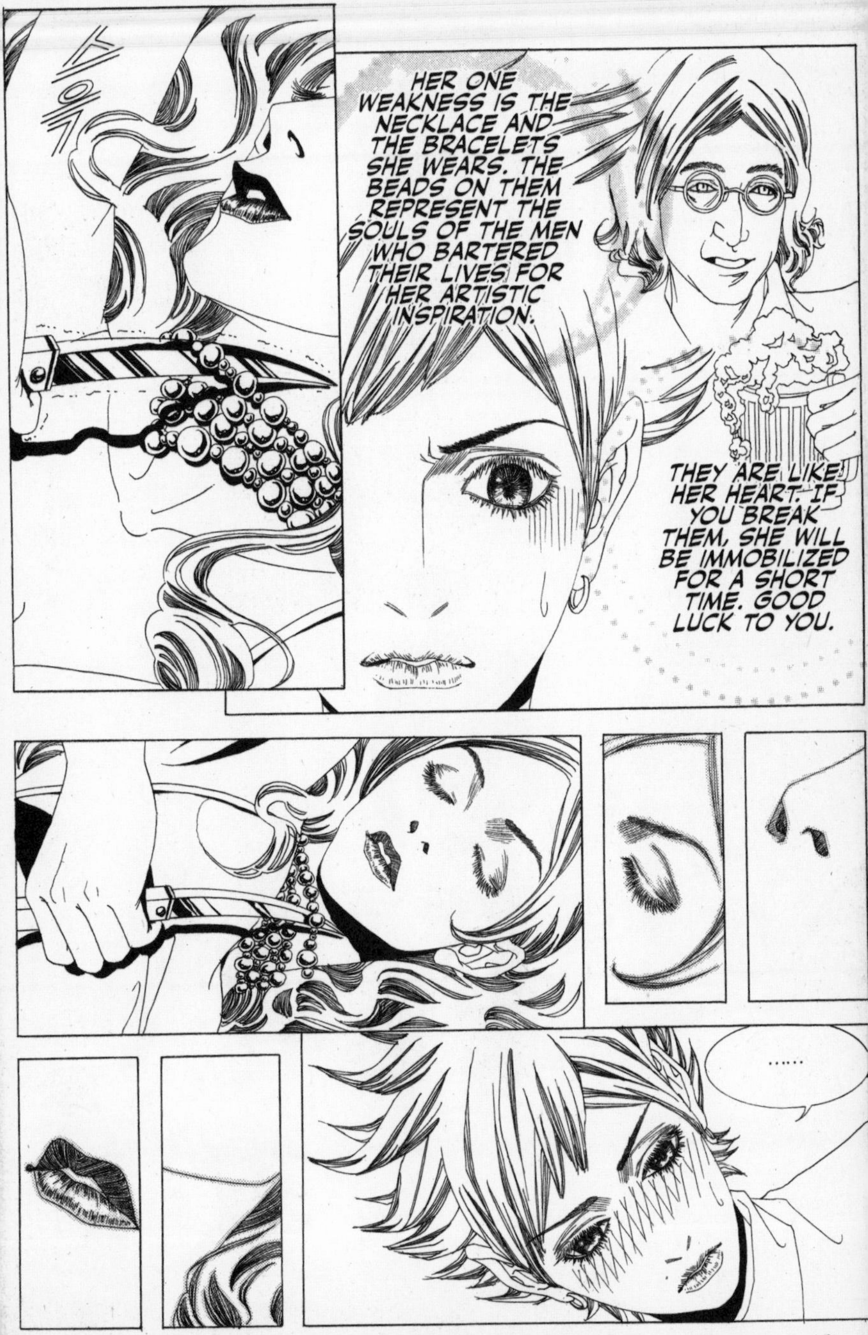
HER ONE WEAKNESS IS THE NECKLACE AND THE BRACELETS SHE WEARS. THE BEADS ON THEM REPRESENT THE SOULS OF THE MEN WHO BARTERED THEIR LIVES FOR HER ARTISTIC INSPIRATION.
THEY ARE LIKE HER HEART. IF YOU BREAK THEM, SHE WILL BE IMMOBILIZED FOR A SHORT TIME. GOOD LUCK TO YOU.
......

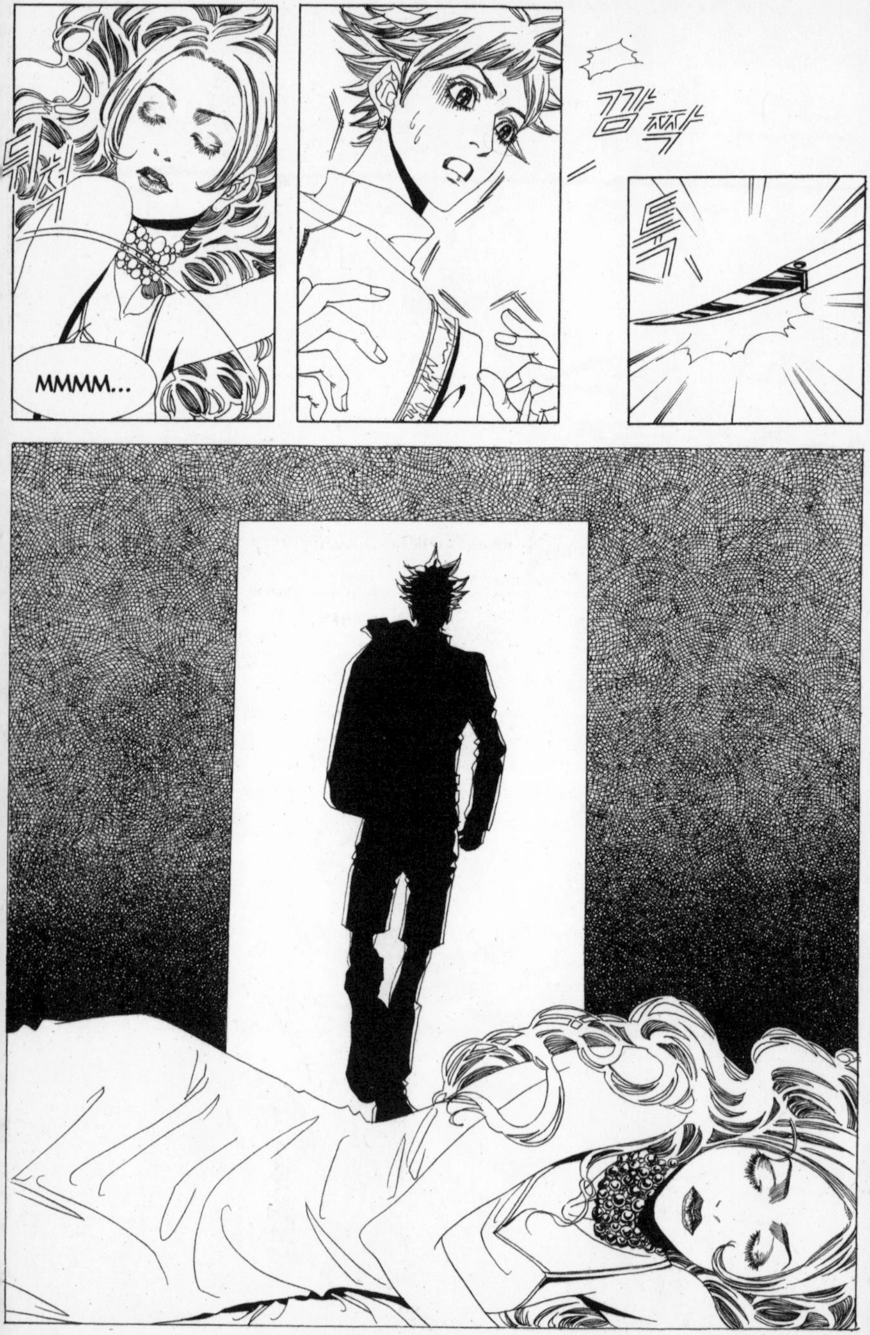
뒤척
MMMM...
깜짝
툭

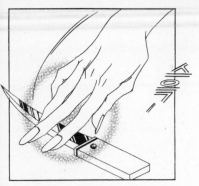

......

WHERE THE HELL ARE YOU GOING SO EARLY IN THE MORNING?

YOU KNOW VERY WELL THAT YOU CAN'T CANCEL THE LONDON CONCERT! I DON'T EVEN NEED TO REMIND YOU THE GRAMMY AWARDS ARE COMING UP.

REMEMBER WHAT YOU'VE WORKED SO HARD FOR!

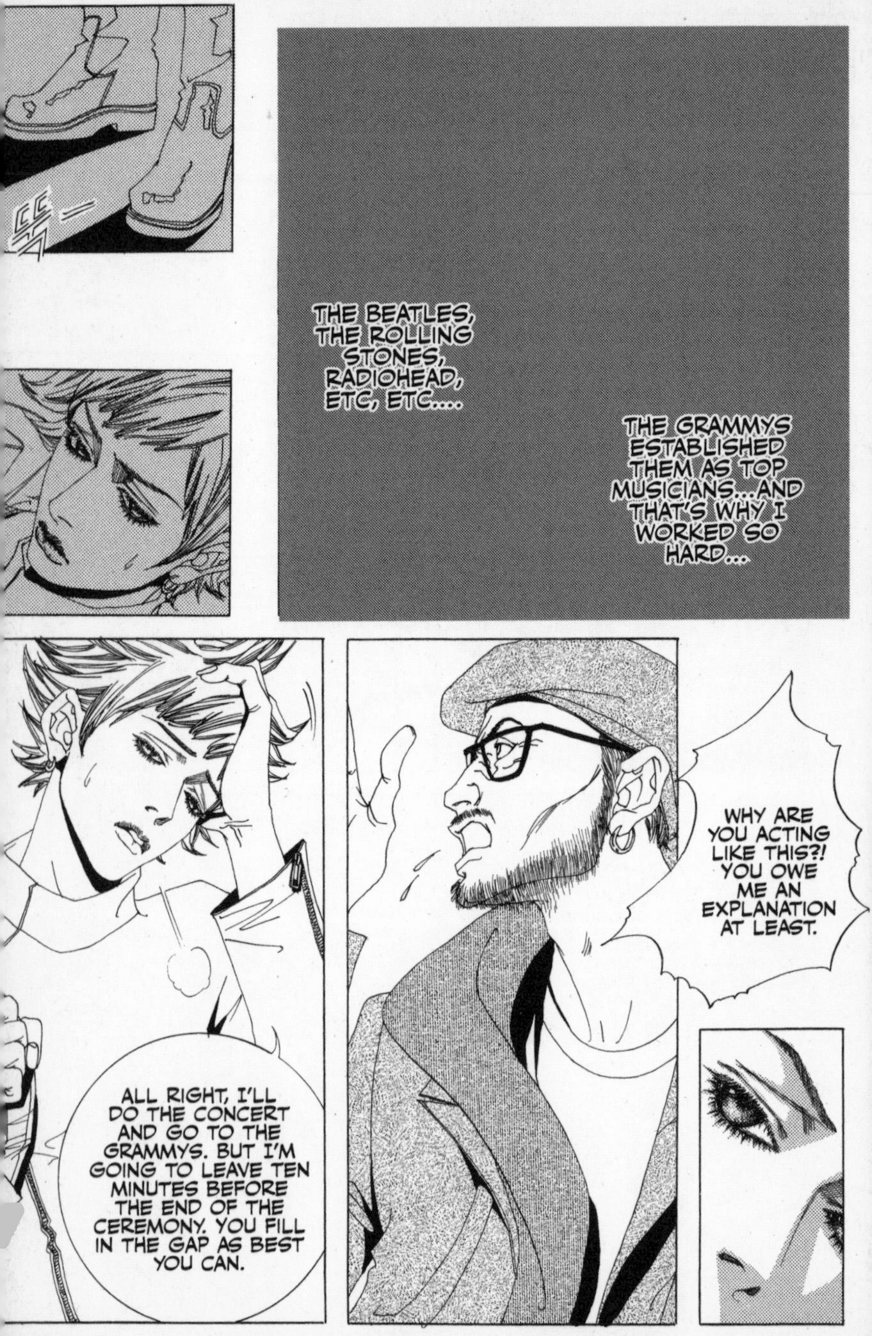
THE BEATLES, THE ROLLING STONES, RADIOHEAD, ETC, ETC....
THE GRAMMYS ESTABLISHED THEM AS TOP MUSICIANS...AND THAT'S WHY I WORKED SO HARD...
ALL RIGHT, I'LL DO THE CONCERT AND GO TO THE GRAMMYS. BUT I'M GOING TO LEAVE TEN MINUTES BEFORE THE END OF THE CEREMONY. YOU FILL IN THE GAP AS BEST YOU CAN.
WHY ARE YOU ACTING LIKE THIS?! YOU OWE ME AN EXPLANATION AT LEAST.

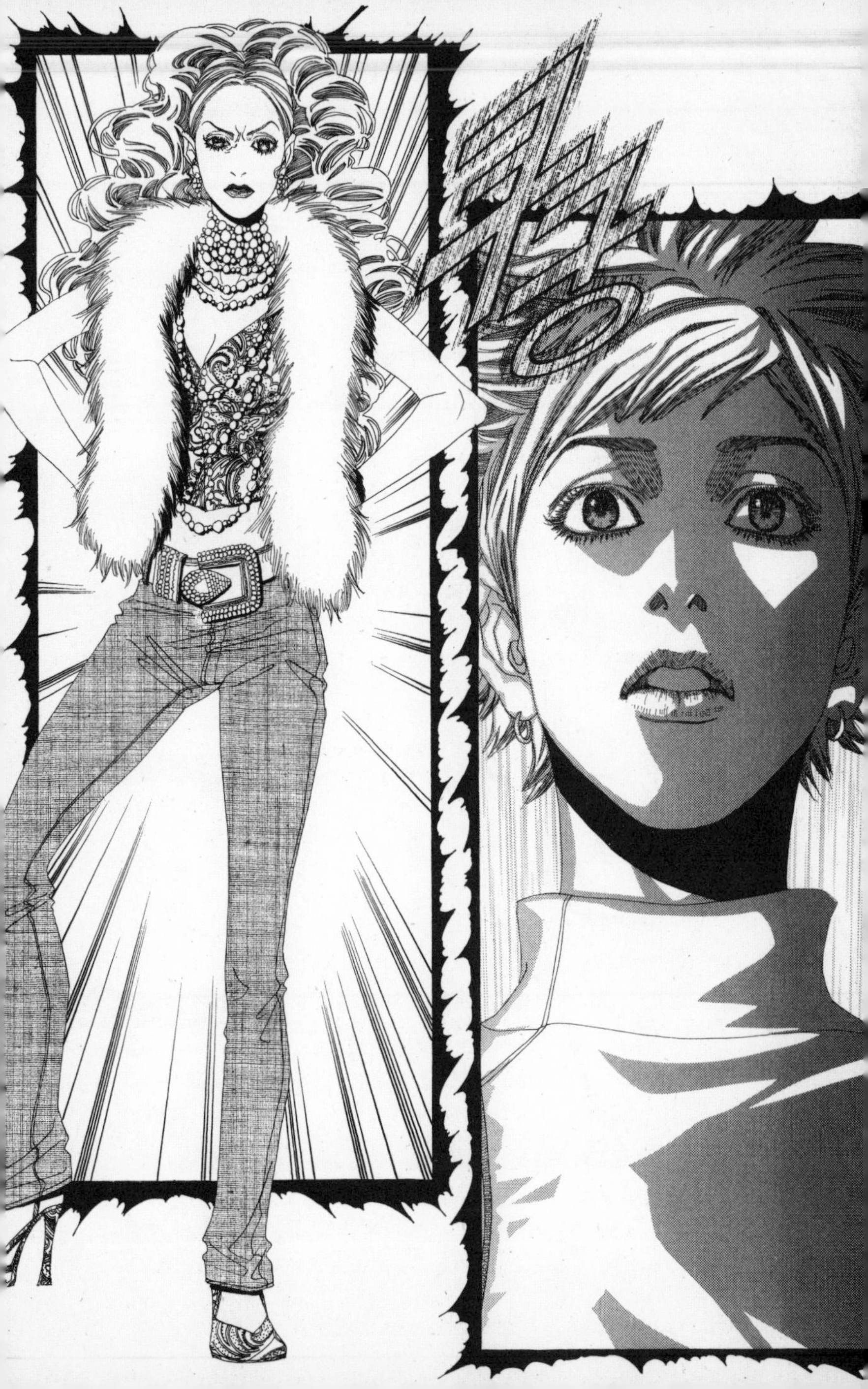

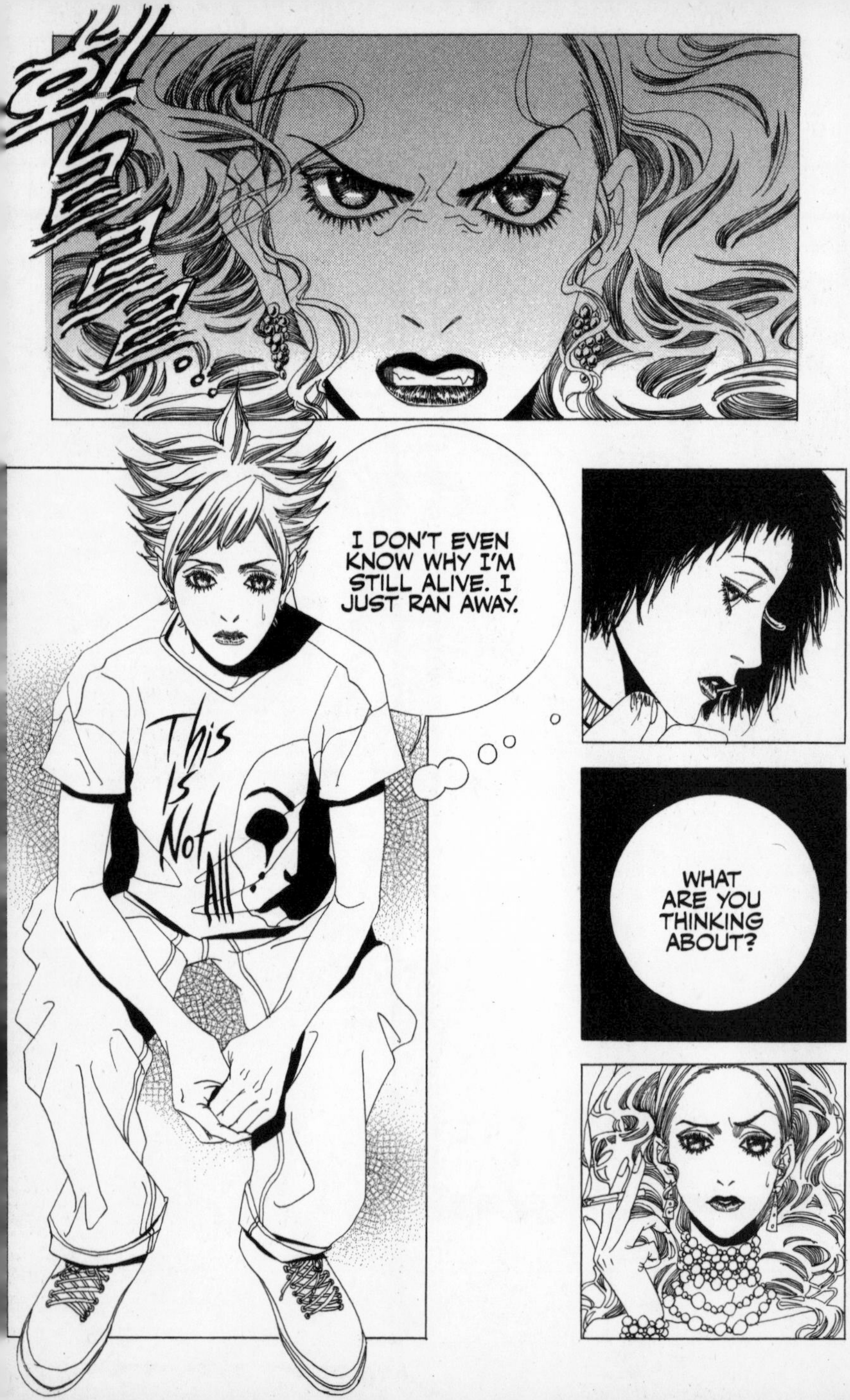
I DON'T EVEN KNOW WHY I'M STILL ALIVE. I JUST RAN AWAY.
This Is Not All
WHAT ARE YOU THINKING ABOUT?

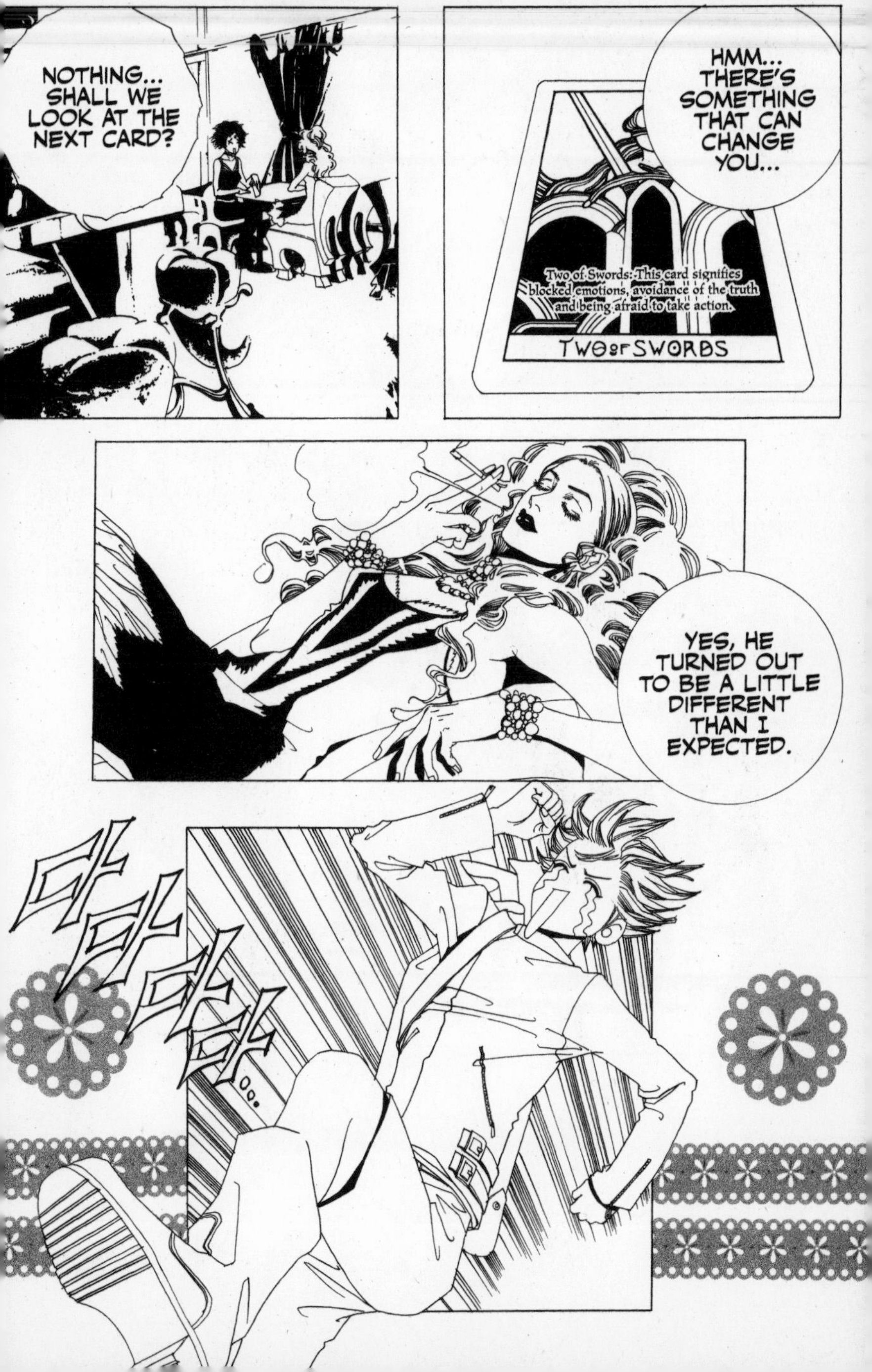
NOTHING... SHALL WE LOOK AT THE NEXT CARD?
HMM... THERE'S SOMETHING THAT CAN CHANGE YOU...
Two of Swords: This card signifies blocked emotions, avoidance of the truth and being afraid to take action.
TWO OF SWORDS
YES, HE TURNED OUT TO BE A LITTLE DIFFERENT THAN I EXPECTED.

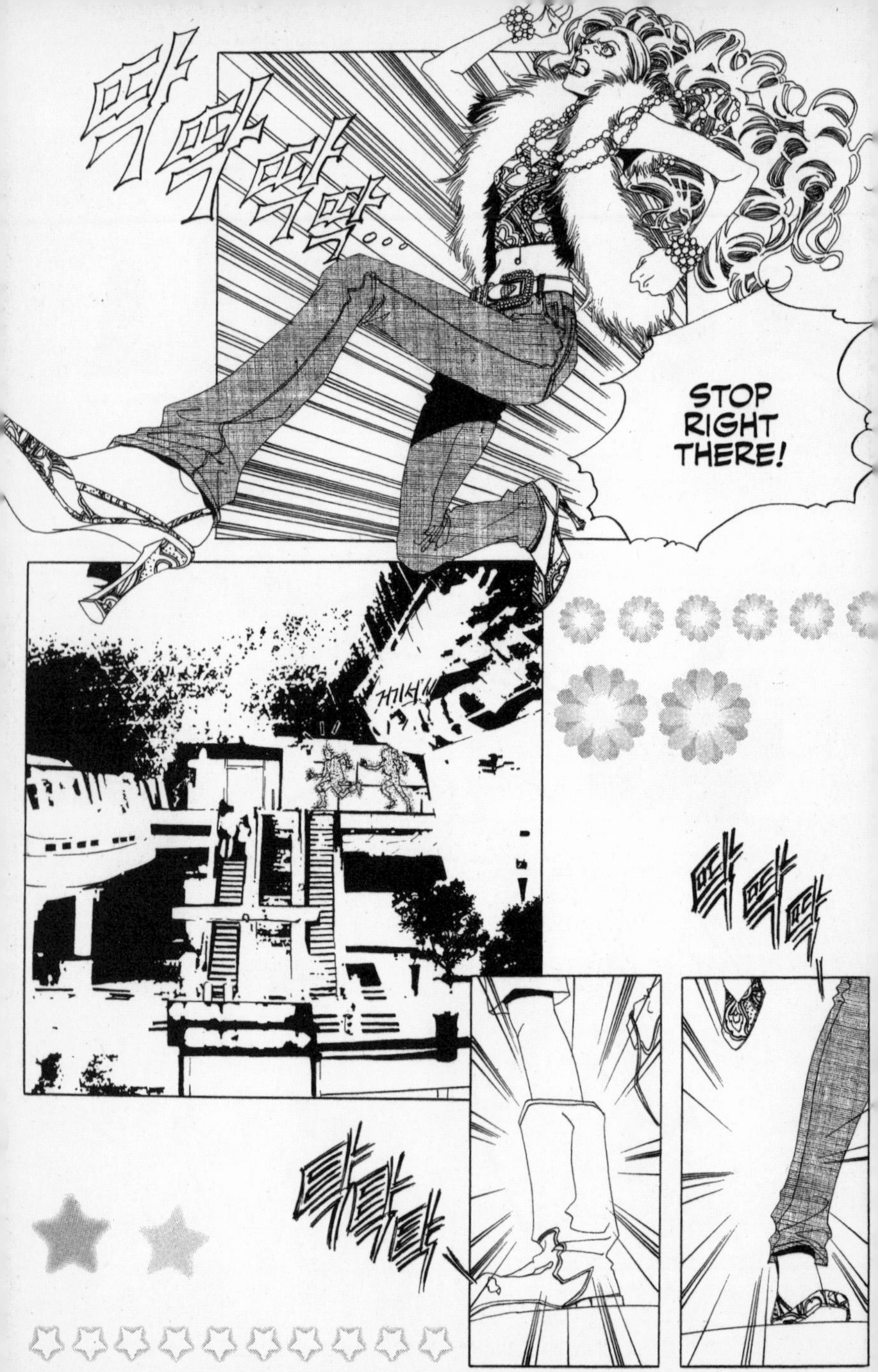
딱딱딱딱...
STOP RIGHT THERE!
거기서!!
딱딱딱
탁탁탁

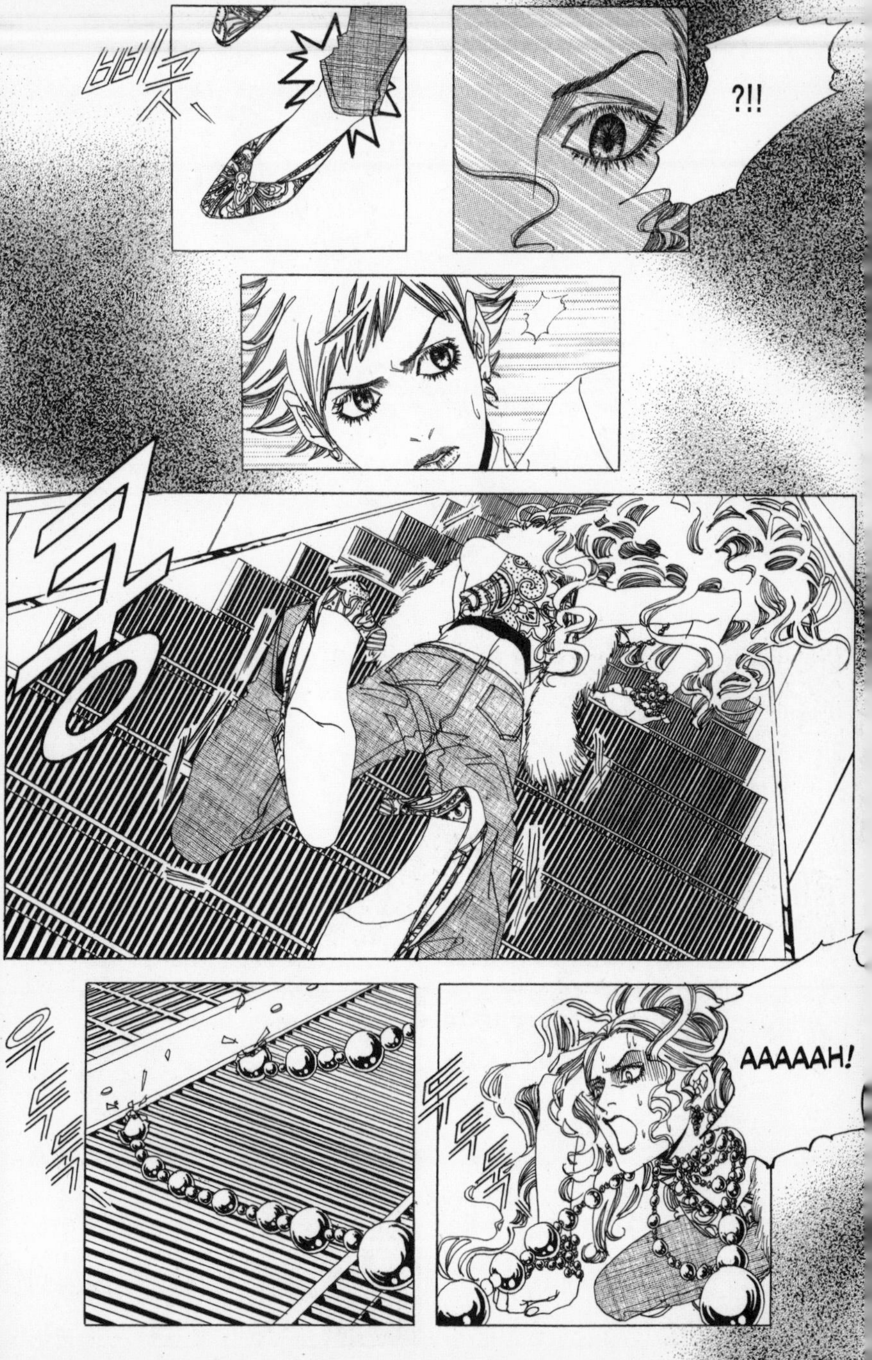
?!!
AAAAAH!

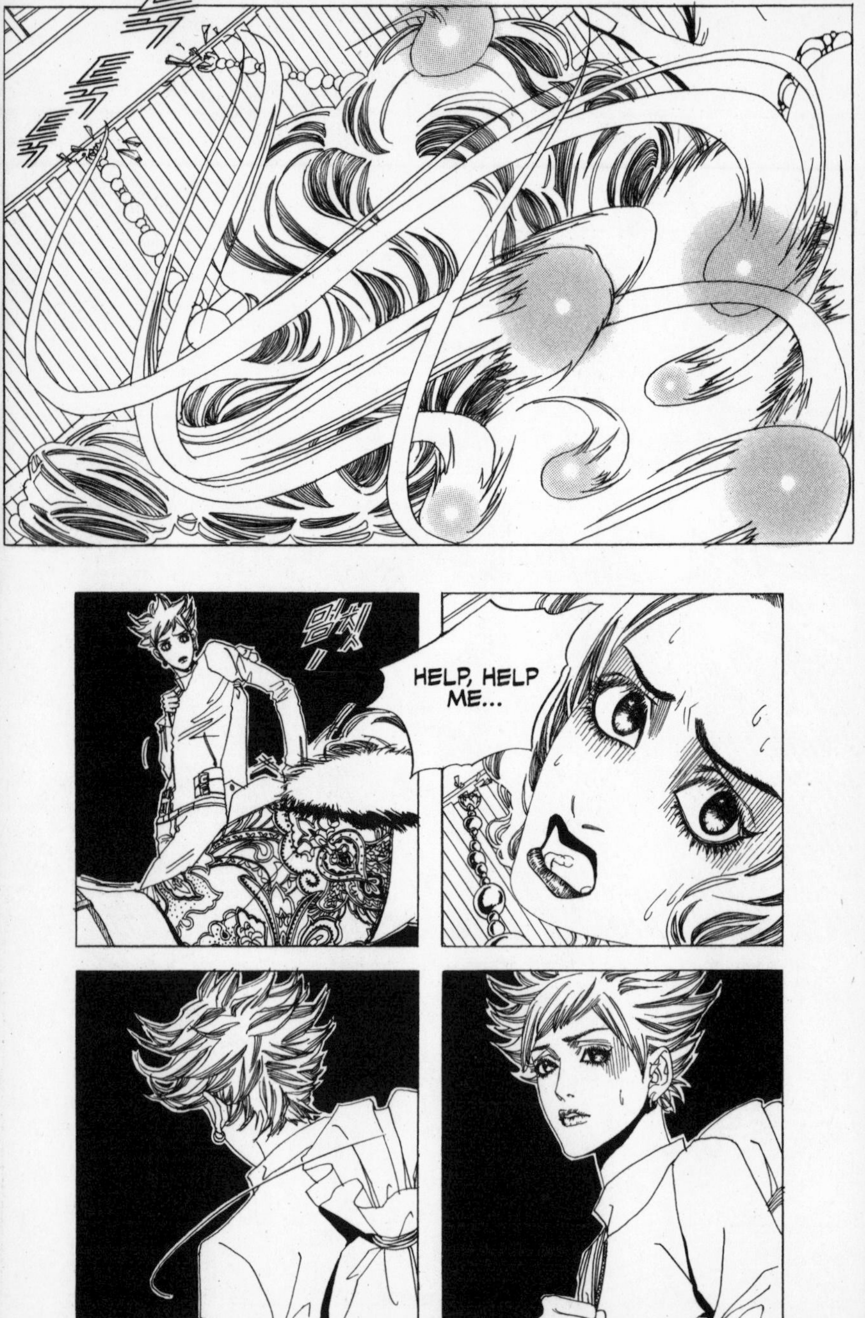
멈칫
HELP, HELP ME...

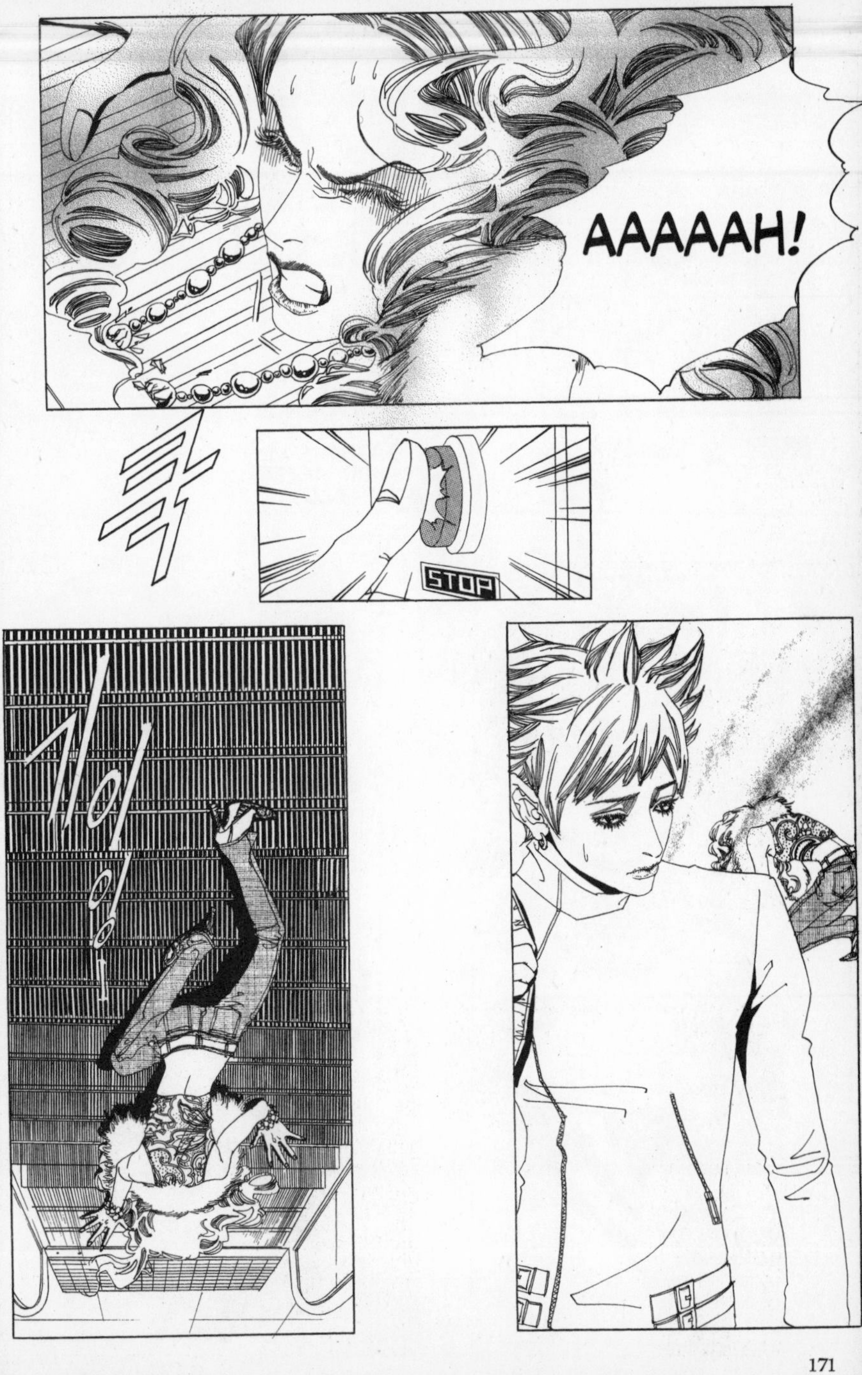
AAAAAH!
쿡
STOP
기이이이

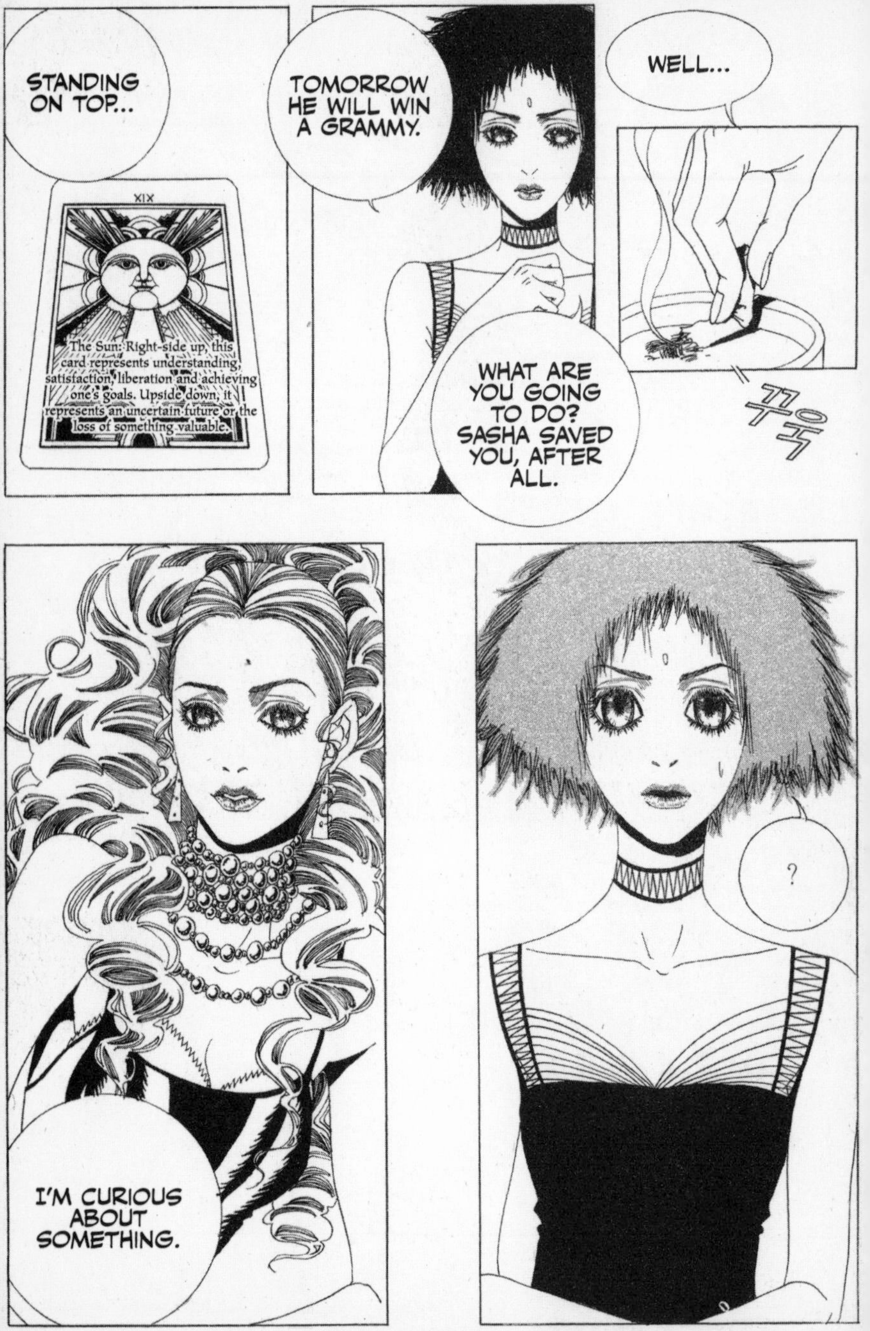

STANDING ON TOP...
XIX
The Sun: Right-side up, this card represents understanding, satisfaction, liberation and achieving one's goals. Upside down, it represents an uncertain future or the loss of something valuable.
TOMORROW HE WILL WIN A GRAMMY.
WHAT ARE YOU GOING TO DO? SASHA SAVED YOU, AFTER ALL.
WELL...
꾸욱
I'M CURIOUS ABOUT SOMETHING.
?

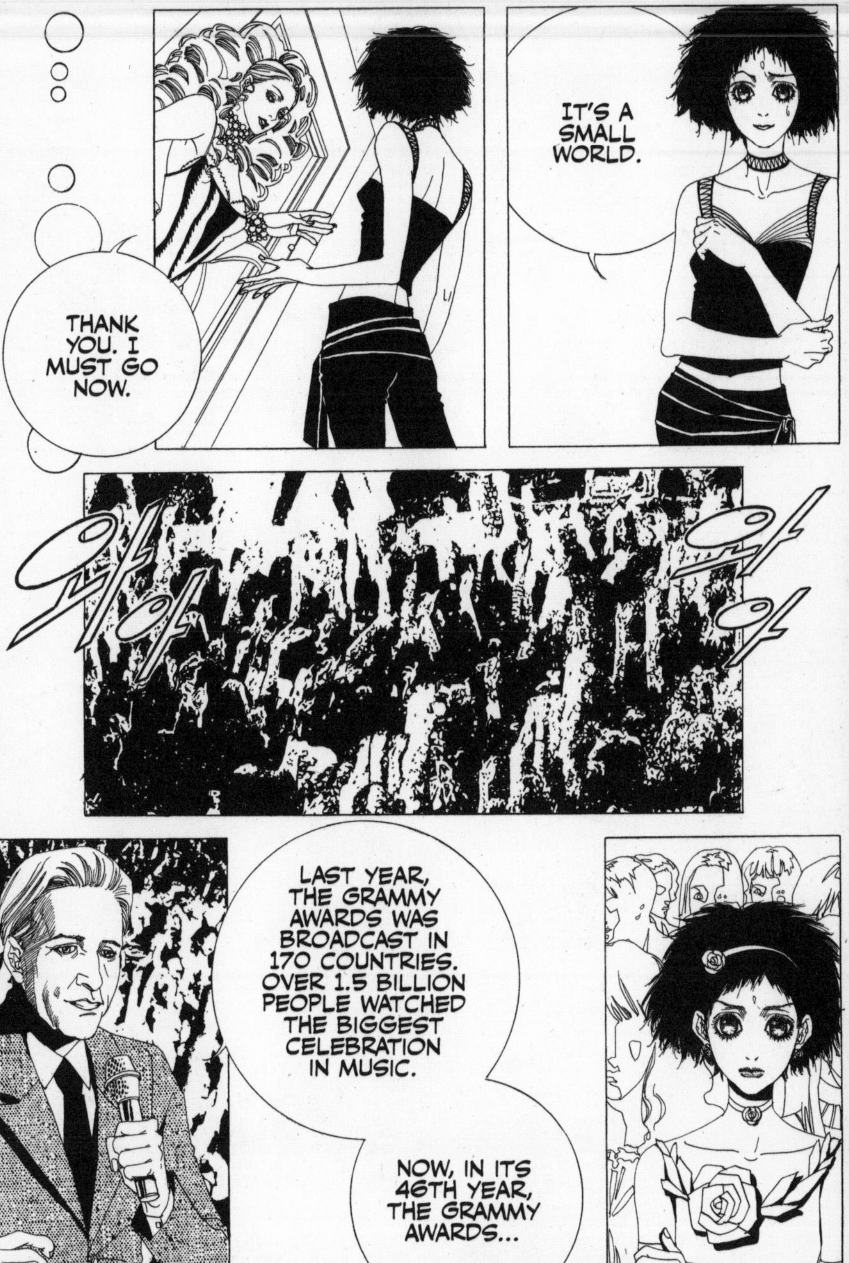
THANK YOU. I MUST GO NOW.
IT'S A SMALL WORLD.
LAST YEAR, THE GRAMMY AWARDS WAS BROADCAST IN 170 COUNTRIES. OVER 1.5 BILLION PEOPLE WATCHED THE BIGGEST CELEBRATION IN MUSIC.
NOW, IN ITS 46TH YEAR, THE GRAMMY AWARDS...

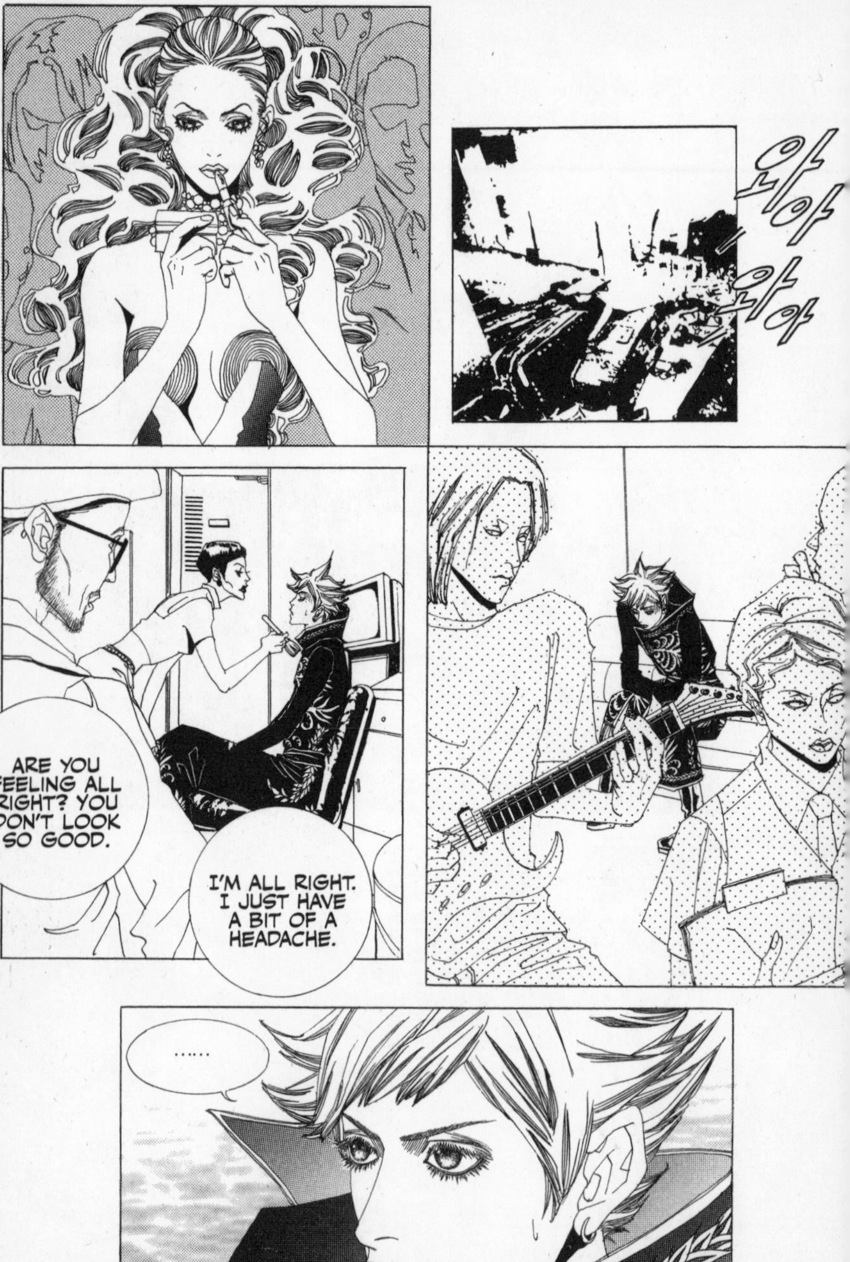
와아 와아
ARE YOU FEELING ALL RIGHT? YOU DON'T LOOK SO GOOD.
I'M ALL RIGHT. I JUST HAVE A BIT OF A HEADACHE.
......

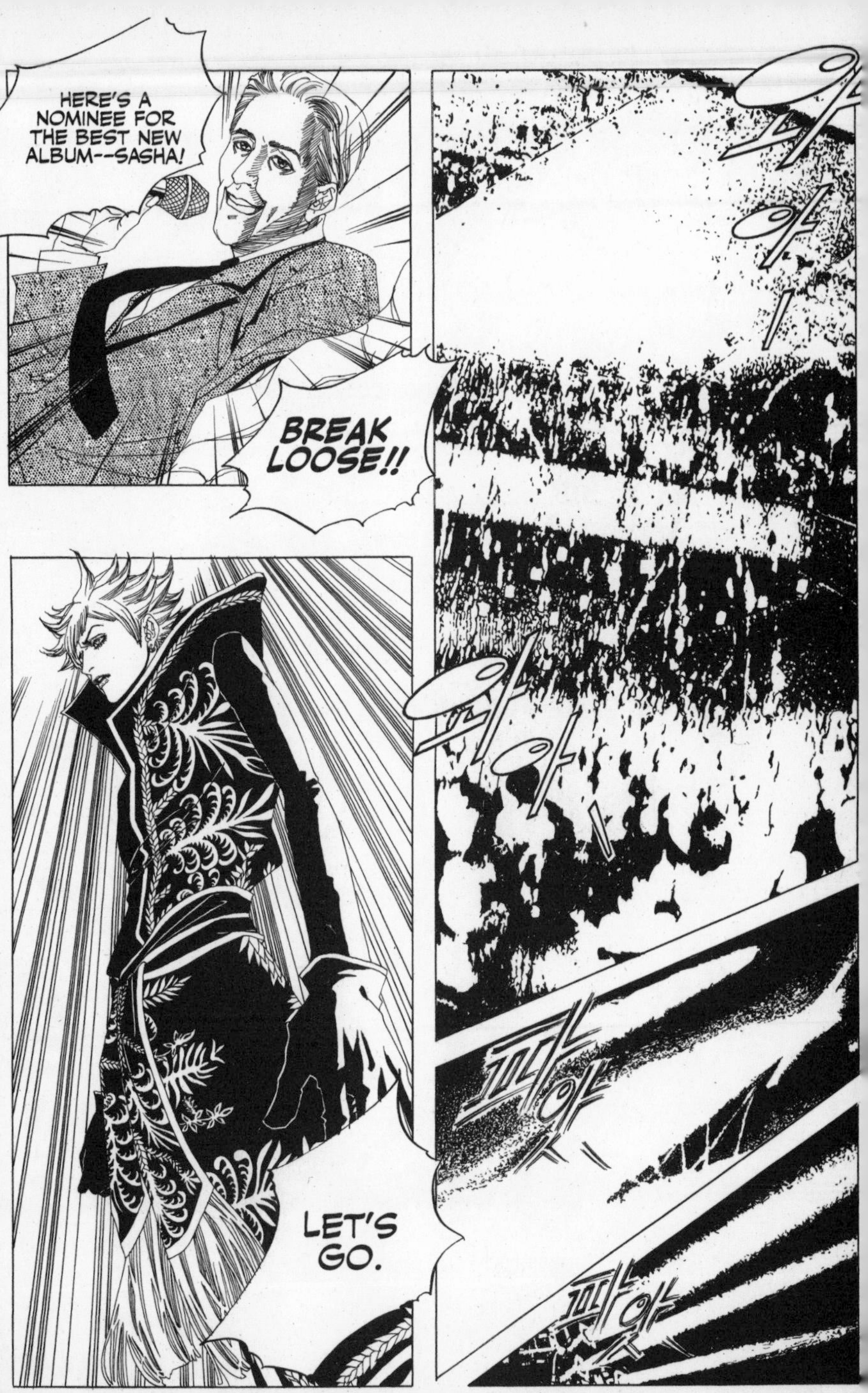
HERE'S A NOMINEE FOR THE BEST NEW ALBUM--SASHA!
BREAK LOOSE!!
LET'S GO.

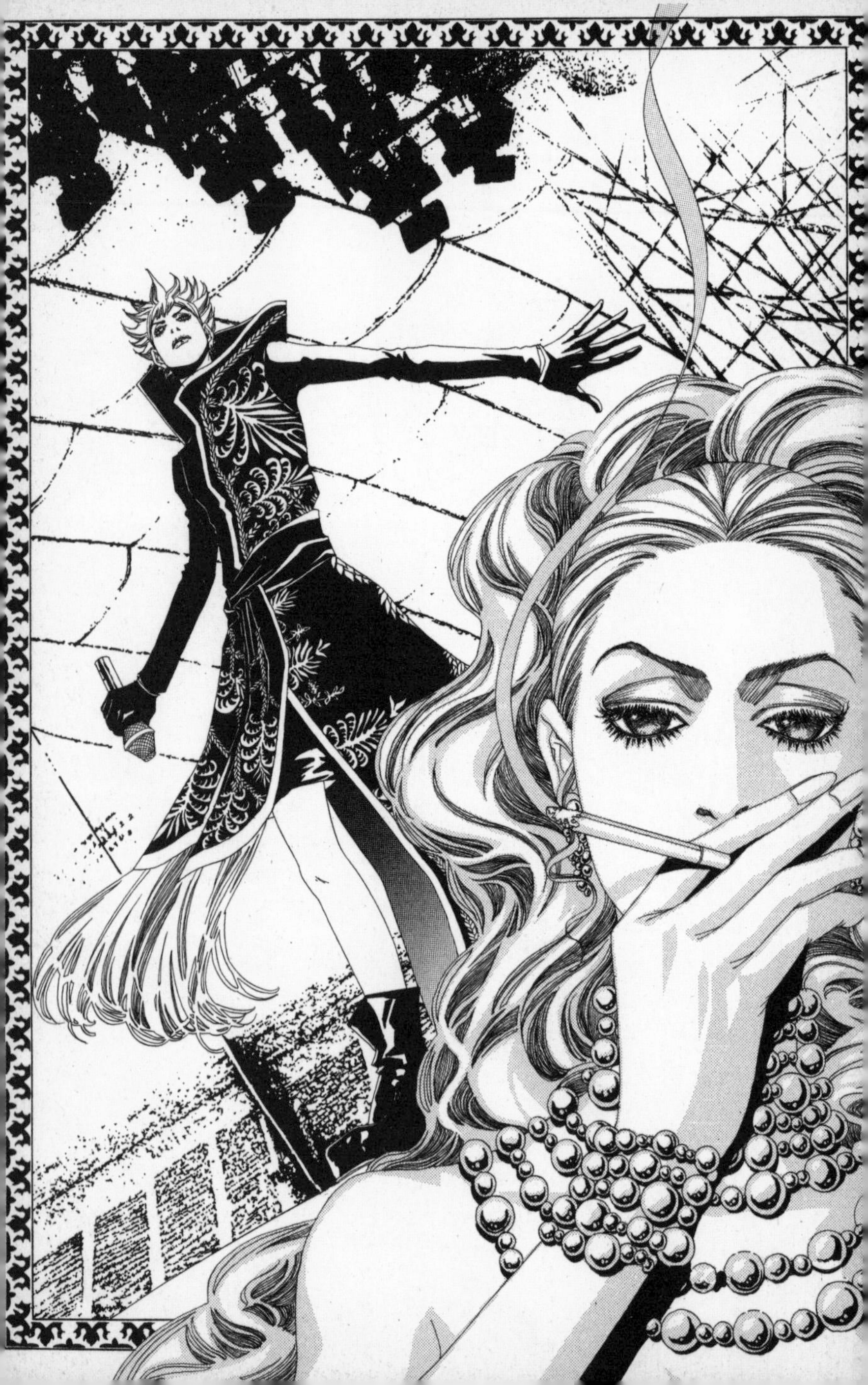

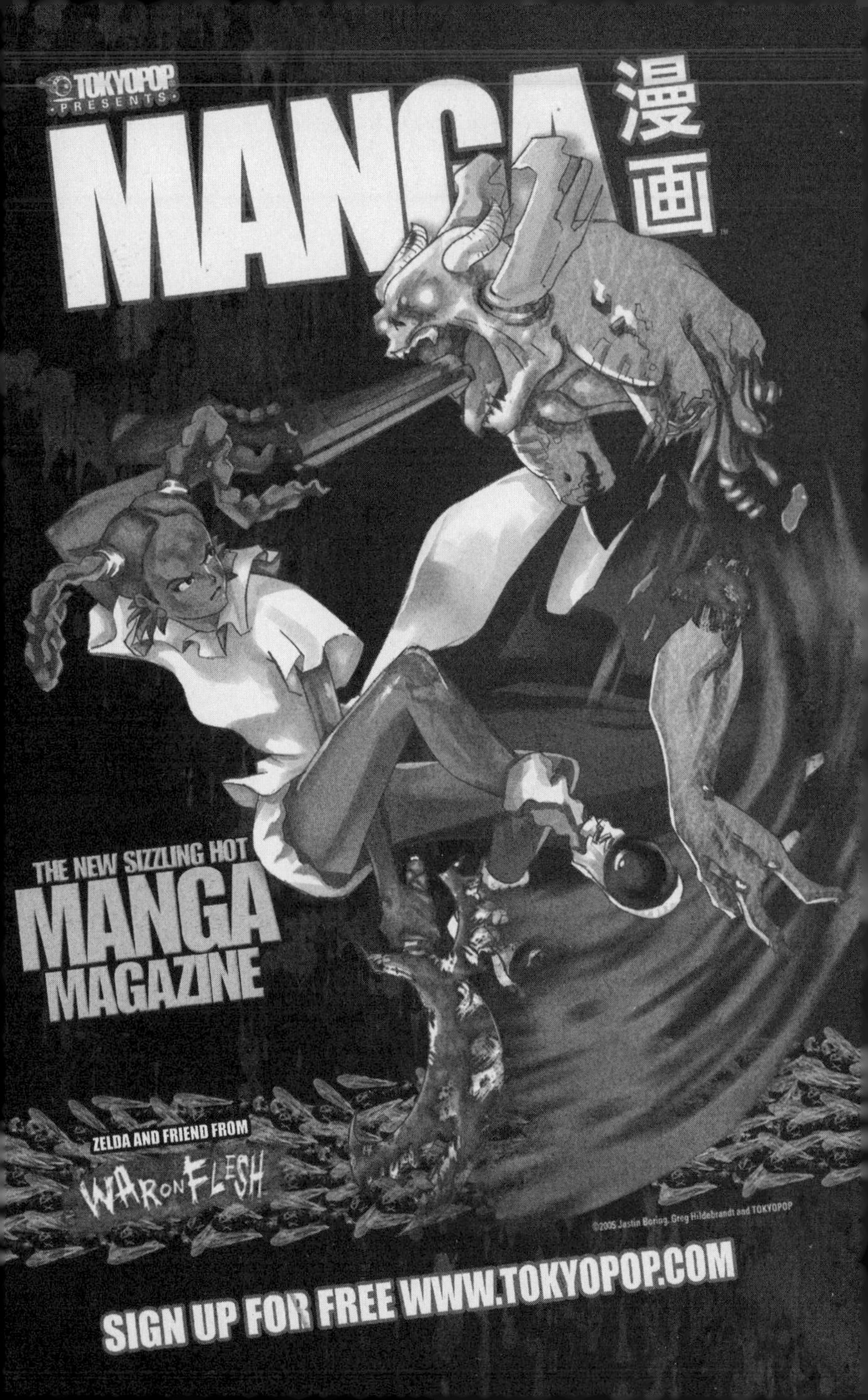
TOKYOPOP
PRESENTS
MANGA 漫画
THE NEW SIZZLING HOT
MANGA
MAGAZINE
ZELDA AND FRIEND FROM
WAR ON FLESH
©2005 Justin Boring, Greg Hildebrandt and TOKYOPOP
SIGN UP FOR FREE WWW.TOKYOPOP.COM

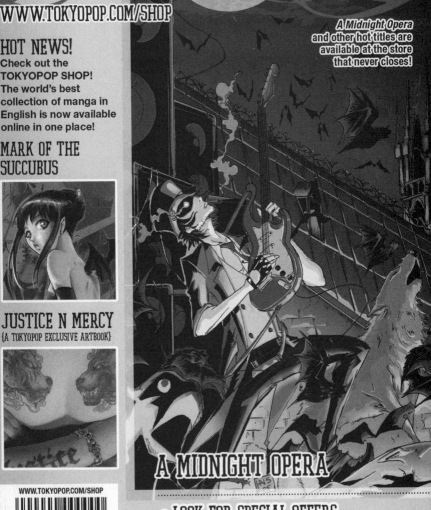

THE DREAMING

BY QUEENIE CHAN

T
TEEN
AGE 13+

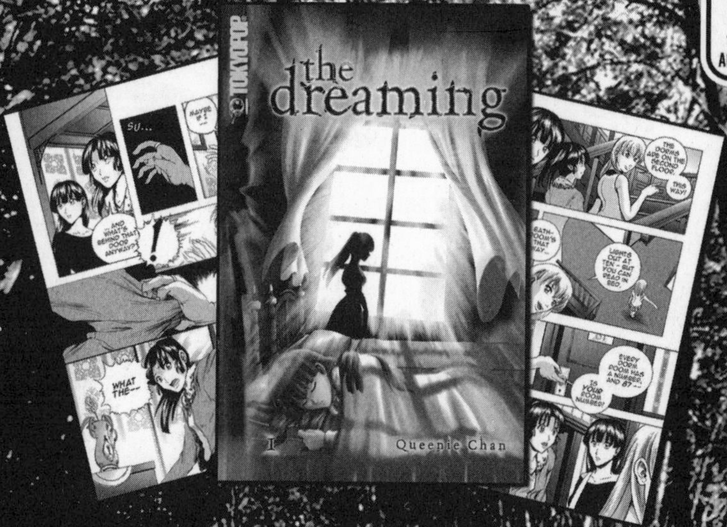
TOKYOPOP
the dreaming
I
Queenie Chan
WHAT THE--

ALL OF THEM VANISHED...WITHOUT A TRACE.

When twin sisters Amber and Jeanie enroll in an Australian boarding school, they soon uncover a dark, unexplained secret: Students have been known to walk off into the surrounding bushlands, where they have vanished completely! Few know how the girls disappeared...fewer yet know why. Amber and Jeanie soon realize that the key to unlocking a secret that has been hidden for years may lie in the world of their dreams!

SUSPENSE-HORROR SHOJO FROM THE CREATOR OF THE HIT WEB MANGA *BLOCK G.*

FOR MORE INFORMATION VISIT: WWW.TOKYOPOP.COM/THEDREAMING

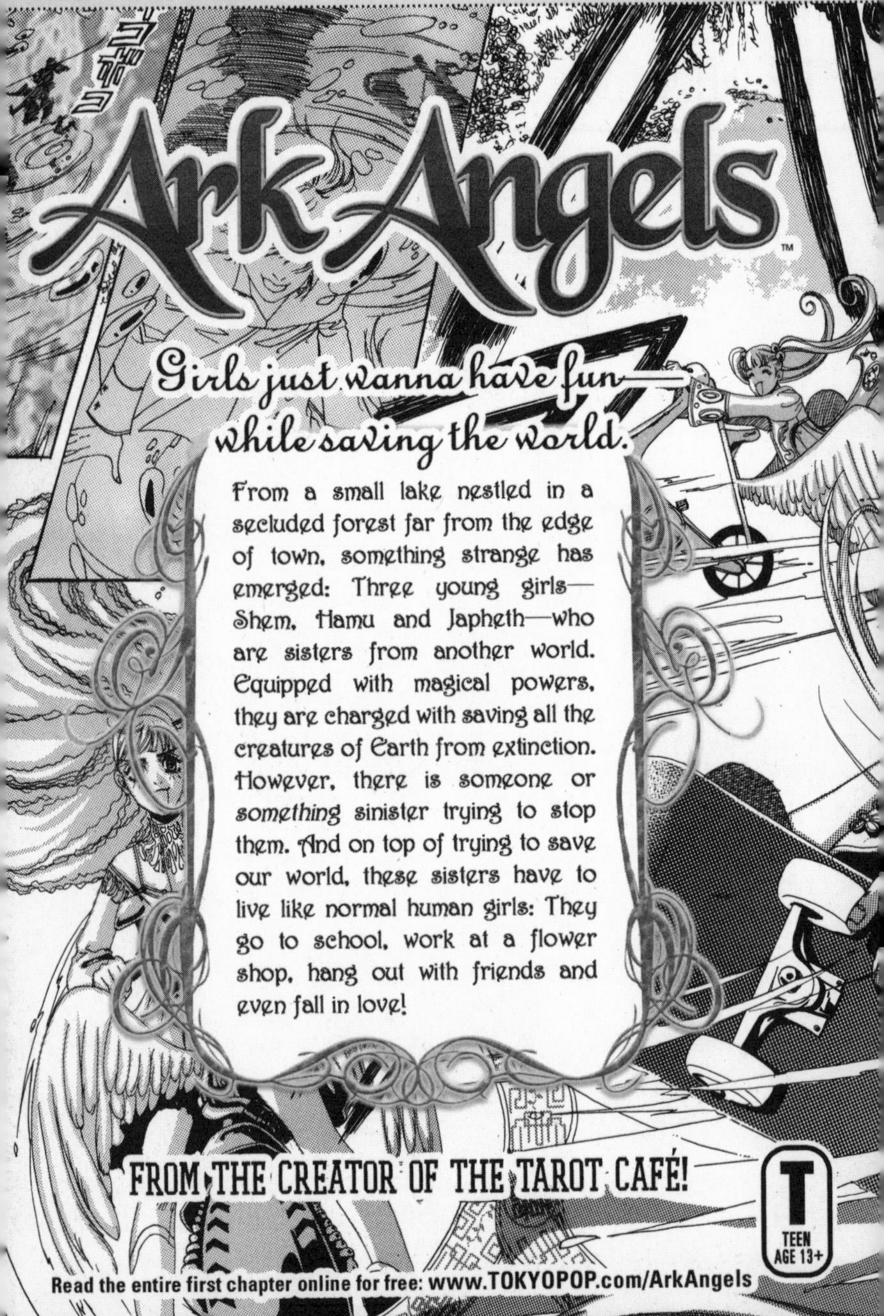
Ark Angels™
Girls just wanna have fun—while saving the world.
From a small lake nestled in a secluded forest far from the edge of town, something strange has emerged: Three young girls—Shem, Hamu and Japheth—who are sisters from another world. Equipped with magical powers, they are charged with saving all the creatures of Earth from extinction. However, there is someone or *something* sinister trying to stop them. And on top of trying to save our world, these sisters have to live like normal human girls: They go to school, work at a flower shop, hang out with friends and even fall in love!
FROM THE CREATOR OF THE TAROT CAFÉ!
T
TEEN AGE 13+
Read the entire first chapter online for free: www.TOKYOPOP.com/ArkAngels

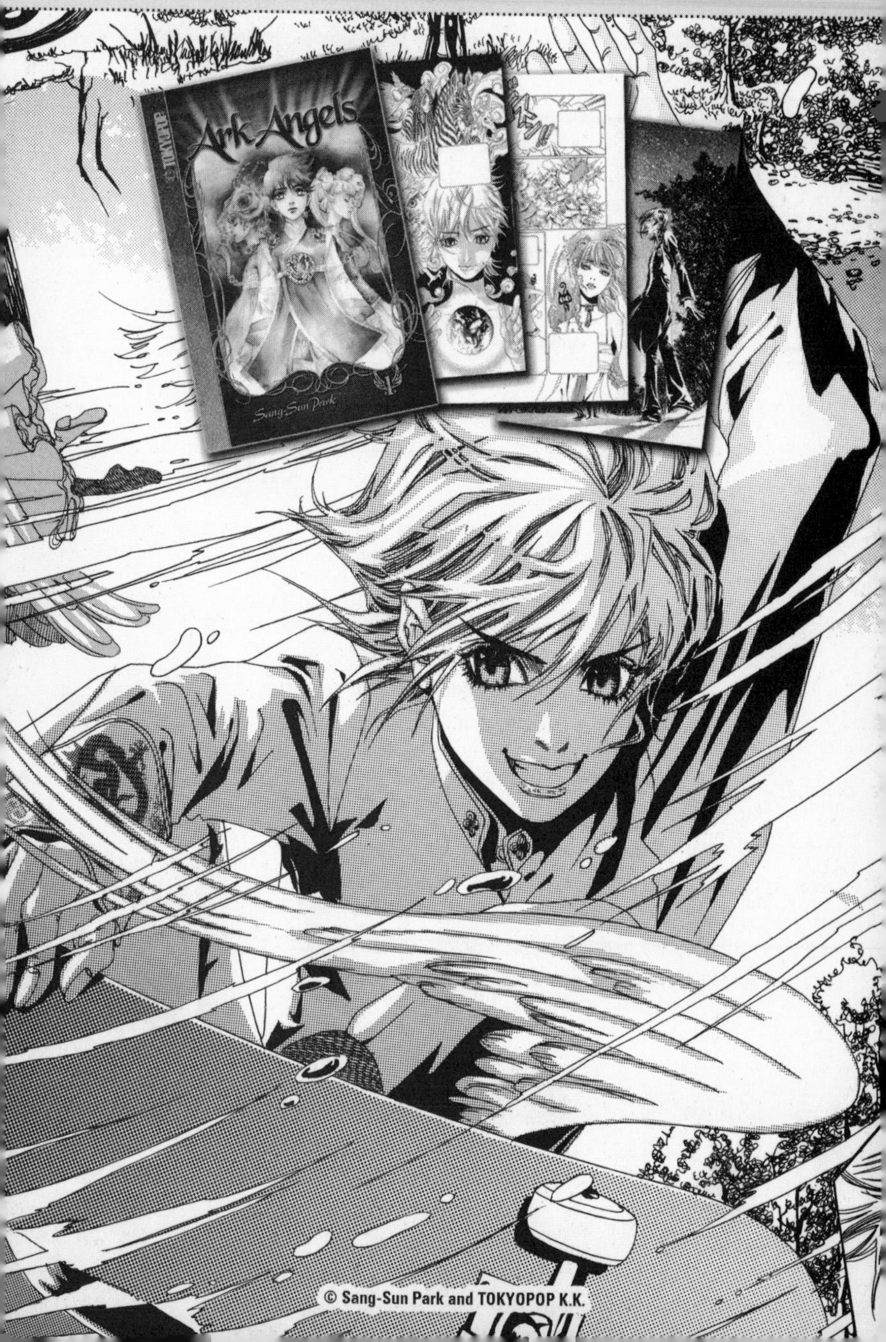
Ark Angels
TOKYOPOP
1
Sang-Sun Park

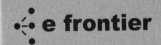

TOKYOPOP
The Tarot Café

BY SANG-SUN PARK

TOKYOPOP®
By the creator of
ARK ANGELS
TOKYOPOP®

THE TAROT CAFÉ

I was always kind of fond of *Petshop of Horrors,* and then along comes *The Tarot Café* and blows me away. It's like *Petshop,* but with a bishonen factor that goes through the roof and into the stratosphere! Sang-Sun Park's art is just unreal. It's beautifully detailed, all the characters are stunning and unique, and while at first the story seems to be yet another Gothy episodic piece of fluff, there is a dark side to Pamela and her powers that I can't wait to read more about. I'm a sucker for teenage werewolves, too.

~Lillian Diaz-Pryzbyl, Editor

TOKYOPOP
DRAMACON
V.I.P.
EEEK!

BY SVETLANA CHMAKOVA

DRAMACON

I love this manga! First of all, Svetlana is amazing. She's the artist who creates "The Adventures of CosmoGIRL!" manga feature in *CosmoGIRL!* magazine, and she totally rules. *Dramacon* is a juicy romance about a guy and a girl who meet up every year at a crazy anime convention. It grabbed me from the first panel and just wouldn't let go. If you love shojo as much as I do, this book will rock your world.

~Julie Taylor, Senior Editor

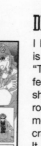

SHOWCASE TOKYOPOP MANGA SUPPLEMENT

© Granger/Henderson/Salvaggio and TOKYOPOP Inc.

PSY-COMM
BY JASON HENDERSON, TONY SALVAGGIO AND SHANE GRANGER

In the not-too-distant future, war is enter-tainment—it is scheduled, televised and rated. It's the new opiate of the masses and its stars are the elite Psychic Commandos—Psy-Comms. Mark Leit, possibly the greatest Psy-Comm of all time, will have to face a tragedy from his past…and abandon everything his life has stood for.

War: The Ultimate Reality Show!

> T
> TEEN
> AGE 13+

© Yasutaka Tsutsui, Sayaka Yamazaki

TELEPATHIC WANDERERS
BY SAYAKA YAMAZAKI AND YASUTAKA TSUTSUI

When Nanase, a beautiful young telepath, returns to her hometown, her life soon becomes more than unsettling. Using her telepathic powers, Nanase stumbles across others who possess similar abilities. On a train she meets Tsuneo, a man with psychic powers who predicts a dire future for the passengers! Will Nanase find her way to safety in time?

A sophisticated and sexy thriller from the guru of Japanese science fiction.

© Koge-Donbo

PITA-TEN OFFICIAL FAN BOOK
BY KOGE-DONBO

Koge-Donbo's lovable characters—Kotarou, Misha and Shia—are all here, illustrated in a unique, fresh style by the some of the biggest fans of the bestselling manga! Different manga-ka from Japan have added their personal touch to the romantic series. And, of course, there's a cool, original tale from Koge-Donbo, too!

Pita-Ten as you've never seen it before!

> T
> TEEN
> AGE 13+